Run Away With Me, Girl

"run away with me, girl," by battan

2

characters

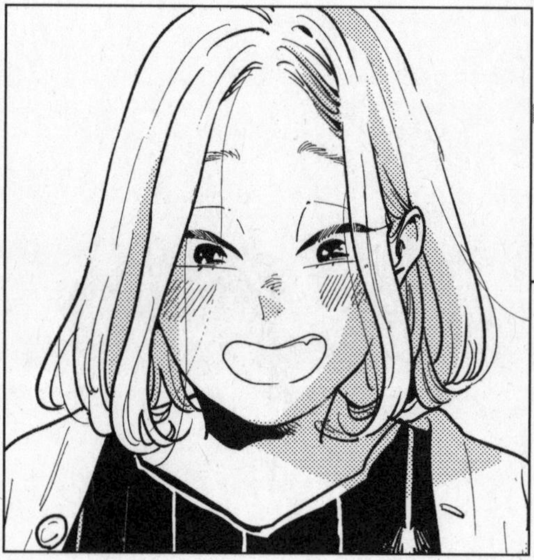

MIDORI ONISHI

WORKS AT A USED CLOTHING STORE. MOMO HADN'T SEEN HER SINCE HIGH SCHOOL, UNTIL THEY RAN INTO EACH OTHER BY SHEER CHANCE.

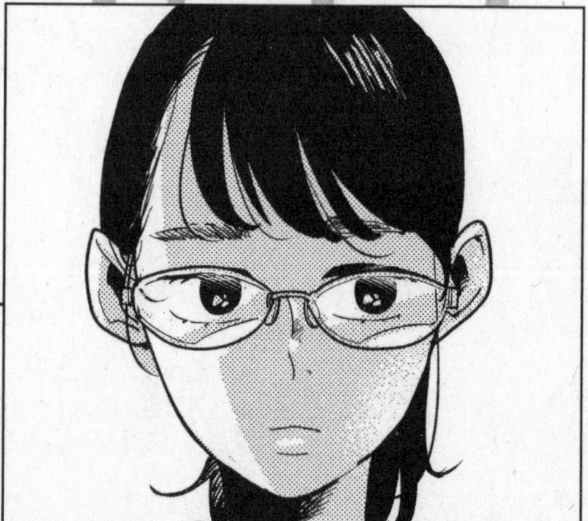

MOMO MAKIMURA

GRADUATE STUDENT. HAS BEEN UNABLE TO FORGET MIDORI SINCE HIGH SCHOOL.

TAZUNE TONOIKE

MIDORI'S FIANCÉ.
VIOLENTLY HIT HER.

KOMARI NIKAIDOU

A HIGH SCHOOLER WHO
LIVES IN SHODOSHIMA.
MOMO MET HER ONLINE
AND OFTEN TURNS TO
HER FOR ADVICE.

AZUSA DOUMYOU

MIDORI'S COLLEAGUE.
IN LOVE WITH TAZUNE.

s t o r y

MOMO AND MIDORI DATED IN HIGH SCHOOL, BUT
THEY HAVEN'T SEEN EACH OTHER SINCE GRADUATION—
UNTIL A SERENDIPITOUS REUNION.

BY THEN, THOUGH, MIDORI IS PREGNANT AND
ABOUT TO GET MARRIED.

THEIR FRIENDSHIP RESUMES AND EVEN GROWS
DEEPER. THEN ONE DAY, MIDORI'S FIANCÉ
TAZUNE VIOLENTLY STRIKES HER...

EPISODE 7
5

EPISODE 8
37

EPISODE 9
69

EPISODE 10
101

EPISODE 11
131

EXTRA EPISODE
166

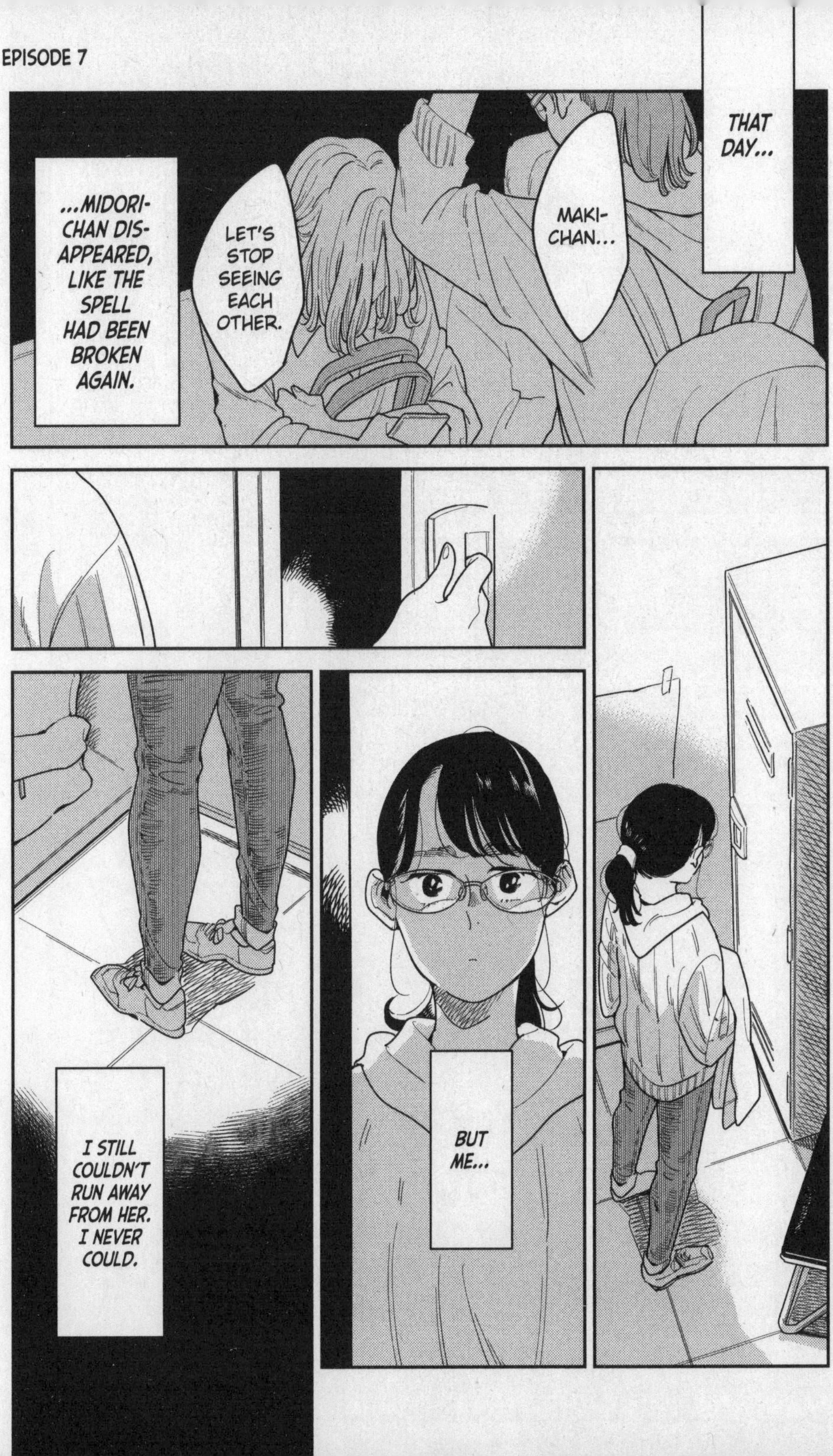
THAT DAY...
MAKI-CHAN...
LET'S STOP SEEING EACH OTHER.
...MIDORI-CHAN DISAPPEARED, LIKE THE SPELL HAD BEEN BROKEN AGAIN.
BUT ME...
I STILL COULDN'T RUN AWAY FROM HER. I NEVER COULD.

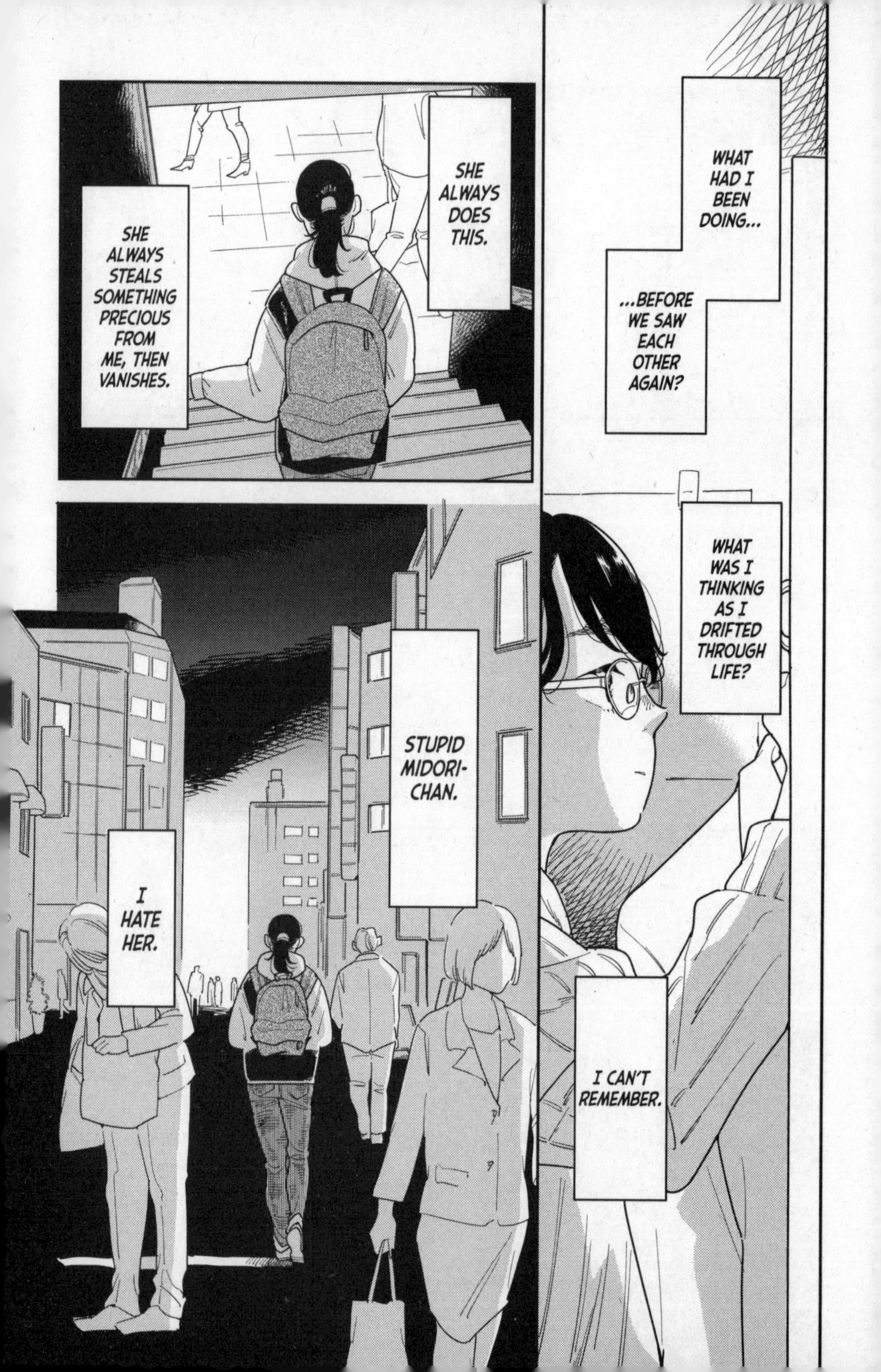
WHAT HAD I BEEN DOING...
...BEFORE WE SAW EACH OTHER AGAIN?
WHAT WAS I THINKING AS I DRIFTED THROUGH LIFE?
I CAN'T REMEMBER.
SHE ALWAYS DOES THIS.
SHE ALWAYS STEALS SOMETHING PRECIOUS FROM ME, THEN VANISHES.
STUPID MIDORI-CHAN.
I HATE HER.

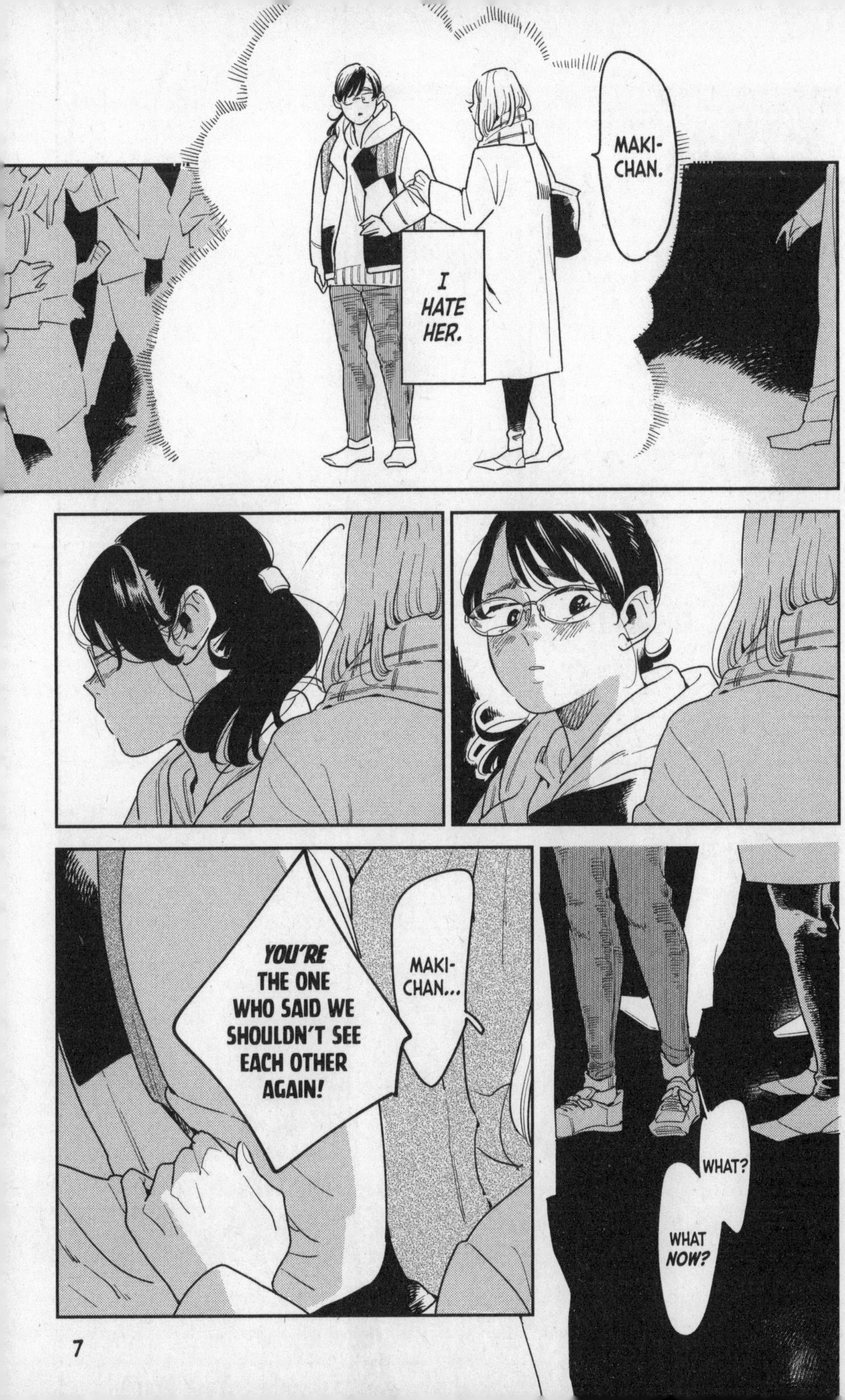
MAKI-CHAN.
I HATE HER.
WHAT?
WHAT *NOW?*
MAKI-CHAN...
YOU'RE THE ONE WHO SAID WE SHOULDN'T SEE EACH OTHER AGAIN!

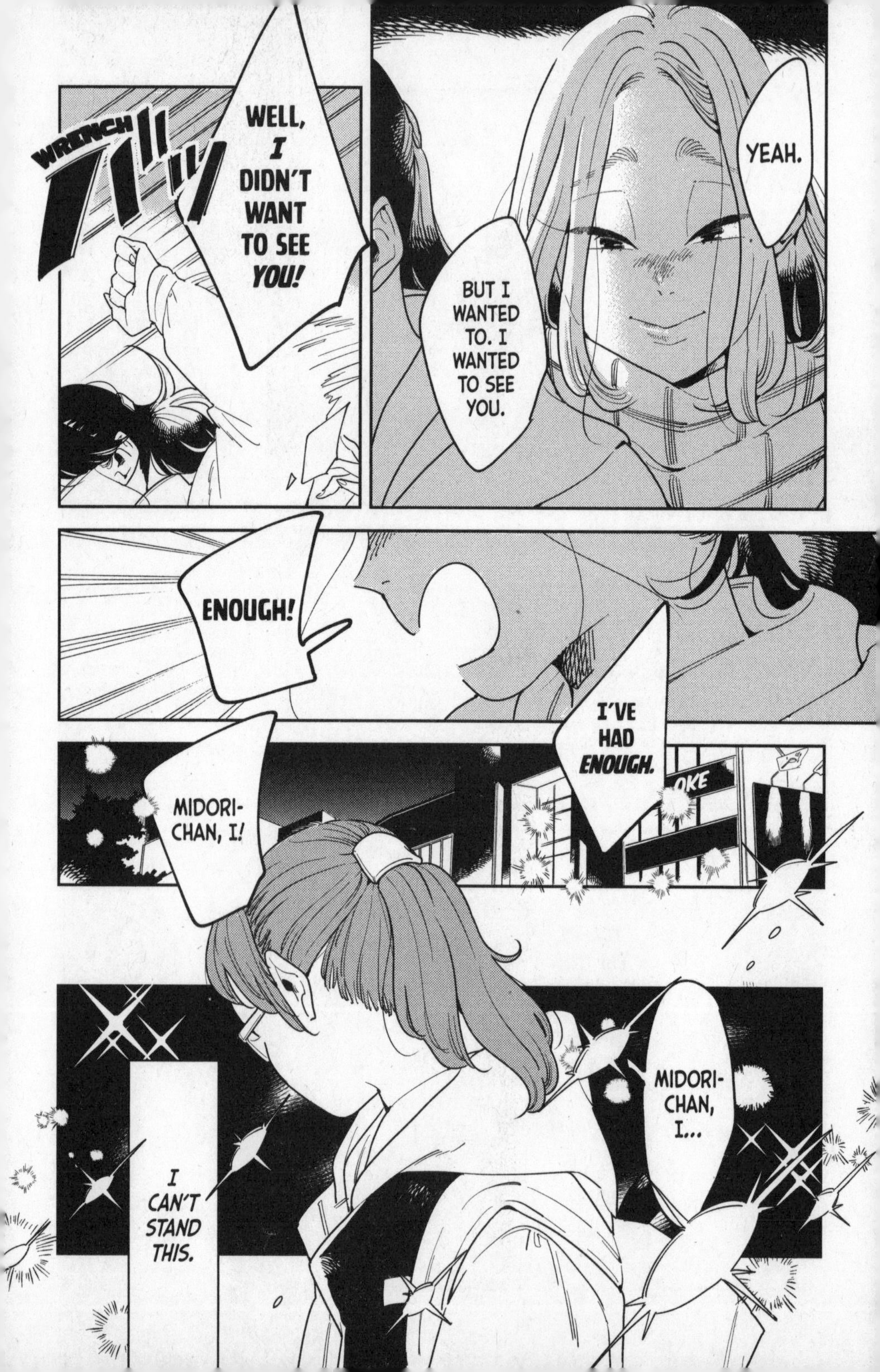
YEAH.
BUT I WANTED TO. I WANTED TO SEE YOU.
WELL, *I* DIDN'T WANT TO SEE *YOU!*
WRENCH
ENOUGH!
I'VE HAD *ENOUGH.*
OKE
MIDORI-CHAN, I!
MIDORI-CHAN, I...
I CAN'T STAND THIS.

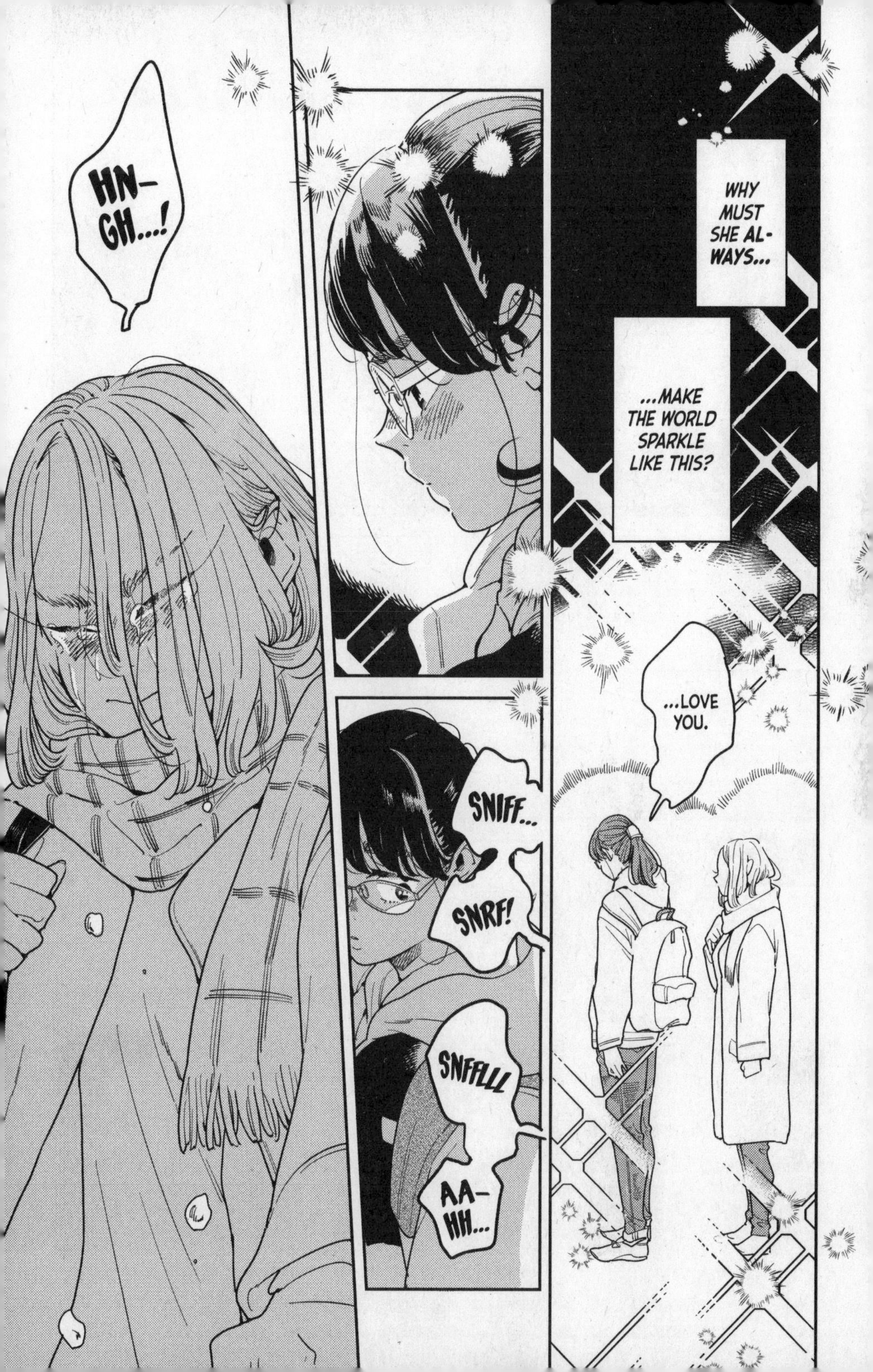
WHY MUST SHE AL-WAYS...
...MAKE THE WORLD SPARKLE LIKE THIS?
...LOVE YOU.
SNIFF...
SNRF!
SNFFLLL
AA-HH...
HN-GH...!

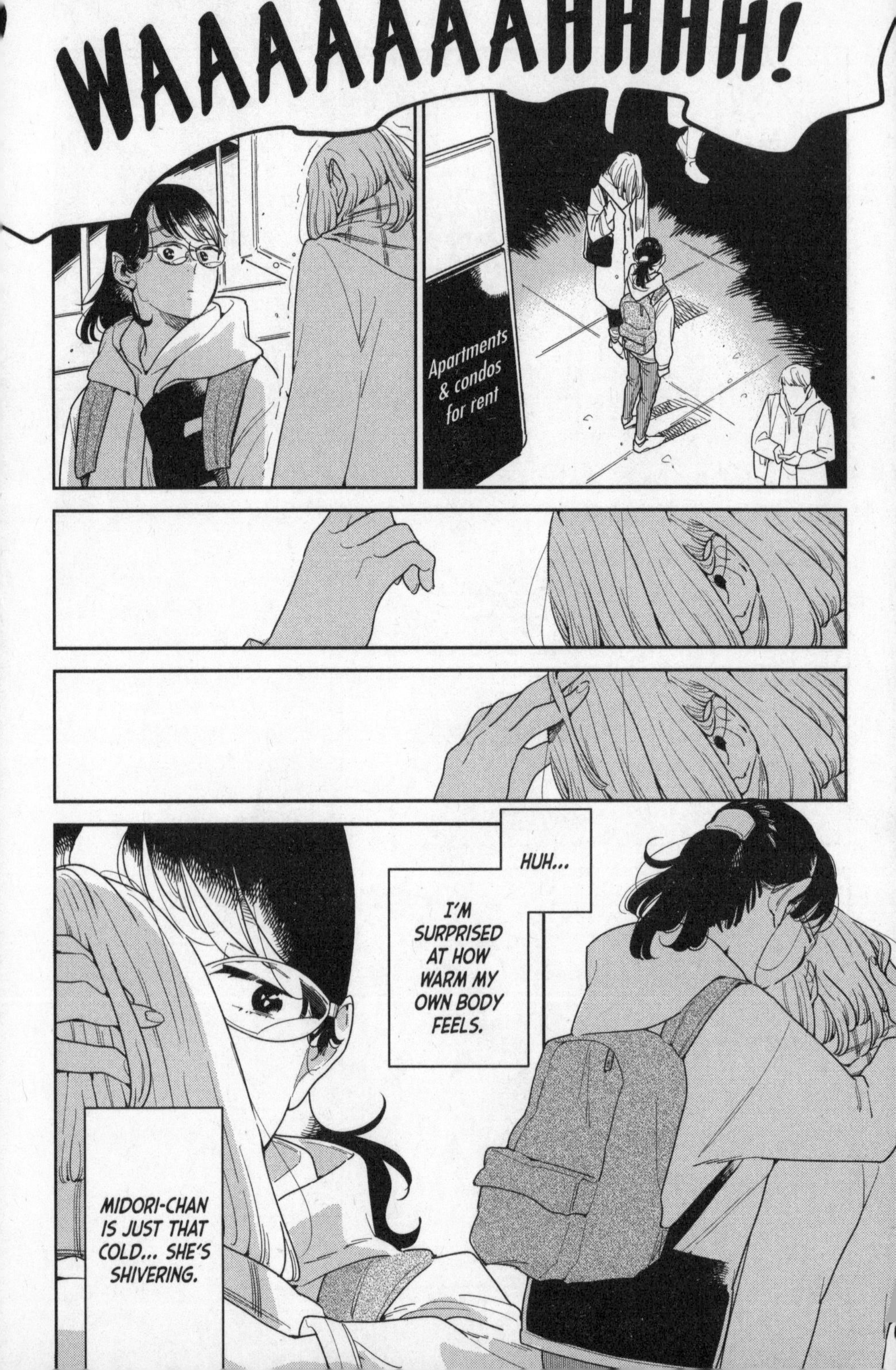
WAAAAAAAHHHH!
Apartments & condos for rent
HUH...
I'M SURPRISED AT HOW WARM MY OWN BODY FEELS.
MIDORI-CHAN IS JUST THAT COLD... SHE'S SHIVERING.

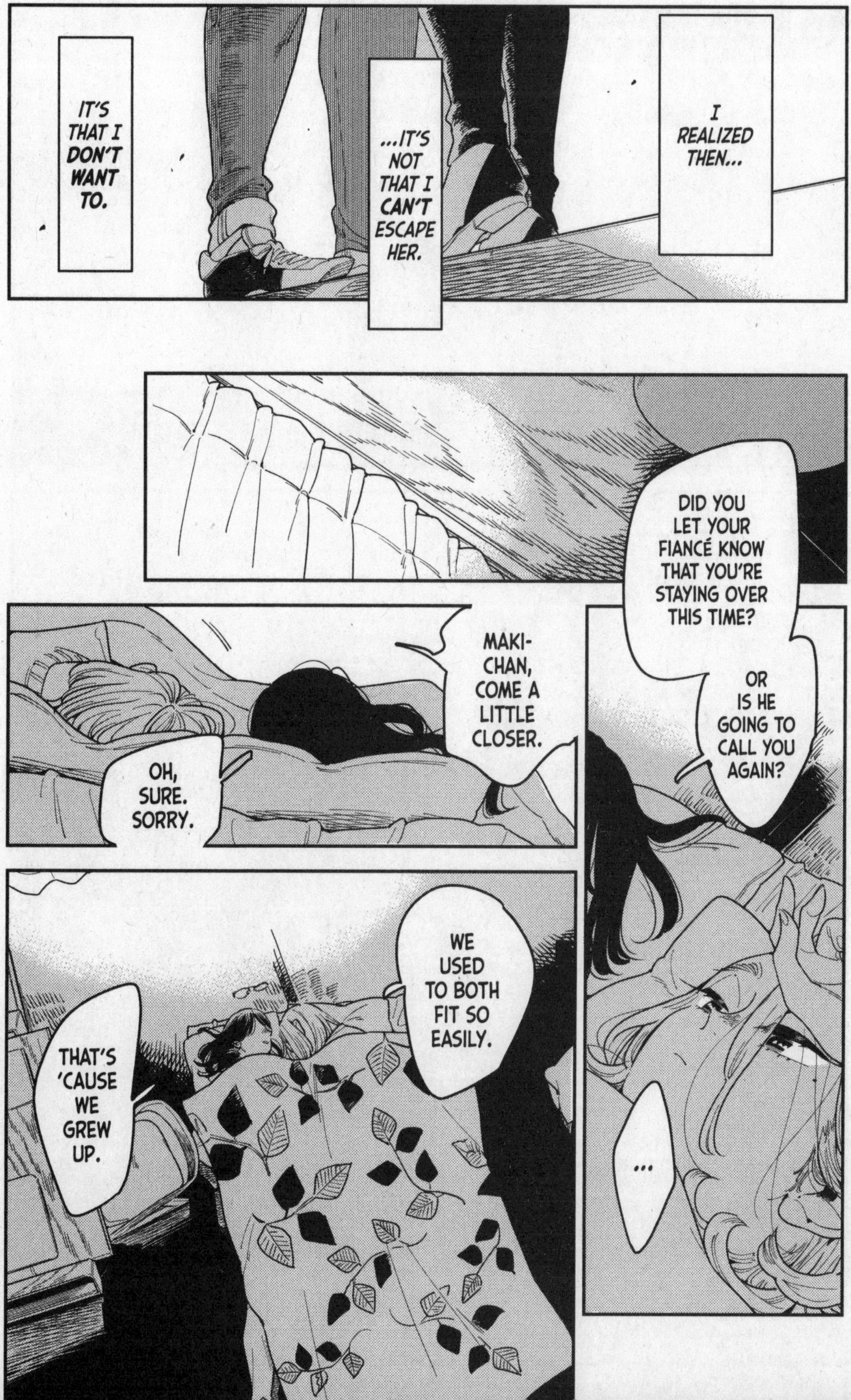
I REALIZED THEN...
...IT'S NOT THAT I CAN'T ESCAPE HER.
IT'S THAT I DON'T WANT TO.
DID YOU LET YOUR FIANCÉ KNOW THAT YOU'RE STAYING OVER THIS TIME?
OR IS HE GOING TO CALL YOU AGAIN?
...
MAKI-CHAN, COME A LITTLE CLOSER.
OH, SURE. SORRY.
WE USED TO BOTH FIT SO EASILY.
THAT'S 'CAUSE WE GREW UP.

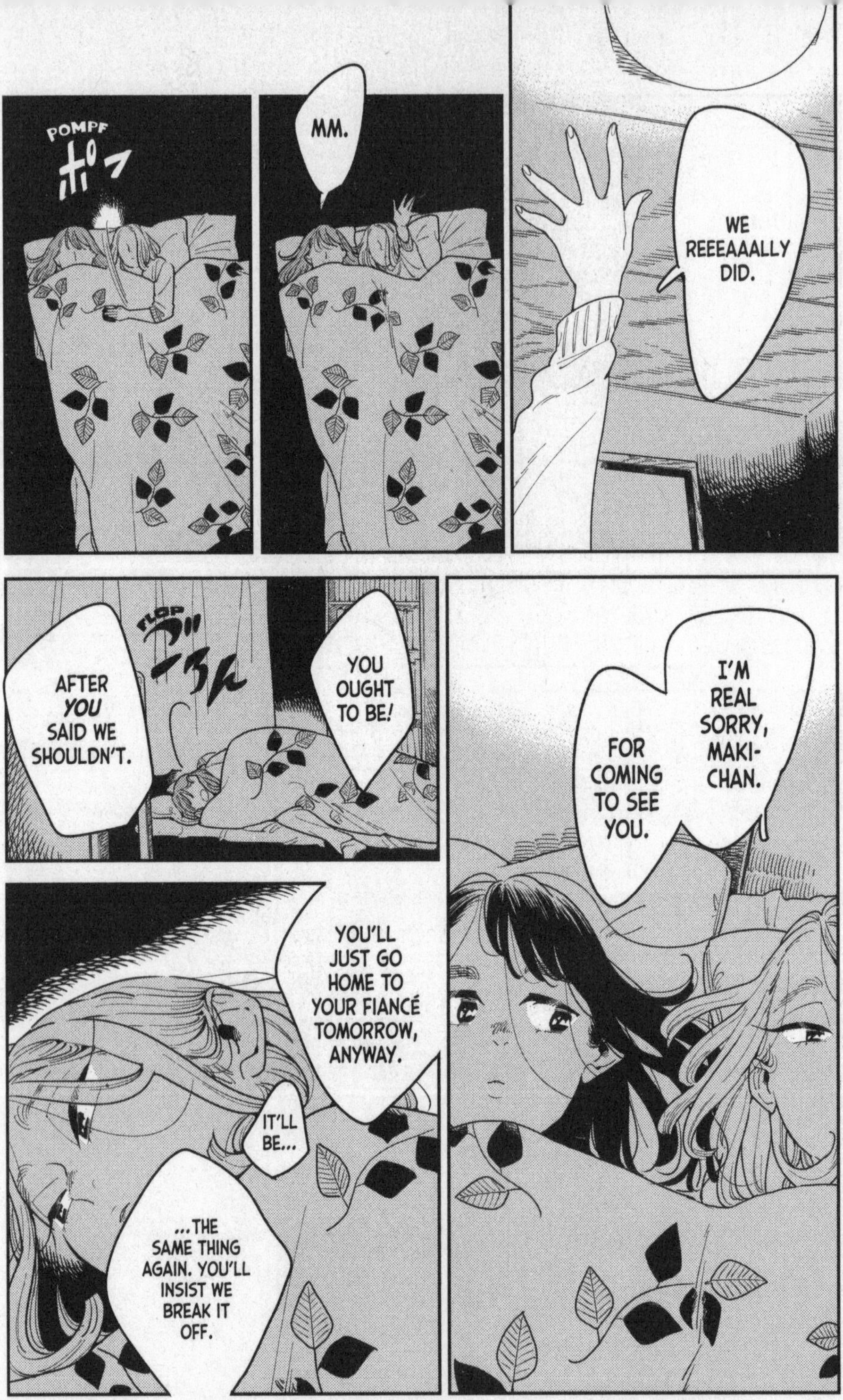
WE REEEAAALLY DID.
MM.
POMPF
I'M REAL SORRY, MAKI-CHAN.
FOR COMING TO SEE YOU.
YOU OUGHT TO BE!
FLOP
AFTER *YOU* SAID WE SHOULDN'T.
YOU'LL JUST GO HOME TO YOUR FIANCÉ TOMORROW, ANYWAY.
IT'LL BE...
...THE SAME THING AGAIN. YOU'LL INSIST WE BREAK IT OFF.

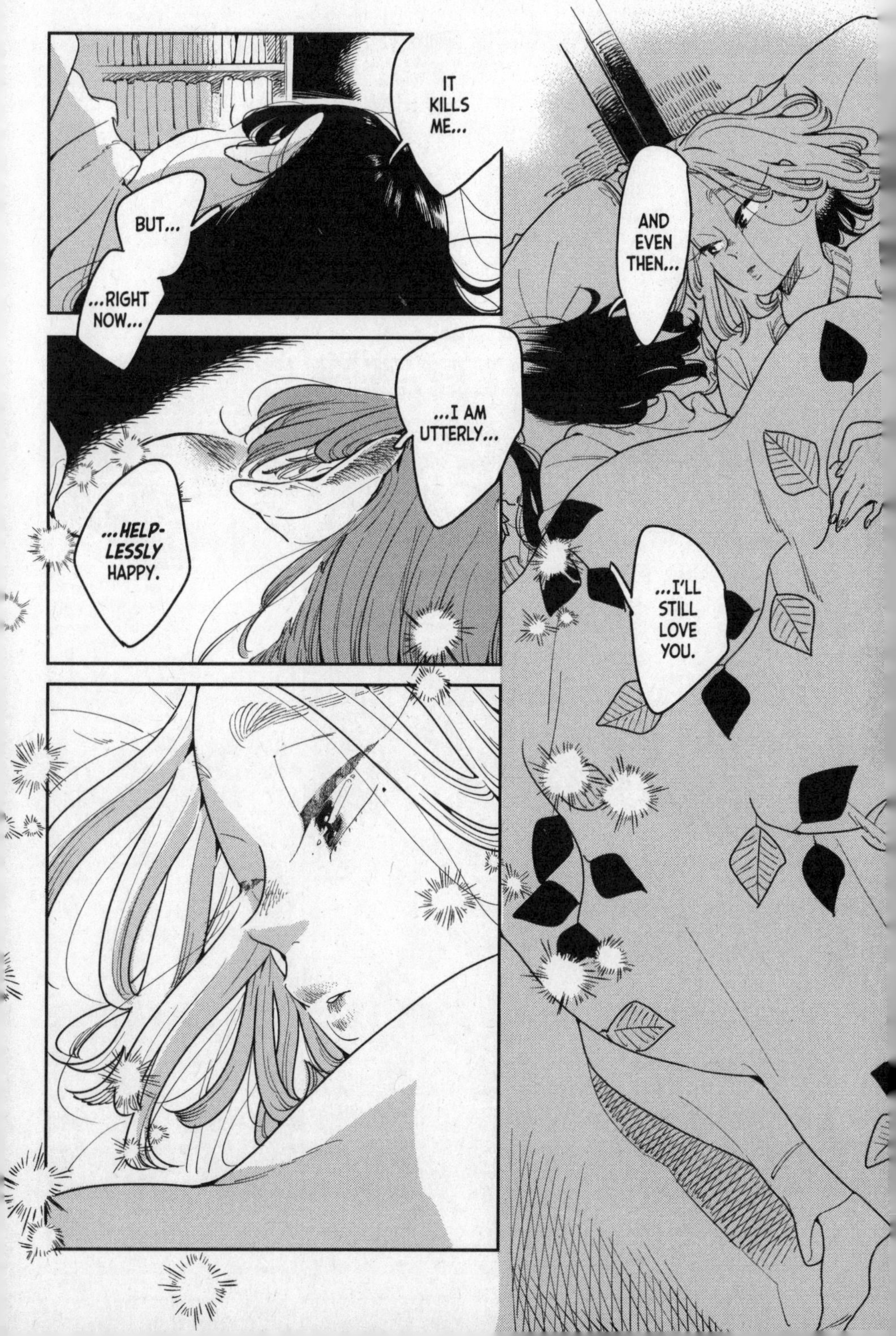
AND EVEN THEN...
...I'LL STILL LOVE YOU.
IT KILLS ME...
BUT...
...RIGHT NOW...
...I AM UTTERLY...
...HELP-LESSLY HAPPY.

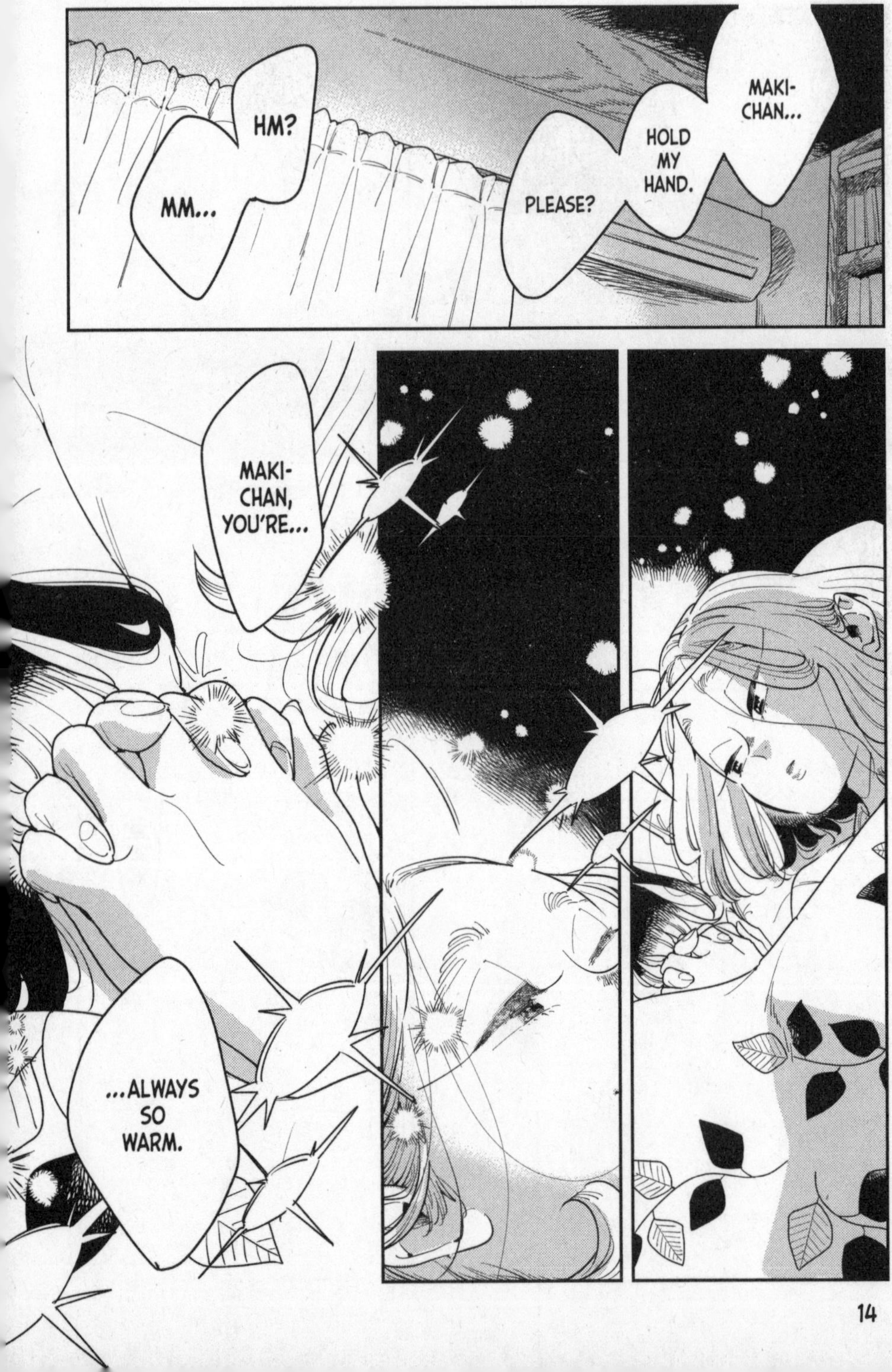
MAKI-CHAN...
HOLD MY HAND.
PLEASE?
HM?
MM...
MAKI-CHAN, YOU'RE...
...ALWAYS SO WARM.

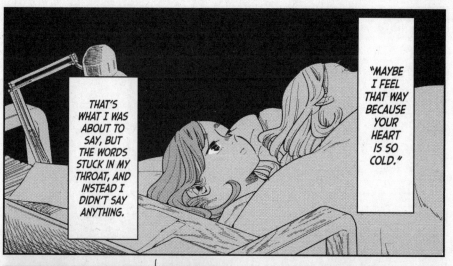

"MAYBE I FEEL THAT WAY BECAUSE YOUR HEART IS SO COLD."
THAT'S WHAT I WAS ABOUT TO SAY, BUT THE WORDS STUCK IN MY THROAT, AND INSTEAD I DIDN'T SAY ANYTHING.
AFTER A FEW MIN-UTES...
ZZZ
ZZZ
...I HEARD MIDORI BREATHING EVENLY, ASLEEP.
ZZZ
ZZZ
ZZZ
Z
I LISTENED UNTIL IT STARTED TO GROW LIGHT OUTSIDE.

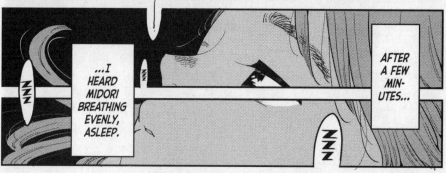

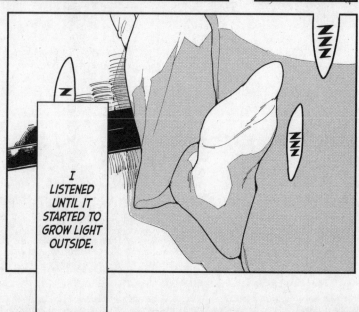

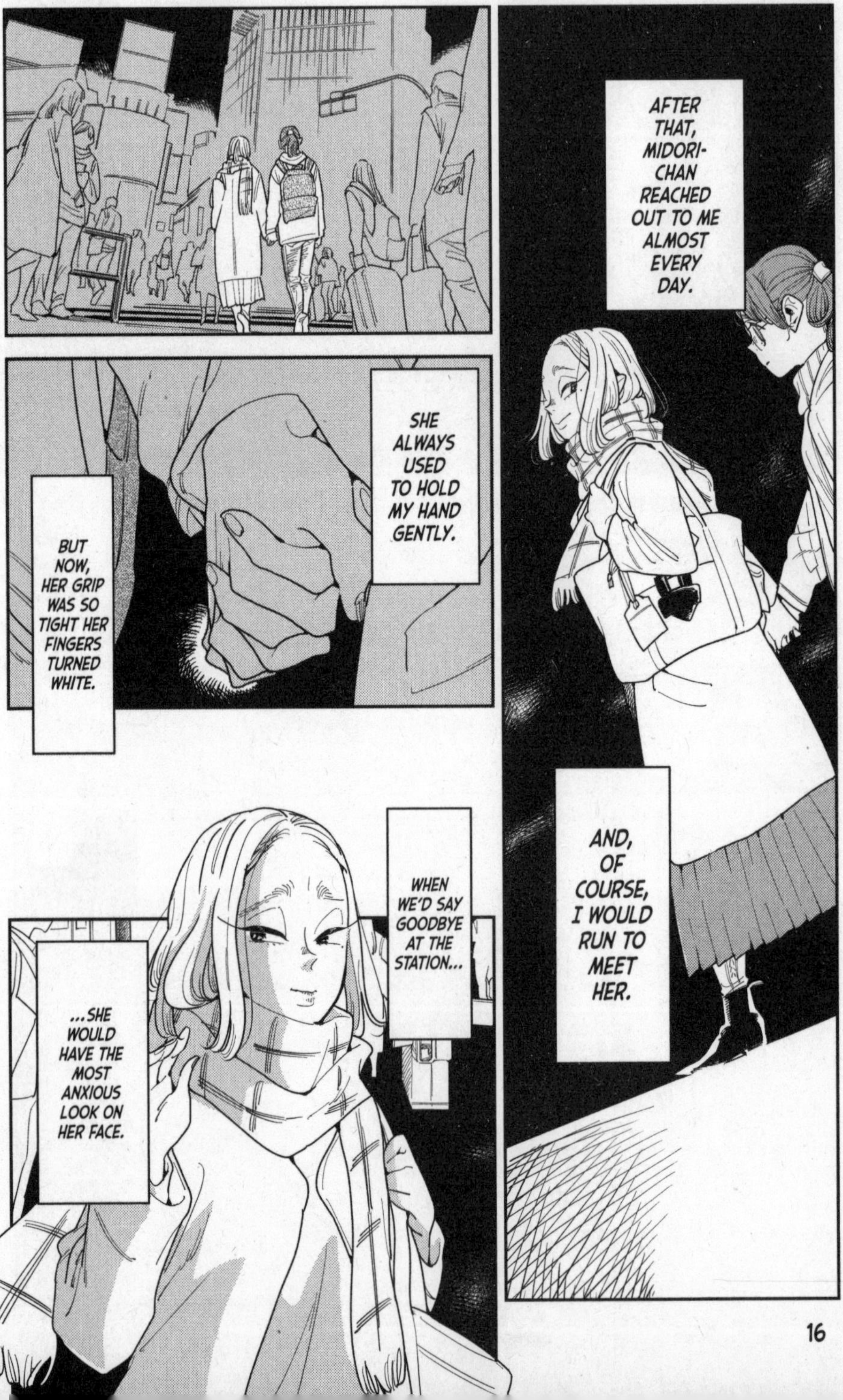
AFTER THAT, MIDORI-CHAN REACHED OUT TO ME ALMOST EVERY DAY.
AND, OF COURSE, I WOULD RUN TO MEET HER.
SHE ALWAYS USED TO HOLD MY HAND GENTLY.
BUT NOW, HER GRIP WAS SO TIGHT HER FINGERS TURNED WHITE.
WHEN WE'D SAY GOODBYE AT THE STATION...
...SHE WOULD HAVE THE MOST ANXIOUS LOOK ON HER FACE.

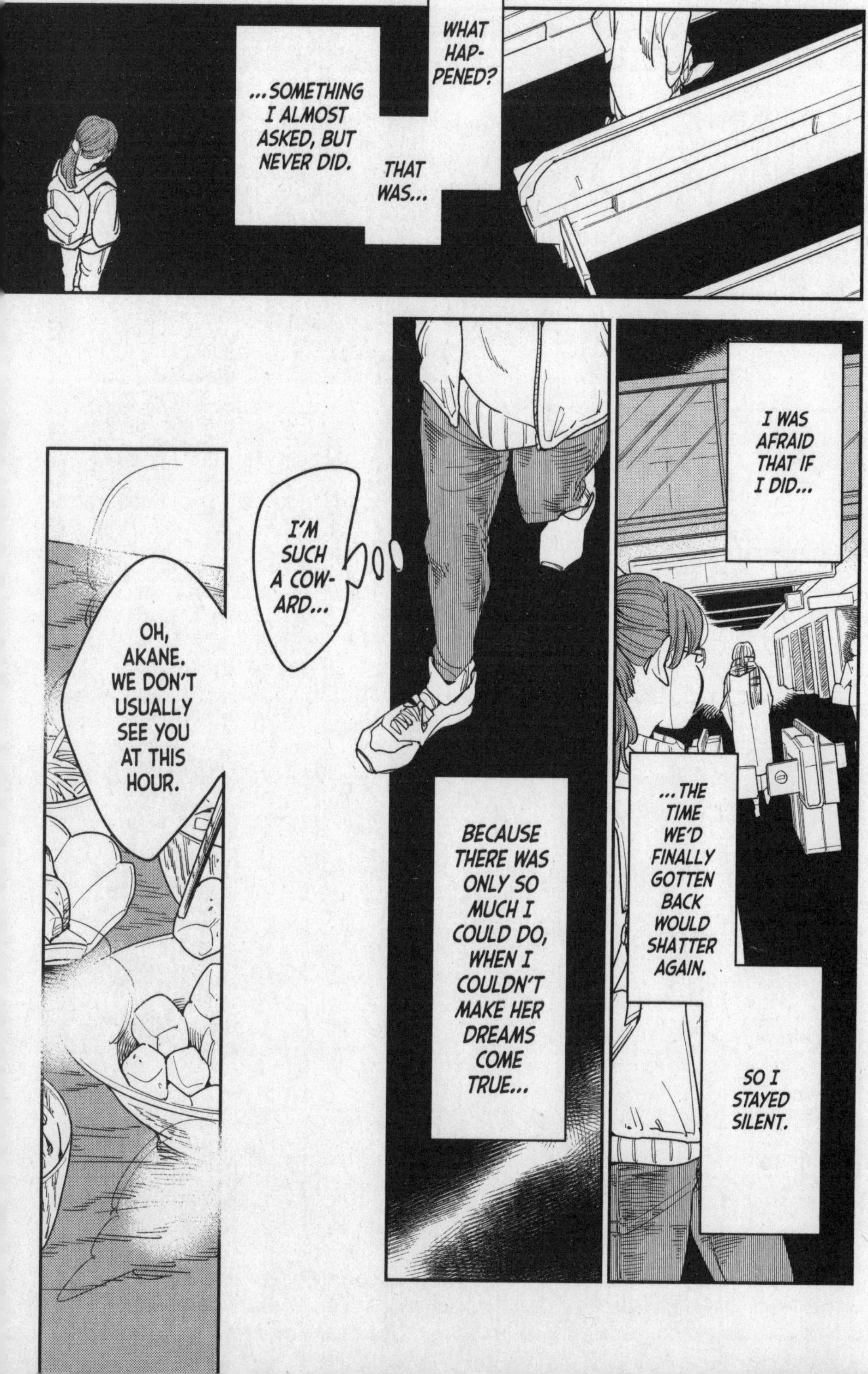
WHAT HAP-PENED?
THAT WAS...
...SOMETHING I ALMOST ASKED, BUT NEVER DID.
I WAS AFRAID THAT IF I DID...
...THE TIME WE'D FINALLY GOTTEN BACK WOULD SHATTER AGAIN.
SO I STAYED SILENT.
I'M SUCH A COW-ARD...
BECAUSE THERE WAS ONLY SO MUCH I COULD DO, WHEN I COULDN'T MAKE HER DREAMS COME TRUE...
OH, AKANE. WE DON'T USUALLY SEE YOU AT THIS HOUR.

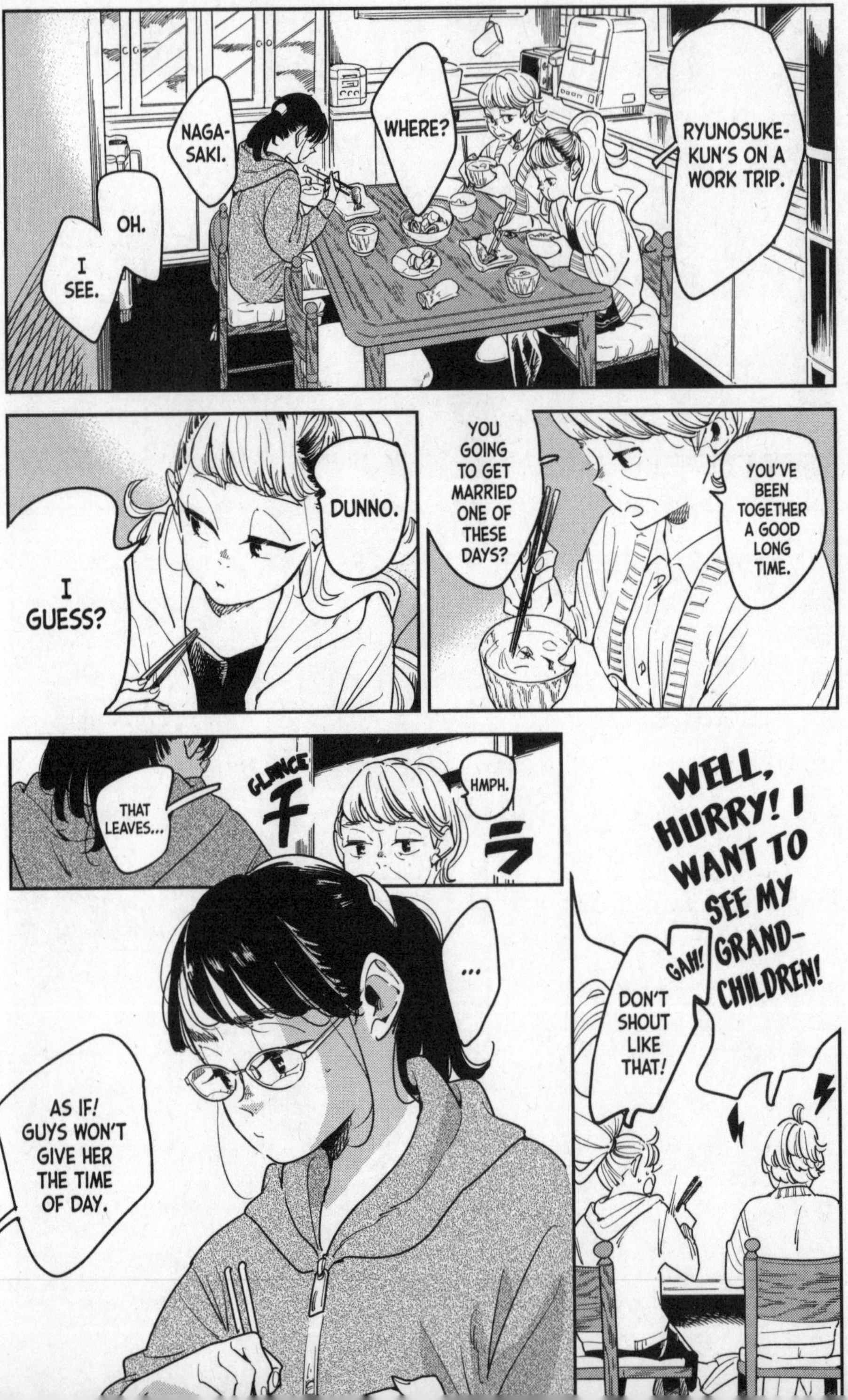
RYUNOSUKE-KUN'S ON A WORK TRIP.
WHERE?
NAGA-SAKI.
OH.
I SEE.
YOU'VE BEEN TOGETHER A GOOD LONG TIME.
YOU GOING TO GET MARRIED ONE OF THESE DAYS?
DUNNO.
I GUESS?
WELL, HURRY! I WANT TO SEE MY GRAND-CHILDREN!
GAH!
DON'T SHOUT LIKE THAT!
HMPH.
ラ
GLANCE
チ
THAT LEAVES...
...
AS IF! GUYS WON'T GIVE HER THE TIME OF DAY.

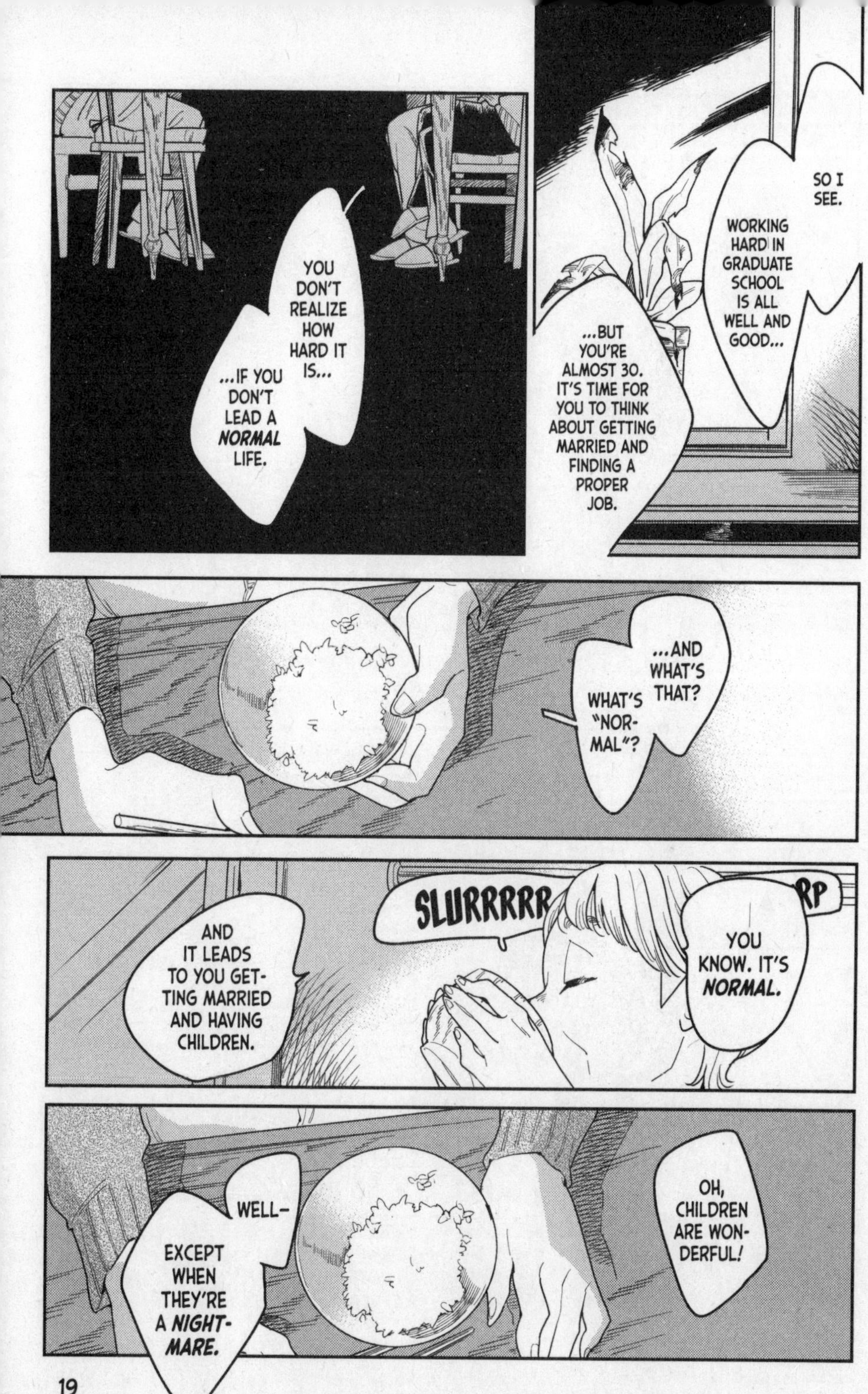
SO I SEE.
WORKING HARD IN GRADUATE SCHOOL IS ALL WELL AND GOOD...
...BUT YOU'RE ALMOST 30. IT'S TIME FOR YOU TO THINK ABOUT GETTING MARRIED AND FINDING A PROPER JOB.
YOU DON'T REALIZE HOW HARD IT IS...
...IF YOU DON'T LEAD A *NORMAL* LIFE.
...AND WHAT'S THAT?
WHAT'S "NOR-MAL"?
SLURRRRR
RP
YOU KNOW. IT'S *NORMAL.*
AND IT LEADS TO YOU GET-TING MARRIED AND HAVING CHILDREN.
OH, CHILDREN ARE WON-DERFUL!
WELL–
EXCEPT WHEN THEY'RE A *NIGHT-MARE.*

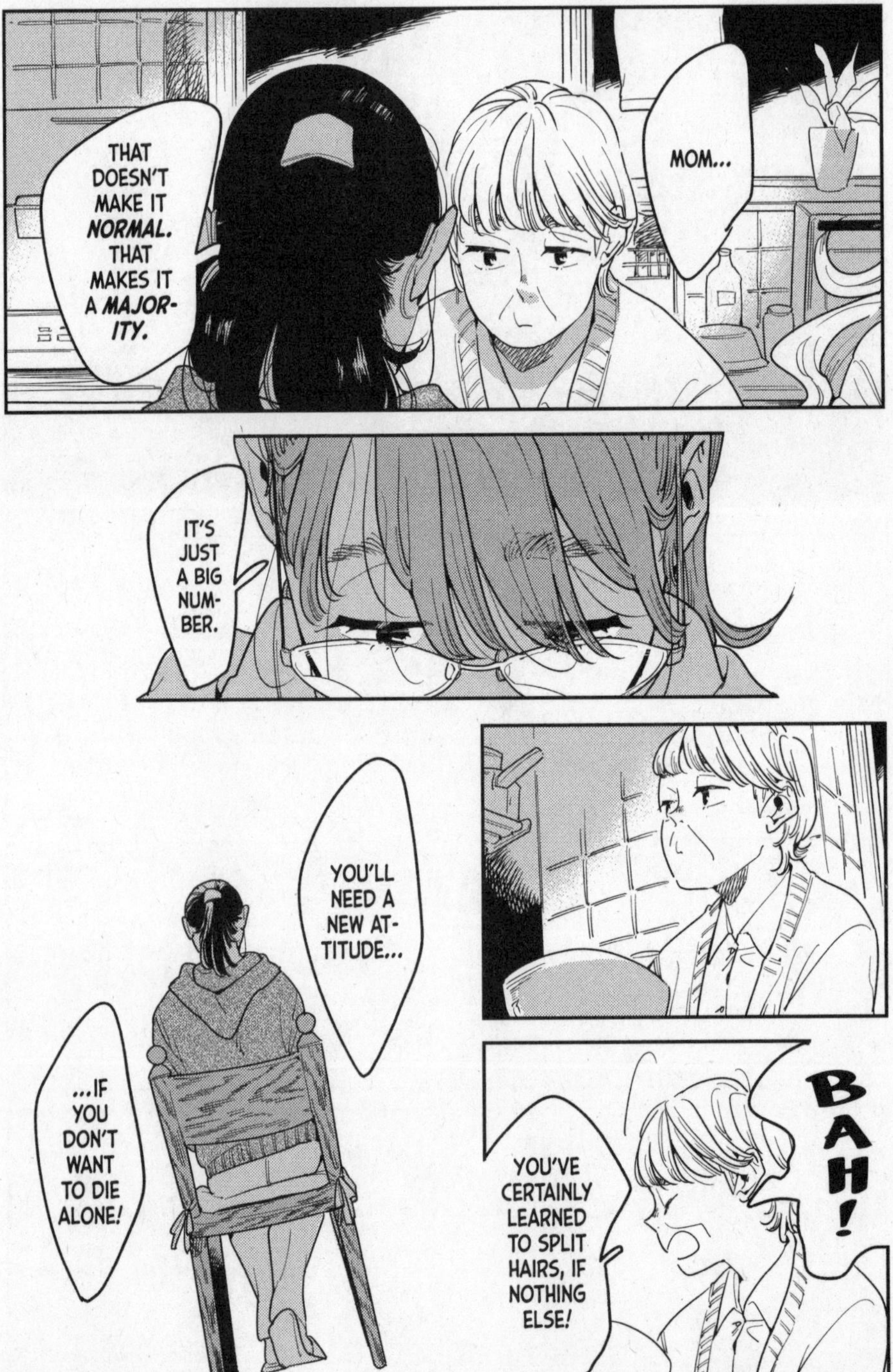
MOM...
THAT DOESN'T MAKE IT *NORMAL.* THAT MAKES IT A *MAJORITY.*
IT'S JUST A BIG NUMBER.
BAH!
YOU'VE CERTAINLY LEARNED TO SPLIT HAIRS, IF NOTHING ELSE!
YOU'LL NEED A NEW ATTITUDE...
...IF YOU DON'T WANT TO DIE ALONE!

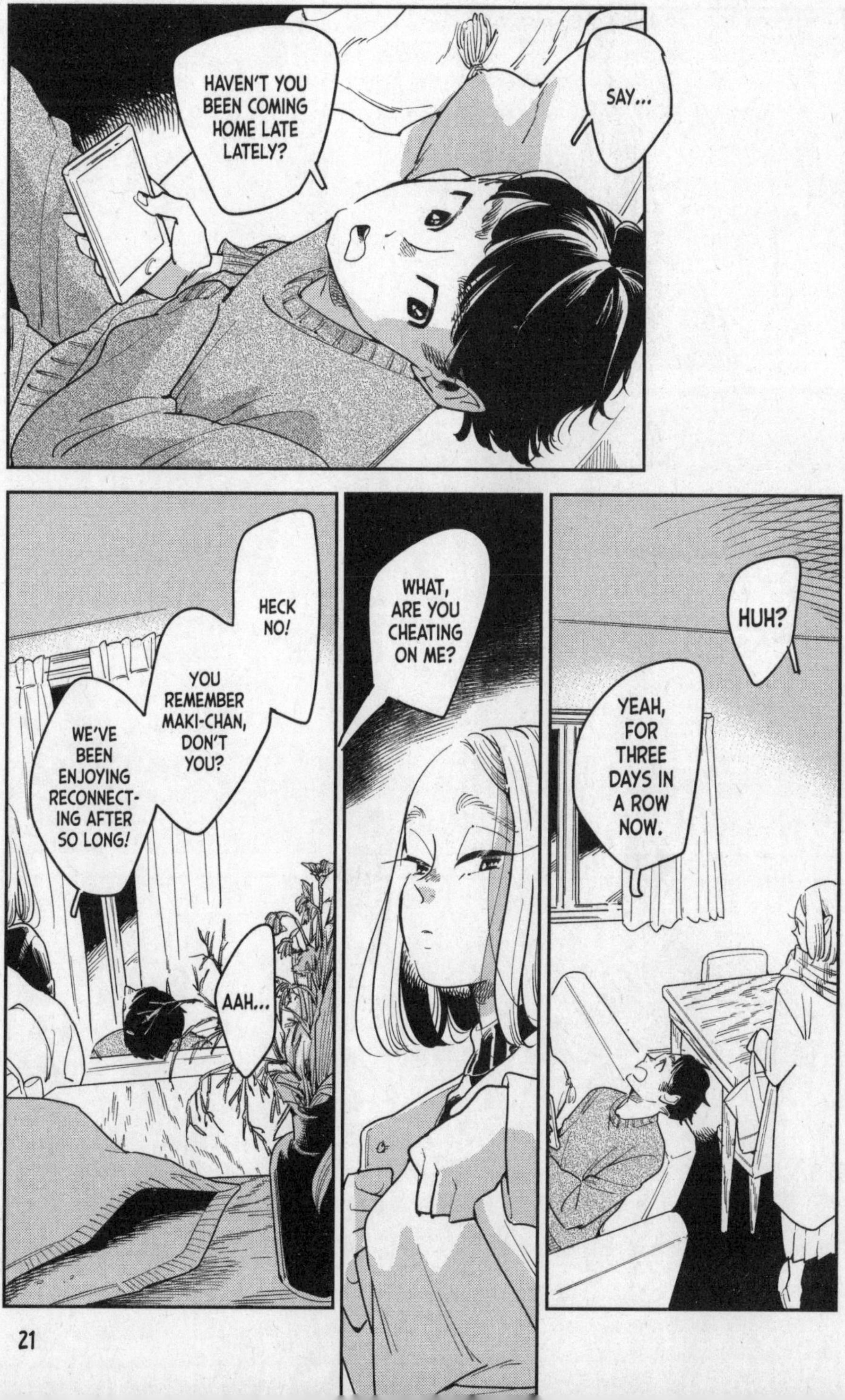
SAY...
HAVEN'T YOU BEEN COMING HOME LATE LATELY?
HUH?
YEAH, FOR THREE DAYS IN A ROW NOW.
WHAT, ARE YOU CHEATING ON ME?
HECK NO!
YOU REMEMBER MAKI-CHAN, DON'T YOU?
WE'VE BEEN ENJOYING RECONNECT-ING AFTER SO LONG!
AAH...

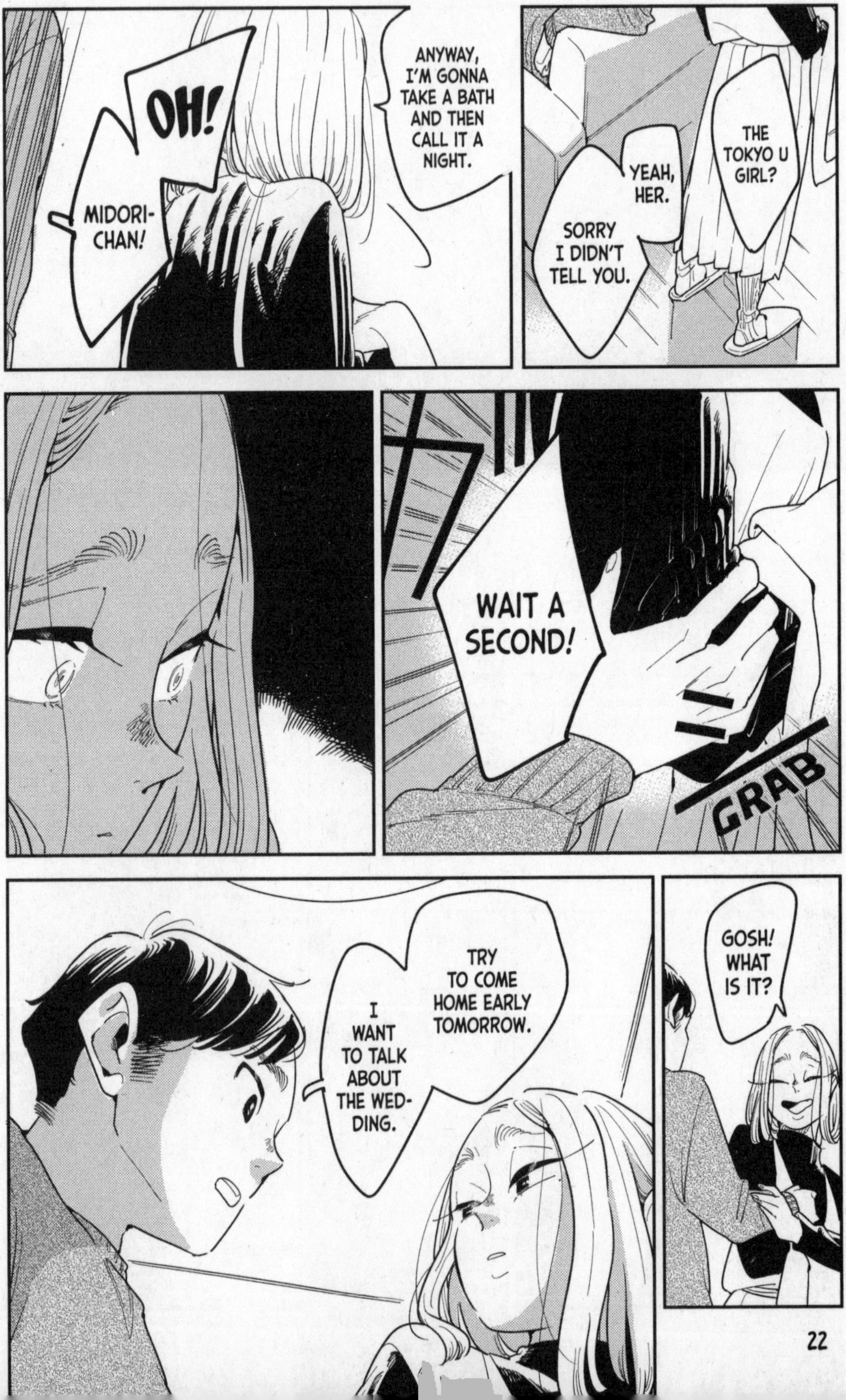
THE TOKYO U GIRL?
YEAH, HER.
SORRY I DIDN'T TELL YOU.
ANYWAY, I'M GONNA TAKE A BATH AND THEN CALL IT A NIGHT.
OH!
MIDORI-CHAN!
WAIT A SECOND!
GRAB
GOSH! WHAT IS IT?
TRY TO COME HOME EARLY TOMORROW.
I WANT TO TALK ABOUT THE WED-DING.

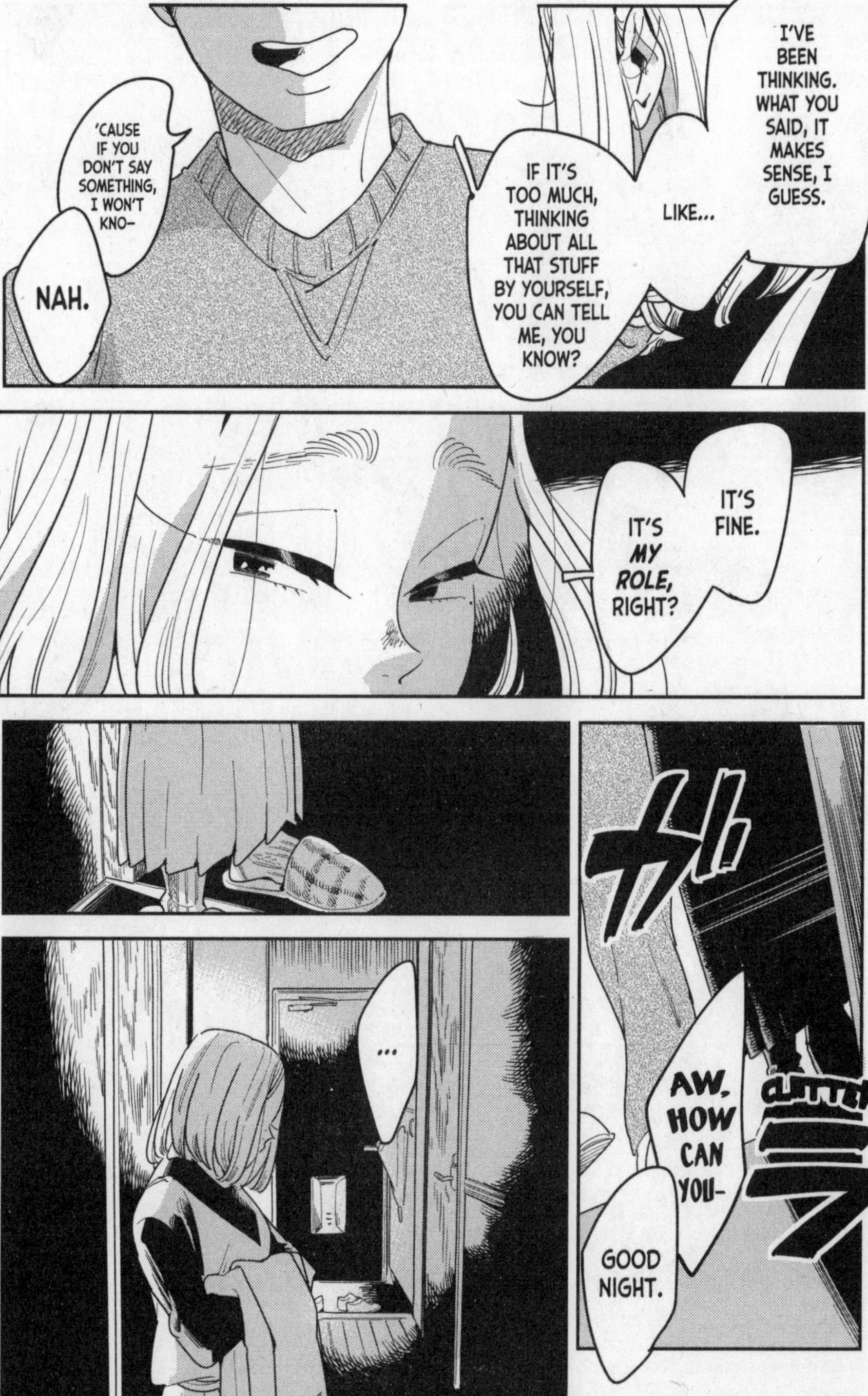
I'VE BEEN THINKING. WHAT YOU SAID, IT MAKES SENSE, I GUESS.
LIKE...
IF IT'S TOO MUCH, THINKING ABOUT ALL THAT STUFF BY YOURSELF, YOU CAN TELL ME, YOU KNOW?
'CAUSE IF YOU DON'T SAY SOMETHING, I WON'T KNO–
NAH.
IT'S FINE.
IT'S *MY ROLE*, RIGHT?
AW, HOW CAN YOU–
CLITTER
GOOD NIGHT.
...

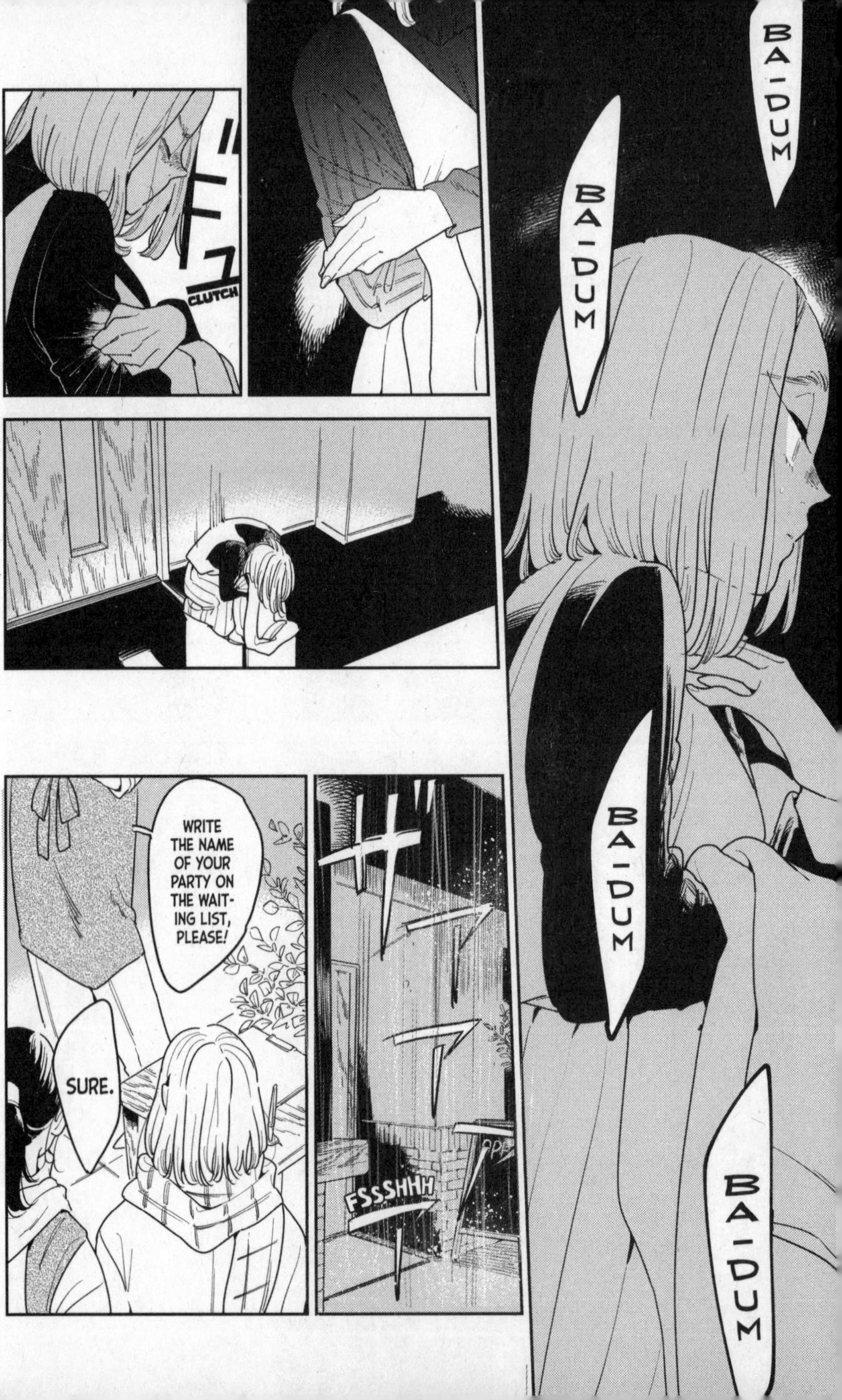
BA-DUM
BA-DUM
BA-DUM
BA-DUM
CLUTCH
FSSSHHH
WRITE THE NAME OF YOUR PARTY ON THE WAITING LIST, PLEASE!
SURE.

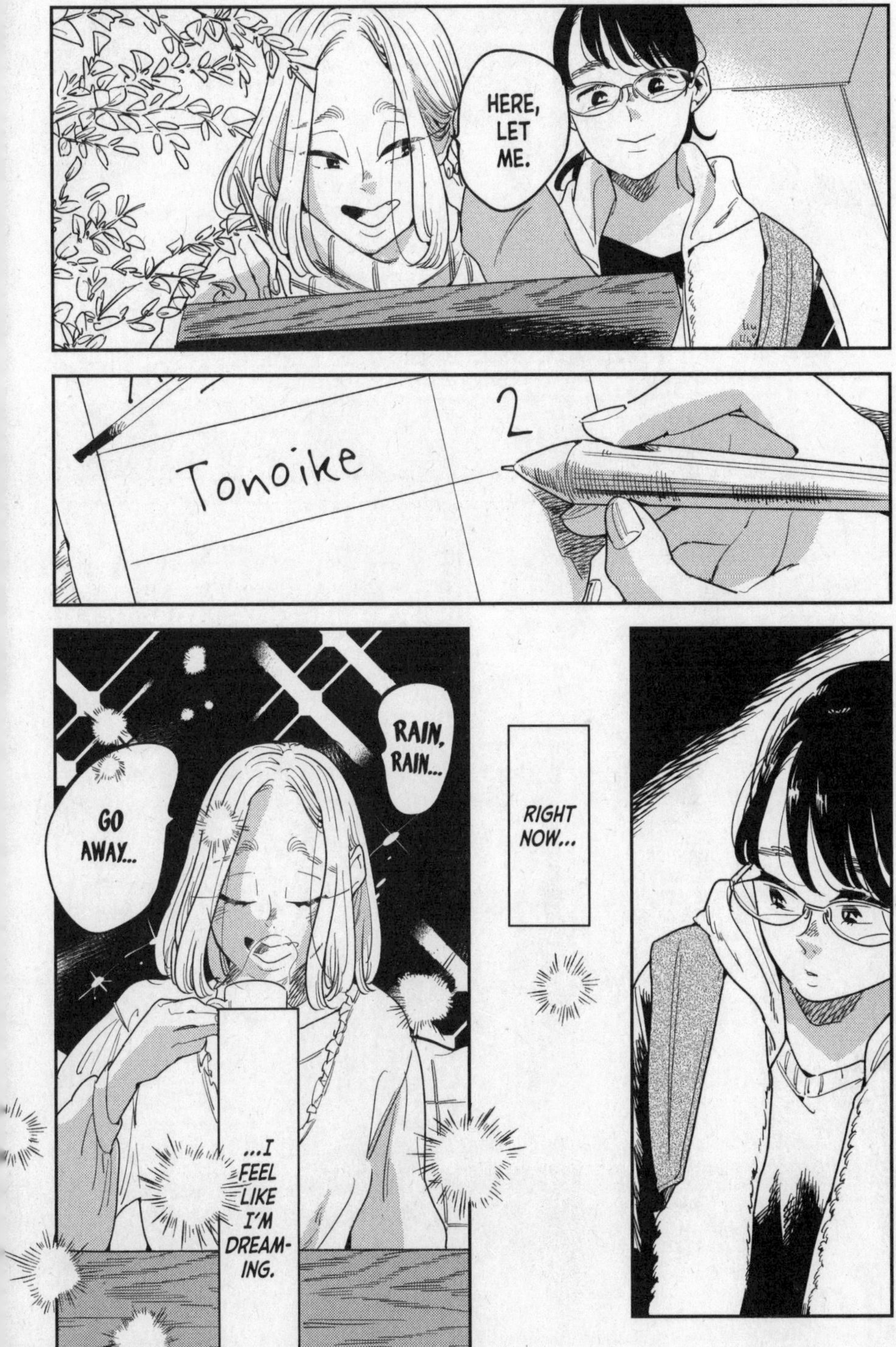
HERE, LET ME.
2
Tonoike
RIGHT NOW...
RAIN, RAIN...
GO AWAY...
...I FEEL LIKE I'M DREAMING.

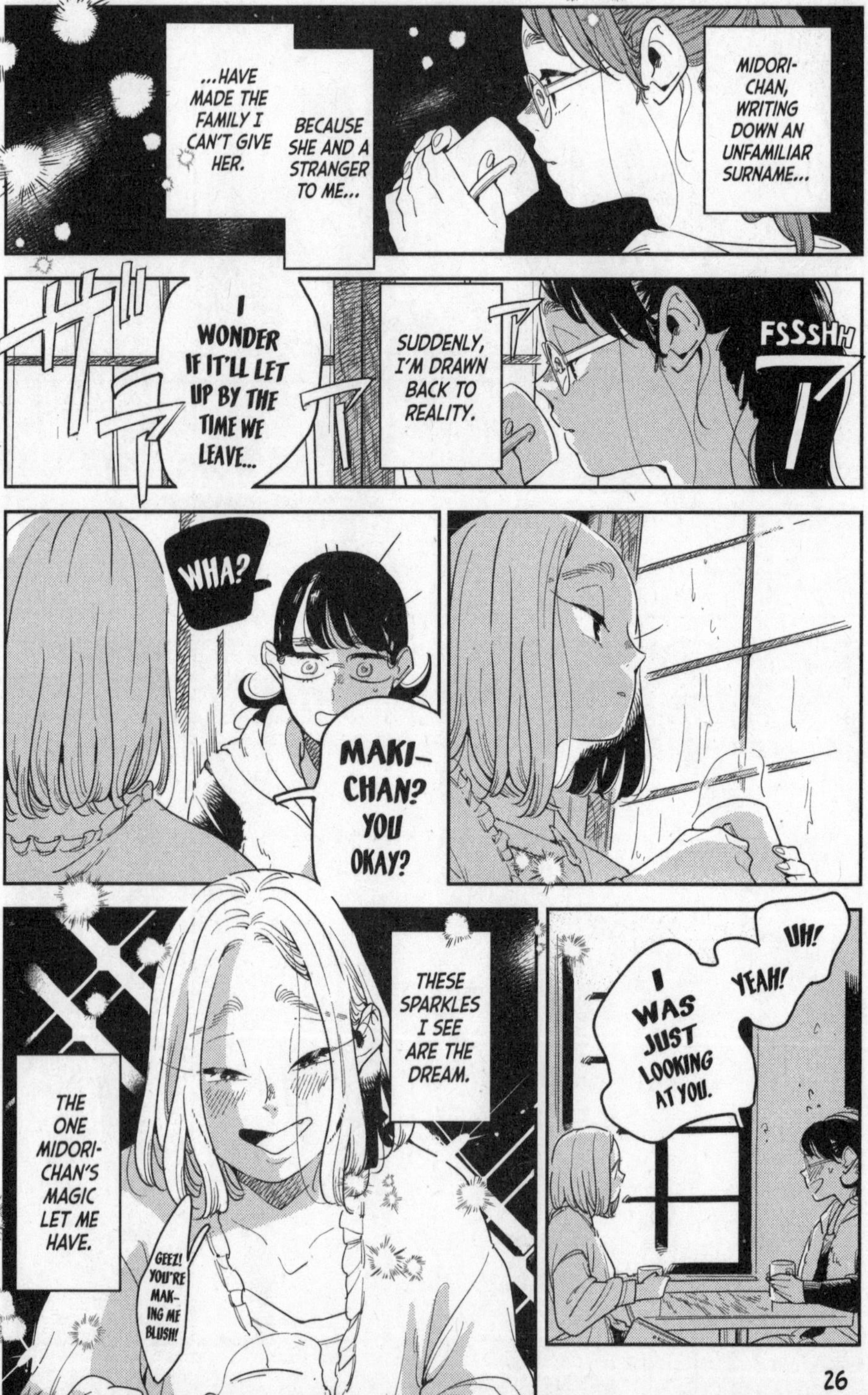
MIDORI-CHAN, WRITING DOWN AN UNFAMILIAR SURNAME...
BECAUSE SHE AND A STRANGER TO ME...
...HAVE MADE THE FAMILY I CAN'T GIVE HER.
FSSSHH
SUDDENLY, I'M DRAWN BACK TO REALITY.
I WONDER IF IT'LL LET UP BY THE TIME WE LEAVE...
WHA?
MAKI-CHAN? YOU OKAY?
UH! YEAH!
I WAS JUST LOOKING AT YOU.
THESE SPARKLES I SEE ARE THE DREAM.
THE ONE MIDORI-CHAN'S MAGIC LET ME HAVE.
GEEZ! YOU'RE MAKING ME BLUSH!

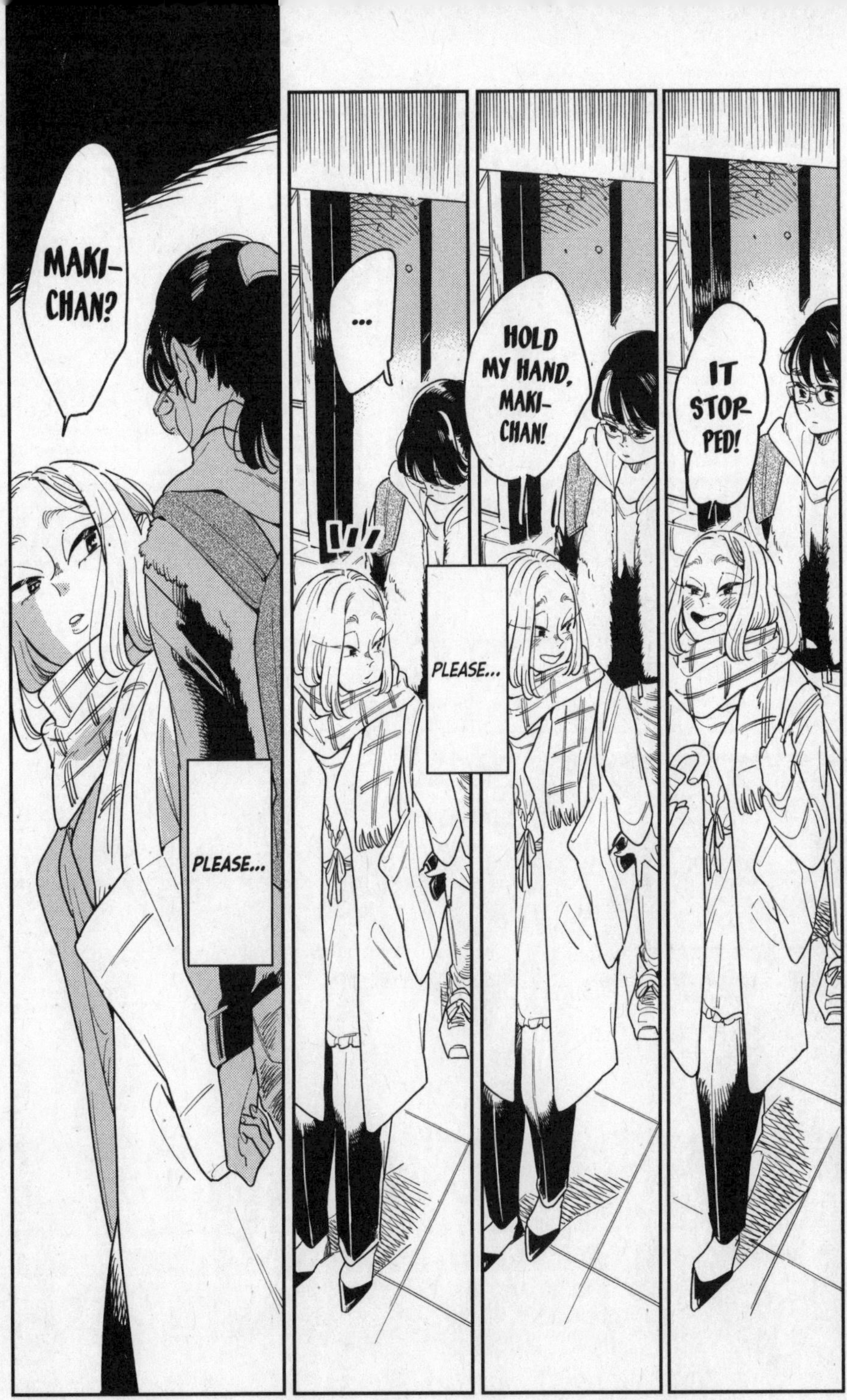
IT STOP-PED!
HOLD MY HAND, MAKI-CHAN!
...
PLEASE...
MAKI-CHAN?
PLEASE...

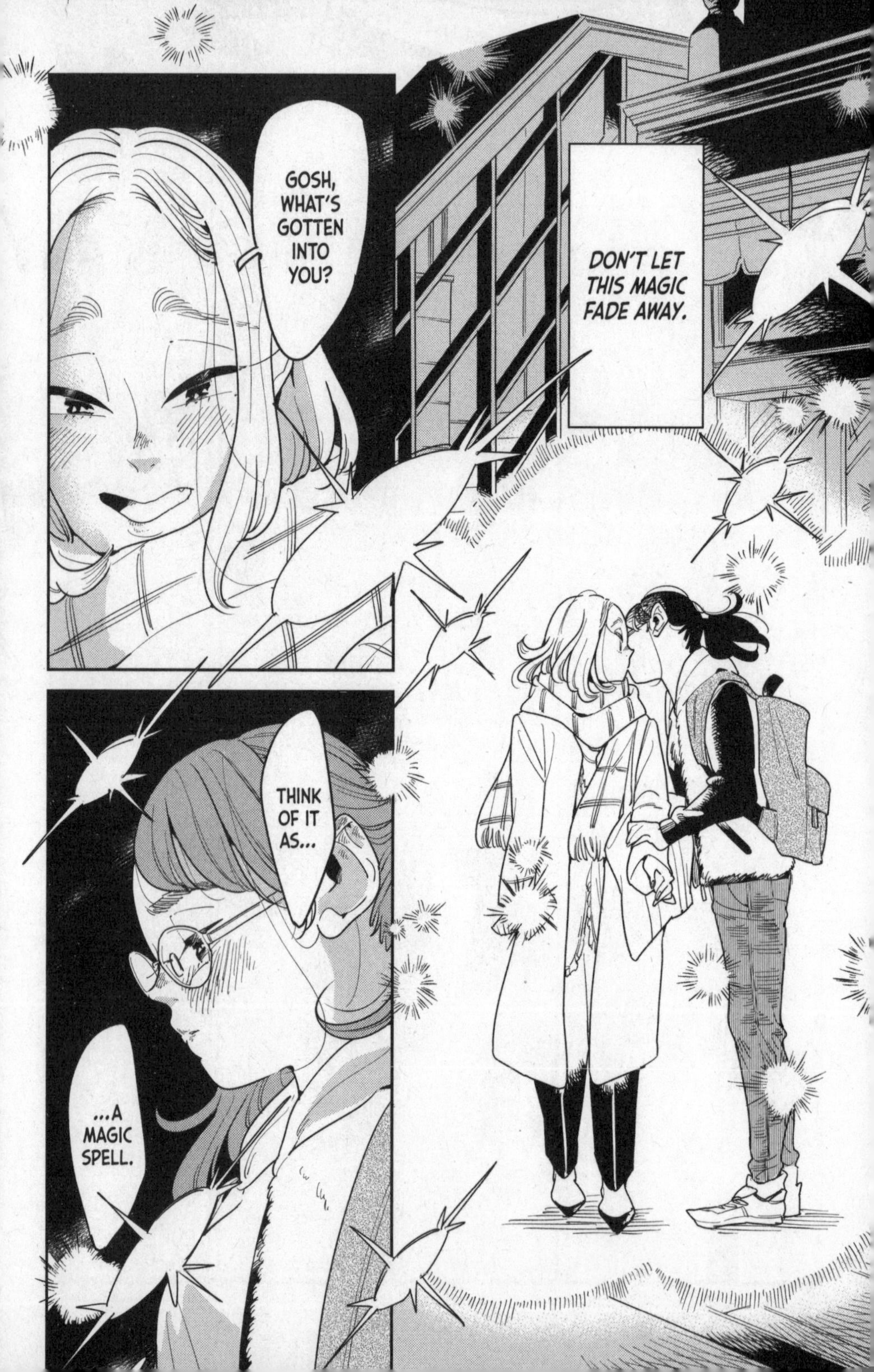
DON'T LET THIS MAGIC FADE AWAY.
GOSH, WHAT'S GOTTEN INTO YOU?
THINK OF IT AS...
...A MAGIC SPELL.

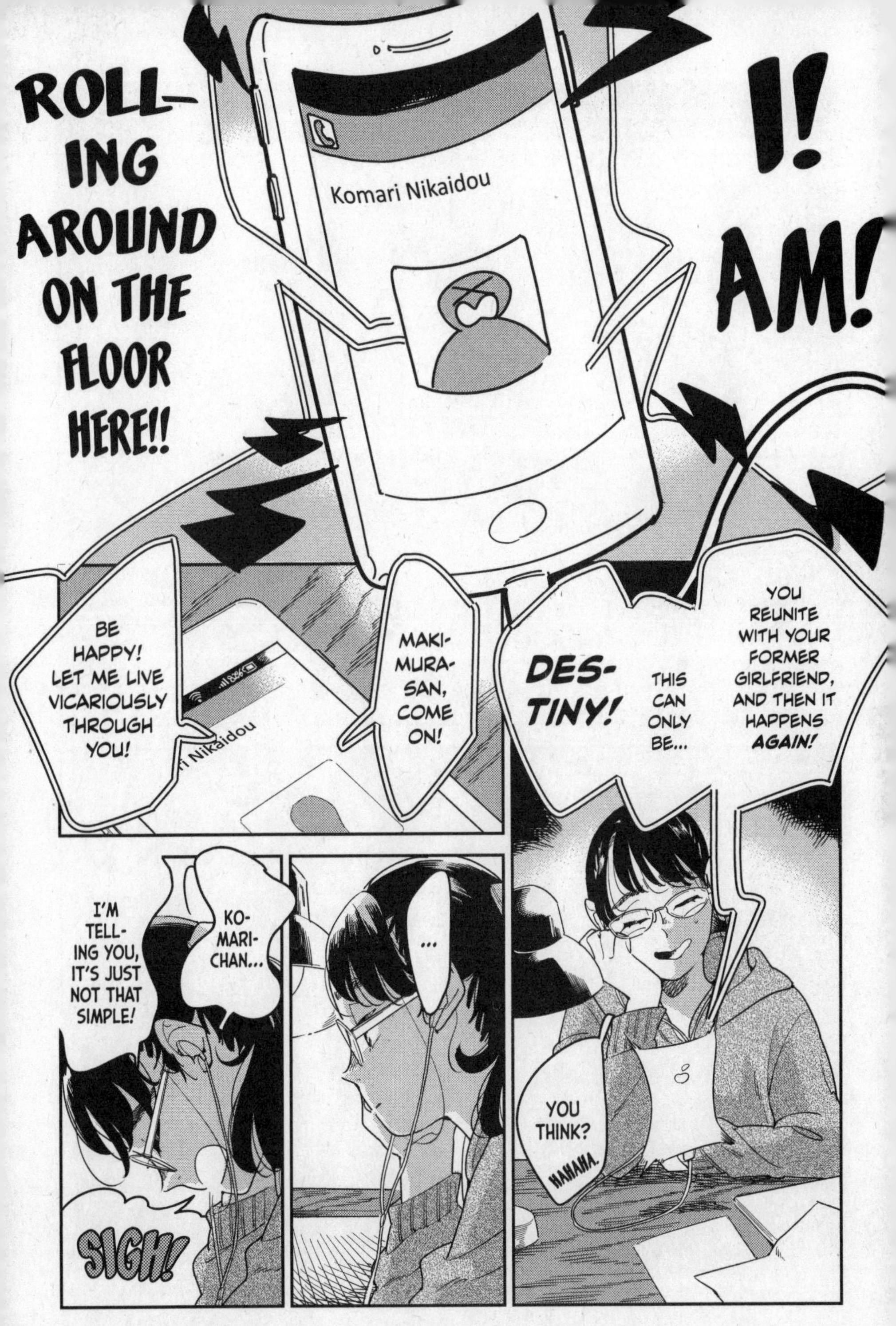
I! AM!
ROLL-ING AROUND ON THE FLOOR HERE!!
Komari Nikaidou
YOU REUNITE WITH YOUR FORMER GIRLFRIEND, AND THEN IT HAPPENS AGAIN!
THIS CAN ONLY BE...
DES-TINY!
YOU THINK?
HAHAHA.
MAKI-MURA-SAN, COME ON!
BE HAPPY! LET ME LIVE VICARIOUSLY THROUGH YOU!
ri Nikaidou
...
KO-MARI-CHAN...
I'M TELL-ING YOU, IT'S JUST NOT THAT SIMPLE!
SIGH!

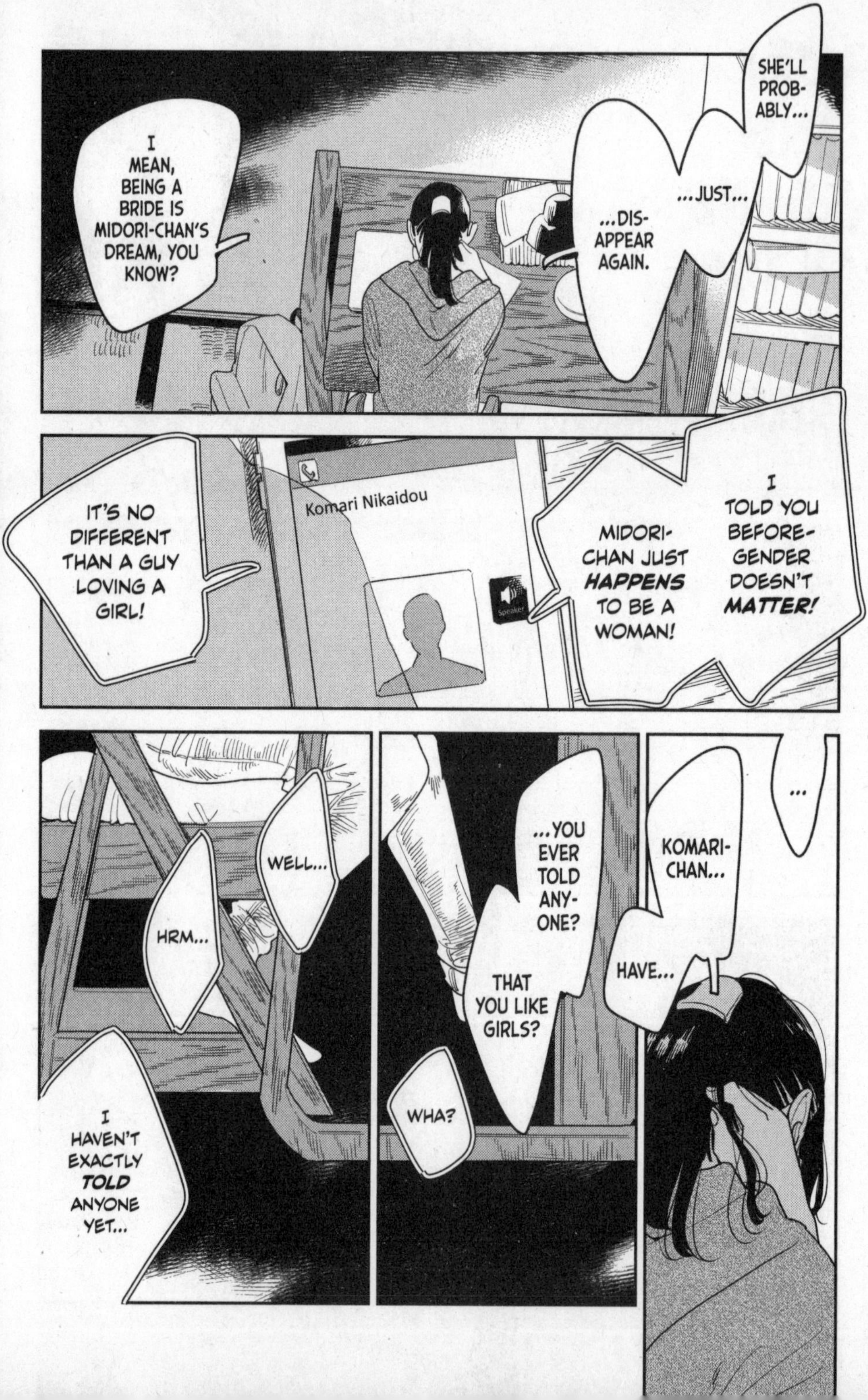
SHE'LL PROBABLY...
...JUST...
...DISAPPEAR AGAIN.
I MEAN, BEING A BRIDE IS MIDORI-CHAN'S DREAM, YOU KNOW?
I TOLD YOU BEFORE-GENDER DOESN'T **MATTER!**
MIDORI-CHAN JUST **HAPPENS** TO BE A WOMAN!
Komari Nikaidou
Speaker
IT'S NO DIFFERENT THAN A GUY LOVING A GIRL!
...
KOMARI-CHAN...
HAVE...
...YOU EVER TOLD ANYONE?
THAT YOU LIKE GIRLS?
WHA?
WELL...
HRM...
I HAVEN'T EXACTLY **TOLD** ANYONE YET...

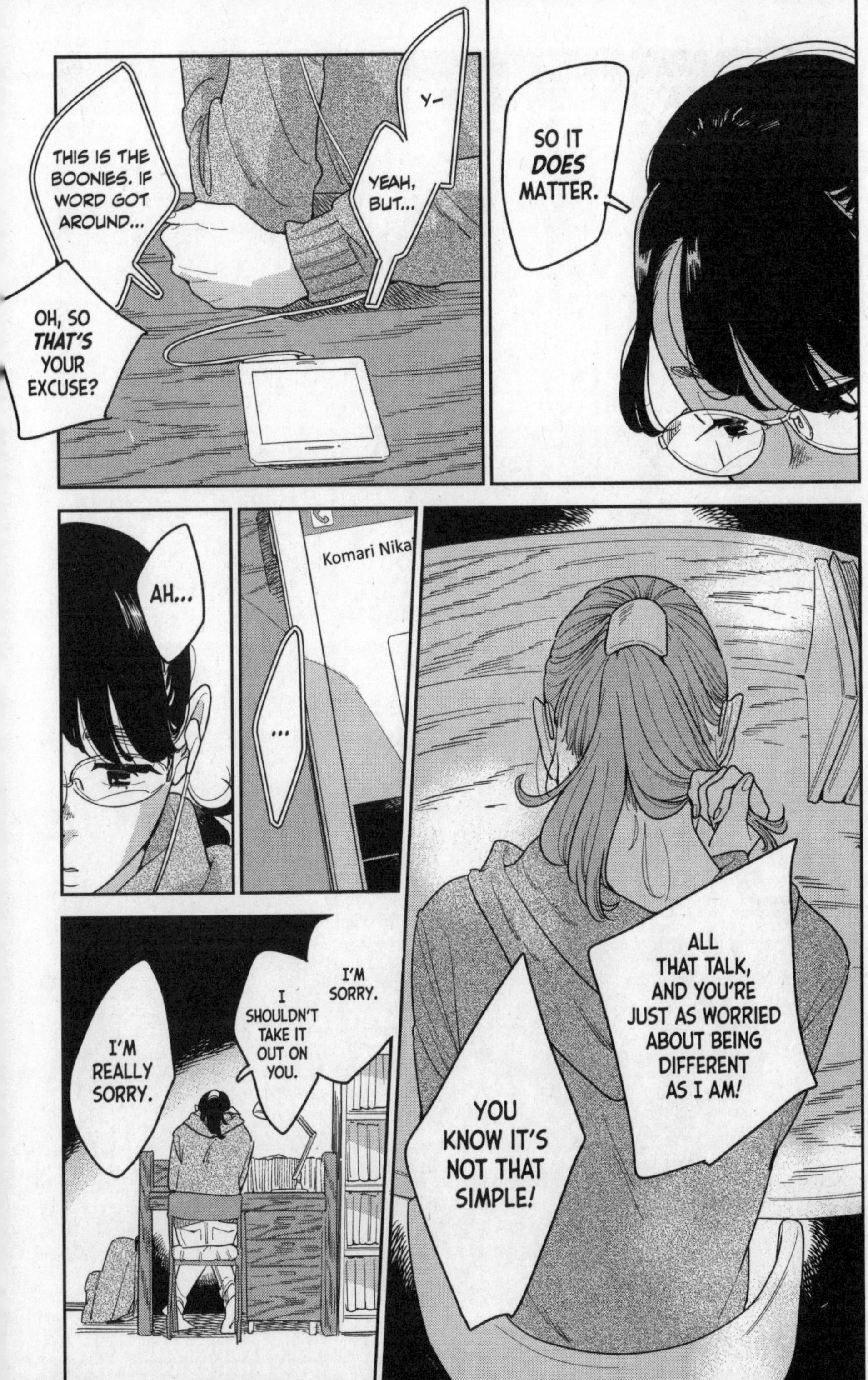
SO IT *DOES* MATTER.
Y-
YEAH, BUT...
THIS IS THE BOONIES. IF WORD GOT AROUND...
OH, SO *THAT'S* YOUR EXCUSE?
ALL THAT TALK, AND YOU'RE JUST AS WORRIED ABOUT BEING DIFFERENT AS I AM!
YOU KNOW IT'S NOT THAT SIMPLE!
Komari Nika
...
AH...
I'M SORRY.
I SHOULDN'T TAKE IT OUT ON YOU.
I'M REALLY SORRY.

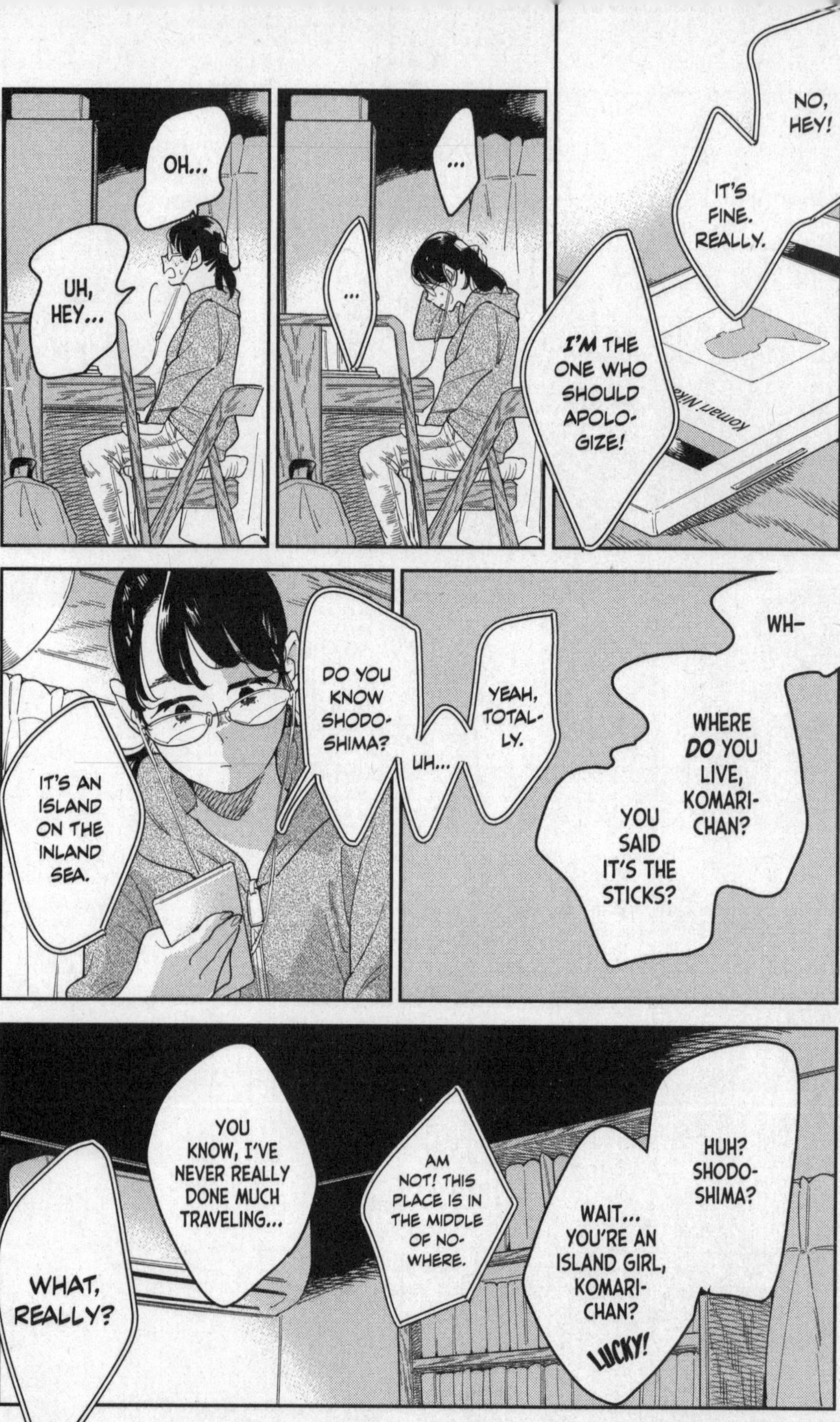

NO, HEY!
IT'S FINE. REALLY.
I'M THE ONE WHO SHOULD APOLOGIZE!
...
...
OH...
UH, HEY...
WH-
WHERE *DO* YOU LIVE, KOMARI-CHAN?
YOU SAID IT'S THE STICKS?
YEAH, TOTALLY.
UH...
DO YOU KNOW SHODOSHIMA?
IT'S AN ISLAND ON THE INLAND SEA.
HUH? SHODOSHIMA?
WAIT... YOU'RE AN ISLAND GIRL, KOMARI-CHAN?
LUCKY!
AM NOT! THIS PLACE IS IN THE MIDDLE OF NOWHERE.
YOU KNOW, I'VE NEVER REALLY DONE MUCH TRAVELING...
WHAT, REALLY?

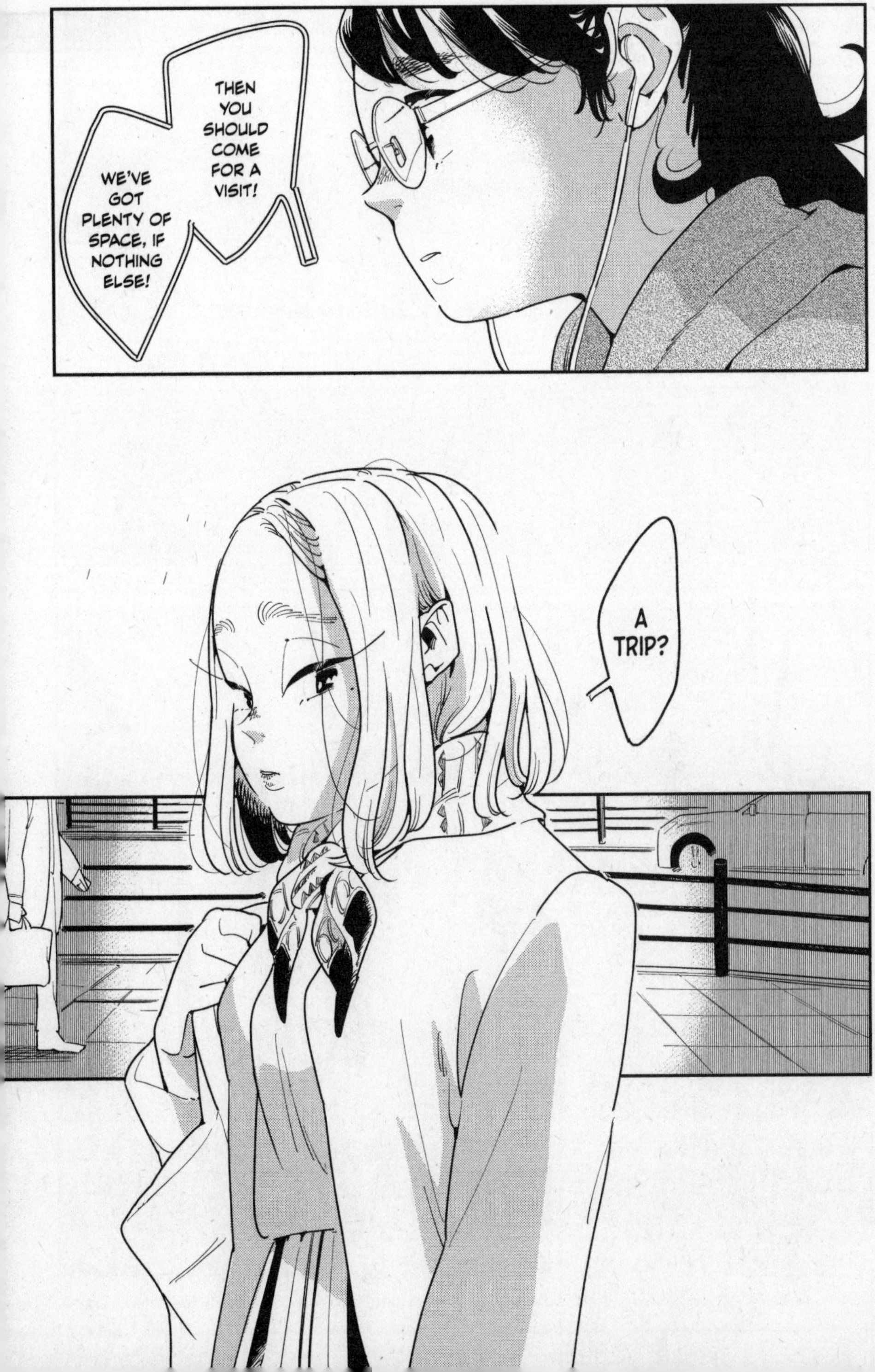
THEN YOU SHOULD COME FOR A VISIT!
WE'VE GOT PLENTY OF SPACE, IF NOTHING ELSE!
A TRIP?

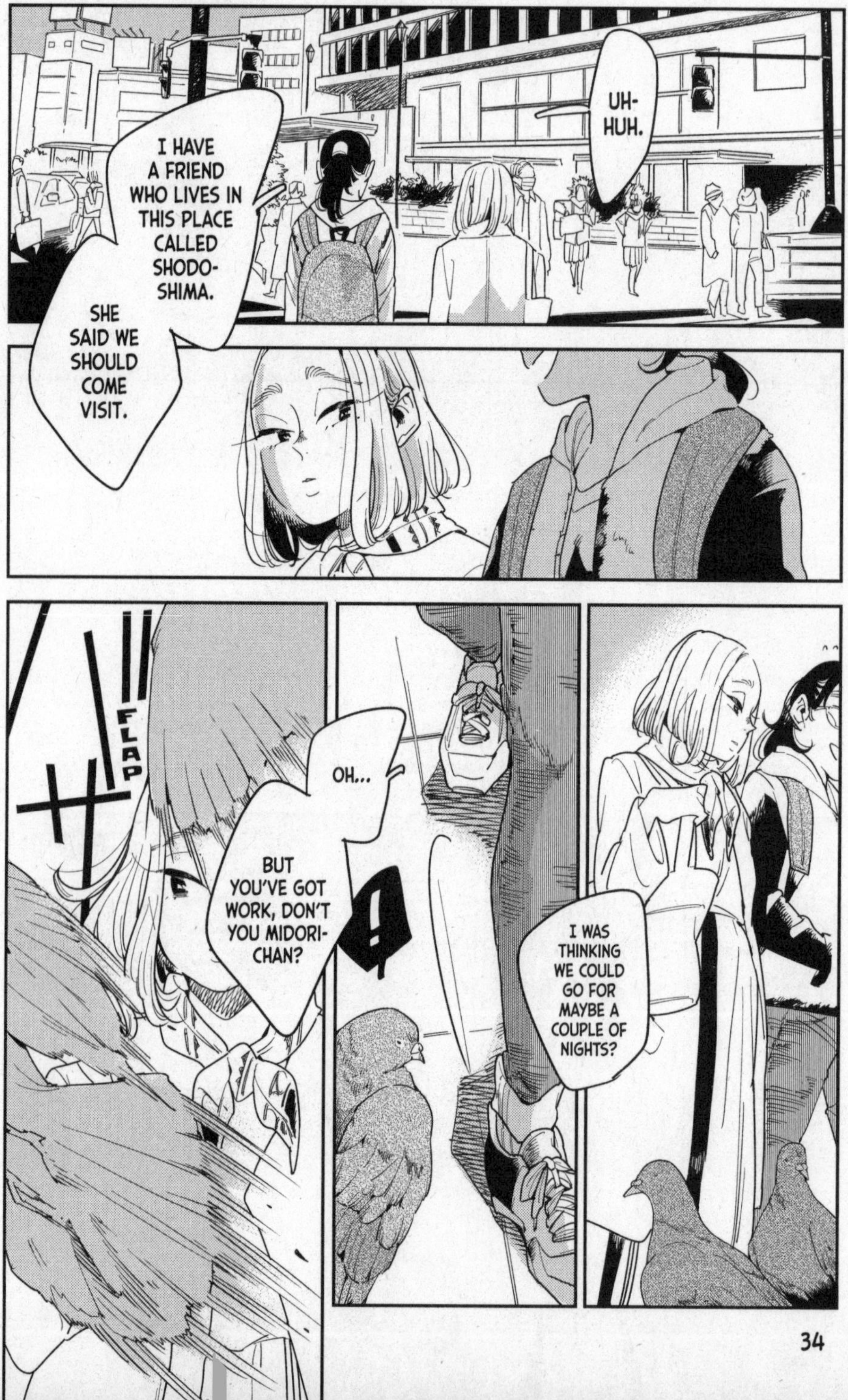
UH-HUH.
I HAVE A FRIEND WHO LIVES IN THIS PLACE CALLED SHODO-SHIMA.
SHE SAID WE SHOULD COME VISIT.
I WAS THINKING WE COULD GO FOR MAYBE A COUPLE OF NIGHTS?
OH...
BUT YOU'VE GOT WORK, DON'T YOU MIDORI-CHAN?
!
FLAP

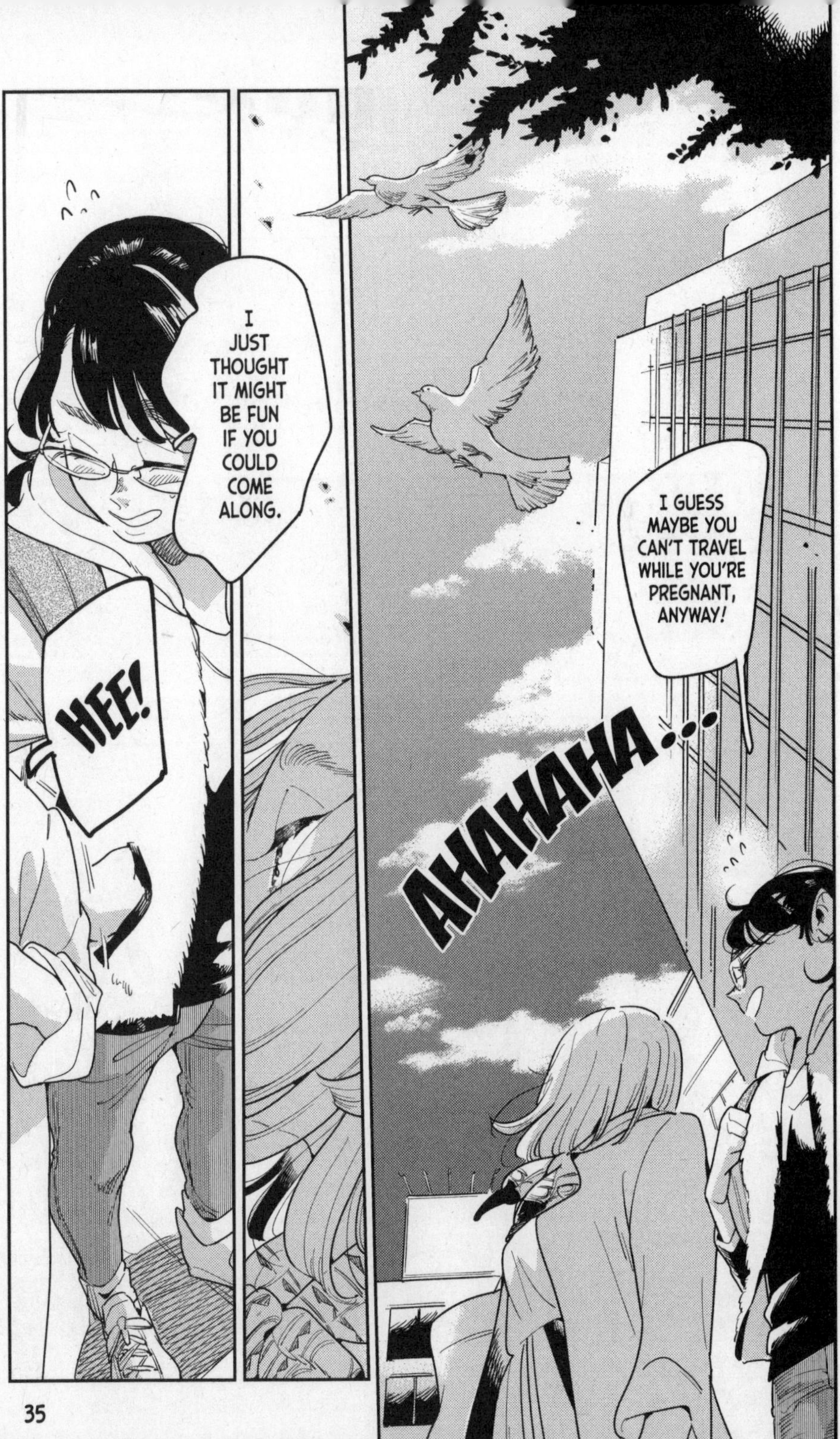
I GUESS MAYBE YOU CAN'T TRAVEL WHILE YOU'RE PREGNANT, ANYWAY!
AHAHAHA...
I JUST THOUGHT IT MIGHT BE FUN IF YOU COULD COME ALONG.
HEE!

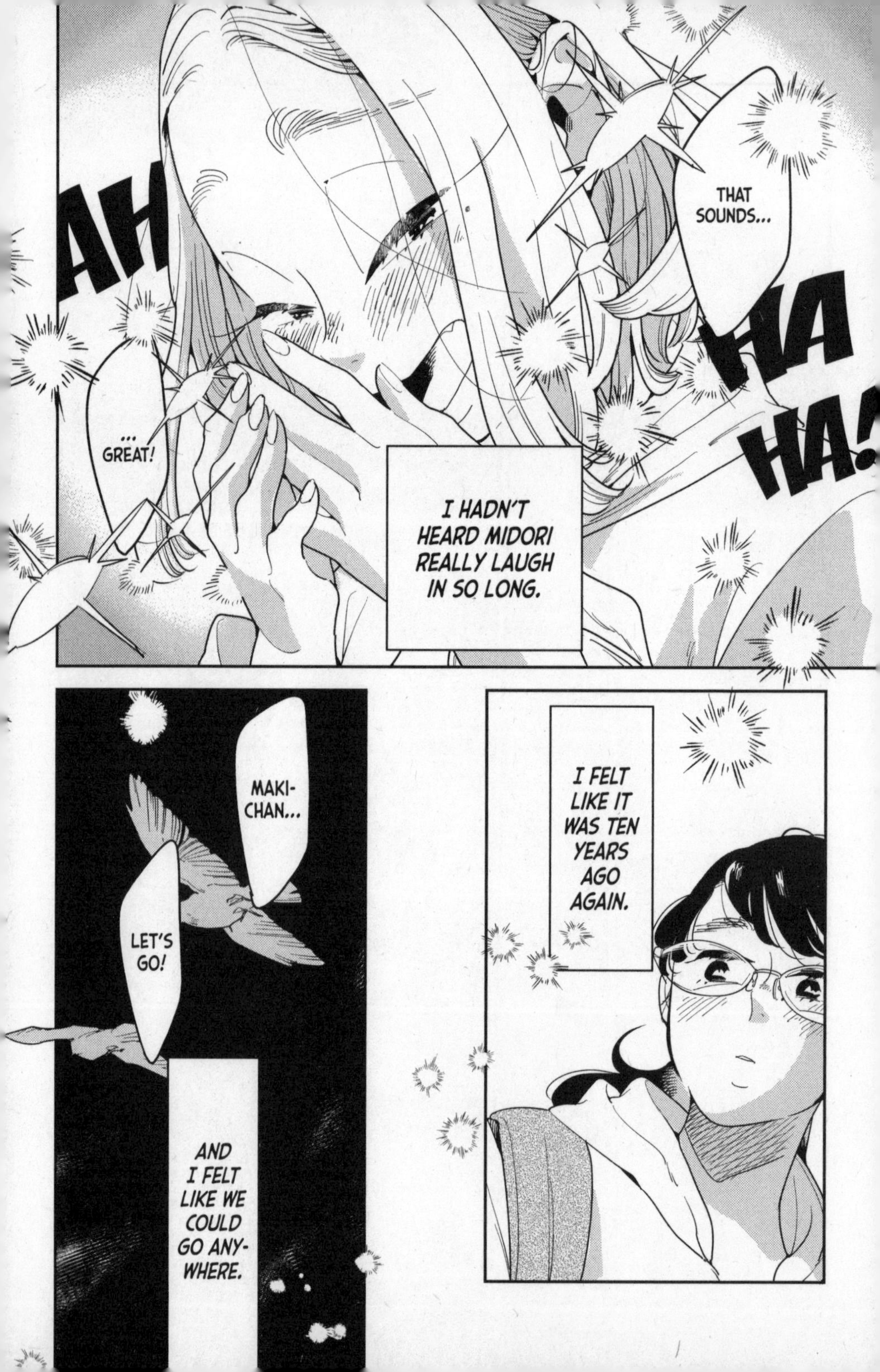
THAT SOUNDS...
AH
HA HA!
...GREAT!
I HADN'T HEARD MIDORI REALLY LAUGH IN SO LONG.
I FELT LIKE IT WAS TEN YEARS AGO AGAIN.
MAKI-CHAN...
LET'S GO!
AND I FELT LIKE WE COULD GO ANY-WHERE.

EPISODE 8

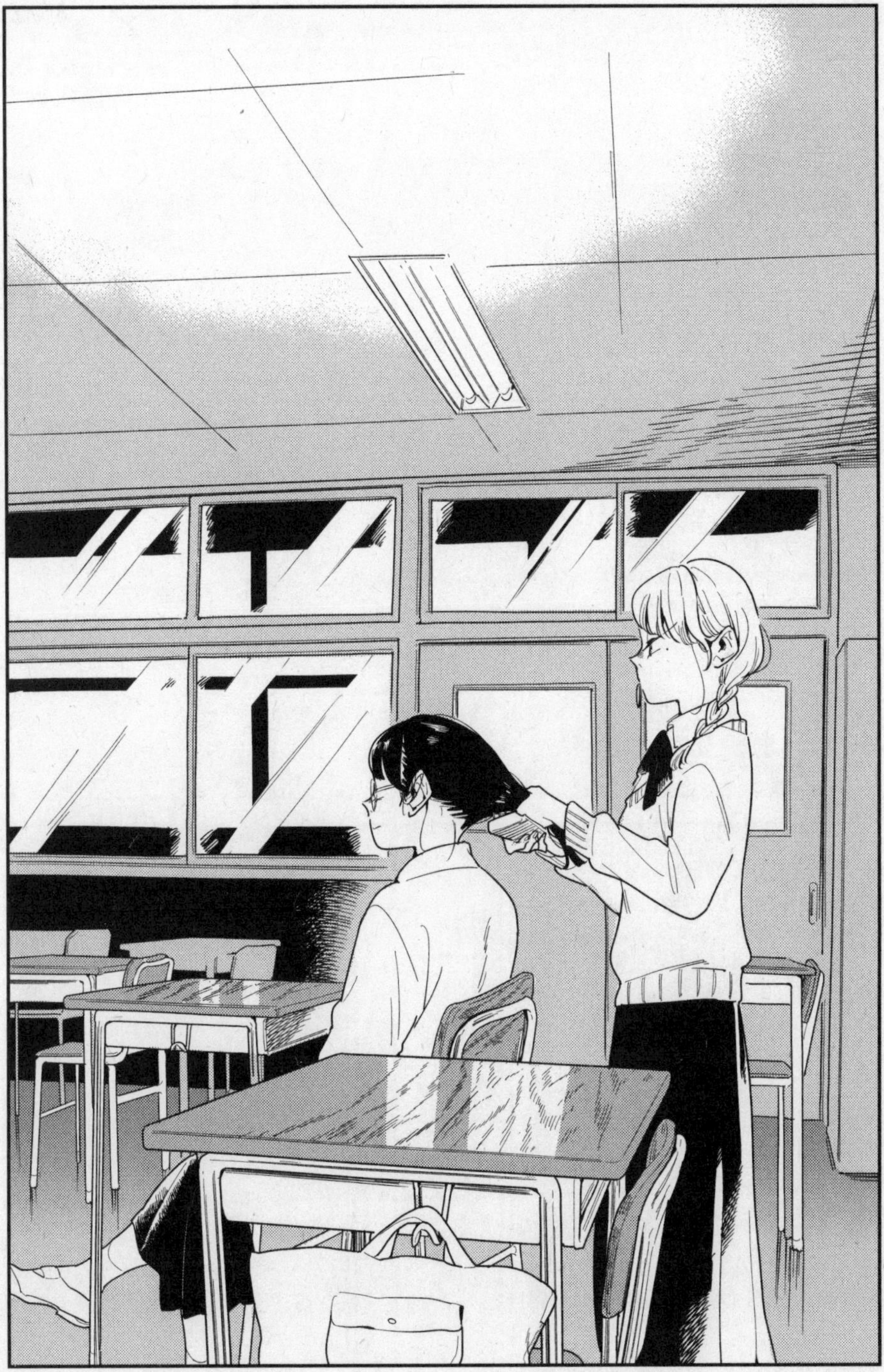

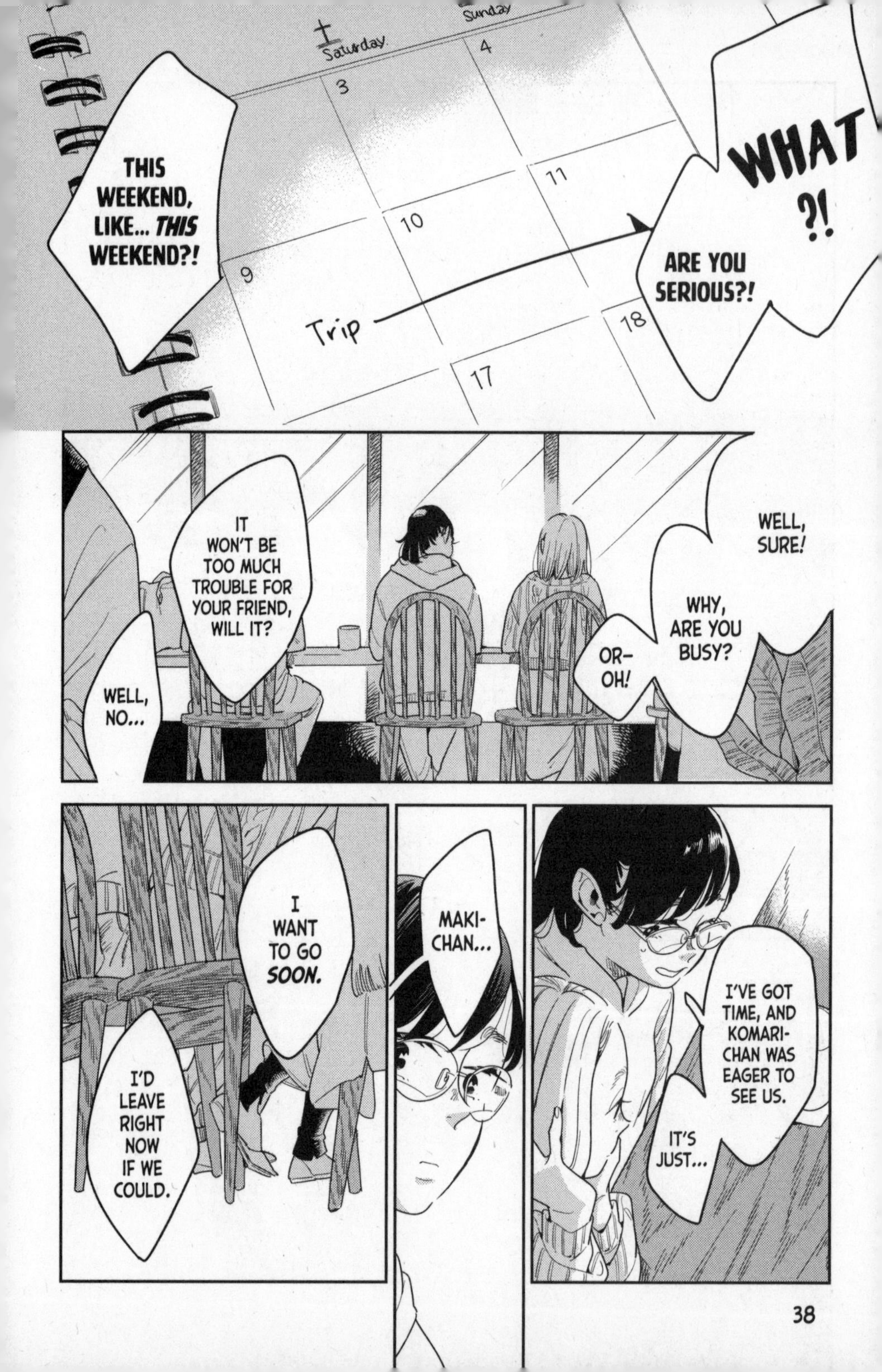
WHAT ?!
ARE YOU SERIOUS?!
Sunday
Saturday
Trip
THIS WEEKEND, LIKE... *THIS* WEEKEND?!
WELL, SURE!
WHY, ARE YOU BUSY?
OR– OH!
IT WON'T BE TOO MUCH TROUBLE FOR YOUR FRIEND, WILL IT?
WELL, NO...
I'VE GOT TIME, AND KOMARI-CHAN WAS EAGER TO SEE US.
IT'S JUST...
MAKI-CHAN...
I WANT TO GO *SOON.*
I'D LEAVE RIGHT NOW IF WE COULD.

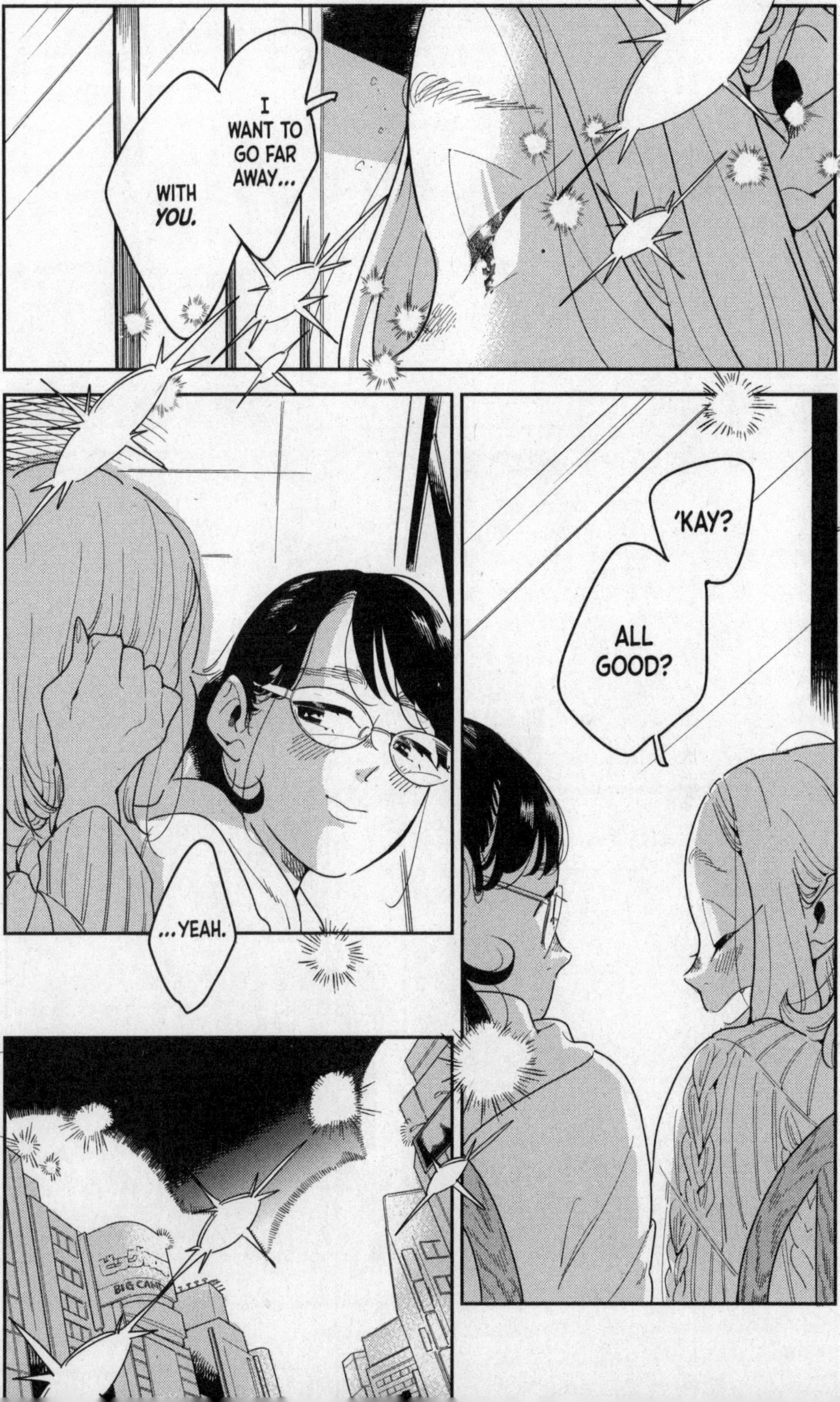
I WANT TO GO FAR AWAY...
WITH *YOU.*
'KAY?
ALL GOOD?
...YEAH.

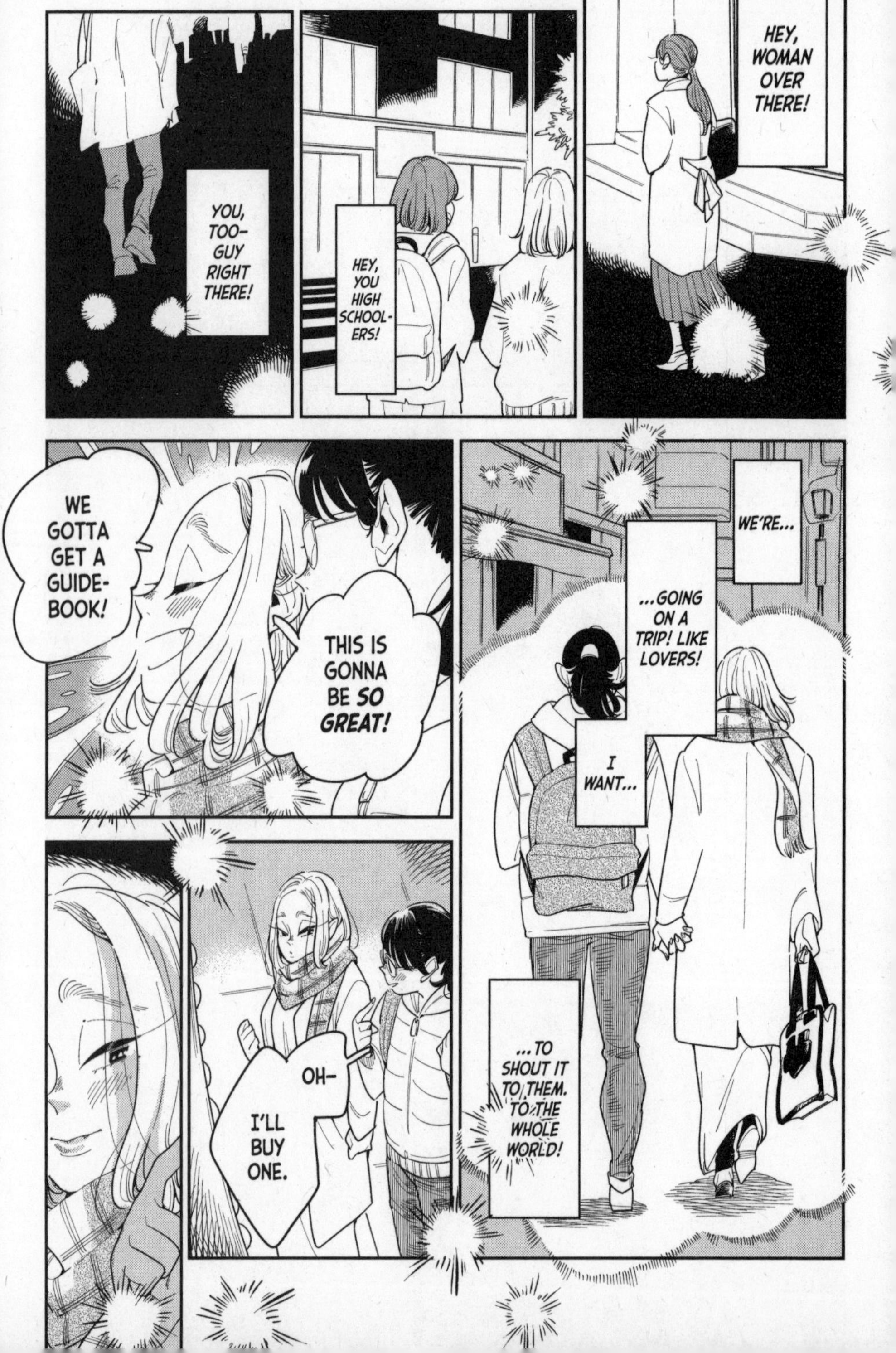
HEY, WOMAN OVER THERE!
HEY, YOU HIGH SCHOOLERS!
YOU, TOO— GUY RIGHT THERE!
WE'RE...
...GOING ON A TRIP! LIKE LOVERS!
I WANT...
...TO SHOUT IT TO THEM. TO THE WHOLE WORLD!
THIS IS GONNA BE SO GREAT!
WE GOTTA GET A GUIDEBOOK!
OH—
I'LL BUY ONE.

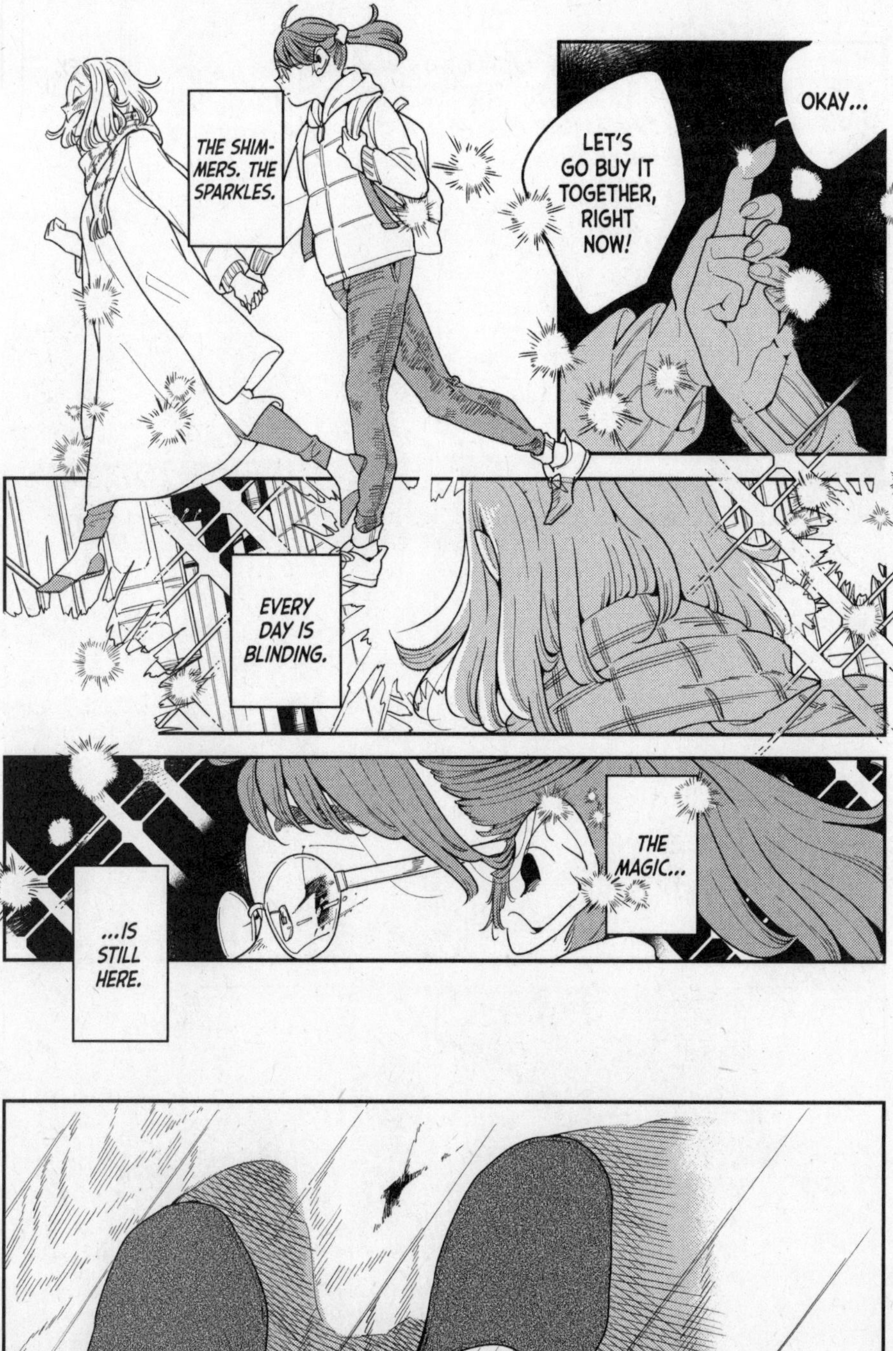
OKAY...
LET'S GO BUY IT TOGETHER, RIGHT NOW!
THE SHIMMERS. THE SPARKLES.
EVERY DAY IS BLINDING.
THE MAGIC...
...IS STILL HERE.

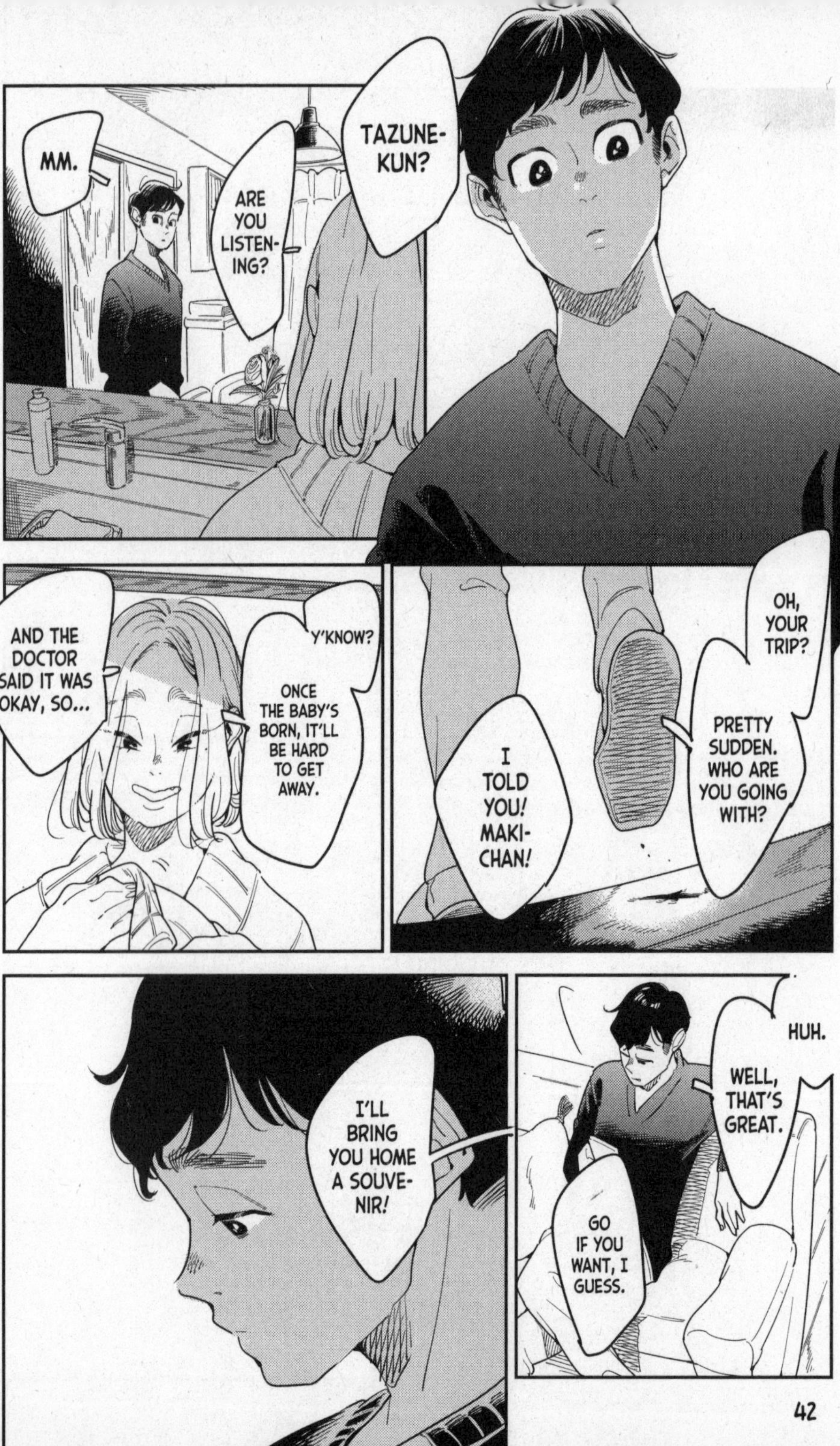
TAZUNE-KUN?
ARE YOU LISTENING?
MM.
OH, YOUR TRIP?
PRETTY SUDDEN. WHO ARE YOU GOING WITH?
I TOLD YOU! MAKI-CHAN!
Y'KNOW?
ONCE THE BABY'S BORN, IT'LL BE HARD TO GET AWAY.
AND THE DOCTOR SAID IT WAS OKAY, SO...
HUH.
WELL, THAT'S GREAT.
GO IF YOU WANT, I GUESS.
I'LL BRING YOU HOME A SOUVENIR!

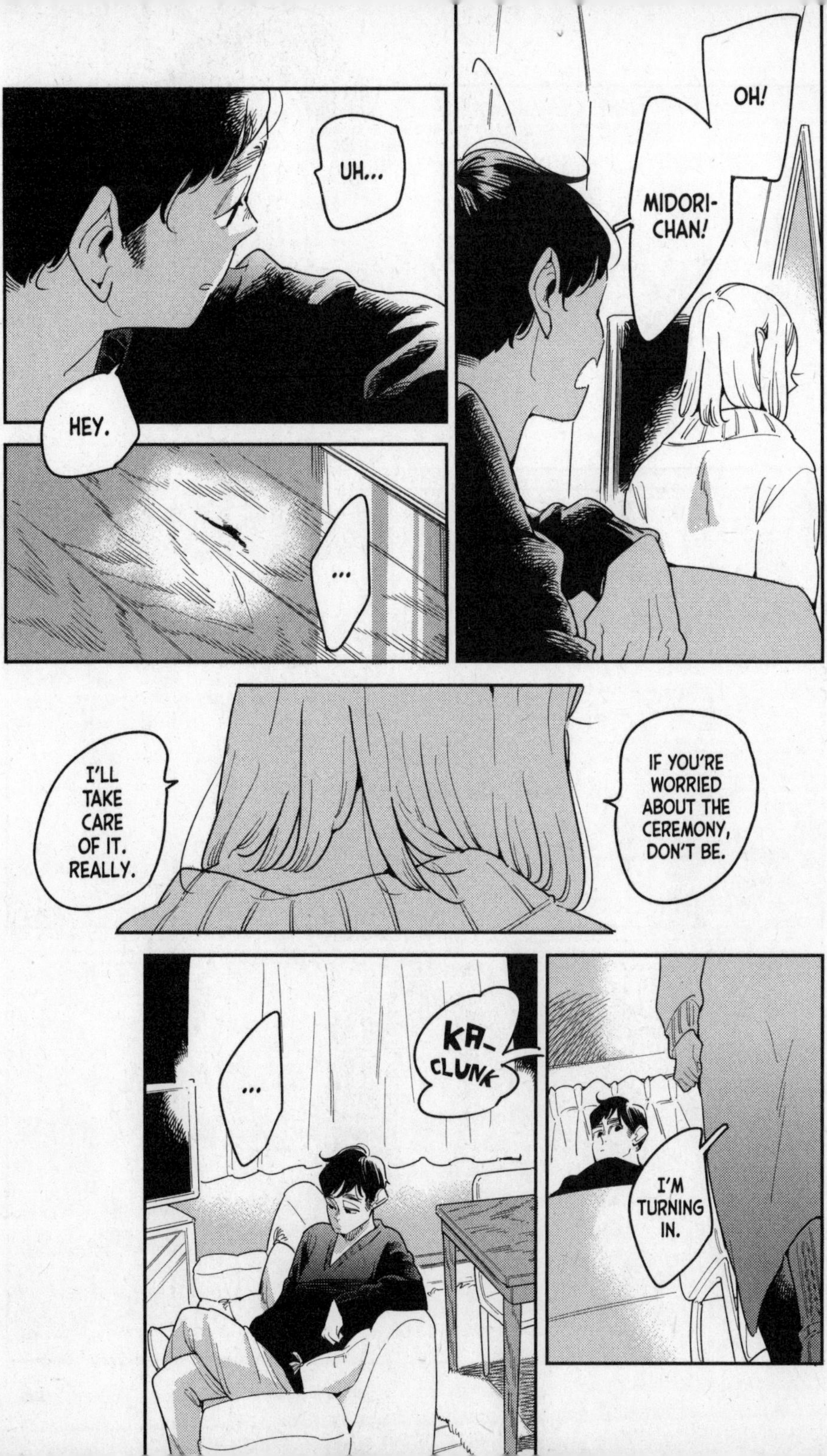
OH!
MIDORI-CHAN!
UH...
HEY.
...
IF YOU'RE WORRIED ABOUT THE CEREMONY, DON'T BE.
I'LL TAKE CARE OF IT. REALLY.
I'M TURNING IN.
KA-CLUNK
...

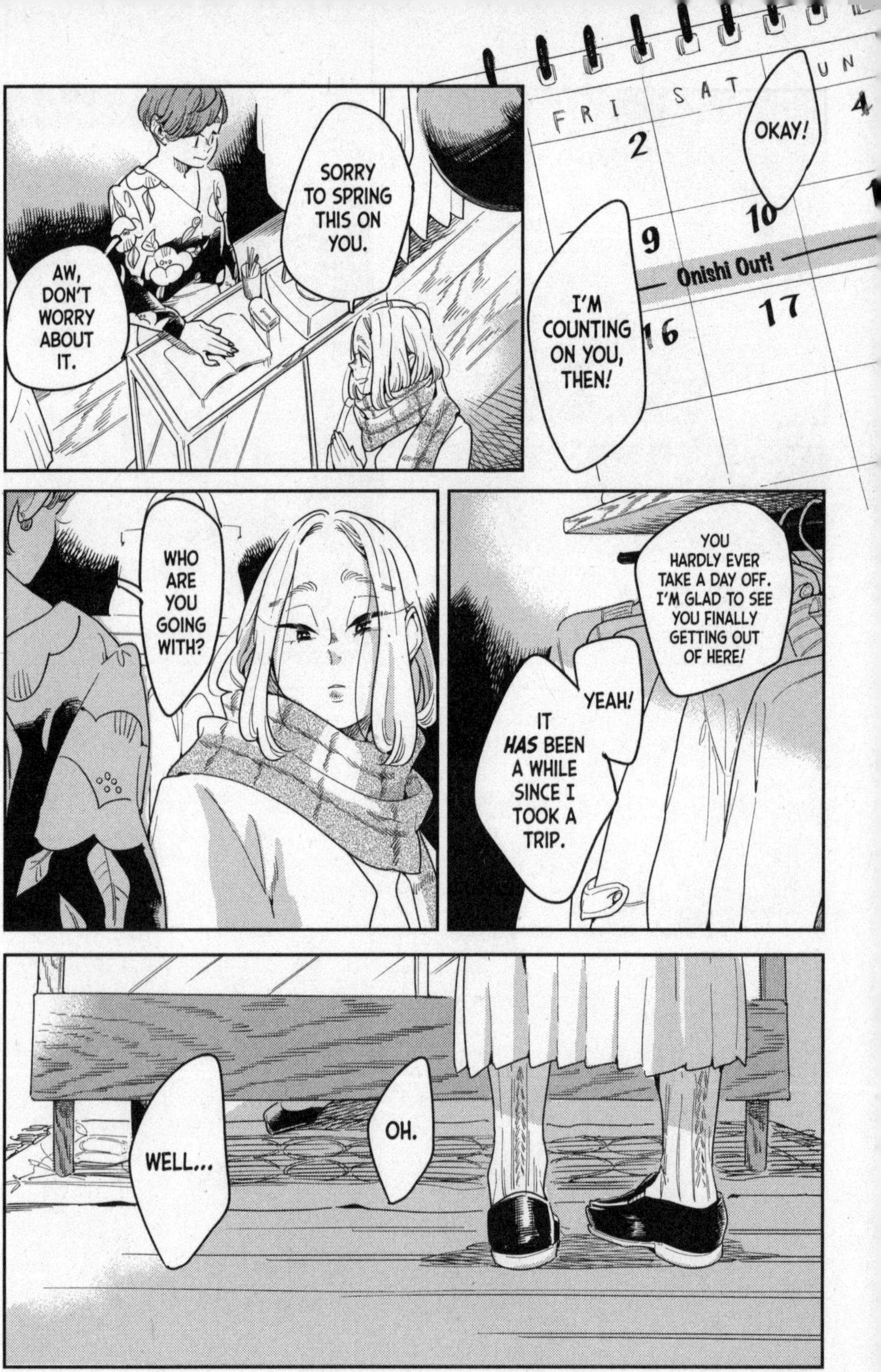

FRI
SAT
2
4
OKAY!
10
9
Onishi Out!
I'M COUNTING ON YOU, THEN!
16
17
SORRY TO SPRING THIS ON YOU.
AW, DON'T WORRY ABOUT IT.
YOU HARDLY EVER TAKE A DAY OFF. I'M GLAD TO SEE YOU FINALLY GETTING OUT OF HERE!
YEAH!
IT *HAS* BEEN A WHILE SINCE I TOOK A TRIP.
WHO ARE YOU GOING WITH?
OH.
WELL...

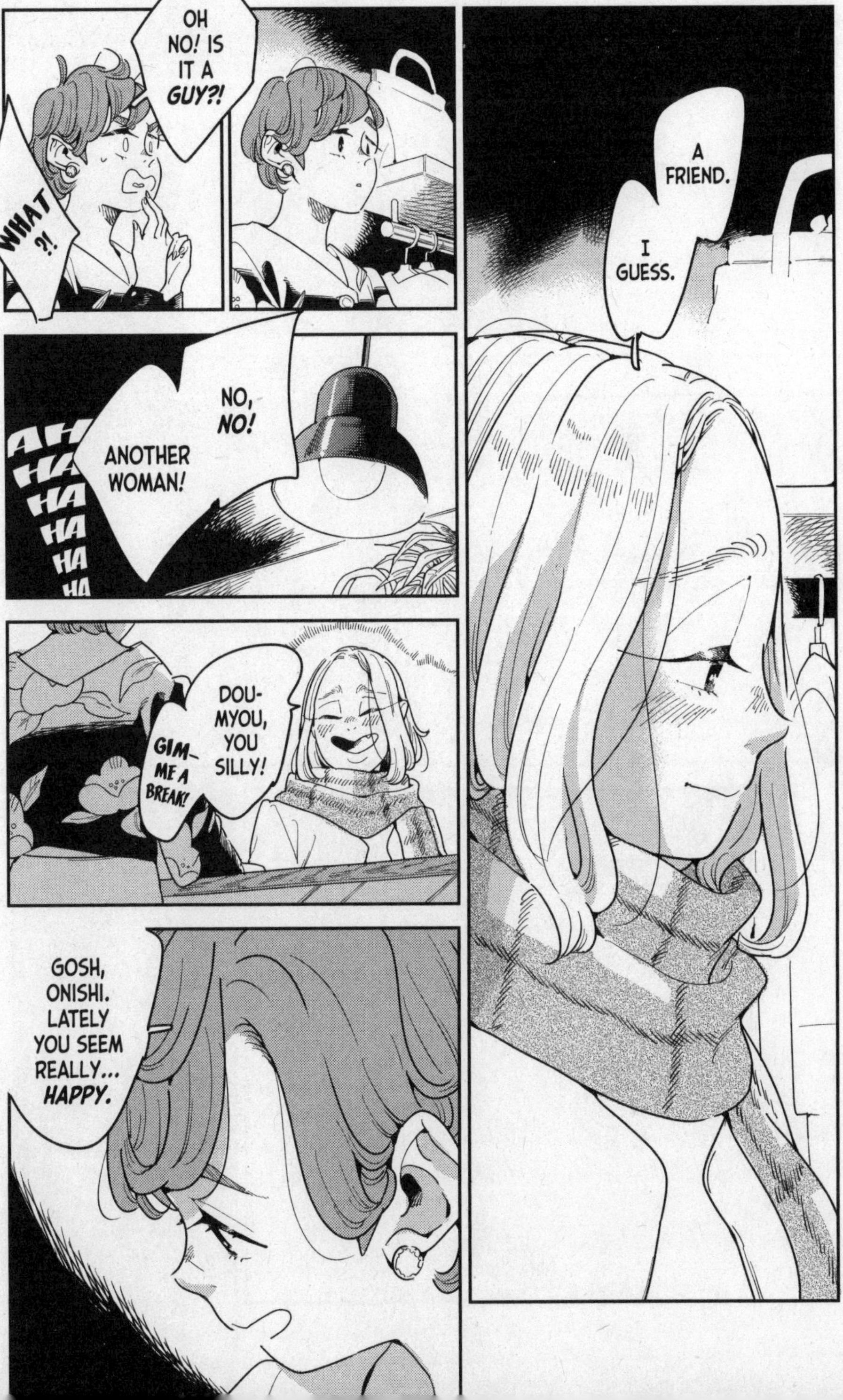
A FRIEND.
I GUESS.
OH NO! IS IT A GUY?!
WHAT ?!
NO, NO!
ANOTHER WOMAN!
AHHAHAHAHAHAHA
DOU-MYOU, YOU SILLY!
GIM-ME A BREAK!
GOSH, ONISHI. LATELY YOU SEEM REALLY... HAPPY.

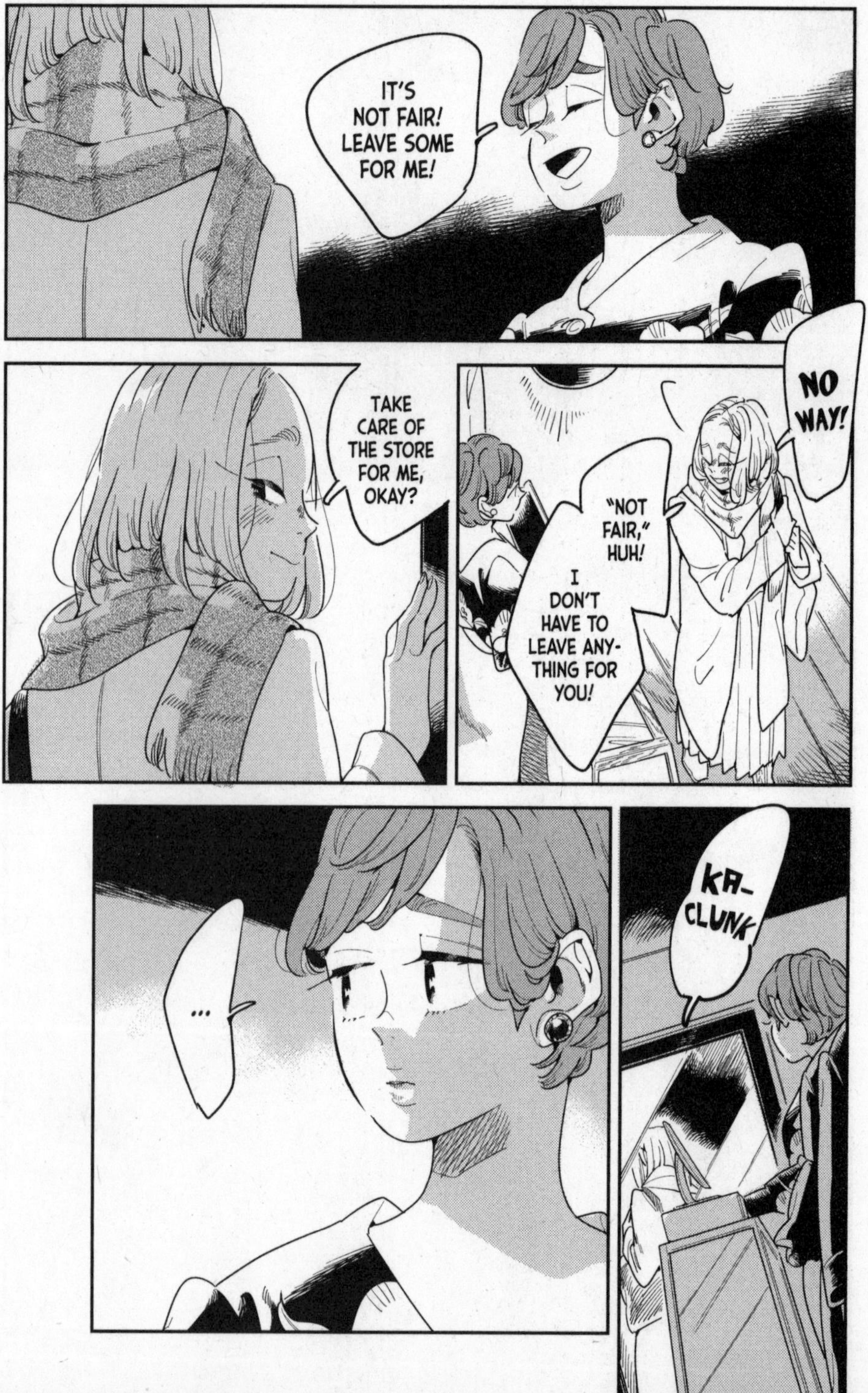
IT'S NOT FAIR! LEAVE SOME FOR ME!
NO WAY!
"NOT FAIR," HUH!
I DON'T HAVE TO LEAVE ANY-THING FOR YOU!
TAKE CARE OF THE STORE FOR ME, OKAY?
KA-CLUNK
...

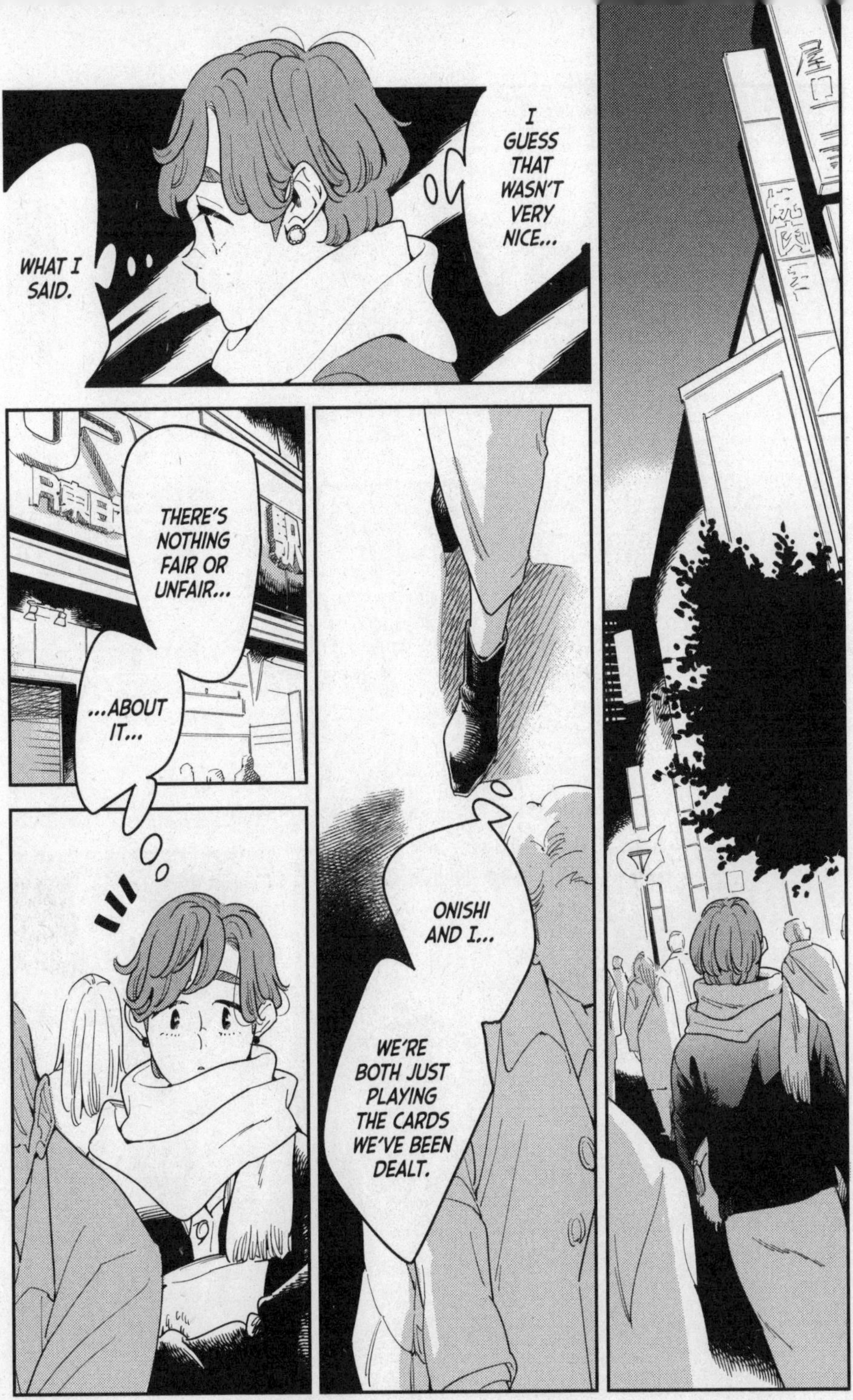
I GUESS THAT WASN'T VERY NICE...
WHAT I SAID.
ONISHI AND I...
WE'RE BOTH JUST PLAYING THE CARDS WE'VE BEEN DEALT.
THERE'S NOTHING FAIR OR UNFAIR...
...ABOUT IT...

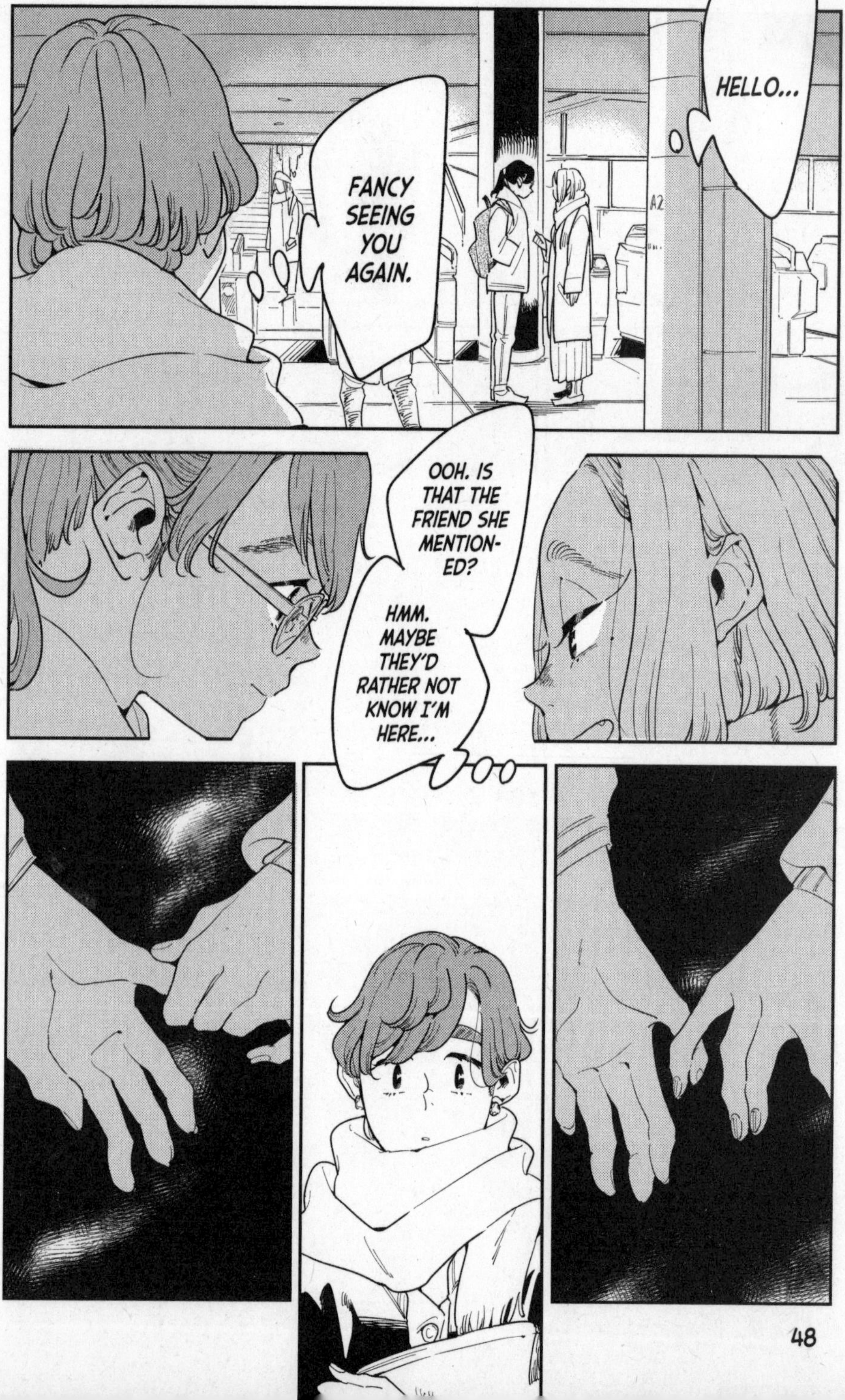
HELLO...
FANCY SEEING YOU AGAIN.
OOH. IS THAT THE FRIEND SHE MENTION-ED?
HMM. MAYBE THEY'D RATHER NOT KNOW I'M HERE...

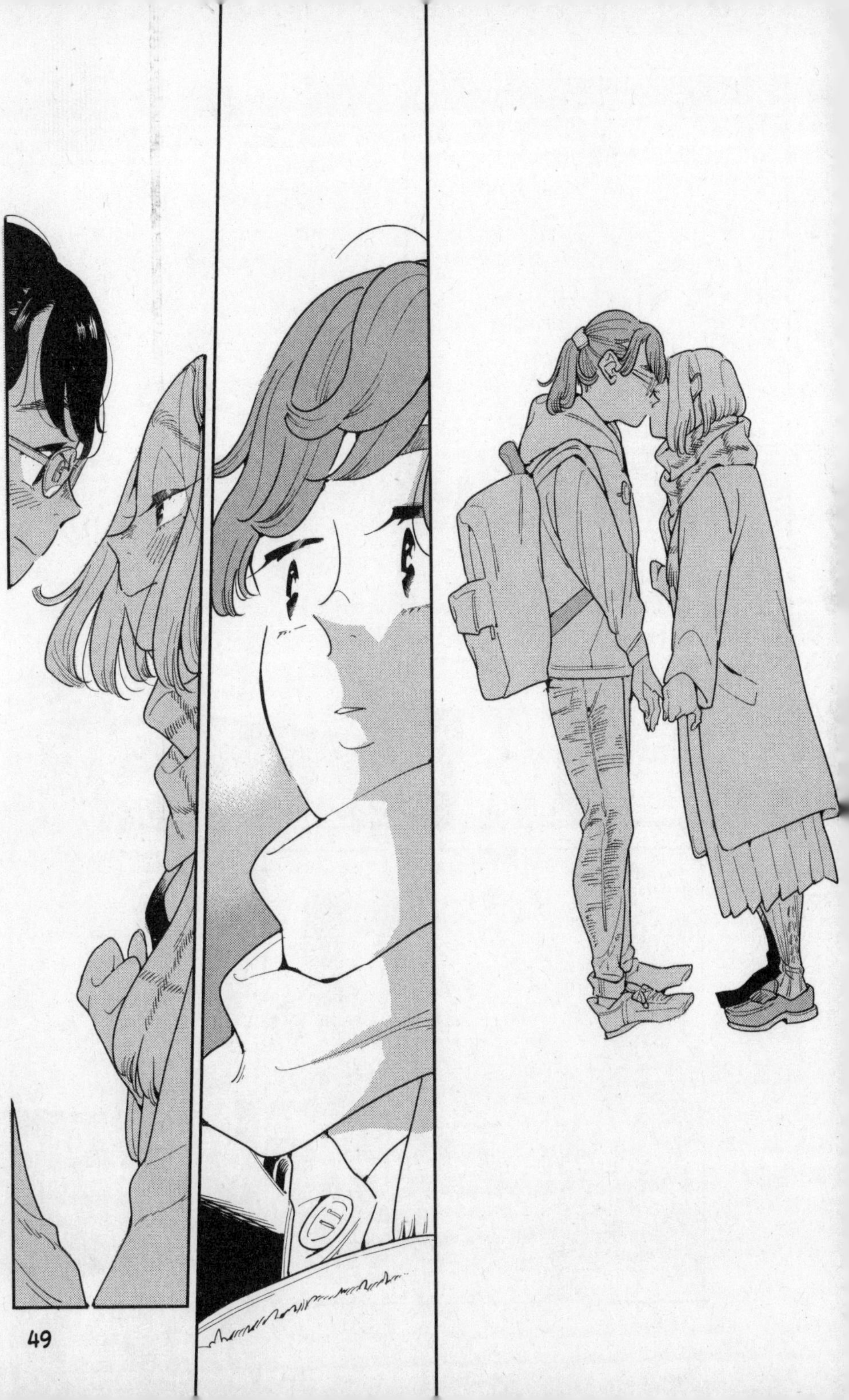

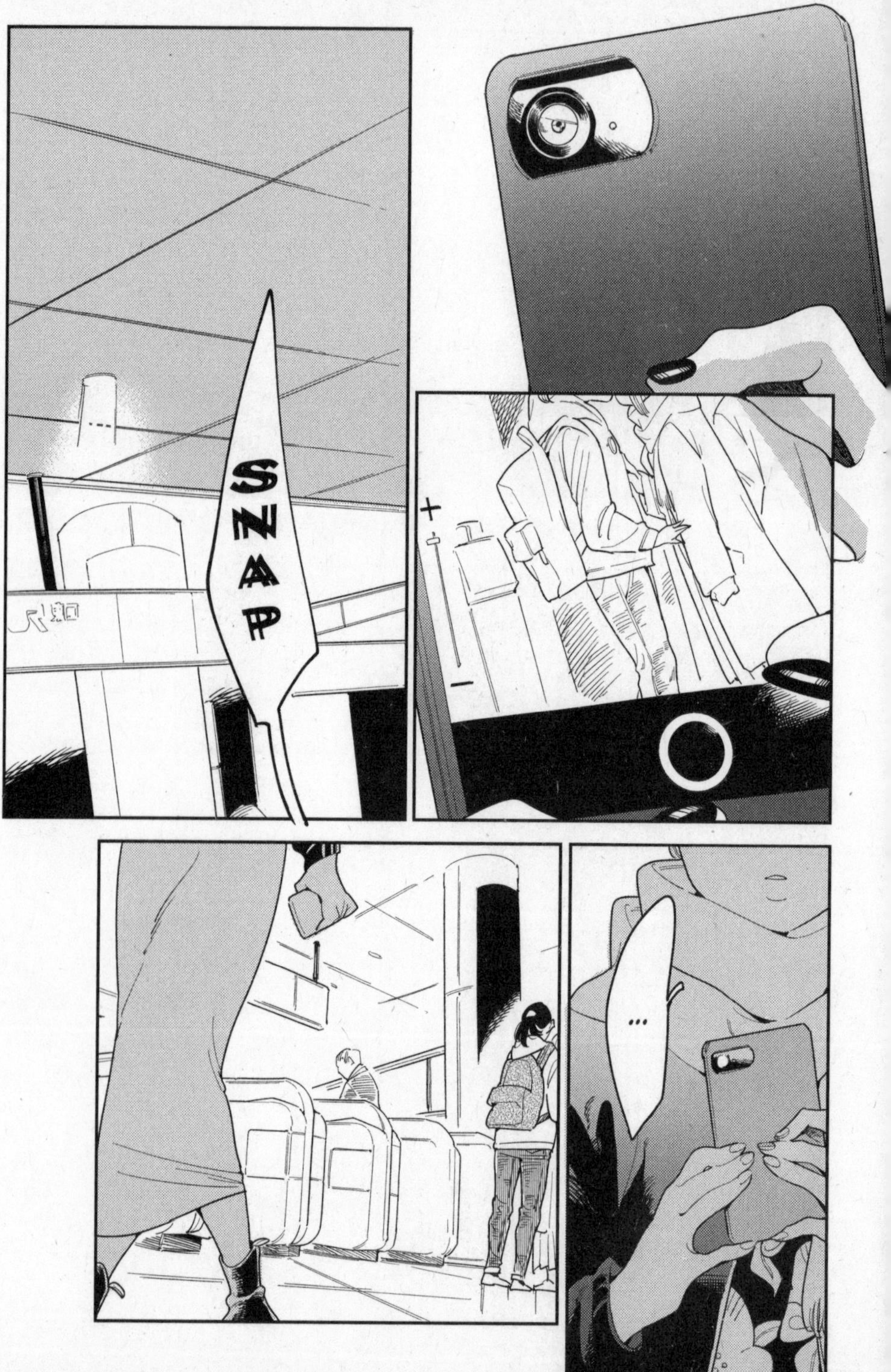
SNAP
...

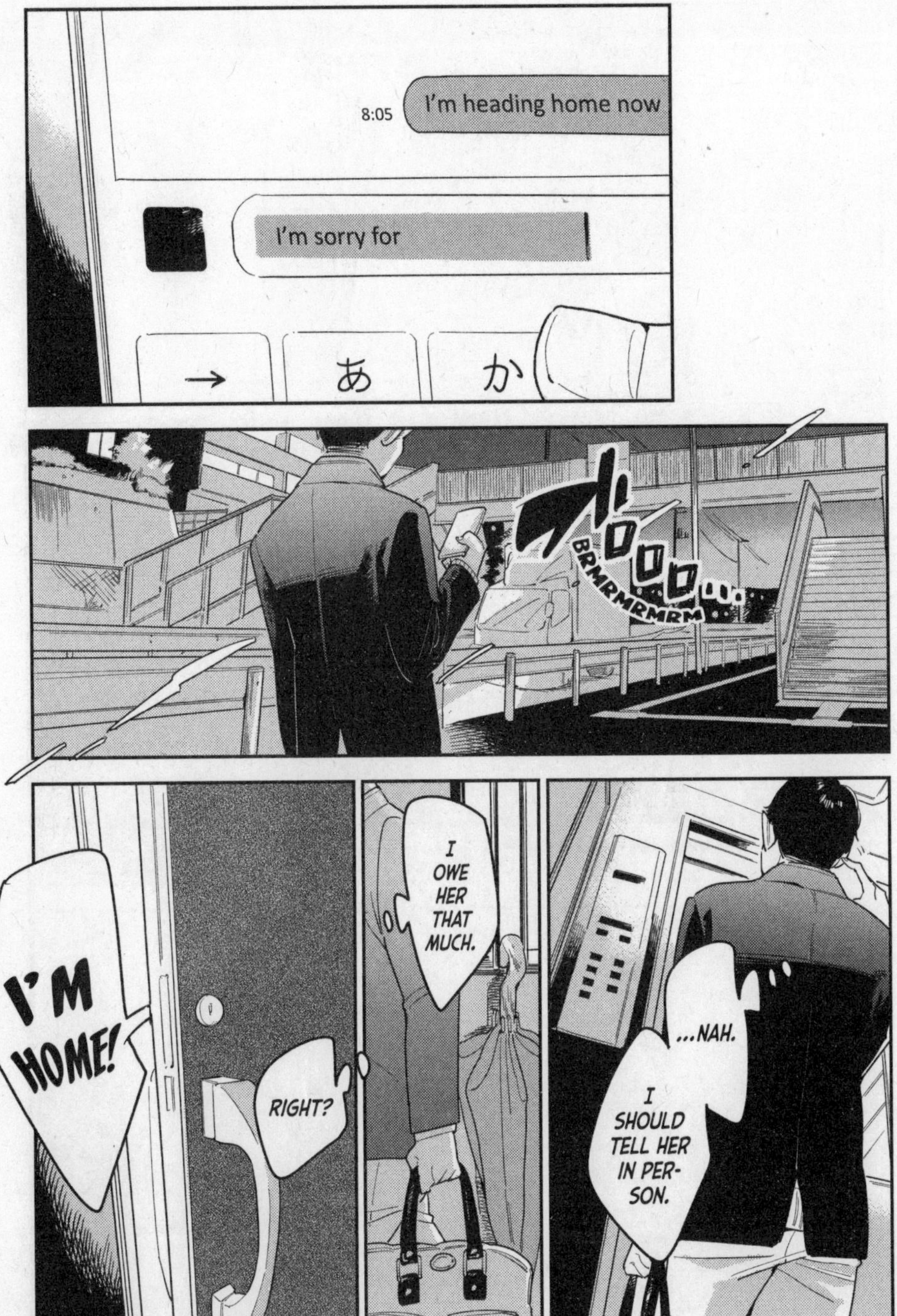
8:05
I'm heading home now
I'm sorry for
→
あ
か
ブロロロ...
BRMRMRMRM
...NAH.
I SHOULD TELL HER IN PER-SON.
I OWE HER THAT MUCH.
RIGHT?
I'M HOME!

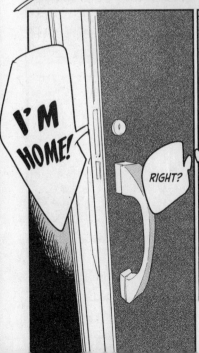

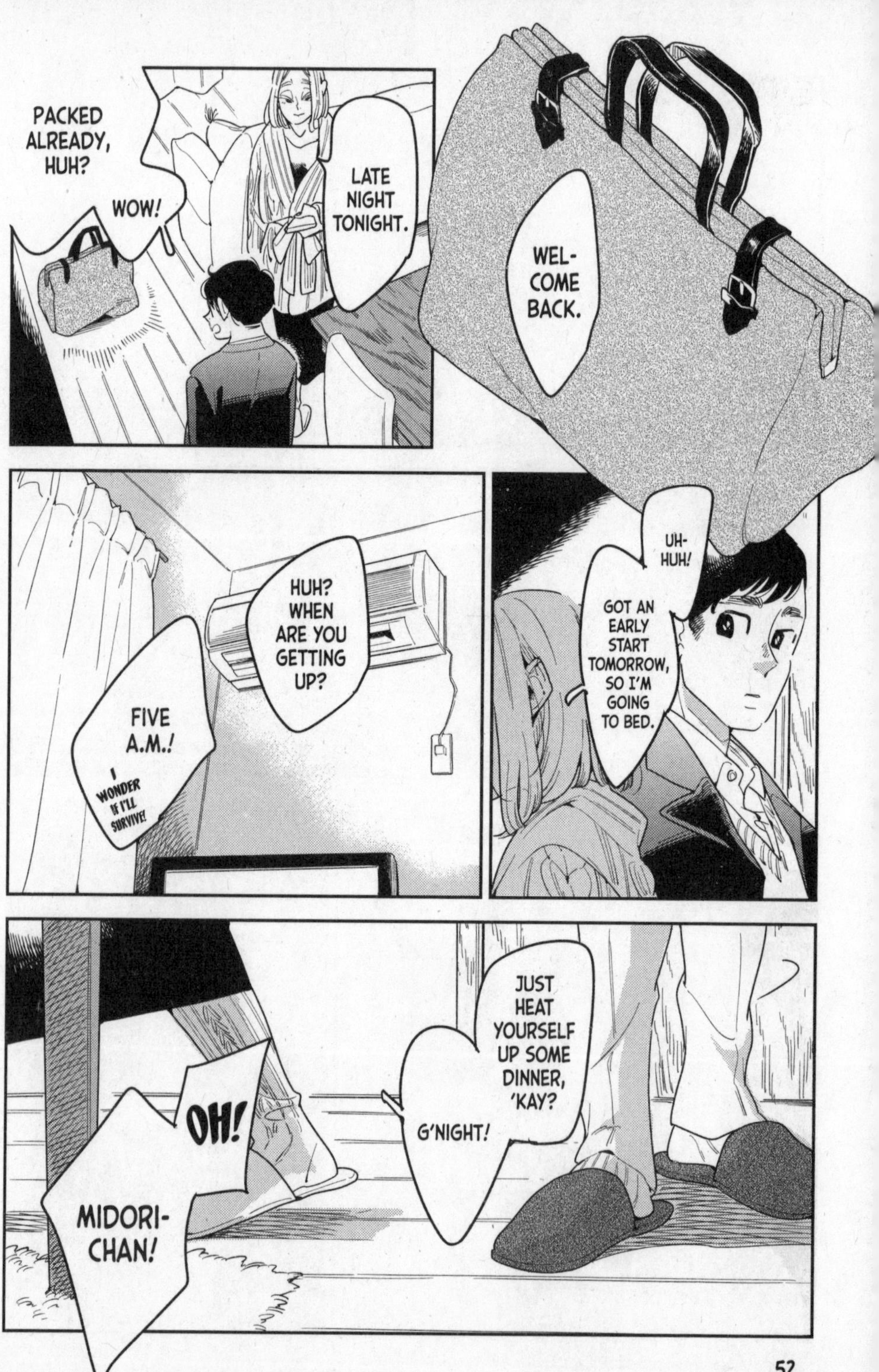
WEL-COME BACK.
LATE NIGHT TONIGHT.
PACKED ALREADY, HUH?
WOW!
UH-HUH!
GOT AN EARLY START TOMORROW, SO I'M GOING TO BED.
HUH? WHEN ARE YOU GETTING UP?
FIVE A.M.!
I WONDER IF I'LL SURVIVE!
JUST HEAT YOURSELF UP SOME DINNER, 'KAY?
G'NIGHT!
OH!
MIDORI-CHAN!

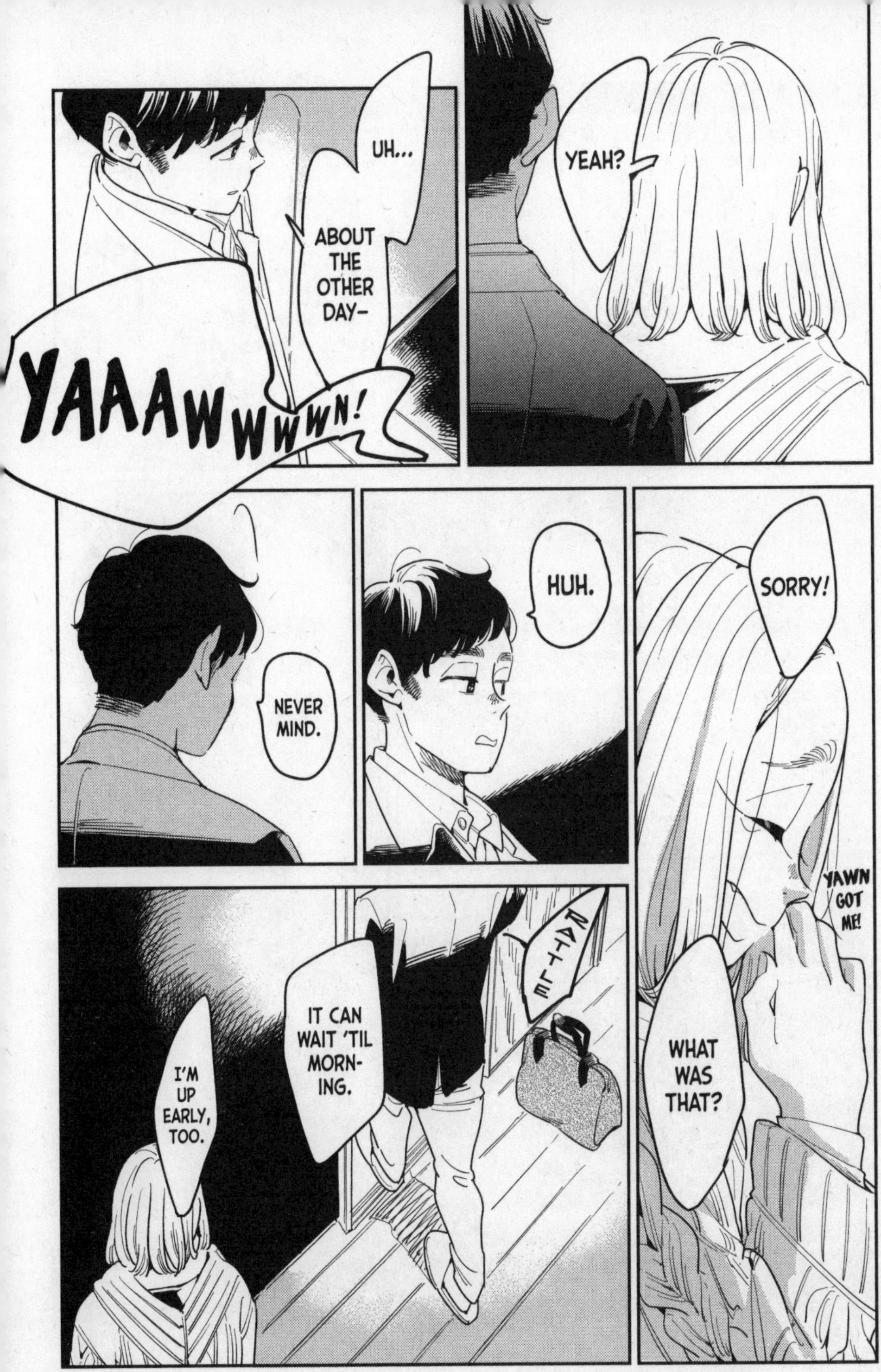
YEAH?
UH...
ABOUT THE OTHER DAY–
YAAAWWWWN!
SORRY!
YAWN GOT ME!
WHAT WAS THAT?
HUH.
NEVER MIND.
RATTLE
IT CAN WAIT 'TIL MORN-ING.
I'M UP EARLY, TOO.

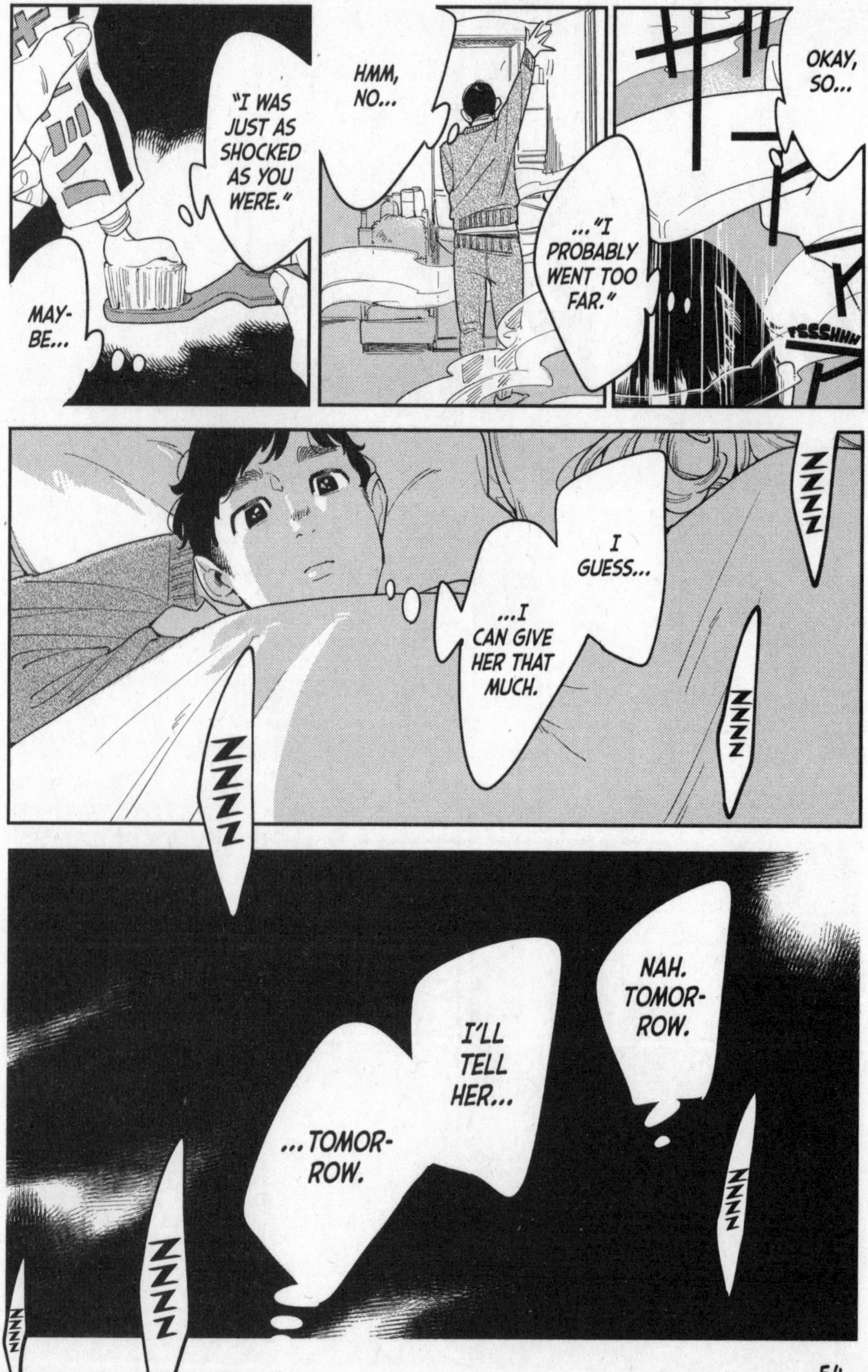
OKAY, SO...
..."I PROBABLY WENT TOO FAR."
HMM, NO...
"I WAS JUST AS SHOCKED AS YOU WERE."
MAY-BE...
ZZZZ
I GUESS...
...I CAN GIVE HER THAT MUCH.
ZZZZ
ZZZZ
NAH. TOMOR-ROW.
I'LL TELL HER...
...TOMOR-ROW.
ZZZZ
ZZZZ
ZZZZ

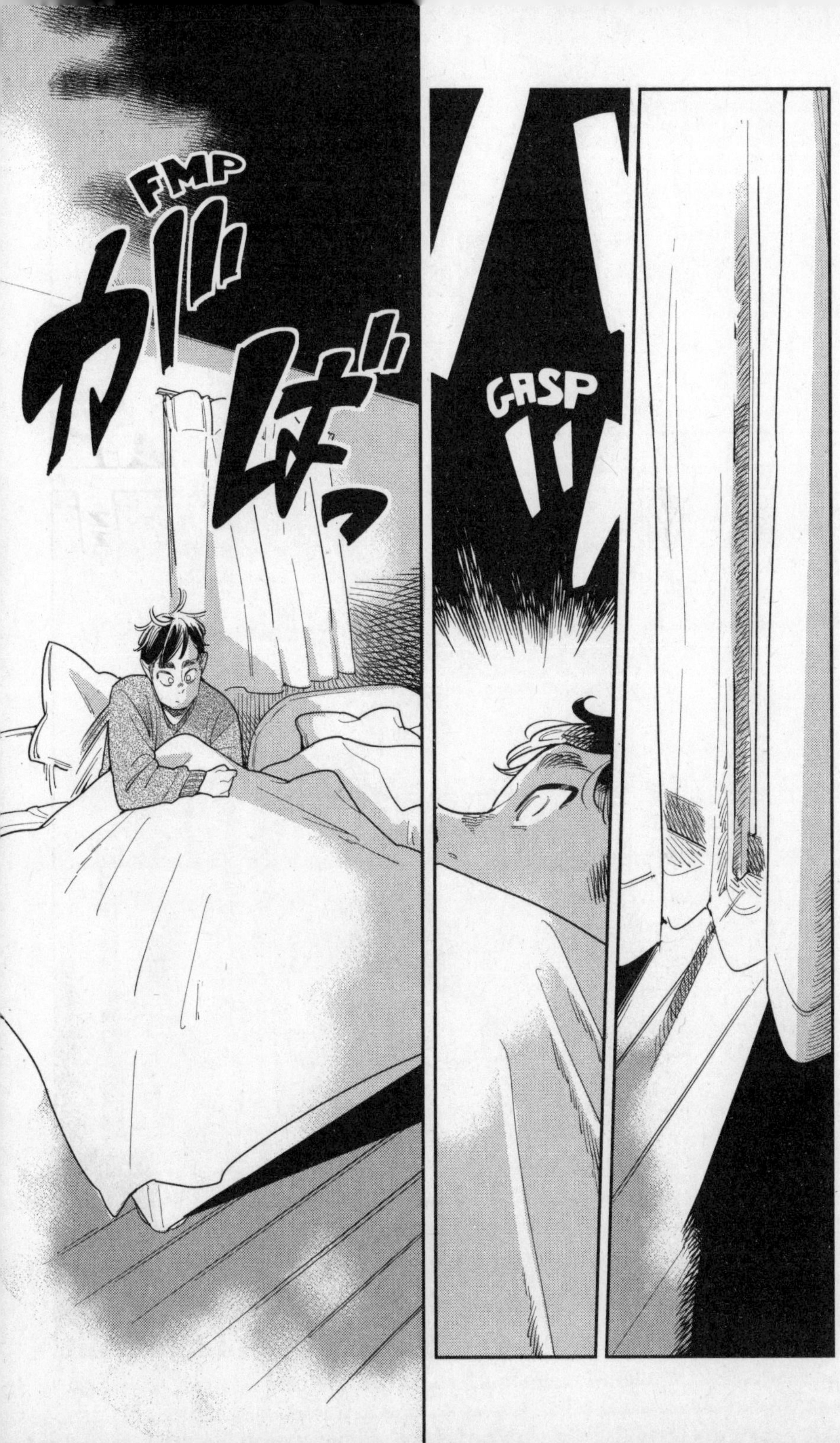
GASP
FMP
がばっ

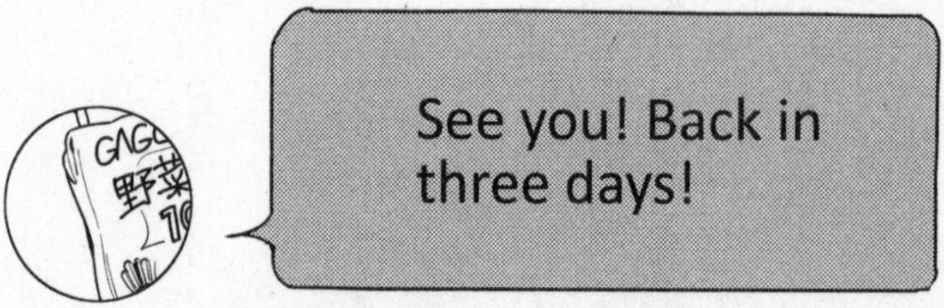
See you! Back in three days!

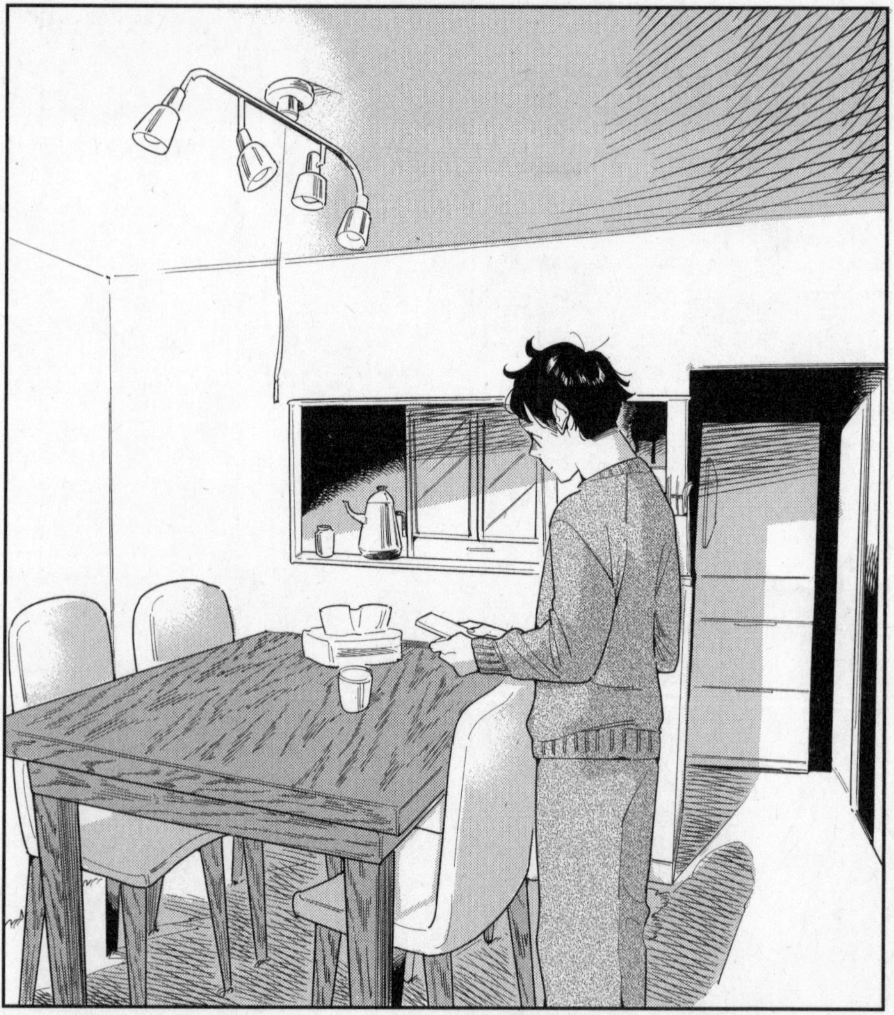

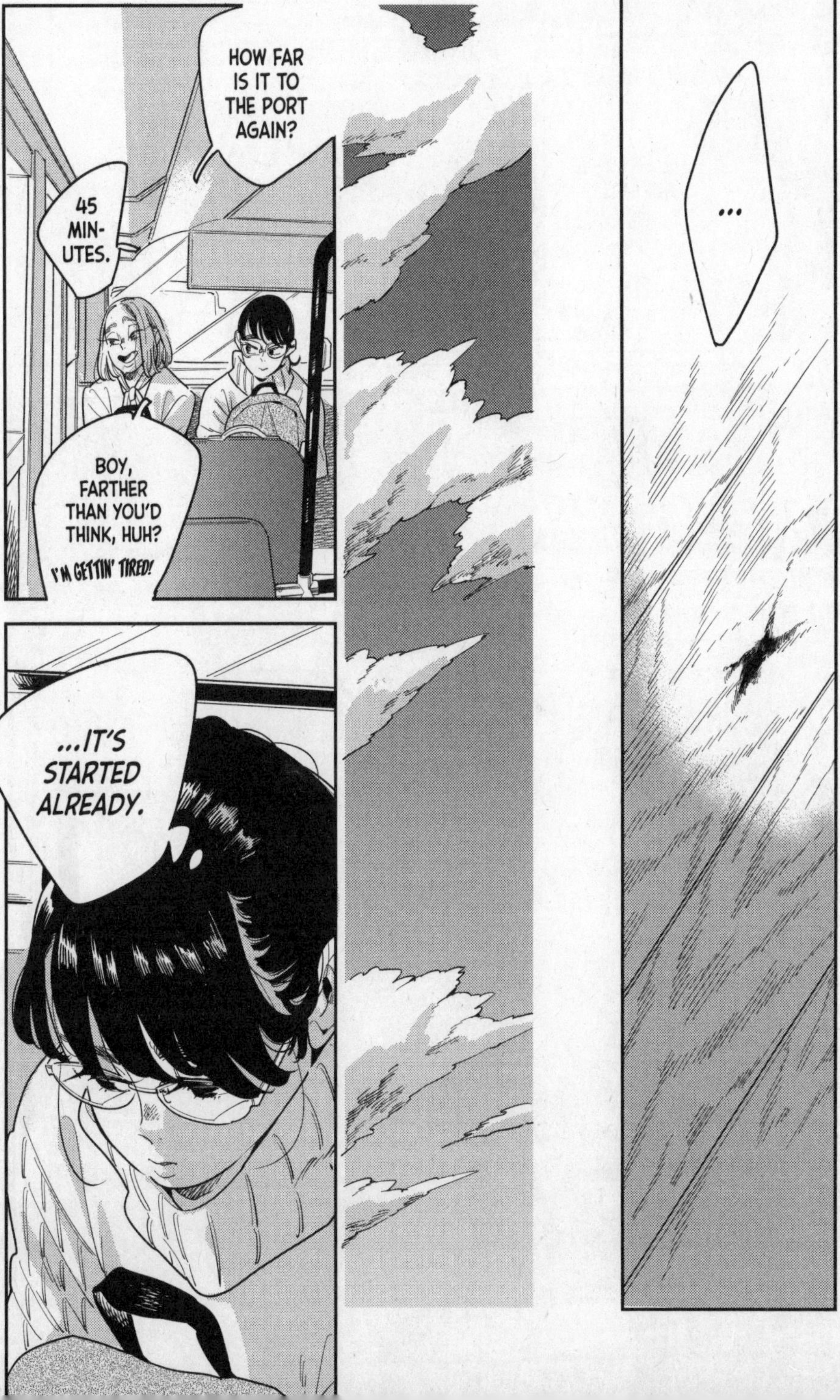
...
HOW FAR IS IT TO THE PORT AGAIN?
45 MIN-UTES.
BOY, FARTHER THAN YOU'D THINK, HUH?
I'M GETTIN' TIRED!
...IT'S STARTED ALREADY.

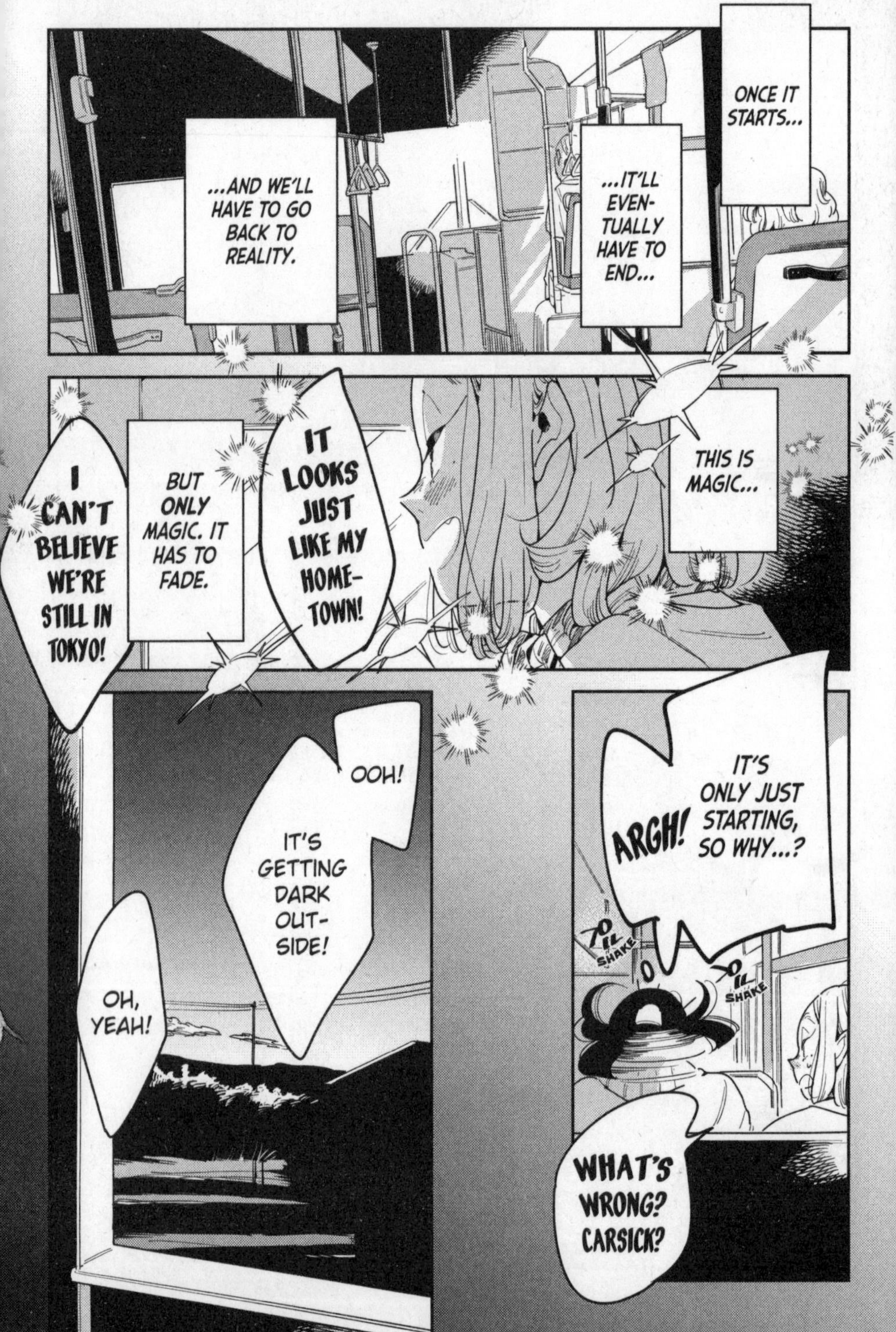
ONCE IT STARTS...
...IT'LL EVENTUALLY HAVE TO END...
...AND WE'LL HAVE TO GO BACK TO REALITY.
THIS IS MAGIC...
IT LOOKS JUST LIKE MY HOME-TOWN!
BUT ONLY MAGIC. IT HAS TO FADE.
I CAN'T BELIEVE WE'RE STILL IN TOKYO!
IT'S ONLY JUST STARTING, SO WHY...?
ARGH!
SHAKE
SHAKE
WHAT'S WRONG? CARSICK?
OOH!
IT'S GETTING DARK OUT-SIDE!
OH, YEAH!

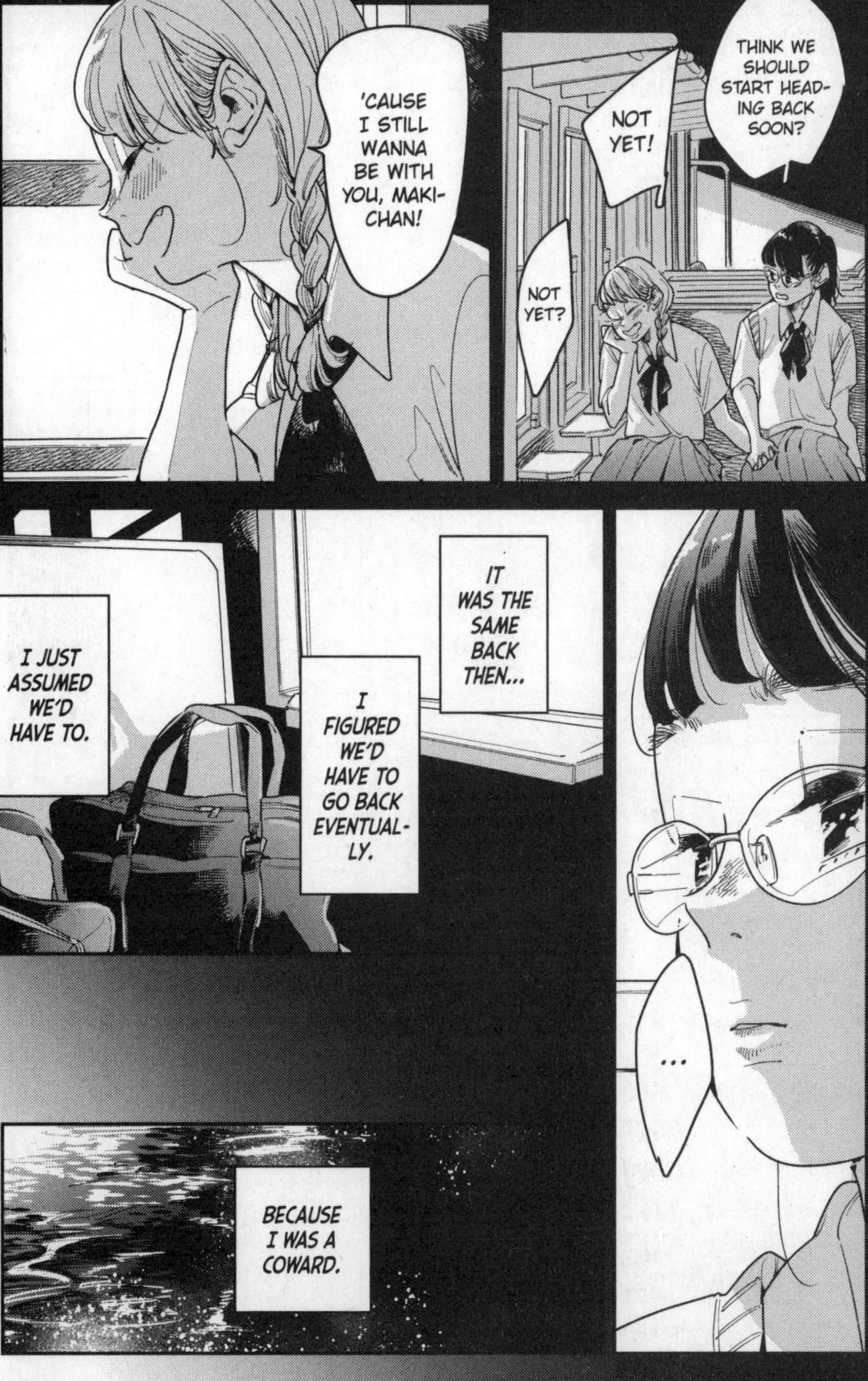
THINK WE SHOULD START HEAD-ING BACK SOON?
NOT YET!
NOT YET?
'CAUSE I STILL WANNA BE WITH YOU, MAKI-CHAN!
...
IT WAS THE SAME BACK THEN...
I FIGURED WE'D HAVE TO GO BACK EVENTUAL-LY.
I JUST ASSUMED WE'D HAVE TO.
BECAUSE I WAS A COWARD.

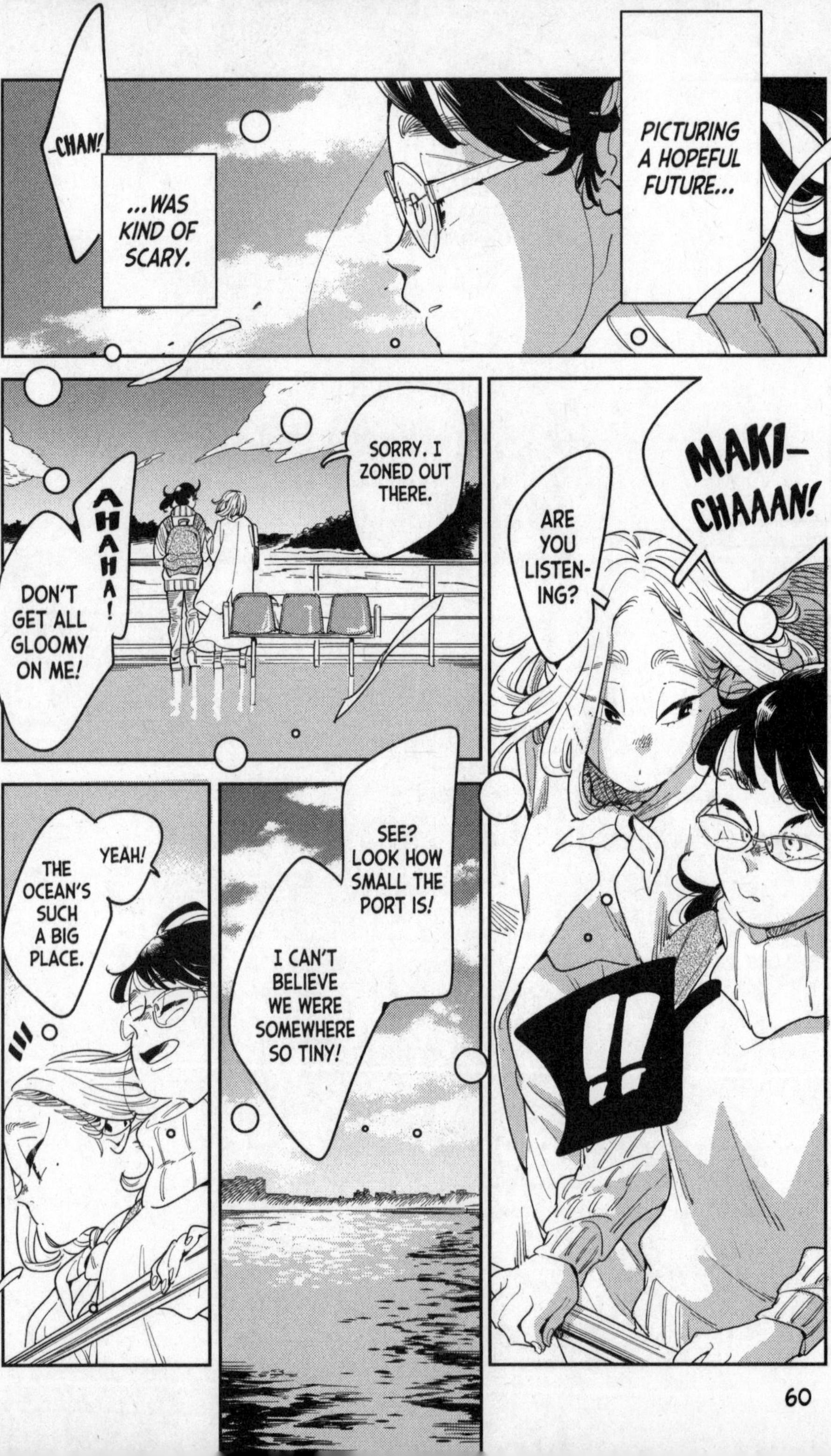
PICTURING A HOPEFUL FUTURE...
...WAS KIND OF SCARY.
-CHAN!
MAKI-CHAAAN!
ARE YOU LISTENING?
!!
SORRY. I ZONED OUT THERE.
AHAHA!
DON'T GET ALL GLOOMY ON ME!
SEE? LOOK HOW SMALL THE PORT IS!
I CAN'T BELIEVE WE WERE SOMEWHERE SO TINY!
YEAH!
THE OCEAN'S SUCH A BIG PLACE.

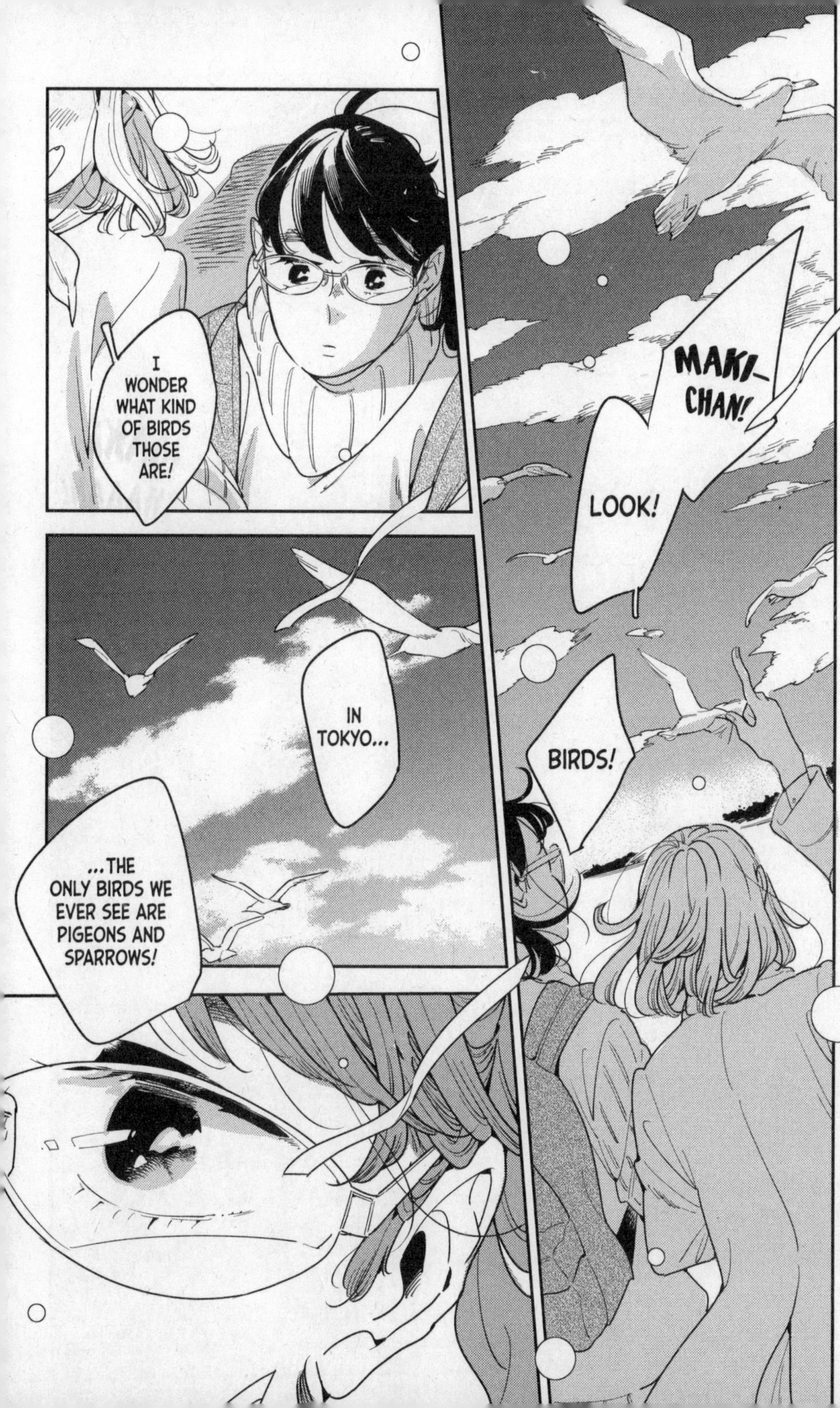
MAKI-CHAN!
LOOK!
BIRDS!
I WONDER WHAT KIND OF BIRDS THOSE ARE!
IN TOKYO...
...THE ONLY BIRDS WE EVER SEE ARE PIGEONS AND SPARROWS!

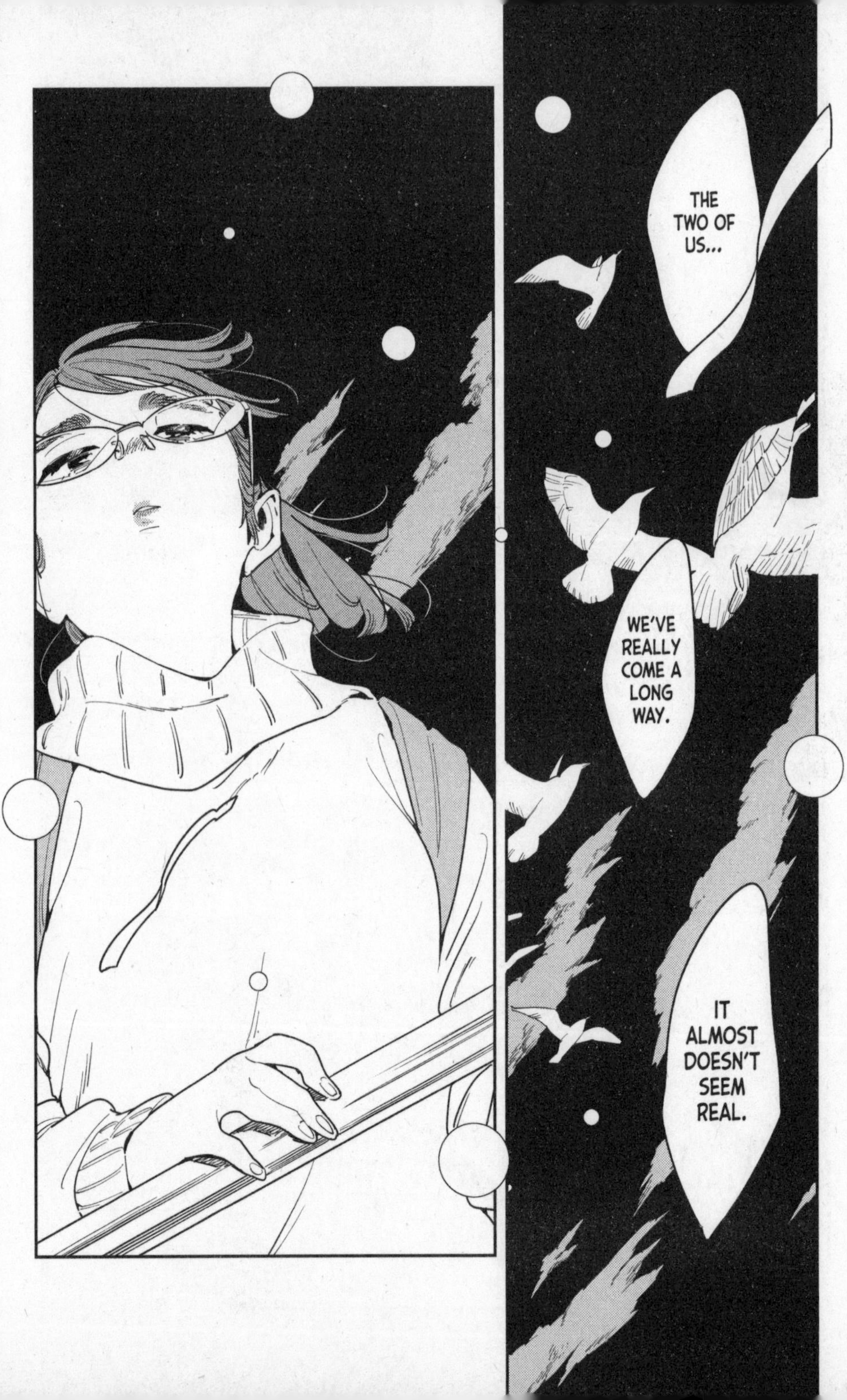
THE TWO OF US...
WE'VE REALLY COME A LONG WAY.
IT ALMOST DOESN'T SEEM REAL.

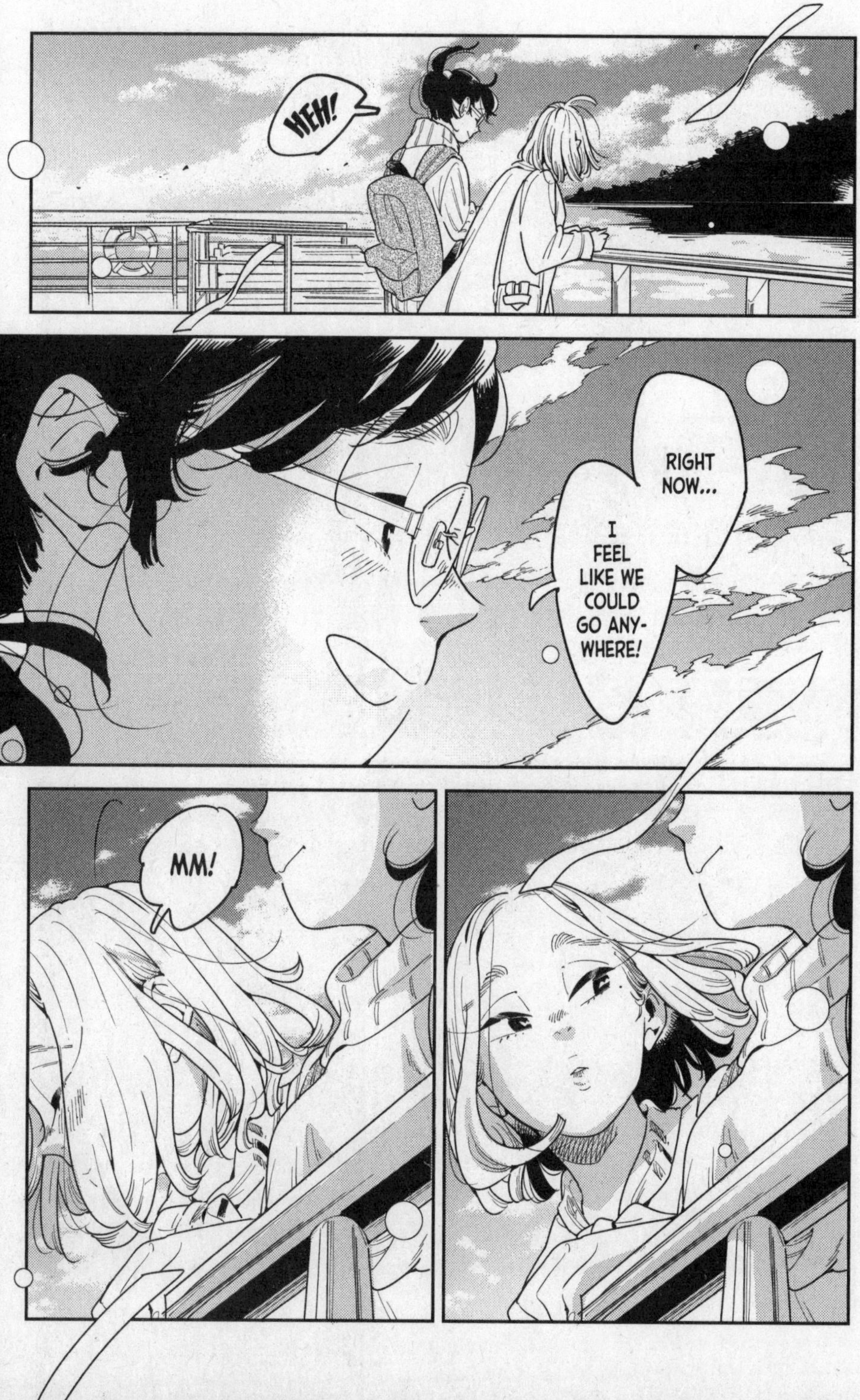
HEH!
RIGHT NOW...
I FEEL LIKE WE COULD GO ANY-WHERE!
MM!

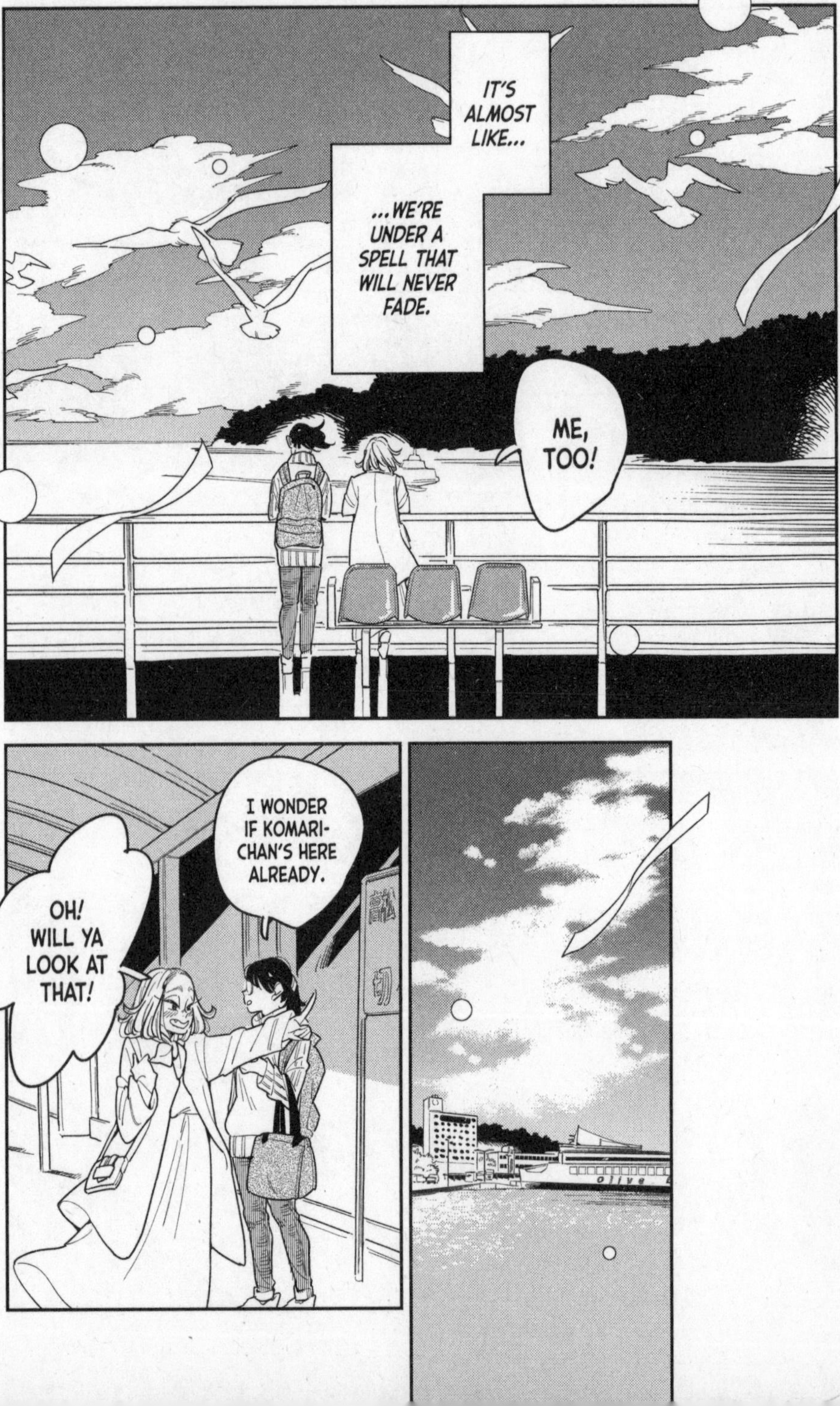
IT'S ALMOST LIKE...
...WE'RE UNDER A SPELL THAT WILL NEVER FADE.
ME, TOO!
I WONDER IF KOMARI-CHAN'S HERE ALREADY.
OH! WILL YA LOOK AT THAT!

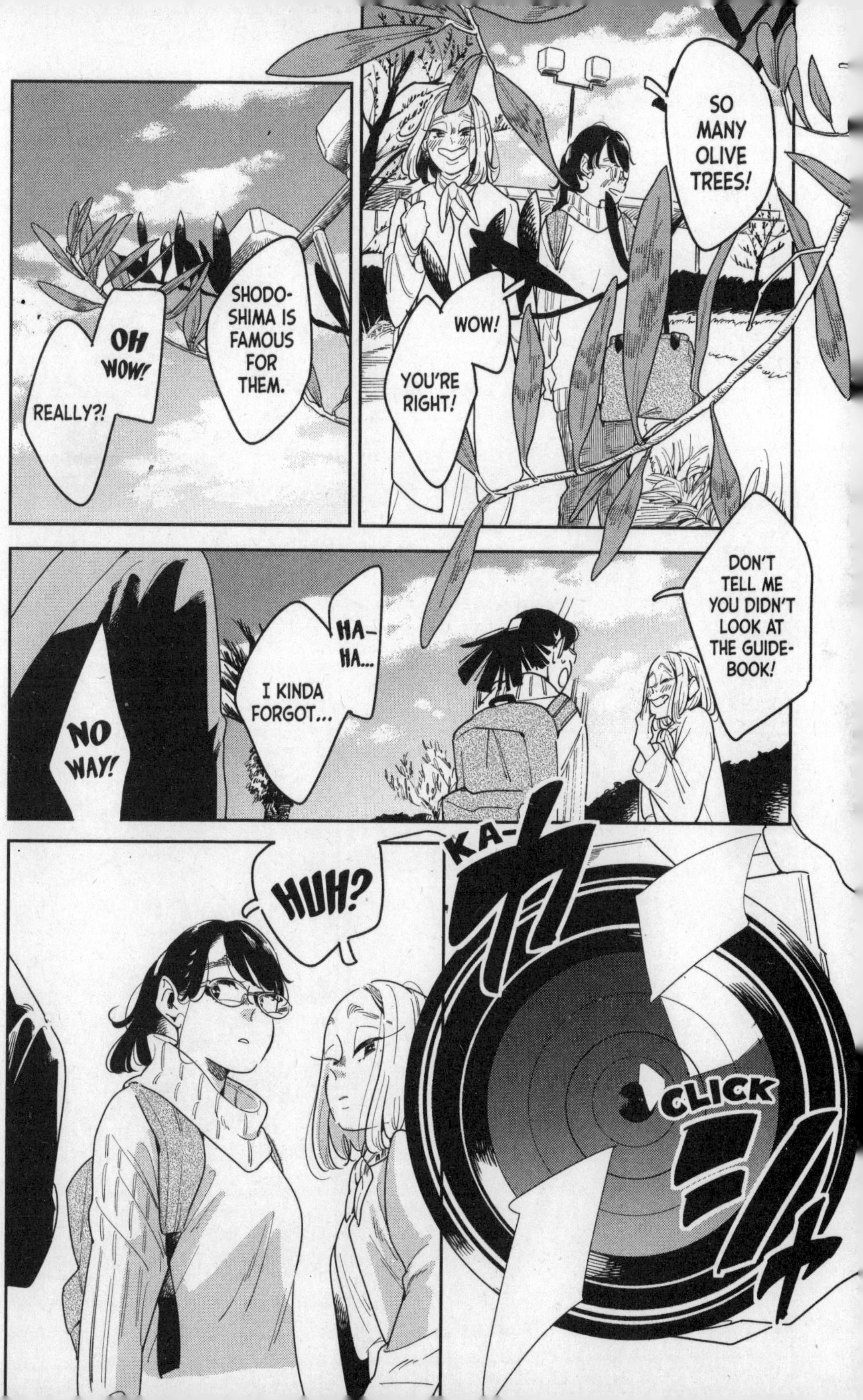
SO MANY OLIVE TREES!
WOW! YOU'RE RIGHT!
SHODO-SHIMA IS FAMOUS FOR THEM.
OH WOW! REALLY?!
DON'T TELL ME YOU DIDN'T LOOK AT THE GUIDE-BOOK!
HA-HA...
I KINDA FORGOT...
NO WAY!
KA-
CLICK
HUH?

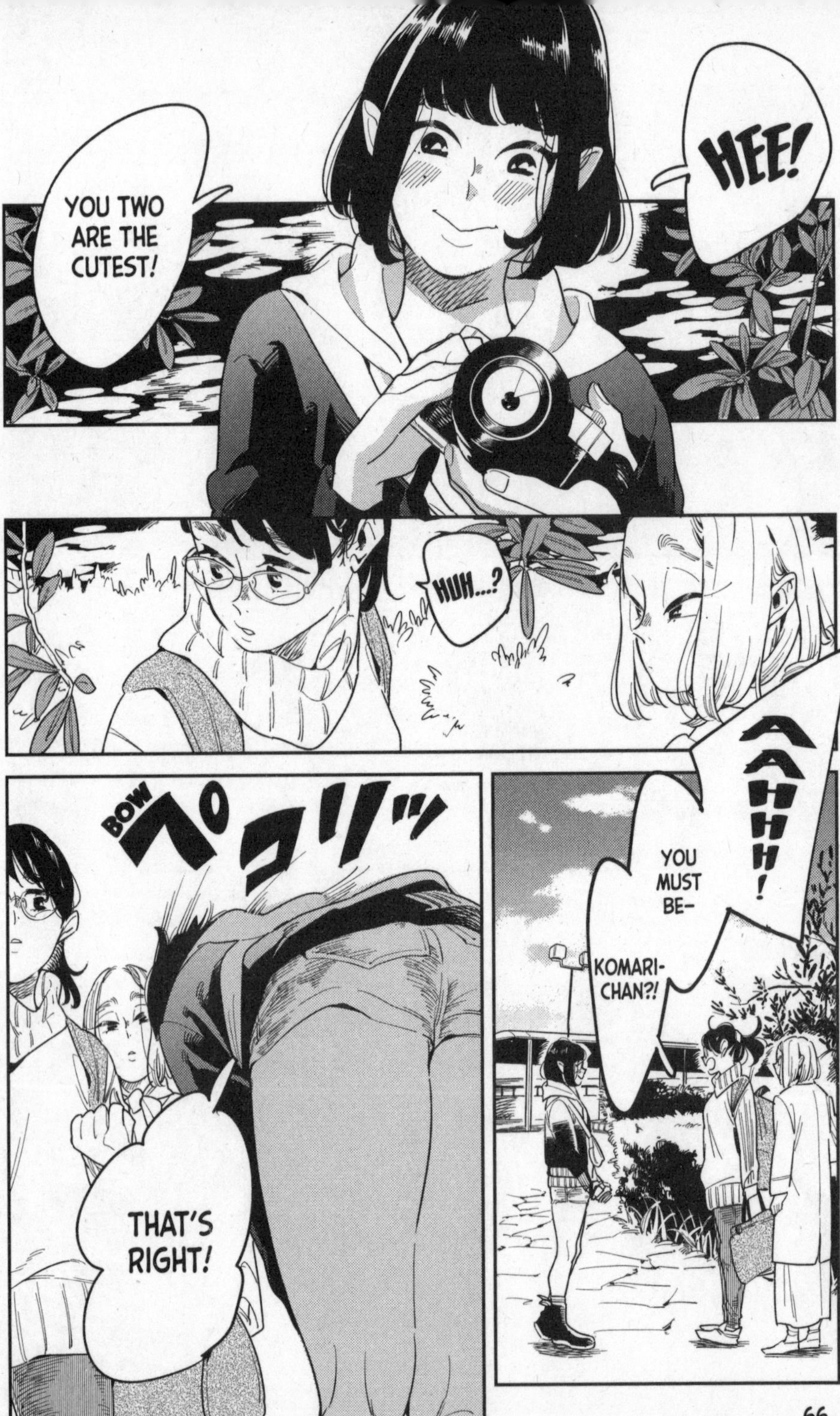
HEE!
YOU TWO ARE THE CUTEST!
HUH...?
AAHHH!
YOU MUST BE–
KOMARI-CHAN?!
BOW
ペコリッ
THAT'S RIGHT!

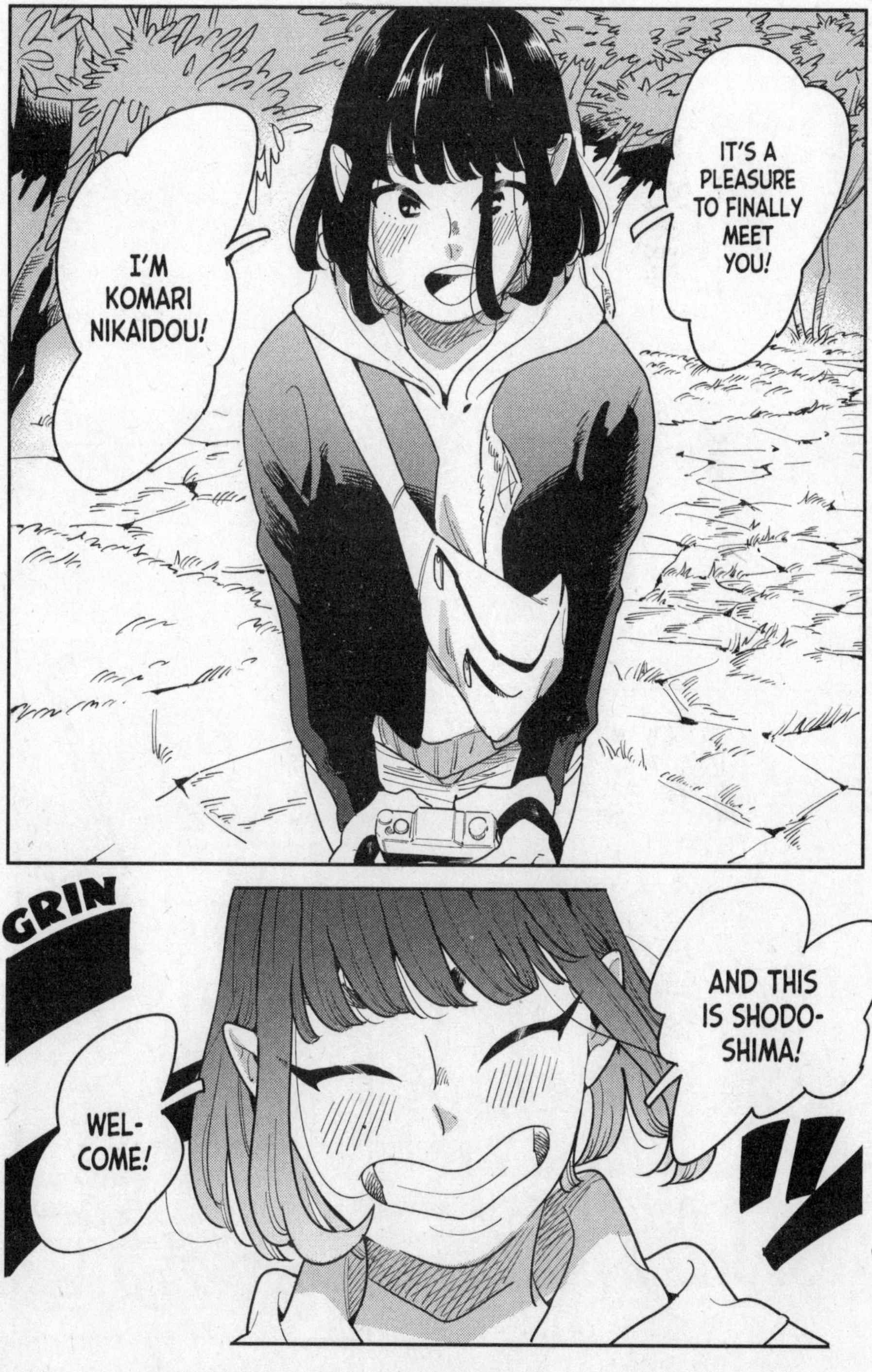
IT'S A PLEASURE TO FINALLY MEET YOU!
I'M KOMARI NIKAIDOU!
AND THIS IS SHODO-SHIMA!
GRIN
WEL-COME!

Run Away
With Me,
Girl

EPISODE 9

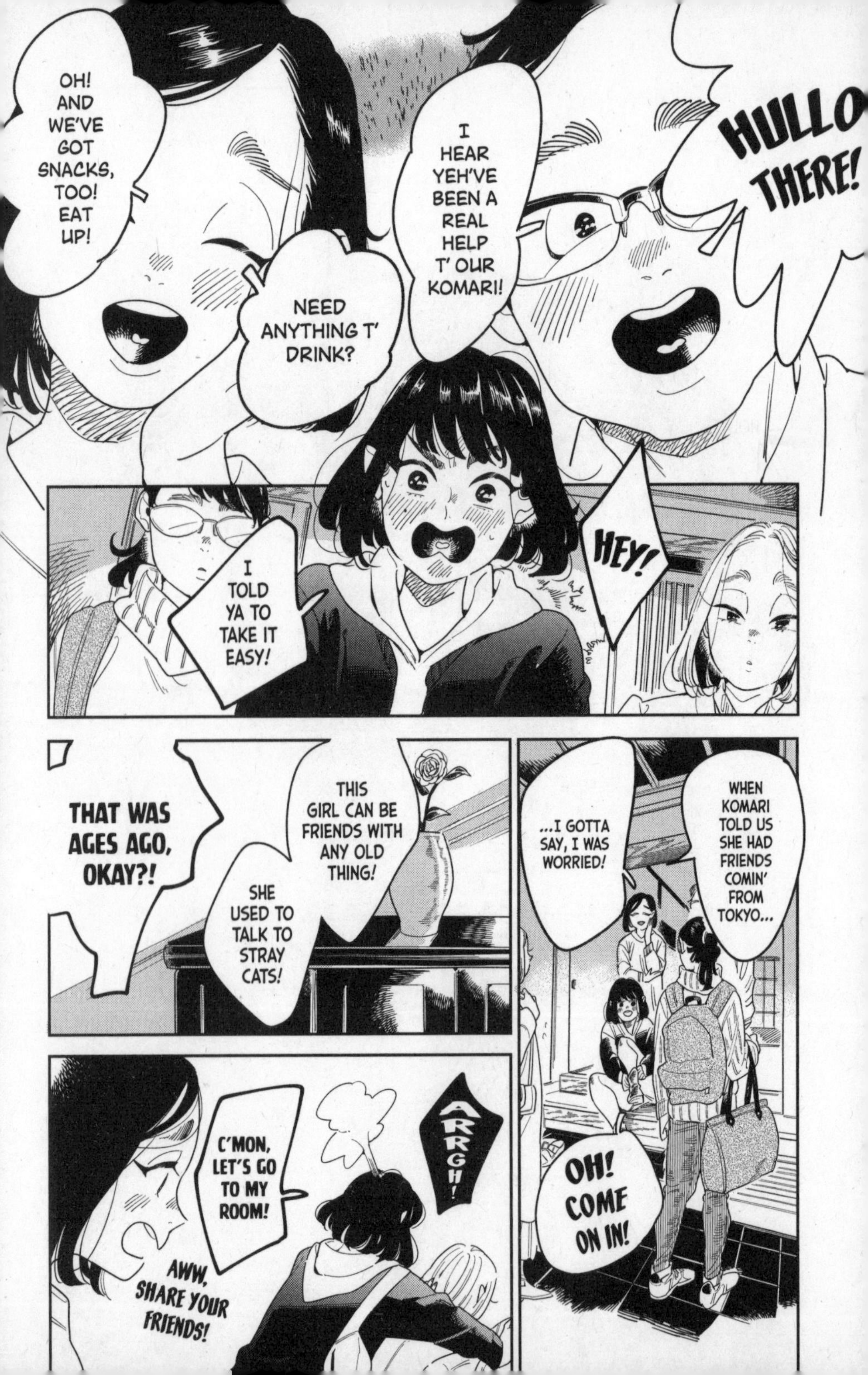
HULLO THERE!
I HEAR YEH'VE BEEN A REAL HELP T' OUR KOMARI!
NEED ANYTHING T' DRINK?
OH! AND WE'VE GOT SNACKS, TOO! EAT UP!
HEY!
I TOLD YA TO TAKE IT EASY!
WHEN KOMARI TOLD US SHE HAD FRIENDS COMIN' FROM TOKYO...
...I GOTTA SAY, I WAS WORRIED!
OH! COME ON IN!
THIS GIRL CAN BE FRIENDS WITH ANY OLD THING!
SHE USED TO TALK TO STRAY CATS!
THAT WAS AGES AGO, OKAY?!
ARRGH!
C'MON, LET'S GO TO MY ROOM!
AWW, SHARE YOUR FRIENDS!

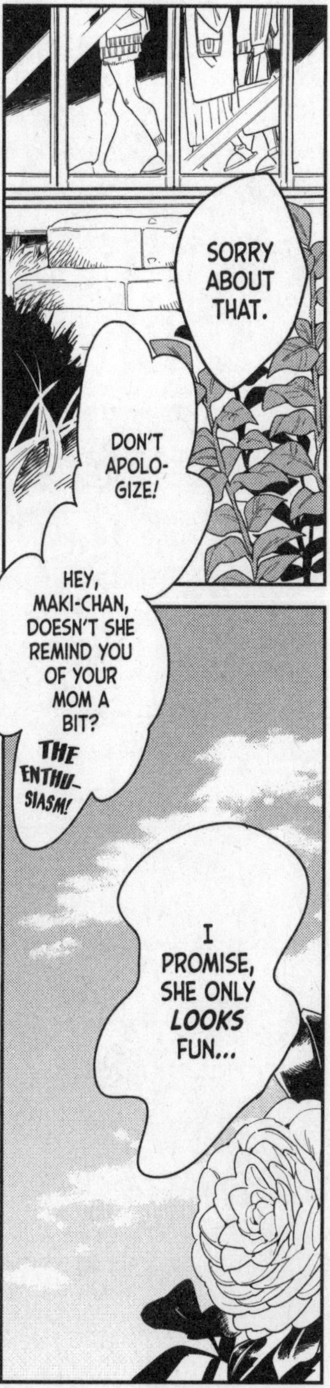
SORRY ABOUT THAT.
DON'T APOLOGIZE!
HEY, MAKI-CHAN, DOESN'T SHE REMIND YOU OF YOUR MOM A BIT?
THE ENTHUSIASM!
I PROMISE, SHE ONLY *LOOKS* FUN...
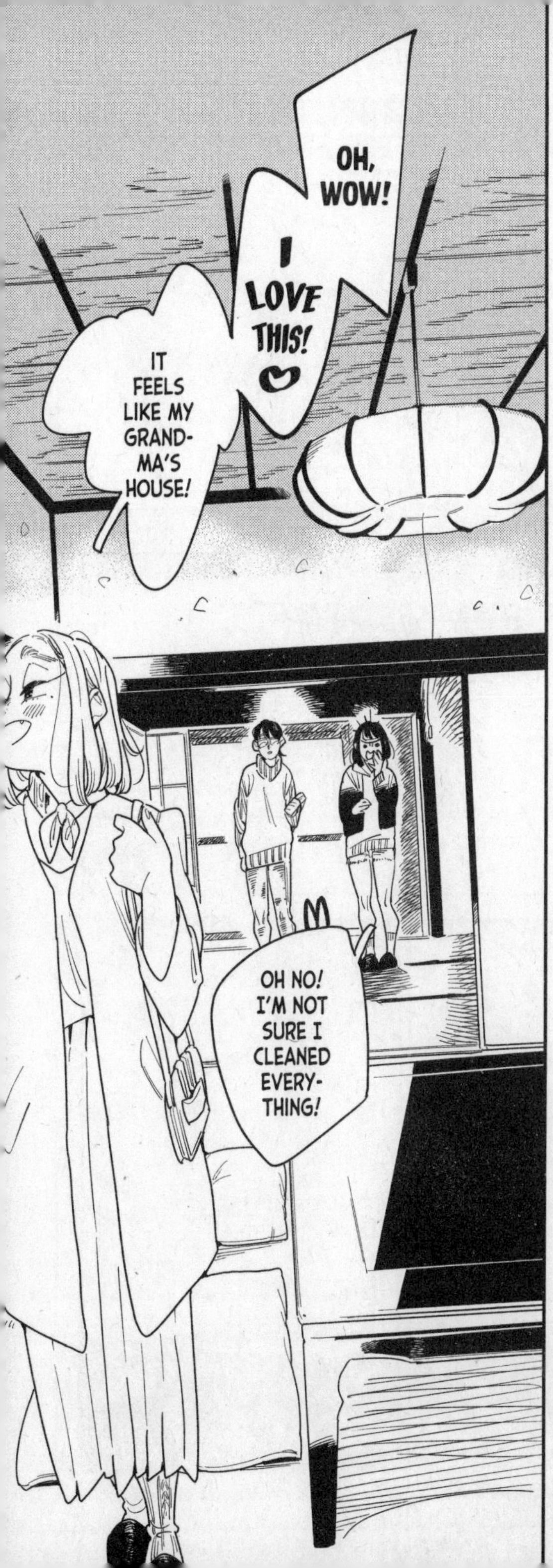
OH, WOW!
I LOVE THIS! ♥
IT FEELS LIKE MY GRAND-MA'S HOUSE!
OH NO! I'M NOT SURE I CLEANED EVERY-THING!

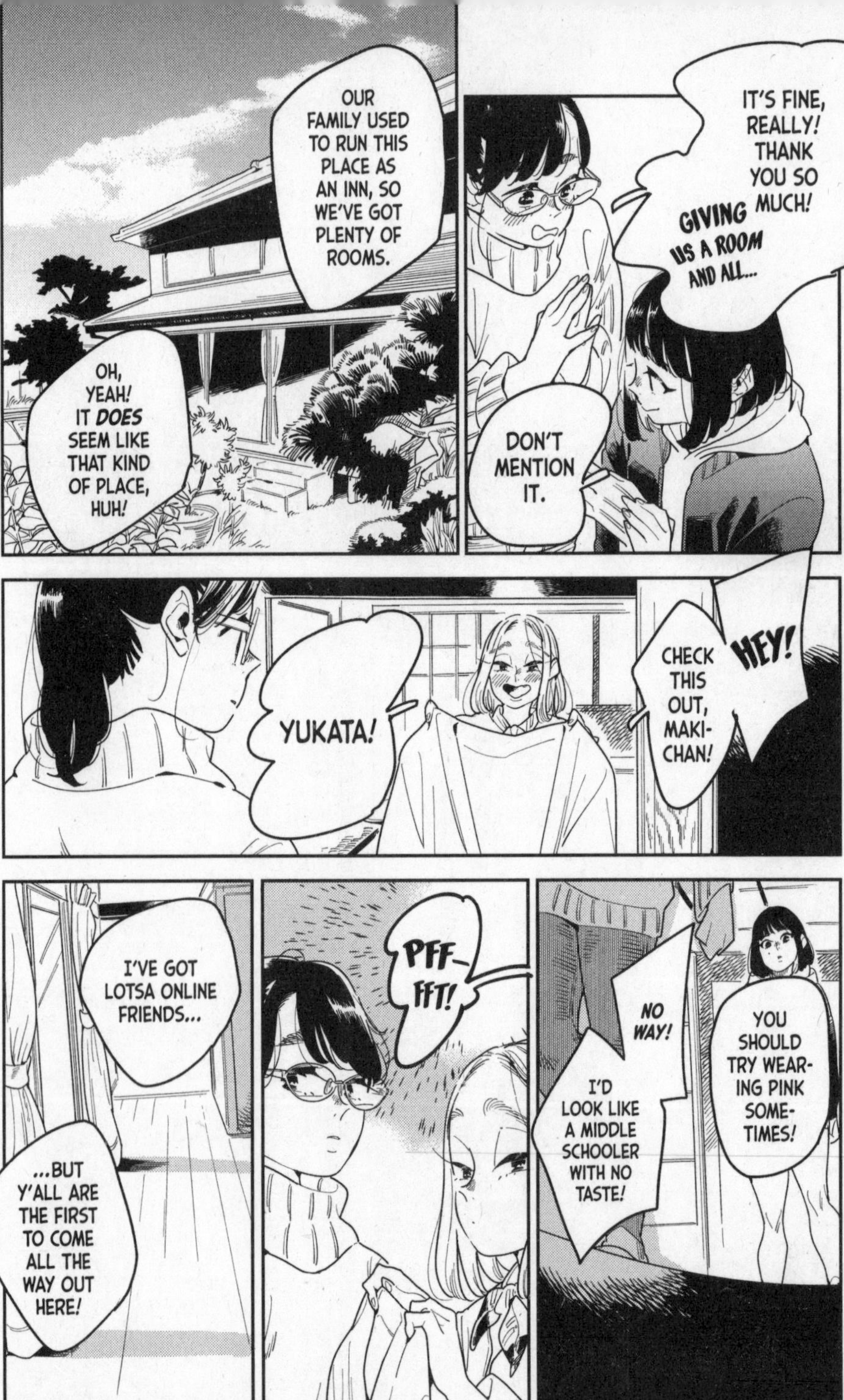

IT'S FINE, REALLY! THANK YOU SO MUCH!
GIVING US A ROOM AND ALL...
DON'T MENTION IT.
OUR FAMILY USED TO RUN THIS PLACE AS AN INN, SO WE'VE GOT PLENTY OF ROOMS.
OH, YEAH! IT *DOES* SEEM LIKE THAT KIND OF PLACE, HUH!
HEY!
CHECK THIS OUT, MAKI-CHAN!
YUKATA!
YOU SHOULD TRY WEAR-ING PINK SOME-TIMES!
NO WAY!
I'D LOOK LIKE A MIDDLE SCHOOLER WITH NO TASTE!
PFF-FFT!
I'VE GOT LOTSA ONLINE FRIENDS...
...BUT Y'ALL ARE THE FIRST TO COME ALL THE WAY OUT HERE!

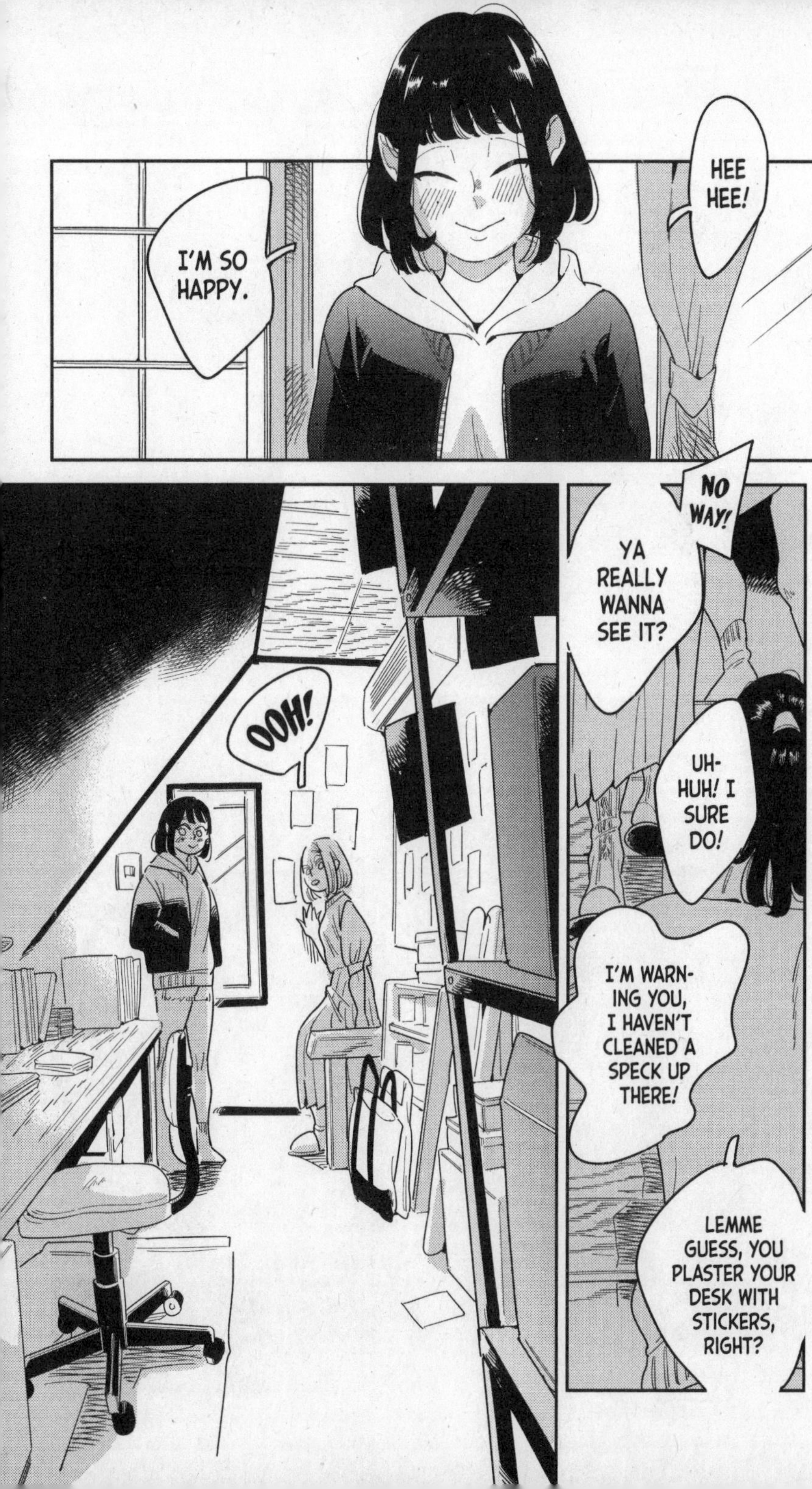
HEE HEE!
I'M SO HAPPY.
NO WAY!
YA REALLY WANNA SEE IT?
UH-HUH! I SURE DO!
I'M WARN-ING YOU, I HAVEN'T CLEANED A SPECK UP THERE!
LEMME GUESS, YOU PLASTER YOUR DESK WITH STICKERS, RIGHT?
OOH!

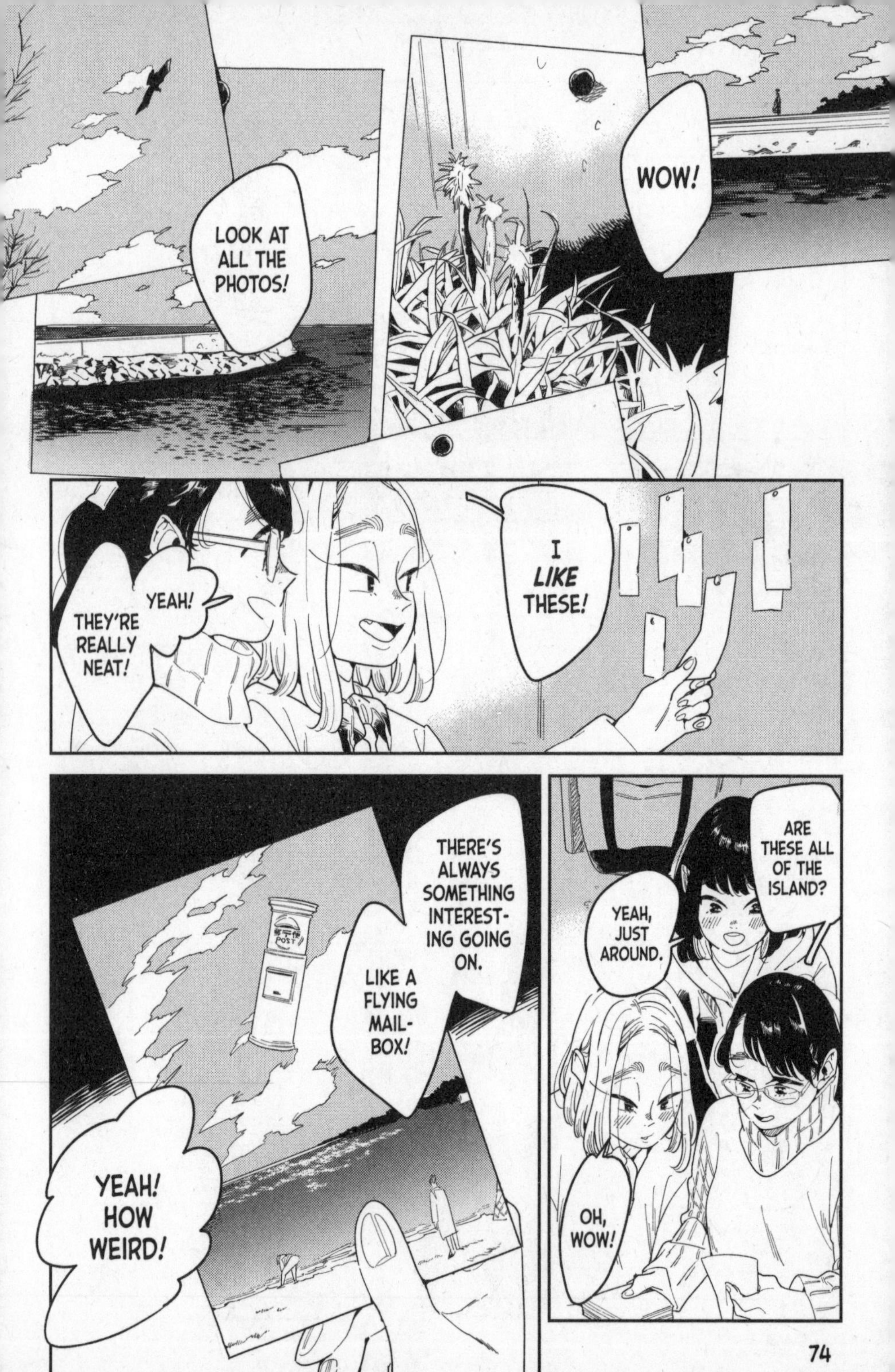
WOW!
LOOK AT ALL THE PHOTOS!
I *LIKE* THESE!
YEAH! THEY'RE REALLY NEAT!
ARE THESE ALL OF THE ISLAND?
YEAH, JUST AROUND.
OH, WOW!
THERE'S ALWAYS SOMETHING INTEREST-ING GOING ON.
LIKE A FLYING MAIL-BOX!
POST
YEAH! HOW WEIRD!

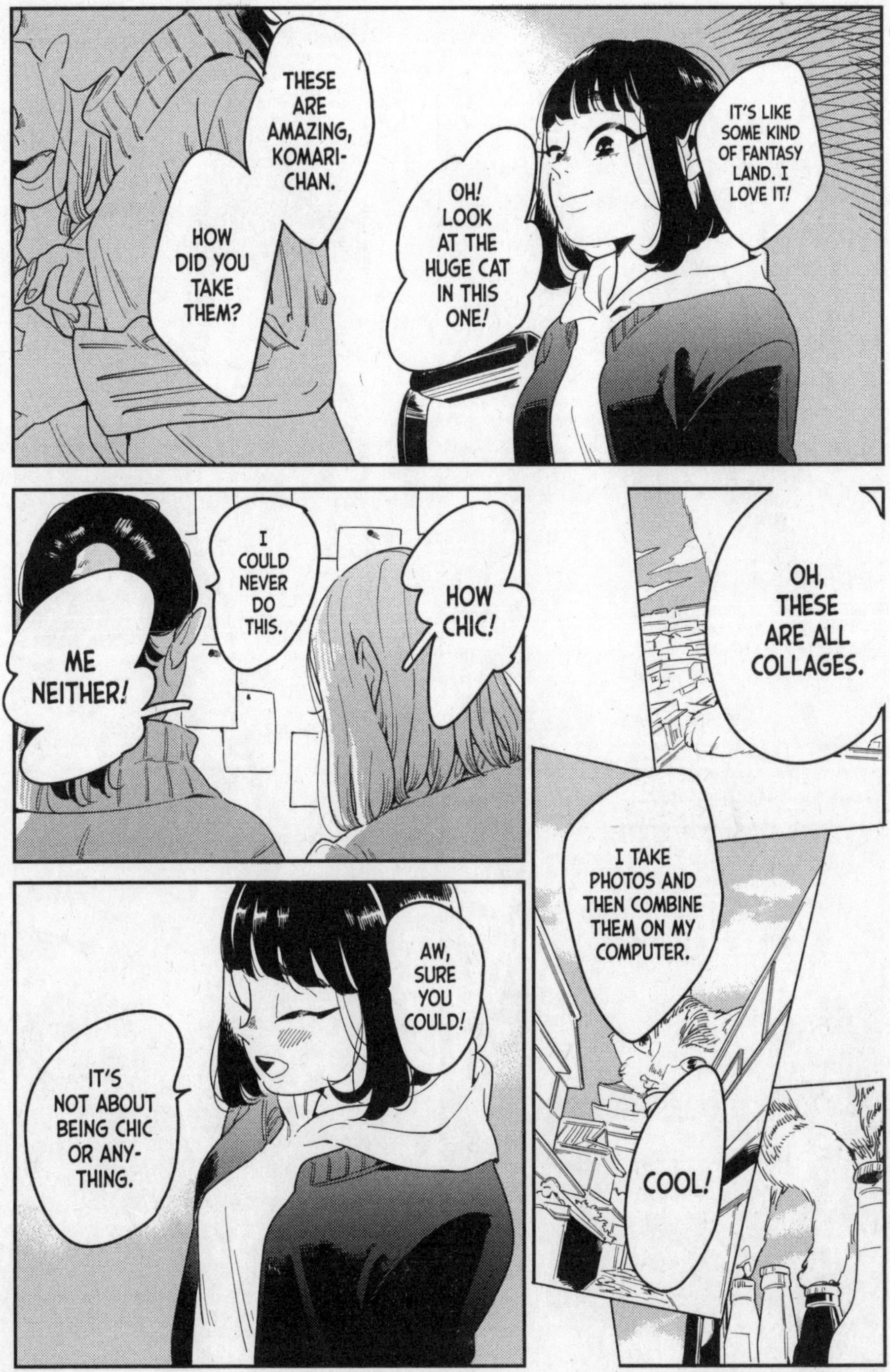
IT'S LIKE SOME KIND OF FANTASY LAND. I LOVE IT!
OH! LOOK AT THE HUGE CAT IN THIS ONE!
THESE ARE AMAZING, KOMARI-CHAN.
HOW DID YOU TAKE THEM?
OH, THESE ARE ALL COLLAGES.
I TAKE PHOTOS AND THEN COMBINE THEM ON MY COMPUTER.
COOL!
HOW CHIC!
I COULD NEVER DO THIS.
ME NEITHER!
AW, SURE YOU COULD!
IT'S NOT ABOUT BEING CHIC OR ANYTHING.

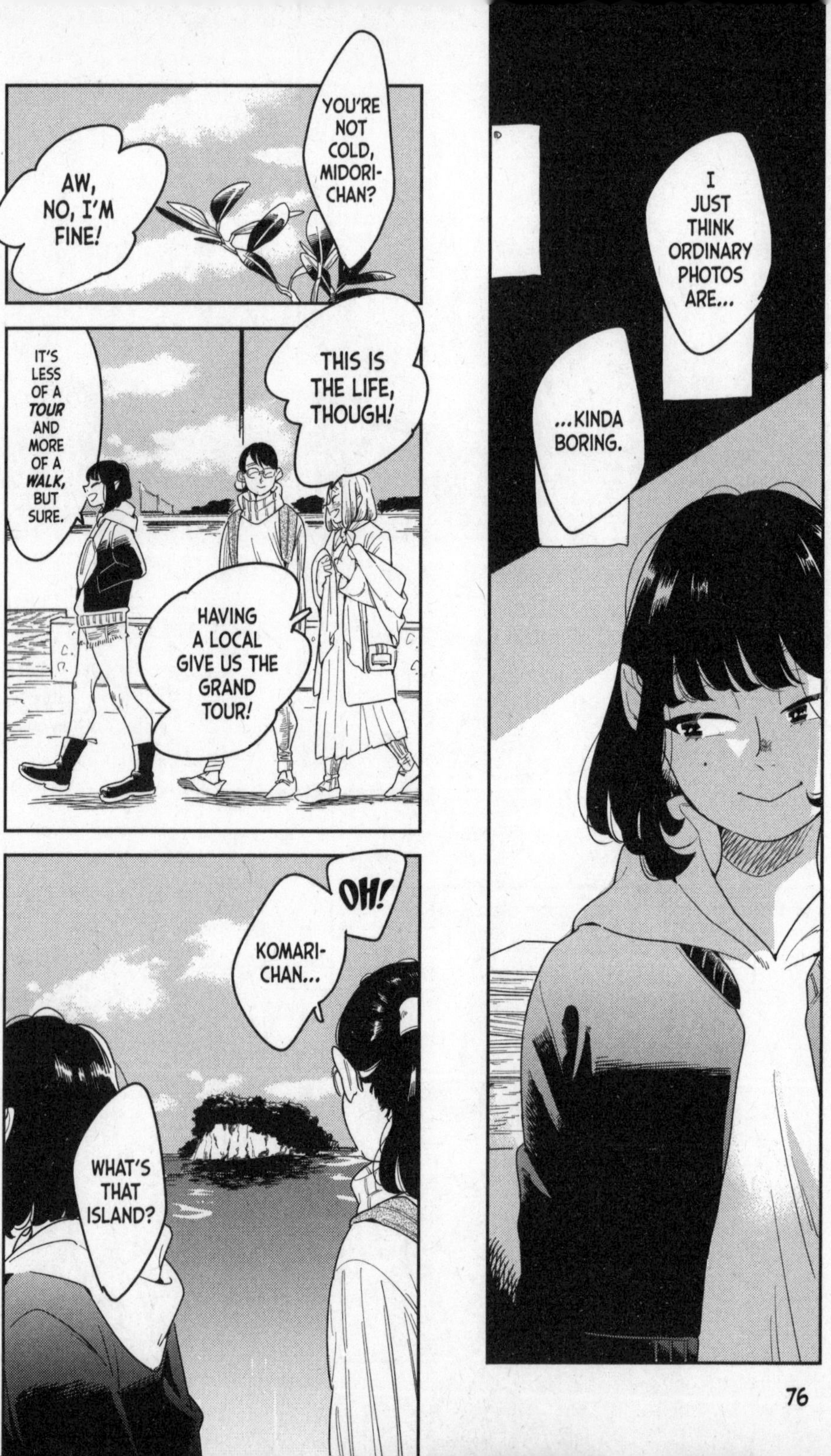
I JUST THINK ORDINARY PHOTOS ARE...
...KINDA BORING.
YOU'RE NOT COLD, MIDORI-CHAN?
AW, NO, I'M FINE!
THIS IS THE LIFE, THOUGH!
HAVING A LOCAL GIVE US THE GRAND TOUR!
IT'S LESS OF A TOUR AND MORE OF A WALK, BUT SURE.
OH!
KOMARI-CHAN...
WHAT'S THAT ISLAND?

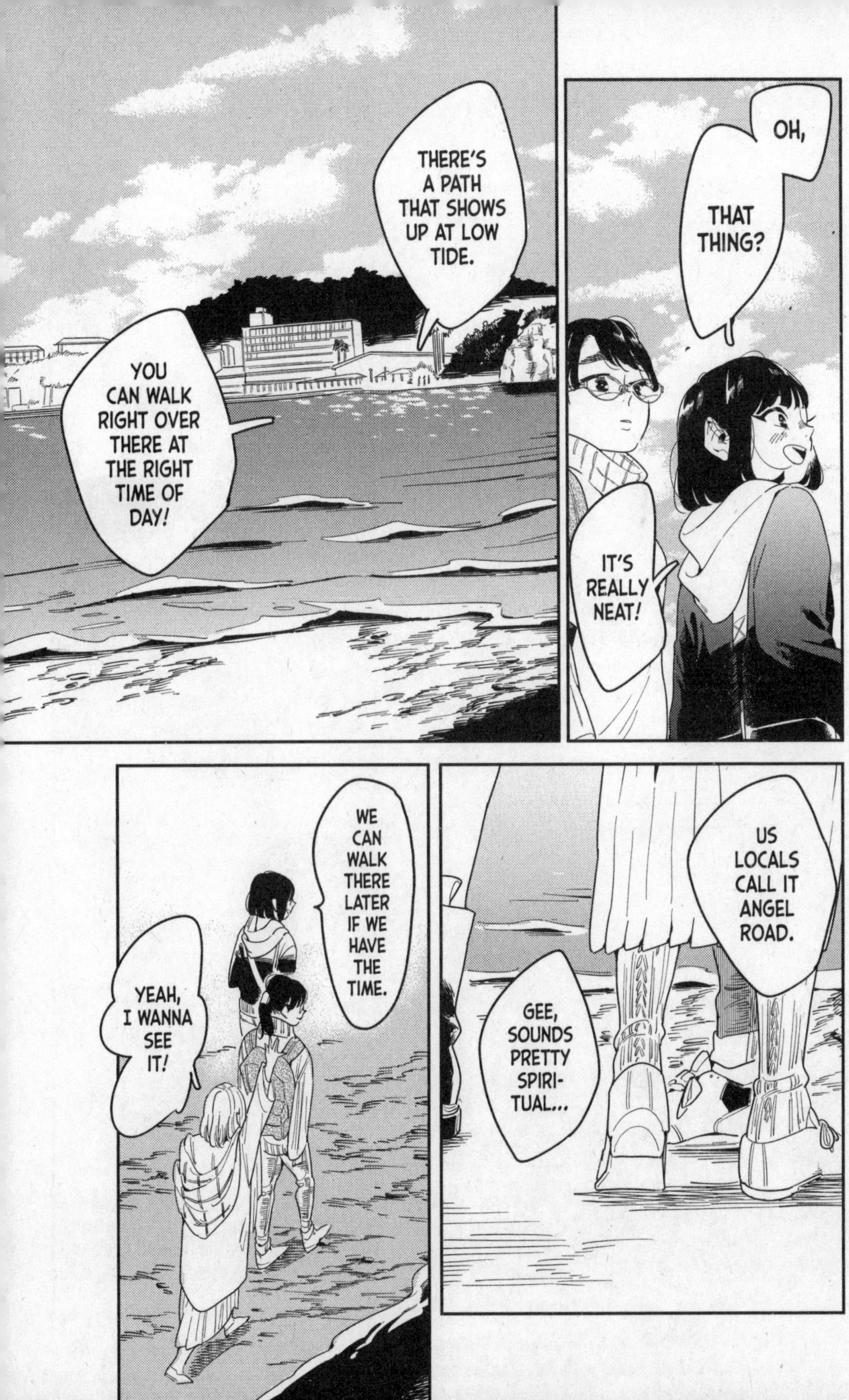
OH,
THAT THING?
IT'S REALLY NEAT!
THERE'S A PATH THAT SHOWS UP AT LOW TIDE.
YOU CAN WALK RIGHT OVER THERE AT THE RIGHT TIME OF DAY!
US LOCALS CALL IT ANGEL ROAD.
GEE, SOUNDS PRETTY SPIRI-TUAL...
WE CAN WALK THERE LATER IF WE HAVE THE TIME.
YEAH, I WANNA SEE IT!

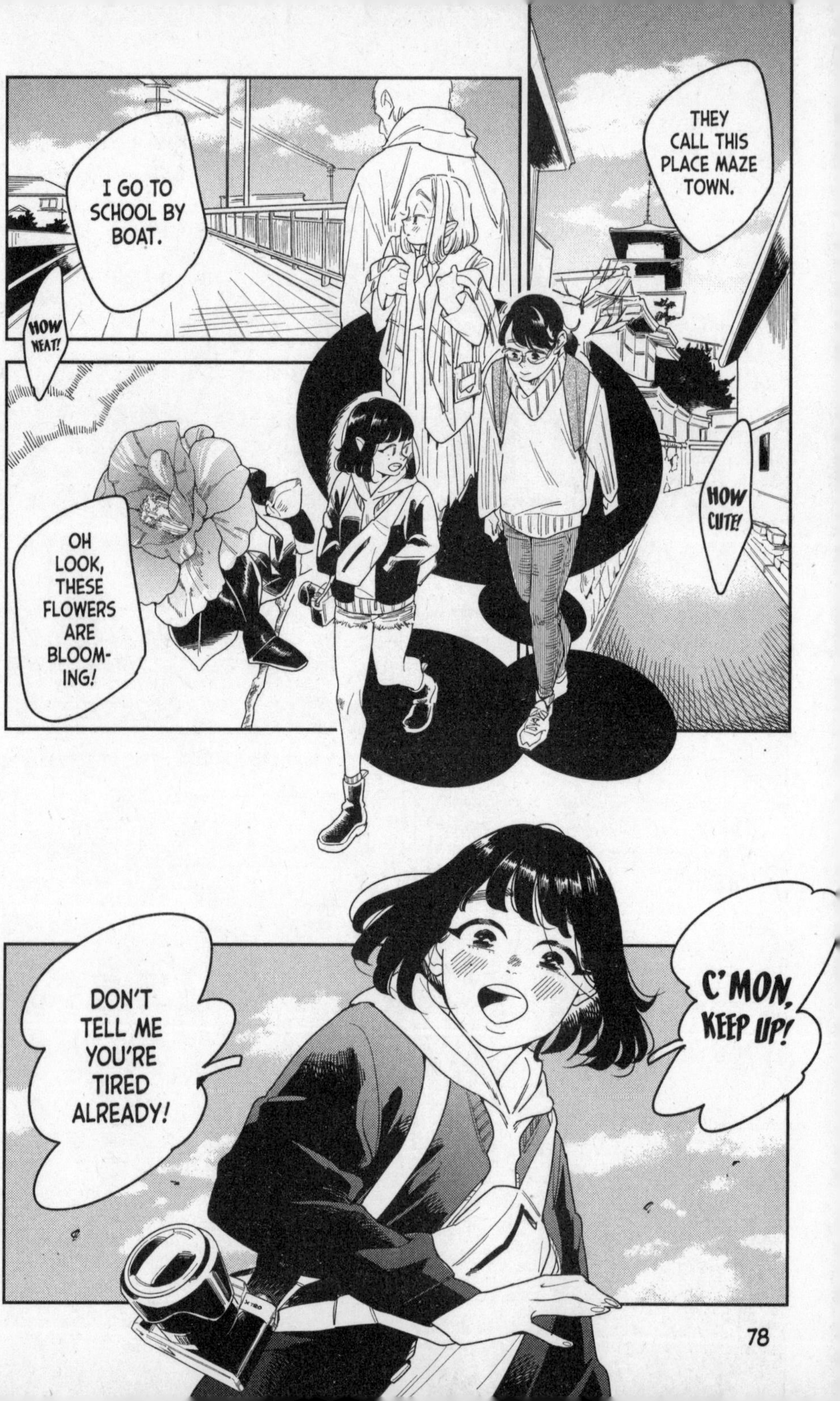
THEY CALL THIS PLACE MAZE TOWN.
HOW CUTE!
I GO TO SCHOOL BY BOAT.
HOW NEAT!
OH LOOK, THESE FLOWERS ARE BLOOM-ING!
C'MON, KEEP UP!
DON'T TELL ME YOU'RE TIRED ALREADY!

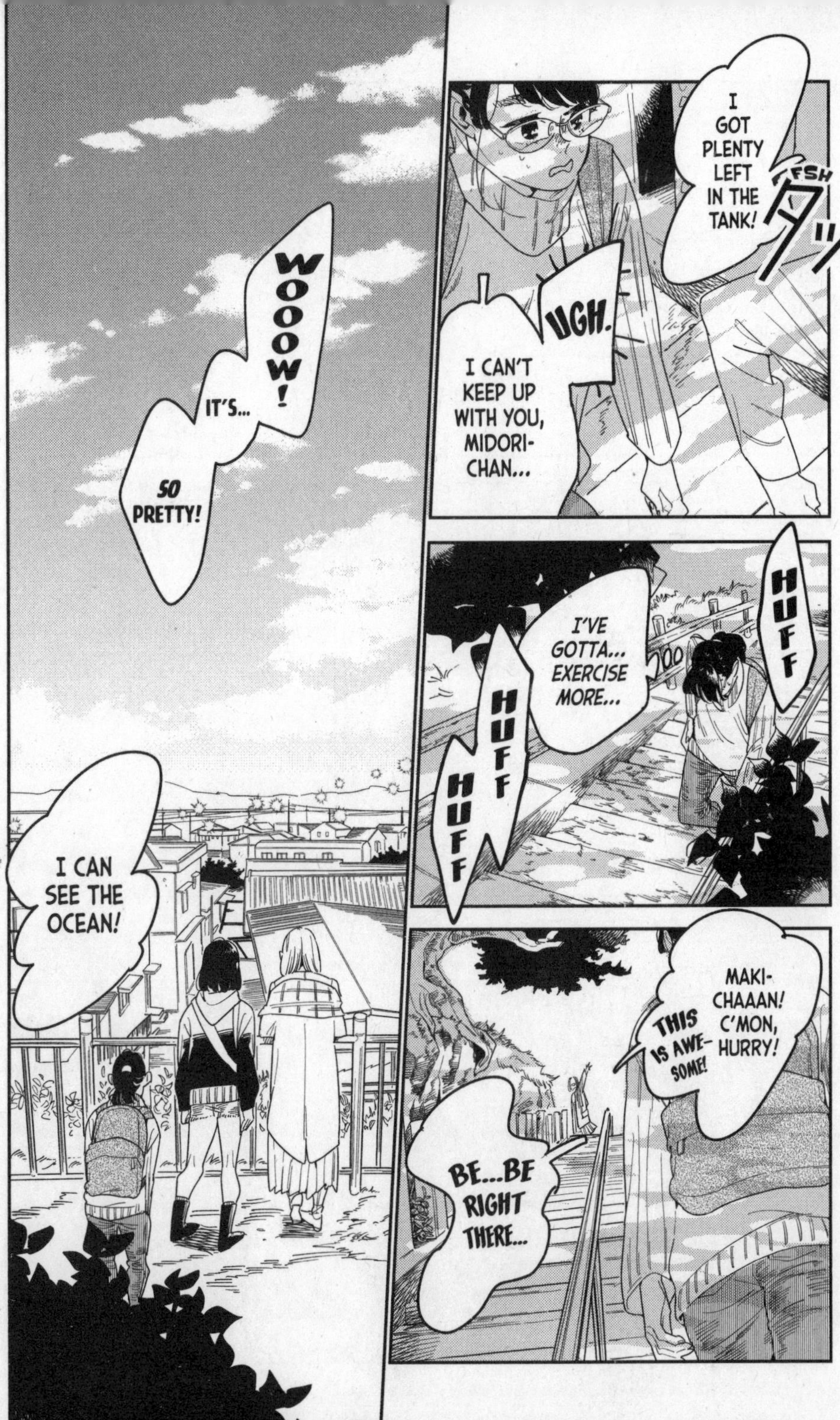
I GOT PLENTY LEFT IN THE TANK!
FSH
UGH.
I CAN'T KEEP UP WITH YOU, MIDORI-CHAN...
HUFF
I'VE GOTTA... EXERCISE MORE...
HUFF
HUFF
MAKI-CHAAAN! C'MON, HURRY!
THIS IS AWE-SOME!
BE...BE RIGHT THERE...
WOOOOW!
IT'S...
SO PRETTY!
I CAN SEE THE OCEAN!

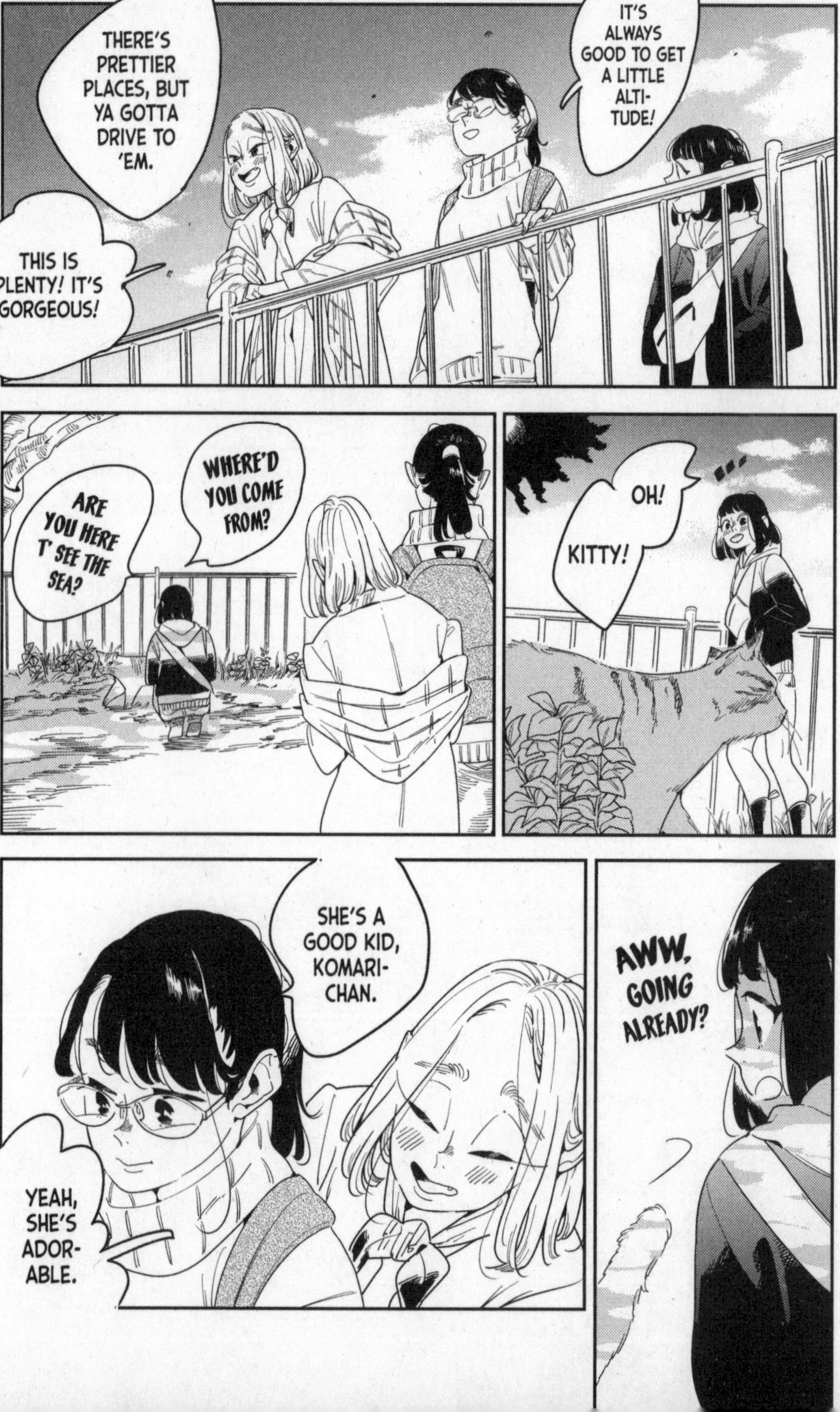
IT'S ALWAYS GOOD TO GET A LITTLE ALTI-TUDE!
THERE'S PRETTIER PLACES, BUT YA GOTTA DRIVE TO 'EM.
THIS IS PLENTY! IT'S GORGEOUS!
OH!
KITTY!
WHERE'D YOU COME FROM?
ARE YOU HERE T' SEE THE SEA?
AWW, GOING ALREADY?
SHE'S A GOOD KID, KOMARI-CHAN.
YEAH, SHE'S ADORABLE.

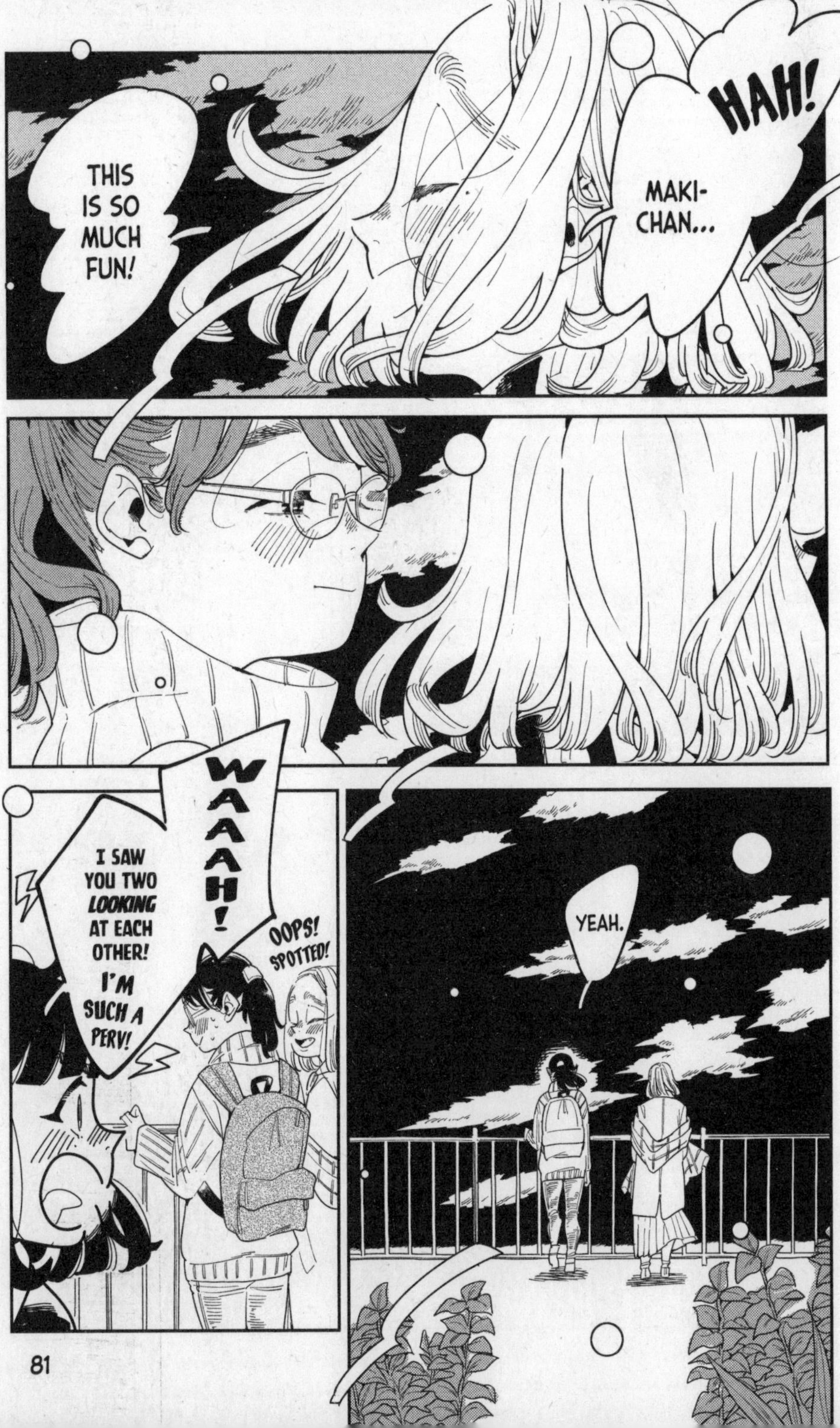
HAH!
MAKI-CHAN...
THIS IS SO MUCH FUN!
YEAH.
WAAAAH!
I SAW YOU TWO *LOOKING* AT EACH OTHER! I'M SUCH A PERV!
OOPS! SPOTTED!

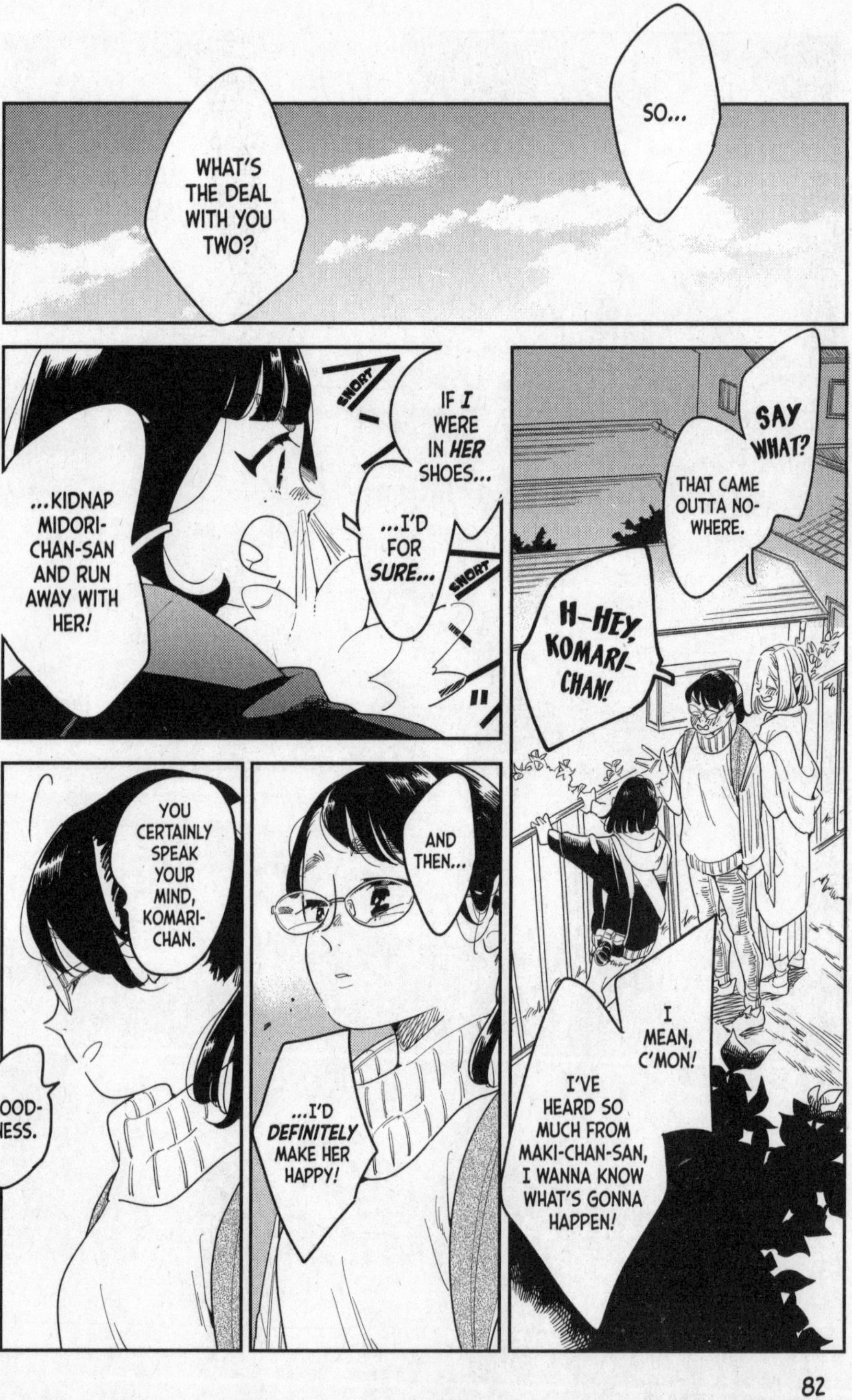
SO...
WHAT'S THE DEAL WITH YOU TWO?
SAY WHAT?
THAT CAME OUTTA NO-WHERE.
H-HEY, KOMARI-CHAN!
I MEAN, C'MON!
I'VE HEARD SO MUCH FROM MAKI-CHAN-SAN, I WANNA KNOW WHAT'S GONNA HAPPEN!
SNORT
IF I WERE IN HER SHOES...
...I'D FOR SURE...
SNORT
...KIDNAP MIDORI-CHAN-SAN AND RUN AWAY WITH HER!
AND THEN...
...I'D DEFINITELY MAKE HER HAPPY!
YOU CERTAINLY SPEAK YOUR MIND, KOMARI-CHAN.
GOOD-NESS.

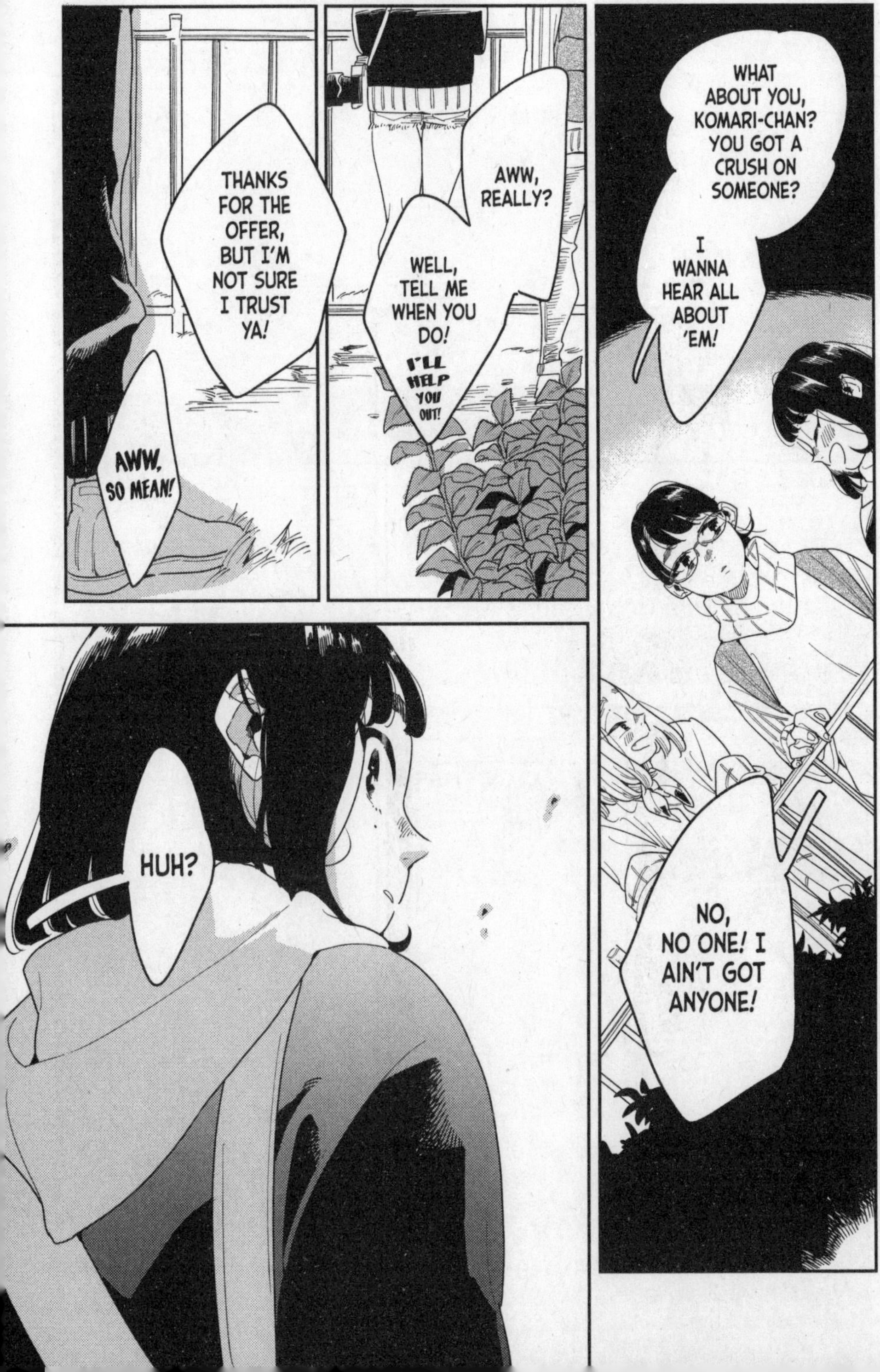
WHAT ABOUT YOU, KOMARI-CHAN? YOU GOT A CRUSH ON SOMEONE?
I WANNA HEAR ALL ABOUT 'EM!
NO, NO ONE! I AIN'T GOT ANYONE!
AWW, REALLY?
WELL, TELL ME WHEN YOU DO!
I'LL HELP YOU OUT!
THANKS FOR THE OFFER, BUT I'M NOT SURE I TRUST YA!
AWW, SO MEAN!
HUH?

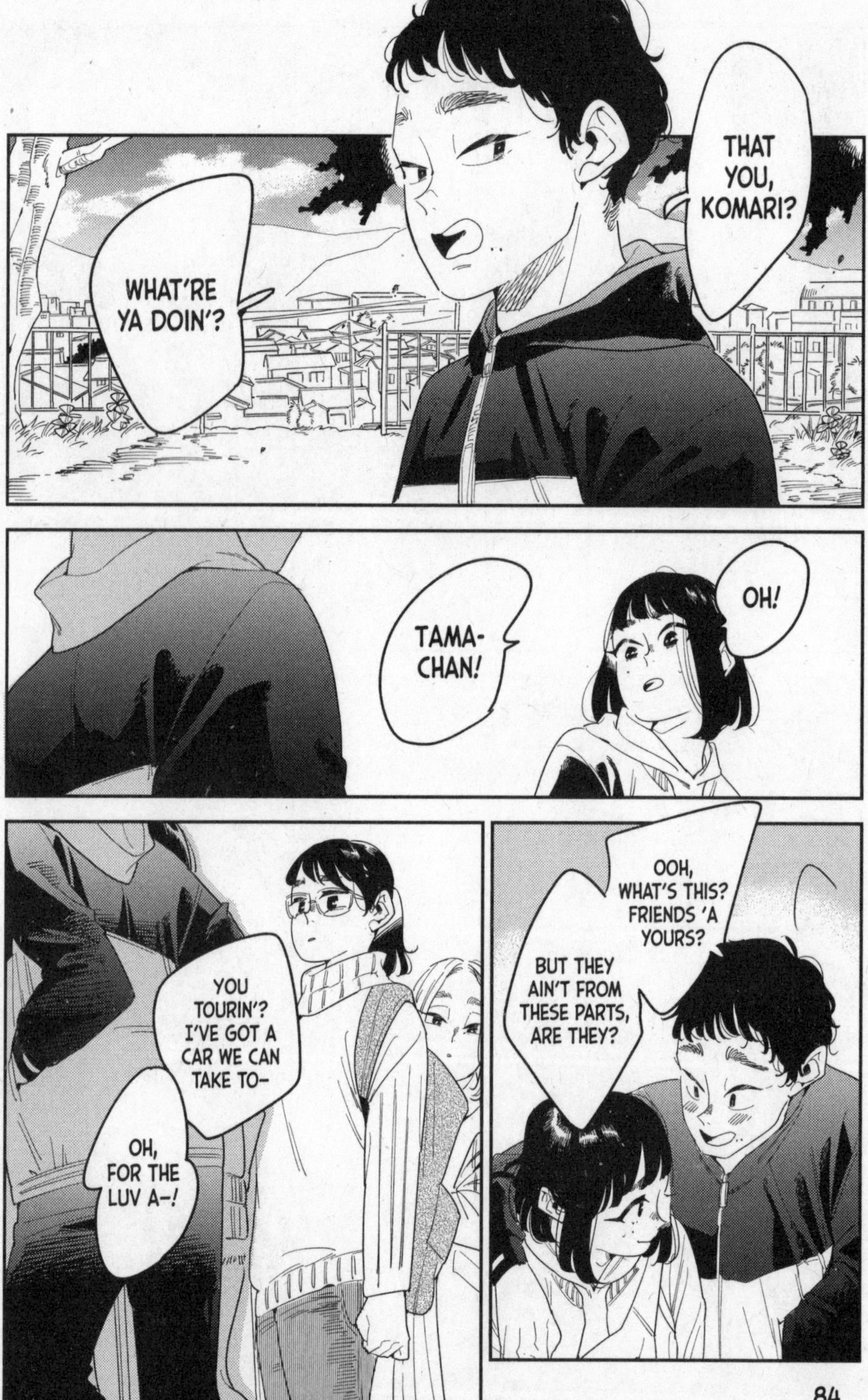
THAT YOU, KOMARI?
WHAT'RE YA DOIN'?
OH!
TAMA-CHAN!
OOH, WHAT'S THIS? FRIENDS 'A YOURS?
BUT THEY AIN'T FROM THESE PARTS, ARE THEY?
YOU TOURIN'? I'VE GOT A CAR WE CAN TAKE TO–
OH, FOR THE LUV A–!

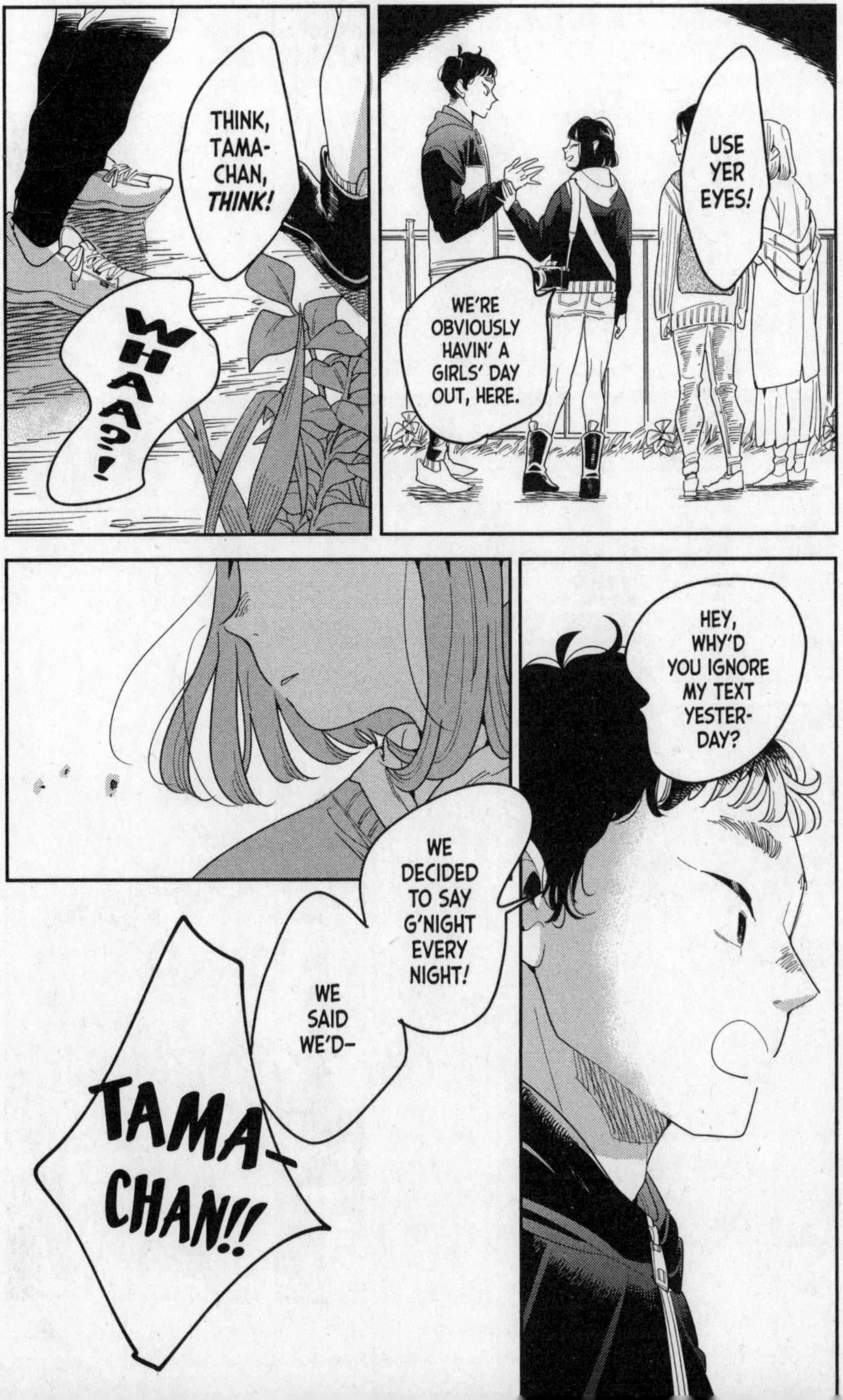
USE YER EYES!
WE'RE OBVIOUSLY HAVIN' A GIRLS' DAY OUT, HERE.
THINK, TAMA-CHAN, *THINK!*
WHAAA?!
HEY, WHY'D YOU IGNORE MY TEXT YESTERDAY?
WE DECIDED TO SAY G'NIGHT EVERY NIGHT!
WE SAID WE'D–
TAMA-CHAN!!

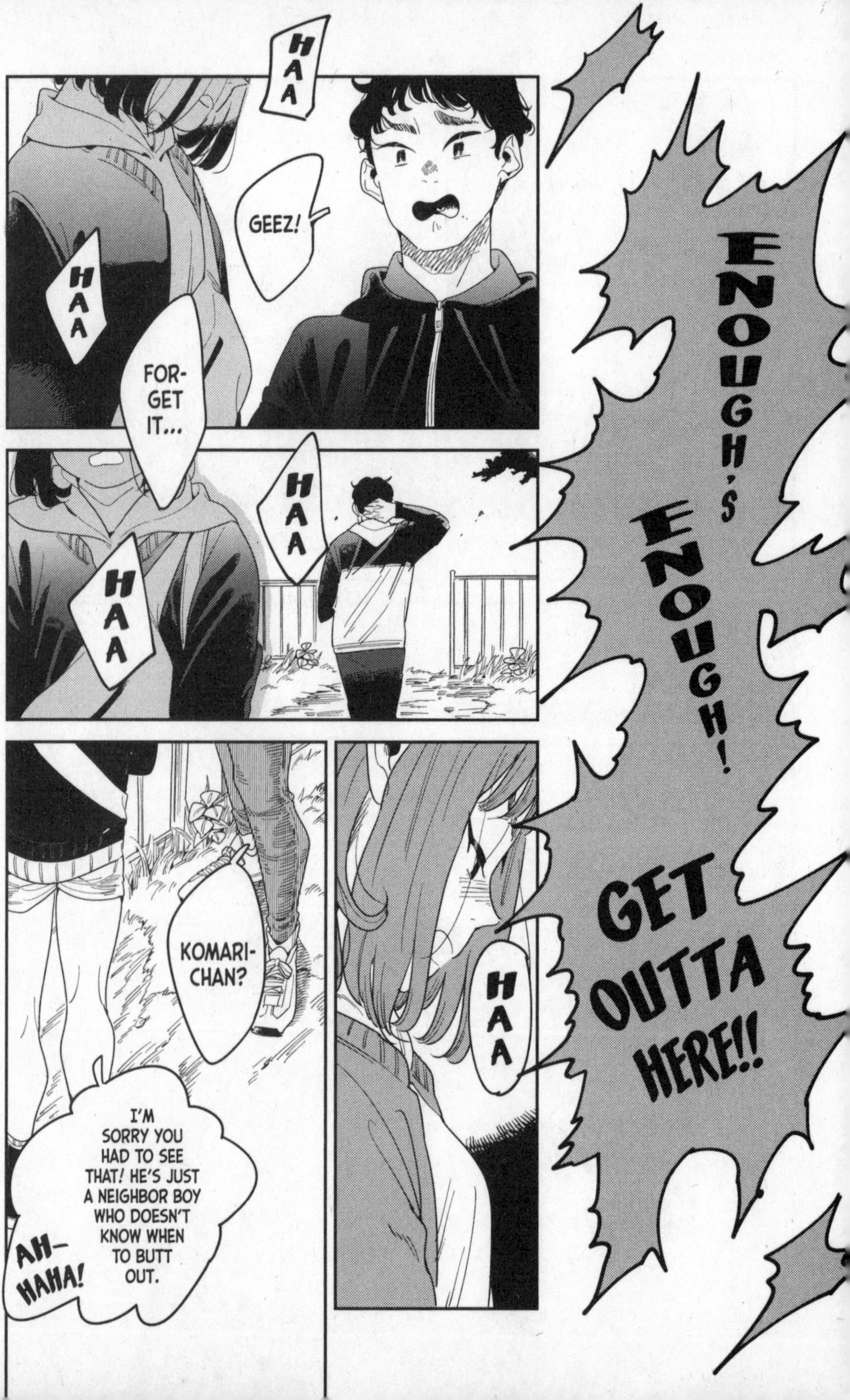
ENOUGH'S ENOUGH!
GET OUTTA HERE!!
HAA
GEEZ!
HAA
FOR-GET IT...
HAA
HAA
HAA
KOMARI-CHAN?
I'M SORRY YOU HAD TO SEE THAT! HE'S JUST A NEIGHBOR BOY WHO DOESN'T KNOW WHEN TO BUTT OUT.
AH-HAHA!

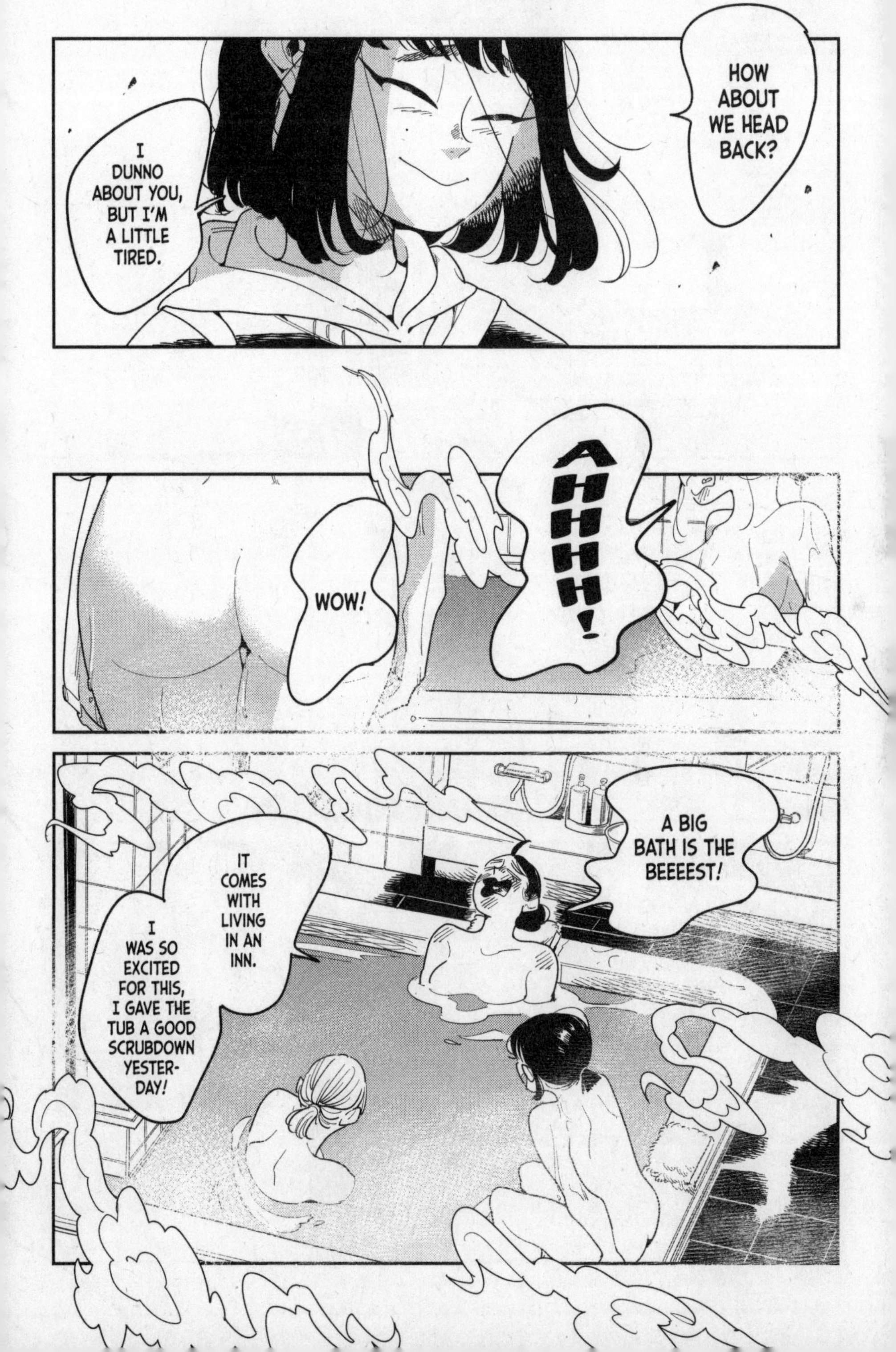
HOW ABOUT WE HEAD BACK?
I DUNNO ABOUT YOU, BUT I'M A LITTLE TIRED.
AHHHHH!
WOW!
A BIG BATH IS THE BEEEEST!
IT COMES WITH LIVING IN AN INN.
I WAS SO EXCITED FOR THIS, I GAVE THE TUB A GOOD SCRUBDOWN YESTER-DAY!

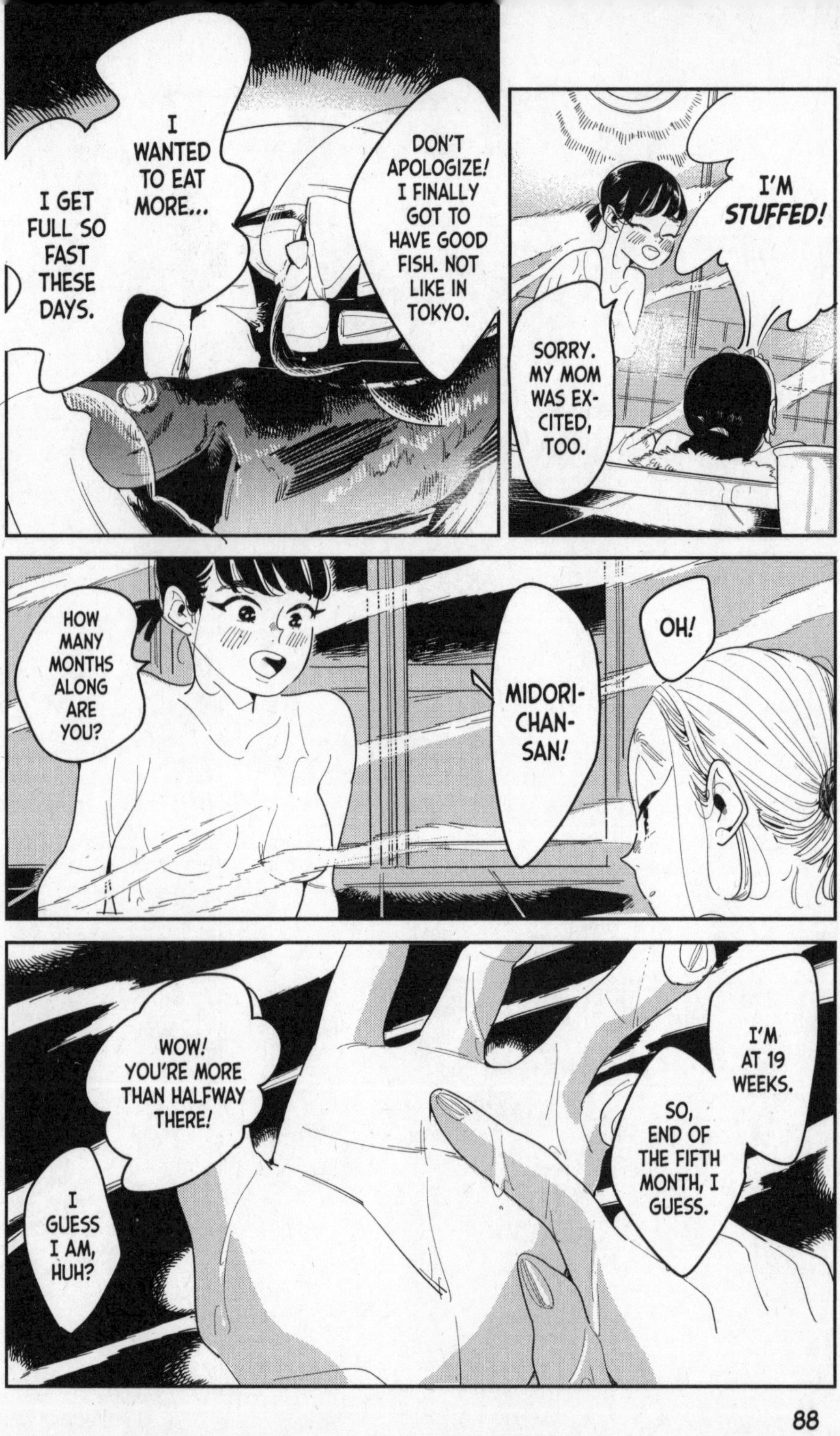
I'M STUFFED!
SORRY. MY MOM WAS EXCITED, TOO.
DON'T APOLOGIZE! I FINALLY GOT TO HAVE GOOD FISH. NOT LIKE IN TOKYO.
I WANTED TO EAT MORE...
I GET FULL SO FAST THESE DAYS.
OH!
MIDORI-CHAN-SAN!
HOW MANY MONTHS ALONG ARE YOU?
I'M AT 19 WEEKS.
SO, END OF THE FIFTH MONTH, I GUESS.
WOW! YOU'RE MORE THAN HALFWAY THERE!
I GUESS I AM, HUH?

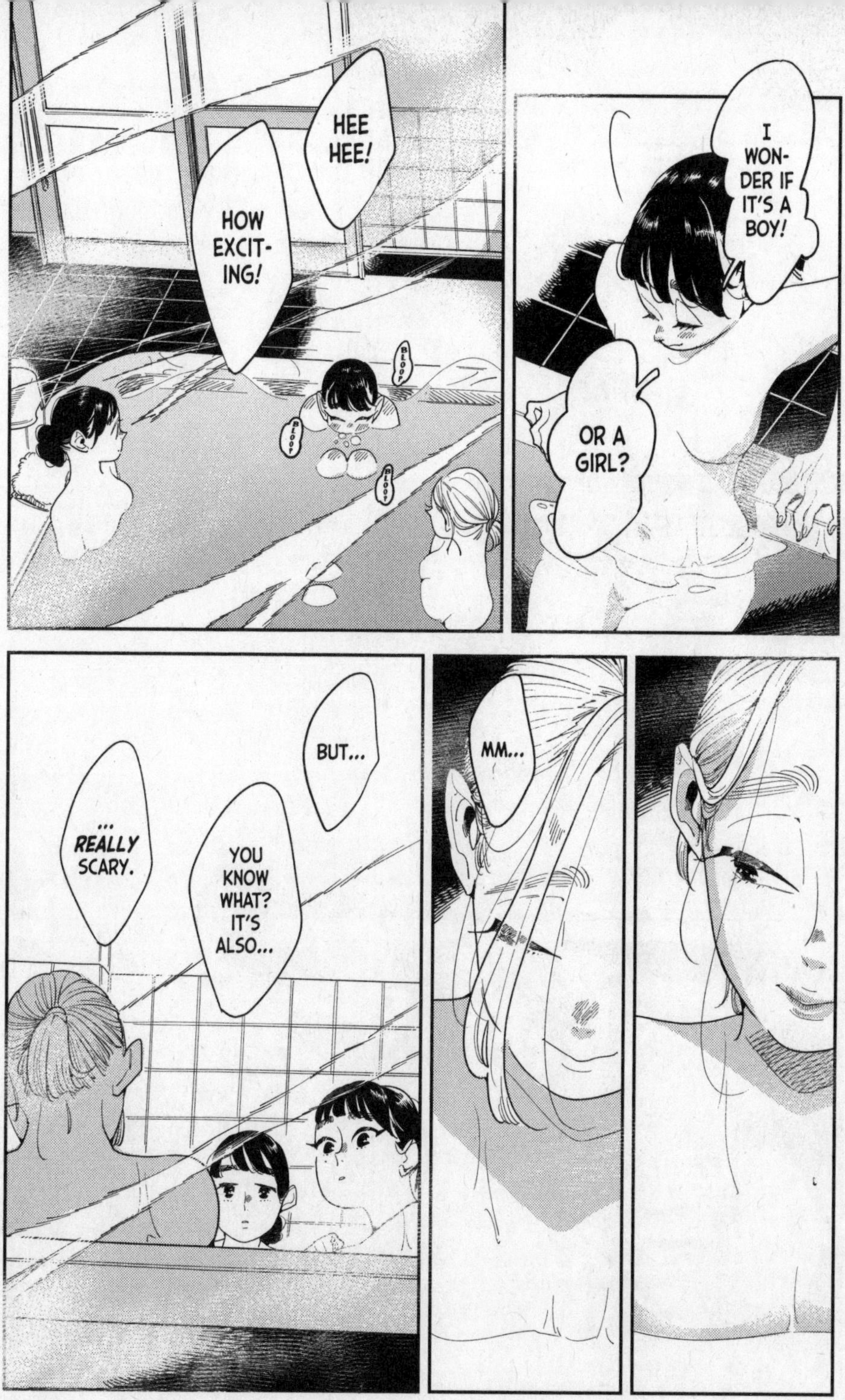
I WONDER IF IT'S A BOY!
OR A GIRL?
HEE HEE!
HOW EXCITING!
BLOOP
BLOOP
BLOOP
MM...
BUT...
YOU KNOW WHAT? IT'S ALSO...
... *REALLY* SCARY.

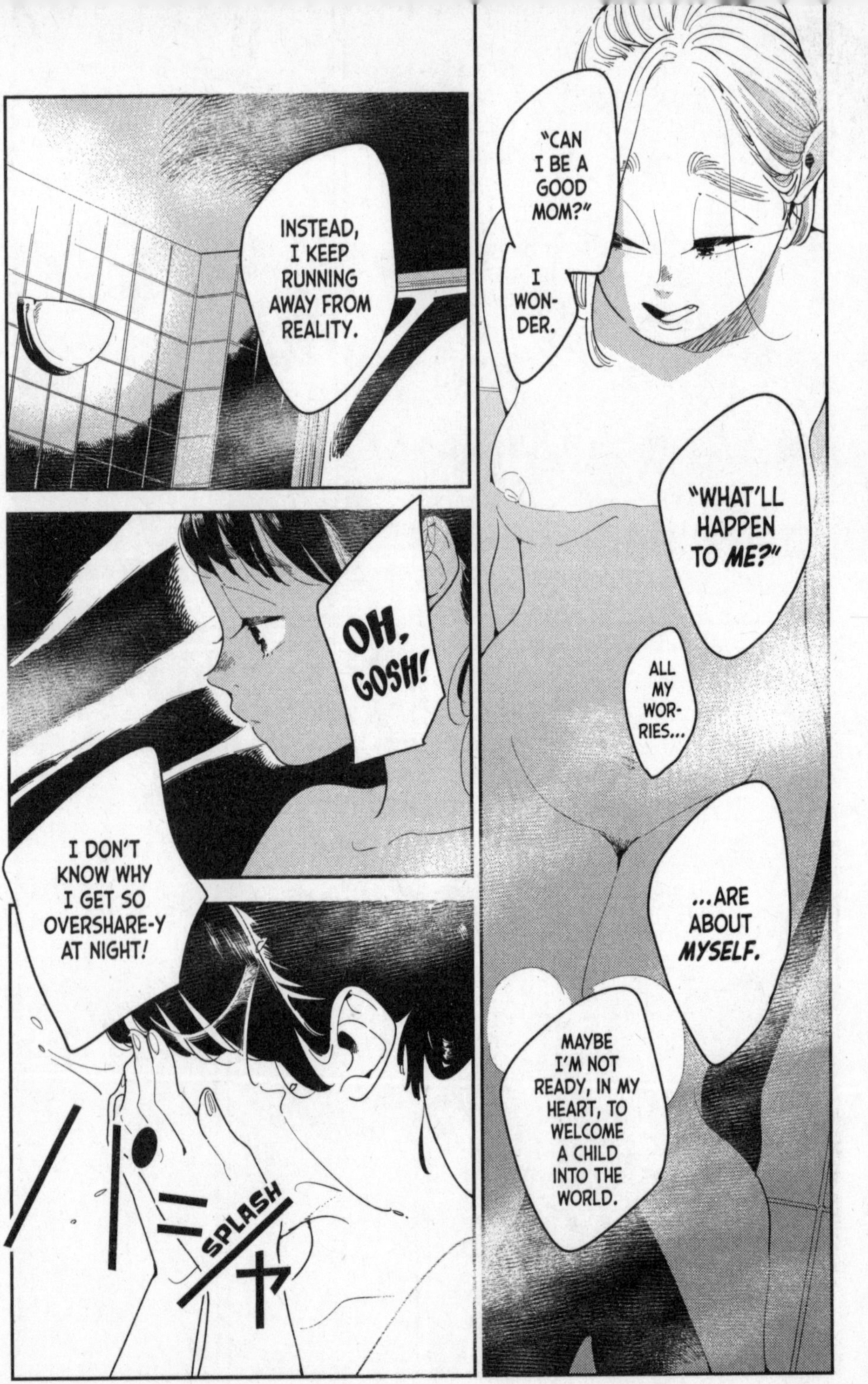
"CAN I BE A GOOD MOM?"
I WONDER.
"WHAT'LL HAPPEN TO *ME?*"
ALL MY WORRIES...
...ARE ABOUT *MYSELF.*
MAYBE I'M NOT READY, IN MY HEART, TO WELCOME A CHILD INTO THE WORLD.
INSTEAD, I KEEP RUNNING AWAY FROM REALITY.
OH, GOSH!
I DON'T KNOW WHY I GET SO OVERSHARE-Y AT NIGHT!
SPLASH

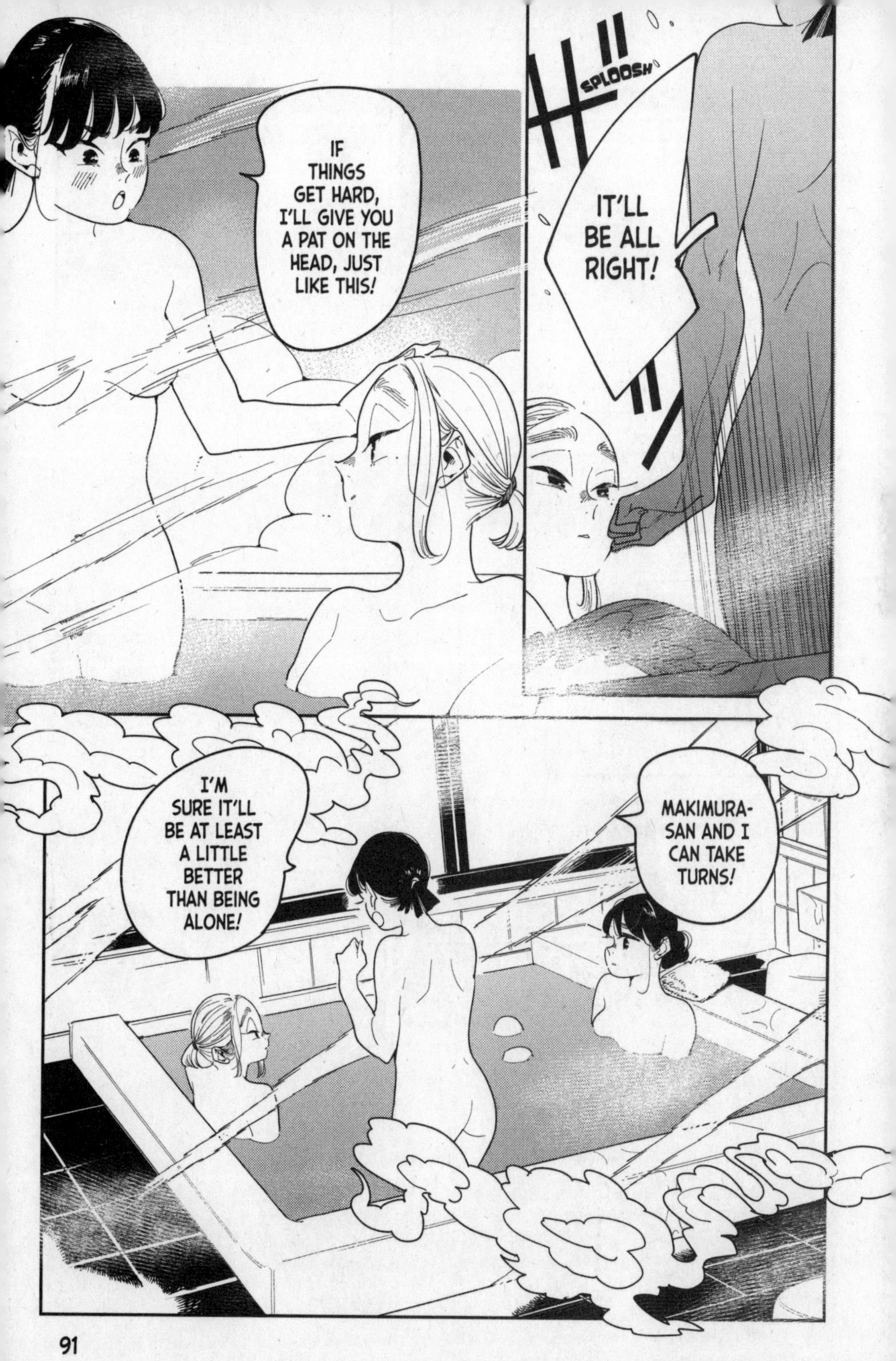
AH!!
SPLOOSH
IT'LL BE ALL RIGHT!
!!
IF THINGS GET HARD, I'LL GIVE YOU A PAT ON THE HEAD, JUST LIKE THIS!
MAKIMURA-SAN AND I CAN TAKE TURNS!
I'M SURE IT'LL BE AT LEAST A LITTLE BETTER THAN BEING ALONE!

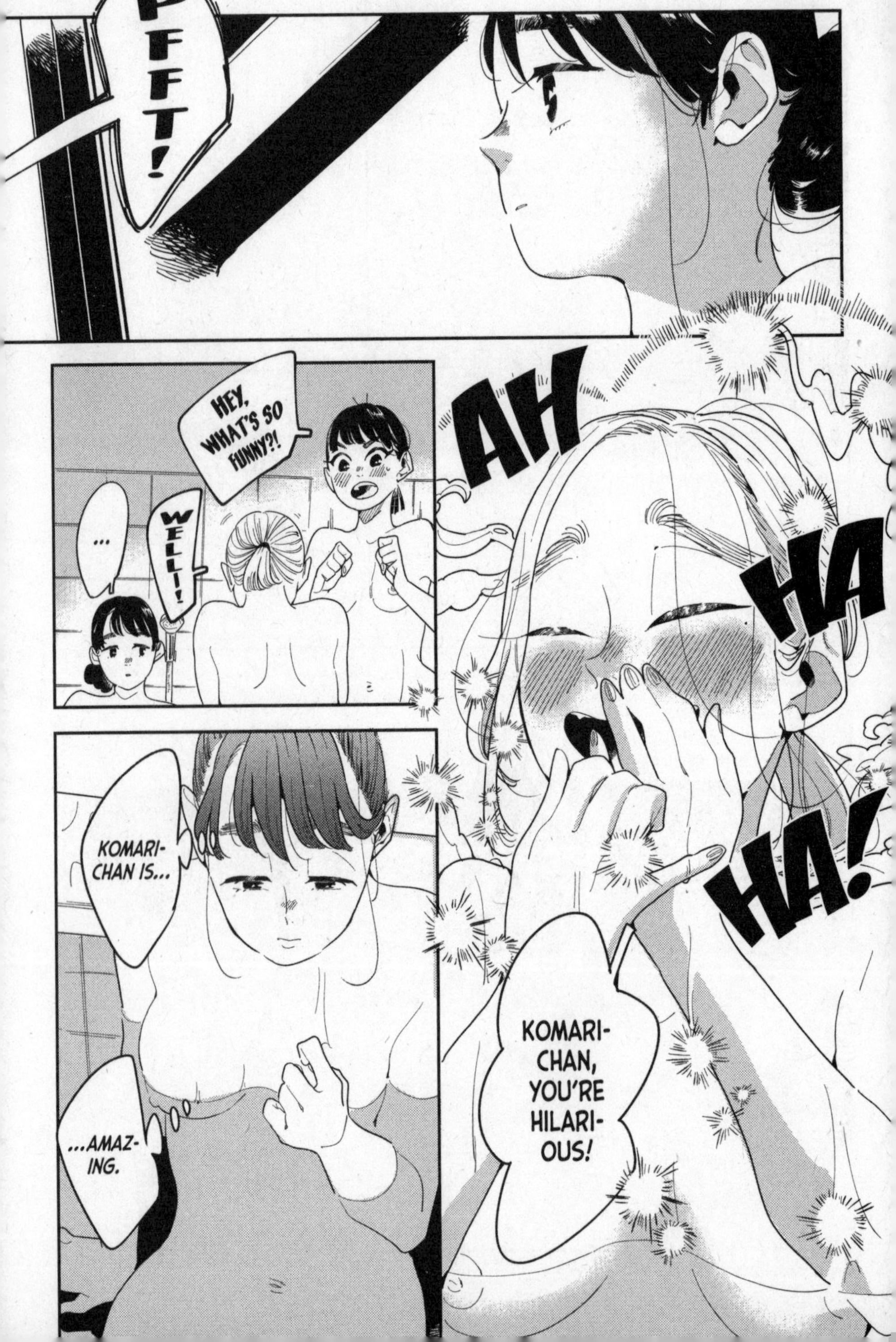
PFFT!
AH HA HA!
KOMARI-CHAN, YOU'RE HILARI-OUS!
HEY, WHAT'S SO FUNNY?!
WELL!
...
KOMARI-CHAN IS...
...AMAZ-ING.

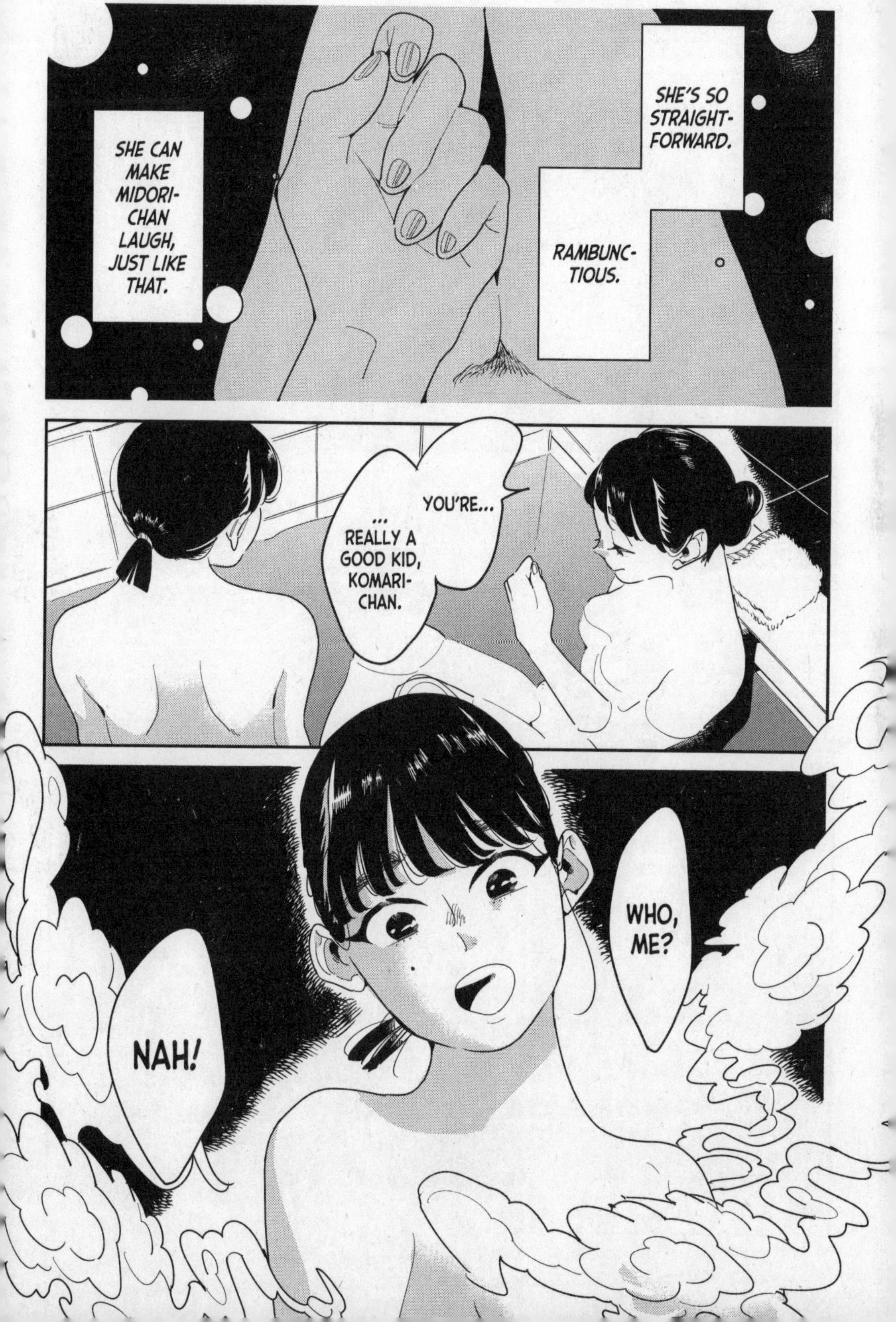
SHE'S SO STRAIGHT-FORWARD.
RAMBUNC-TIOUS.
SHE CAN MAKE MIDORI-CHAN LAUGH, JUST LIKE THAT.
YOU'RE...
... REALLY A GOOD KID, KOMARI-CHAN.
WHO, ME?
NAH!

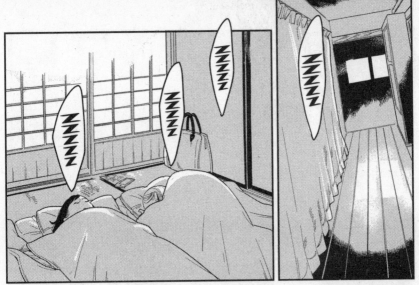

ZZZZZ
ZZZZZ
ZZZZZ
ZZZZZ

CLACK

YOU'RE GOING OUT?

ISN'T IT DANGER-OUS TO GO ALONE?

OH—

I'M SORRY.

MRRRF?

DID I WAKE YOU?

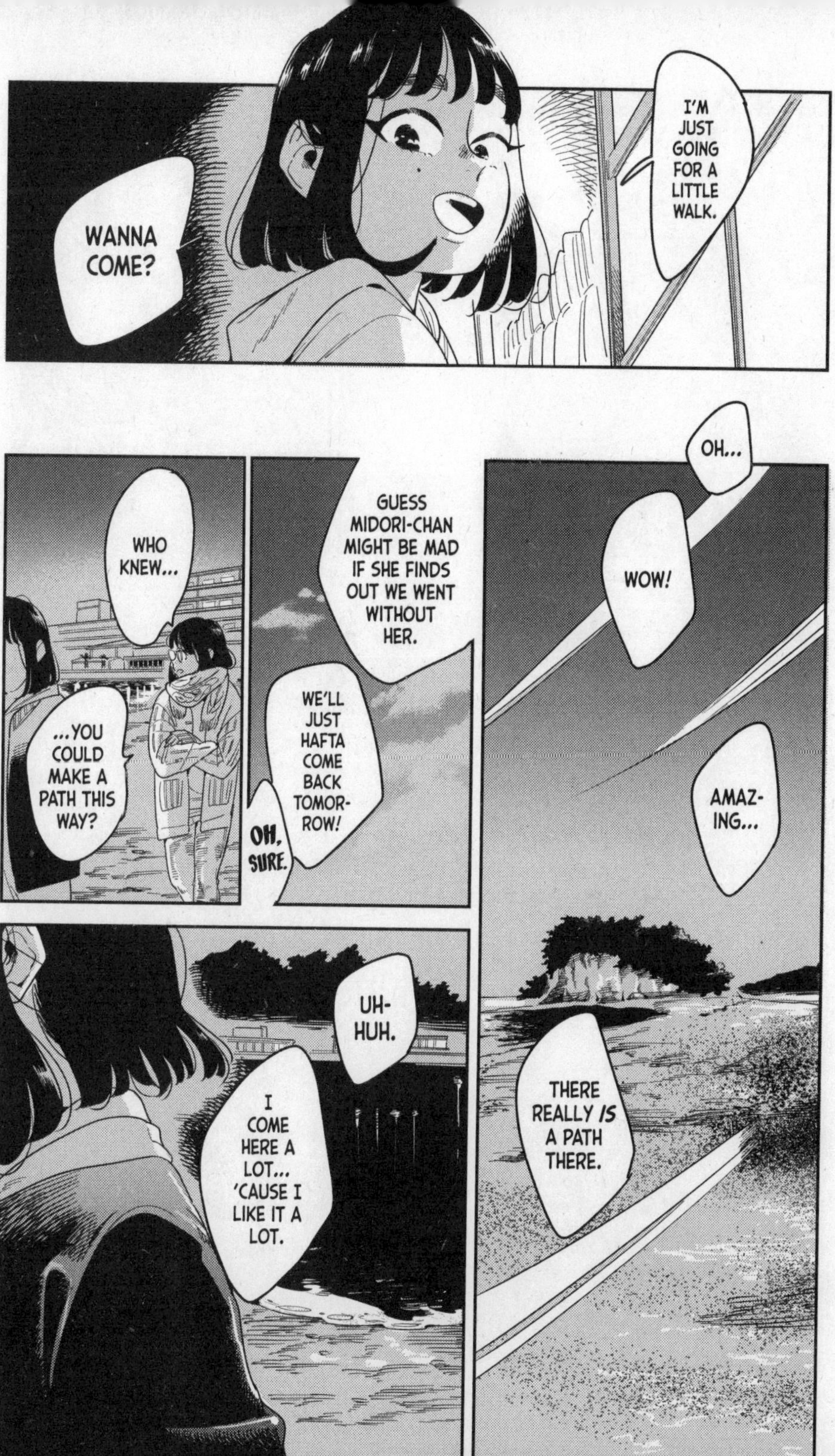
I'M JUST GOING FOR A LITTLE WALK.
WANNA COME?
OH...
WOW!
AMAZ-ING...
THERE REALLY *IS* A PATH THERE.
GUESS MIDORI-CHAN MIGHT BE MAD IF SHE FINDS OUT WE WENT WITHOUT HER.
WE'LL JUST HAFTA COME BACK TOMOR-ROW!
OH, SURE.
WHO KNEW...
...YOU COULD MAKE A PATH THIS WAY?
UH-HUH.
I COME HERE A LOT... 'CAUSE I LIKE IT A LOT.

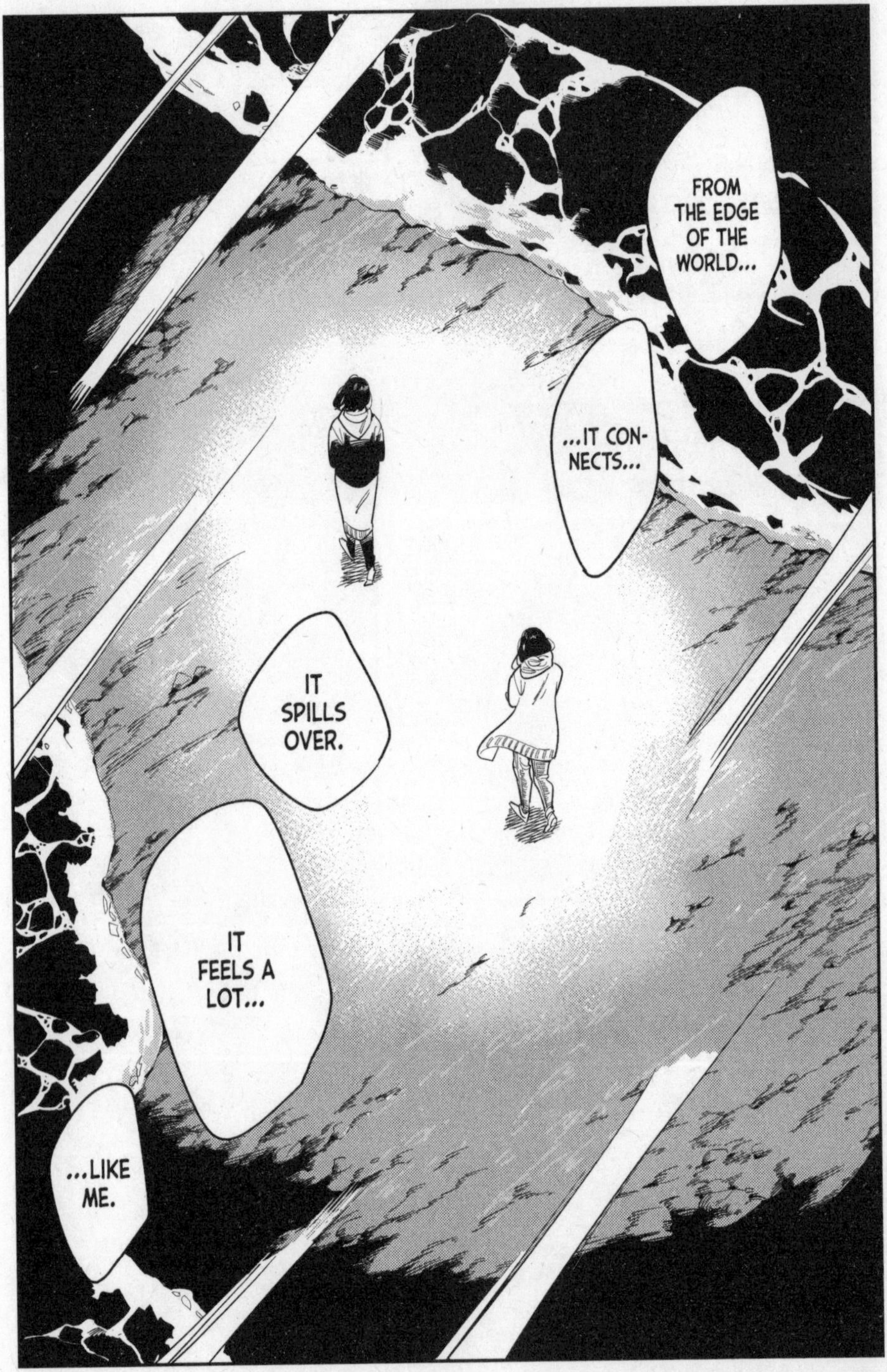
FROM THE EDGE OF THE WORLD...
...IT CONNECTS...
IT SPILLS OVER.
IT FEELS A LOT...
...LIKE ME.

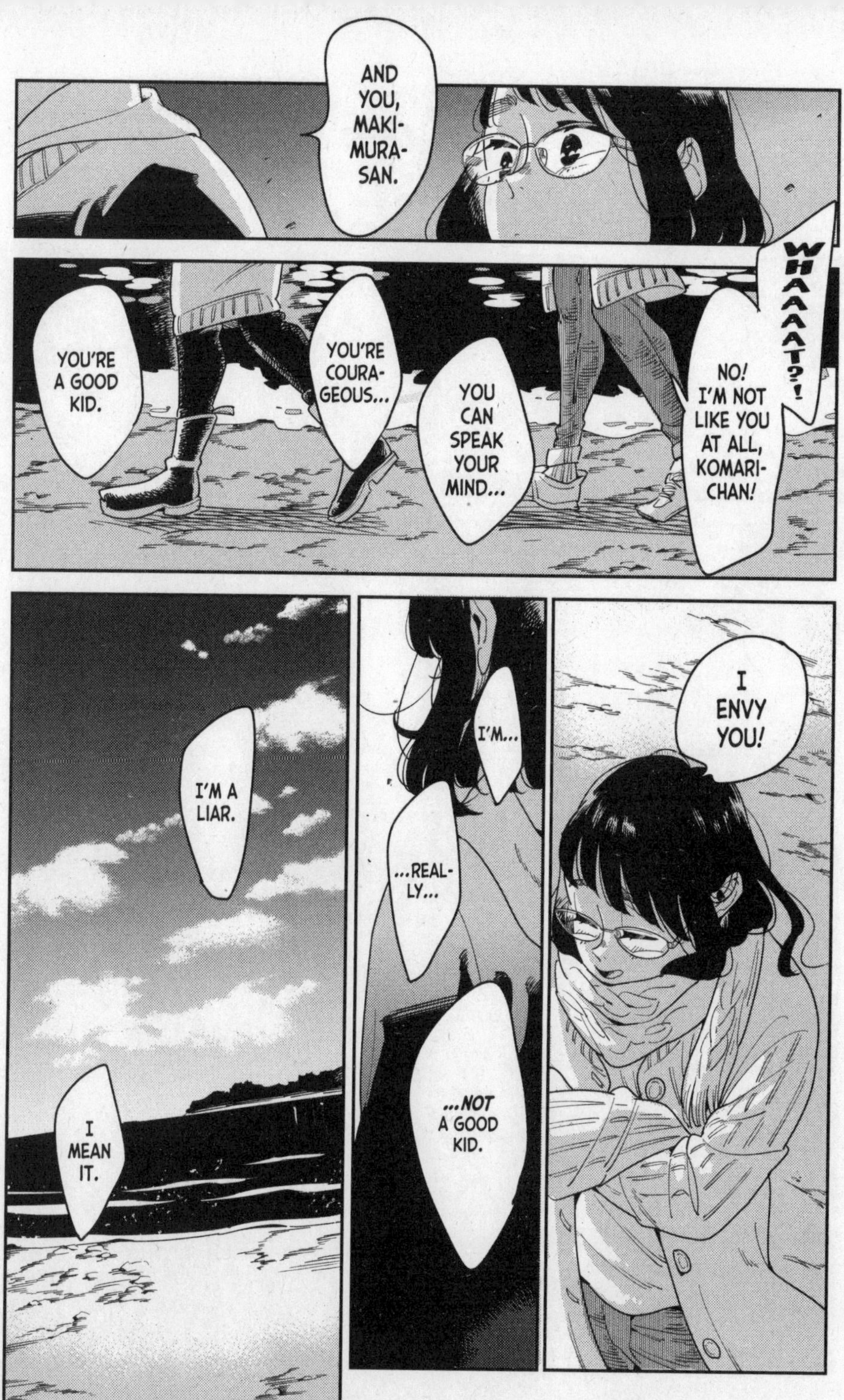
AND YOU, MAKI-MURA-SAN.
WHAAAAAT?!
NO! I'M NOT LIKE YOU AT ALL, KOMARI-CHAN!
YOU CAN SPEAK YOUR MIND...
YOU'RE COURA-GEOUS...
YOU'RE A GOOD KID.
I ENVY YOU!
I'M...
...REAL-LY...
...NOT A GOOD KID.
I'M A LIAR.
I MEAN IT.

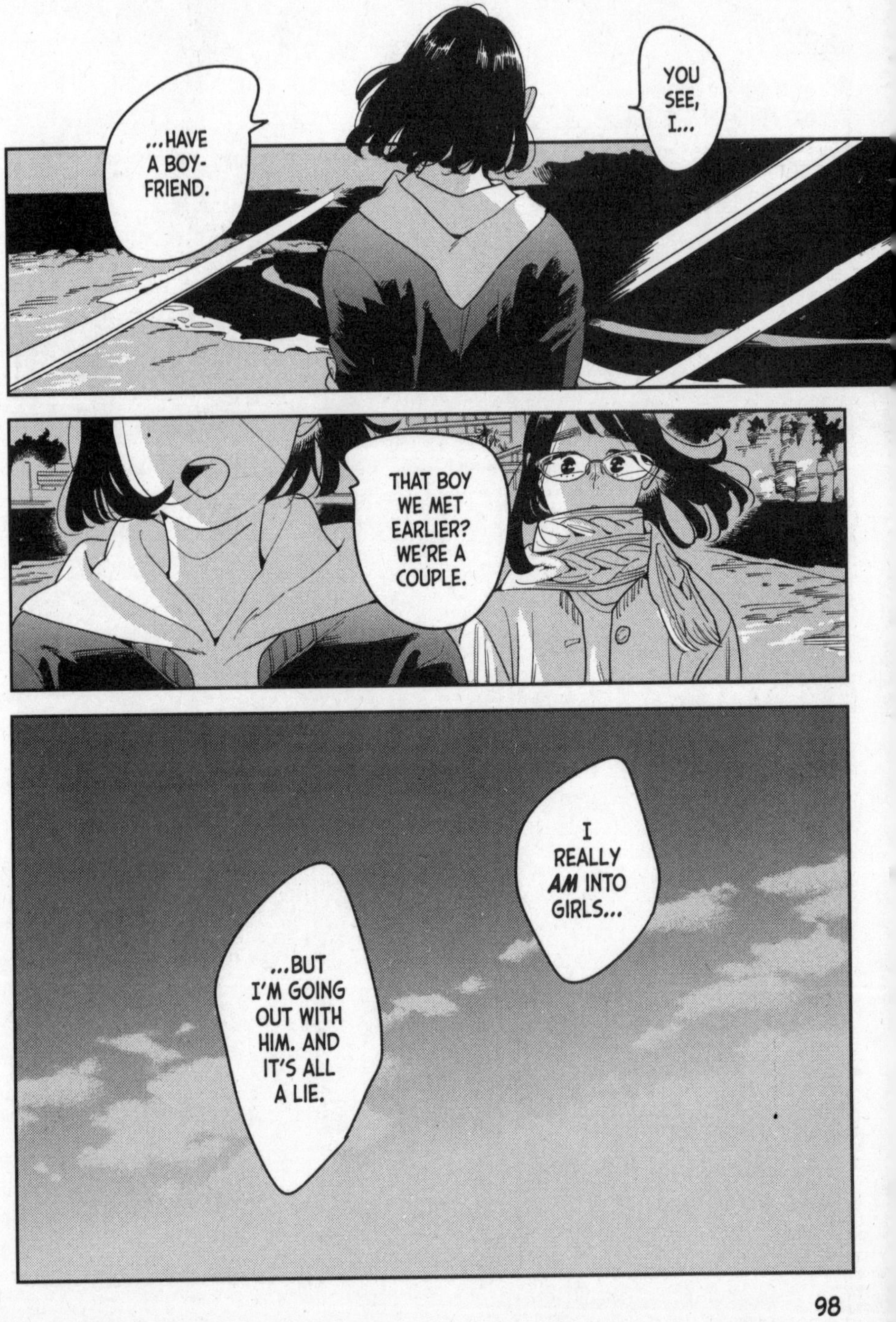
YOU SEE, I...
...HAVE A BOY-FRIEND.
THAT BOY WE MET EARLIER? WE'RE A COUPLE.
I REALLY *AM* INTO GIRLS...
...BUT I'M GOING OUT WITH HIM. AND IT'S ALL A LIE.

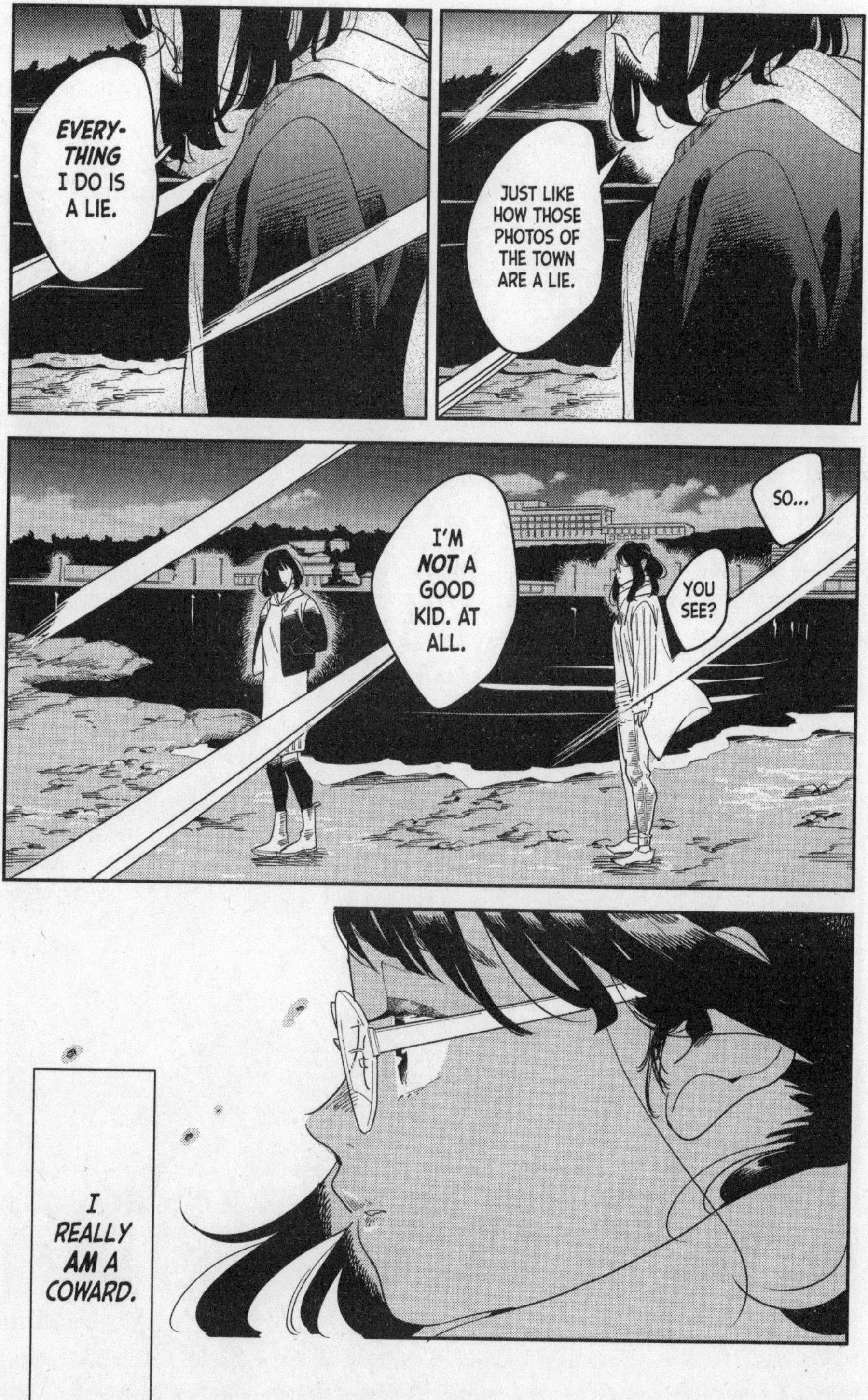
JUST LIKE HOW THOSE PHOTOS OF THE TOWN ARE A LIE.
EVERY-THING I DO IS A LIE.
SO...
YOU SEE?
I'M *NOT* A GOOD KID. AT ALL.
I REALLY AM A COWARD.

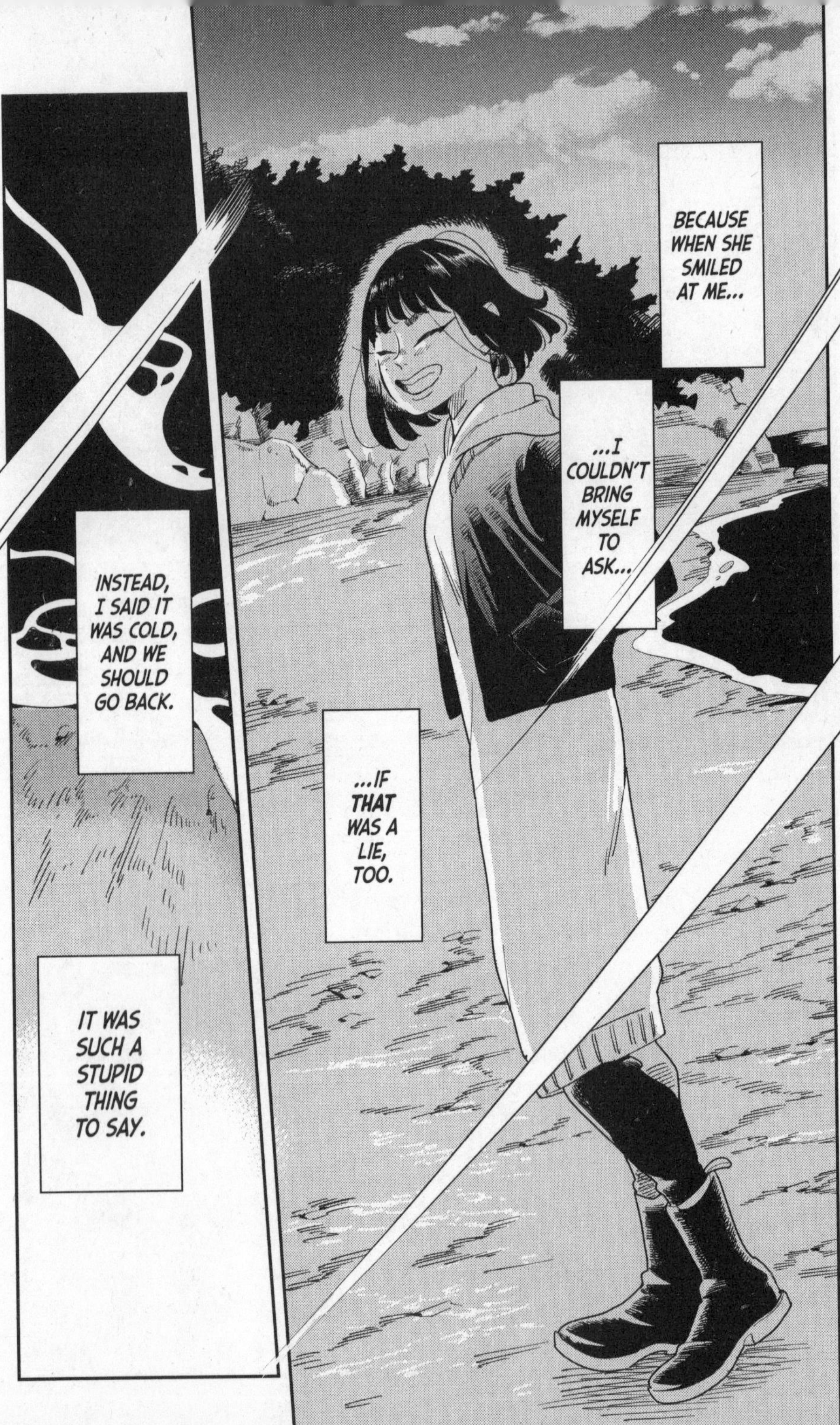
BECAUSE WHEN SHE SMILED AT ME...
...I COULDN'T BRING MYSELF TO ASK...
...IF THAT WAS A LIE, TOO.
INSTEAD, I SAID IT WAS COLD, AND WE SHOULD GO BACK.
IT WAS SUCH A STUPID THING TO SAY.

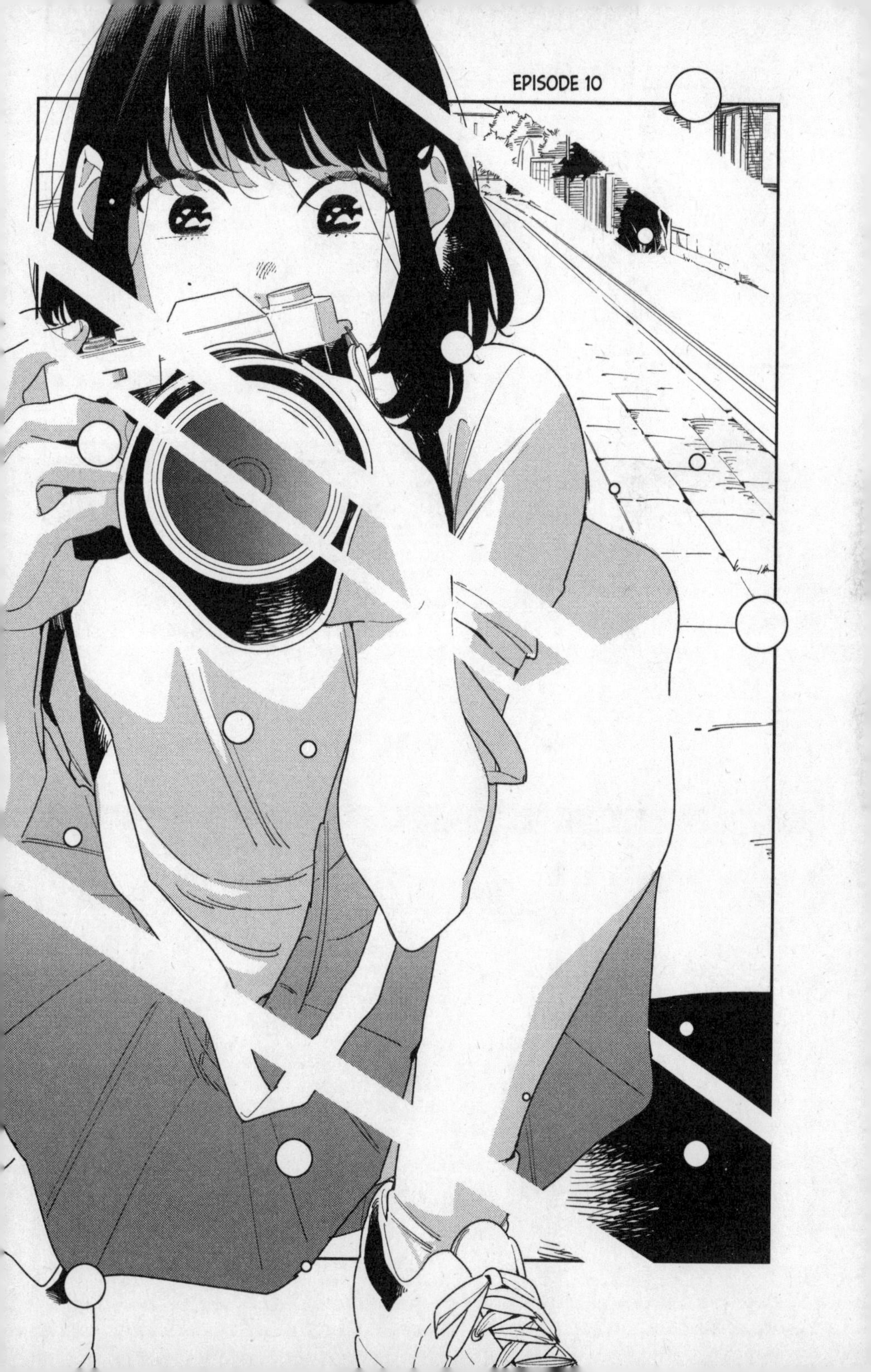
EPISODE 10

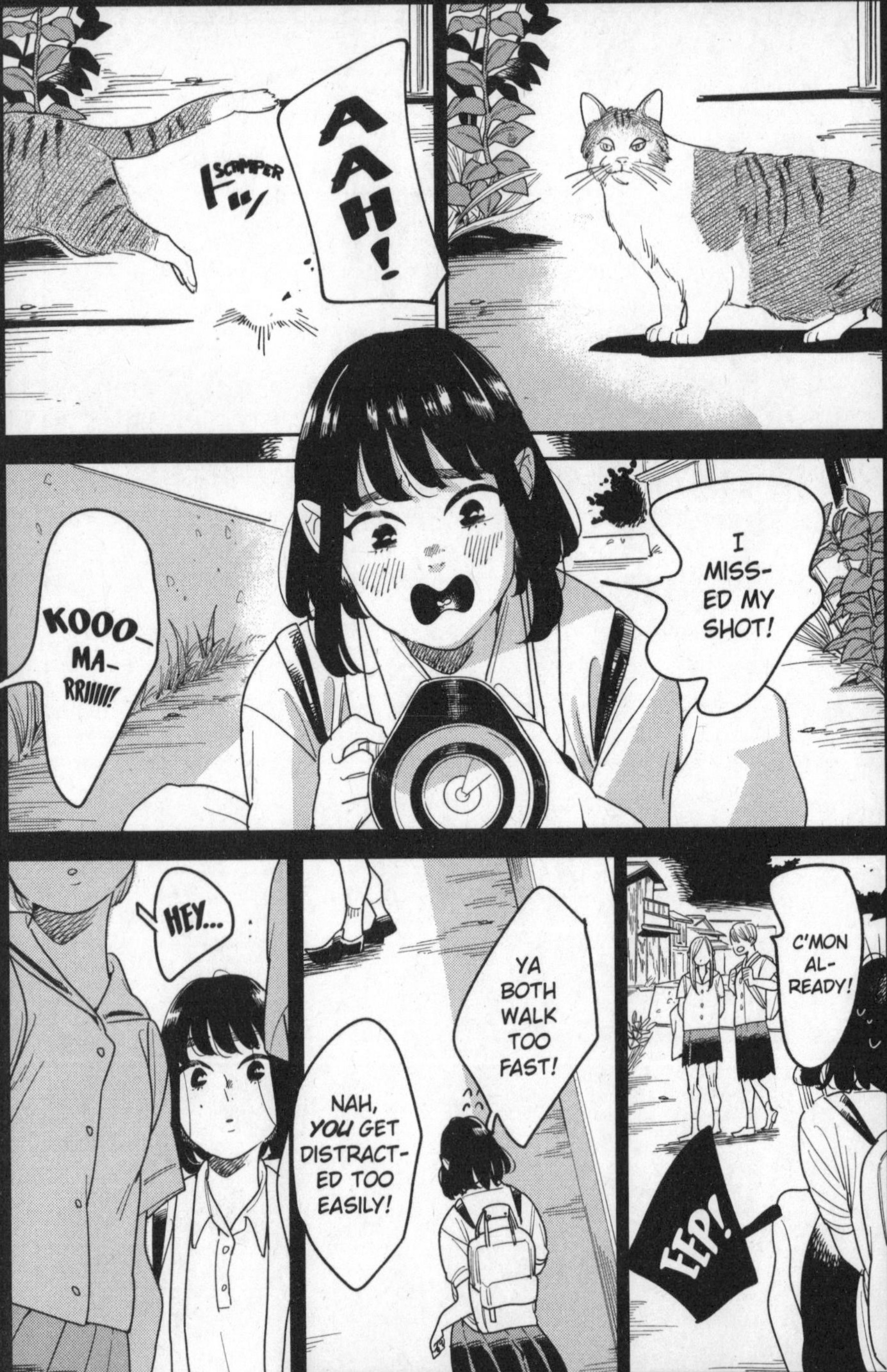
AAH!
SCAMPER
I MISSED MY SHOT!
KOOOMARRIIIII!
C'MON ALREADY!
EEP!
YA BOTH WALK TOO FAST!
NAH, YOU GET DISTRACTED TOO EASILY!
HEY...

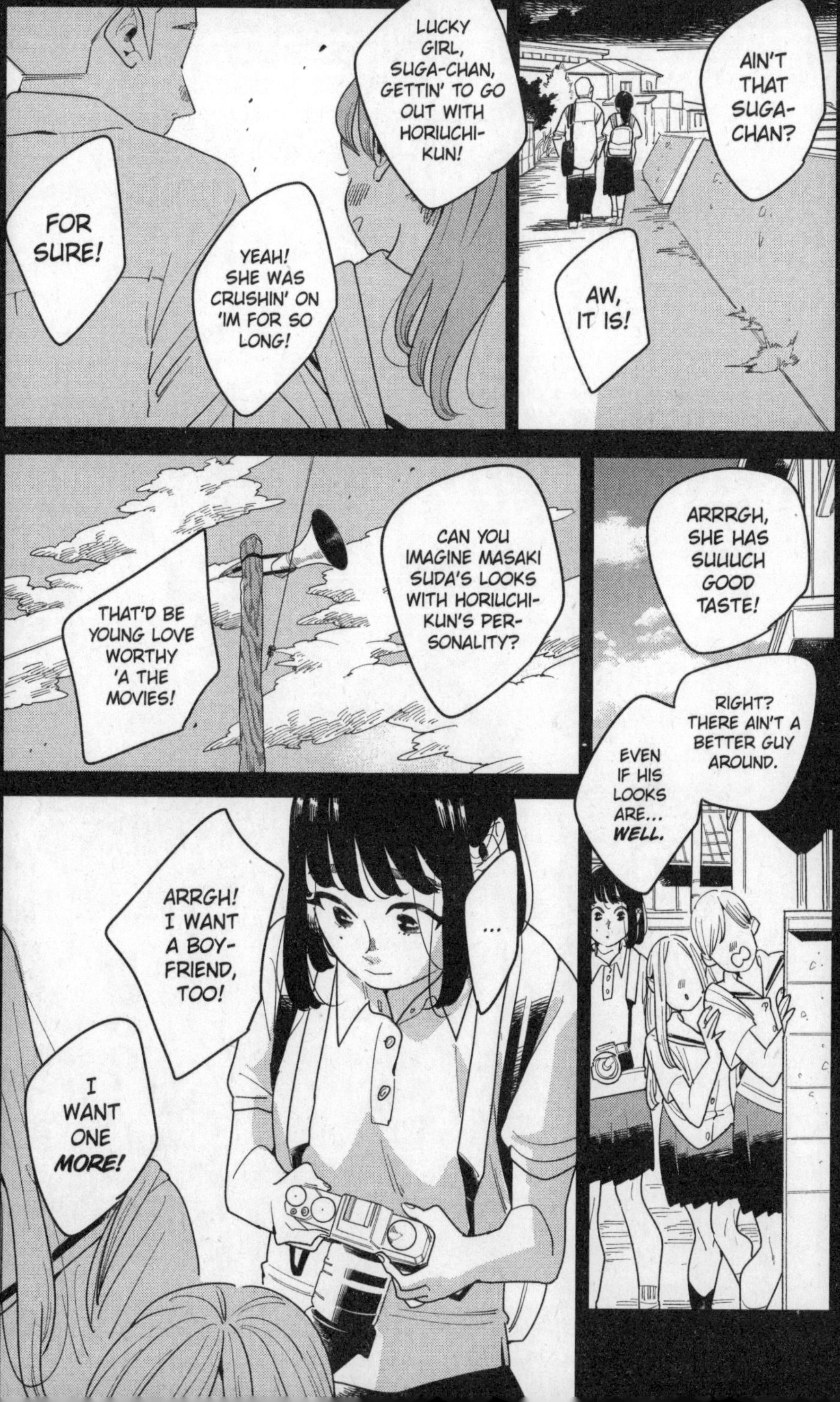
AIN'T THAT SUGA-CHAN?
AW, IT IS!
LUCKY GIRL, SUGA-CHAN, GETTIN' TO GO OUT WITH HORIUCHI-KUN!
YEAH! SHE WAS CRUSHIN' ON 'IM FOR SO LONG!
FOR SURE!
ARRRGH, SHE HAS SUUUCH GOOD TASTE!
RIGHT? THERE AIN'T A BETTER GUY AROUND.
EVEN IF HIS LOOKS ARE... ***WELL.***
CAN YOU IMAGINE MASAKI SUDA'S LOOKS WITH HORIUCHI-KUN'S PER-SONALITY?
THAT'D BE YOUNG LOVE WORTHY 'A THE MOVIES!
ARRGH! I WANT A BOY-FRIEND, TOO!
...
I WANT ONE ***MORE!***

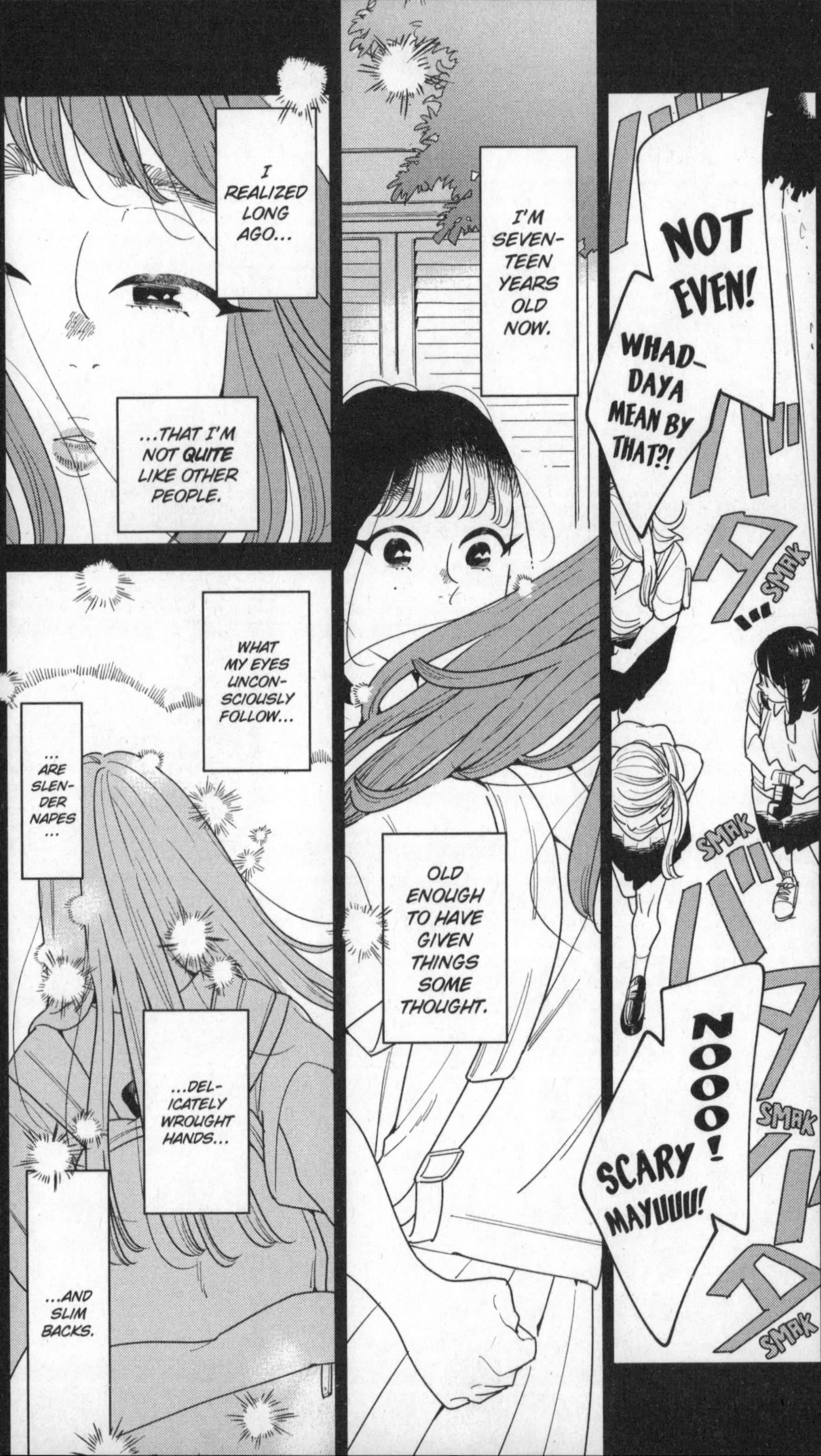
NOT EVEN!
WHADDAYA MEAN BY THAT?!
SMAK
SMAK
NOOOO!
SCARY MAYUUU!
SMAK
SMAK
I'M SEVENTEEN YEARS OLD NOW.
OLD ENOUGH TO HAVE GIVEN THINGS SOME THOUGHT.
I REALIZED LONG AGO...
...THAT I'M NOT QUITE LIKE OTHER PEOPLE.
WHAT MY EYES UNCONSCIOUSLY FOLLOW...
...ARE SLENDER NAPES...
...DELICATELY WROUGHT HANDS...
...AND SLIM BACKS.

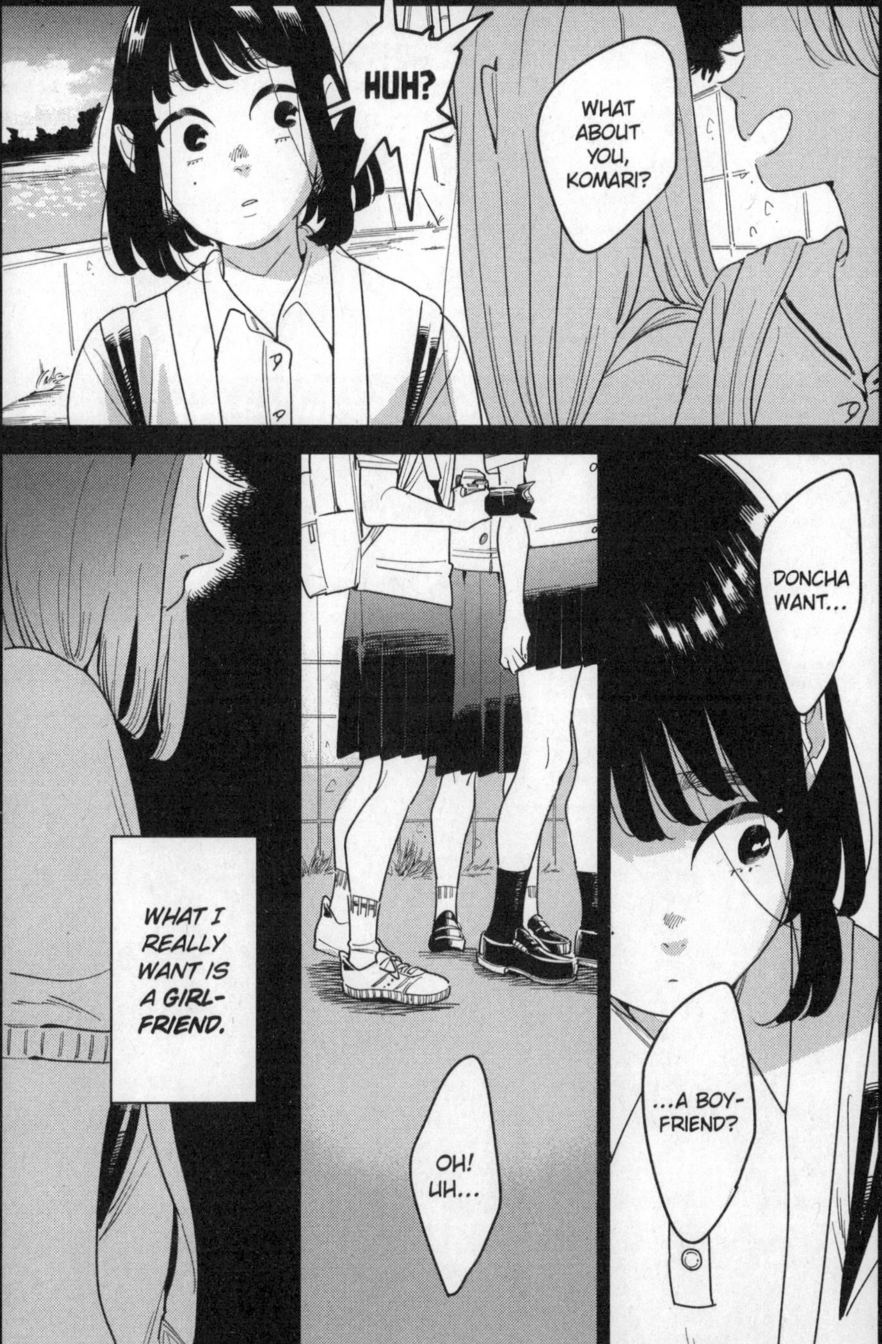
WHAT ABOUT YOU, KOMARI?
HUH?
DONCHA WANT...
...A BOY-FRIEND?
OH! UH...
WHAT I REALLY WANT IS A GIRL-FRIEND.

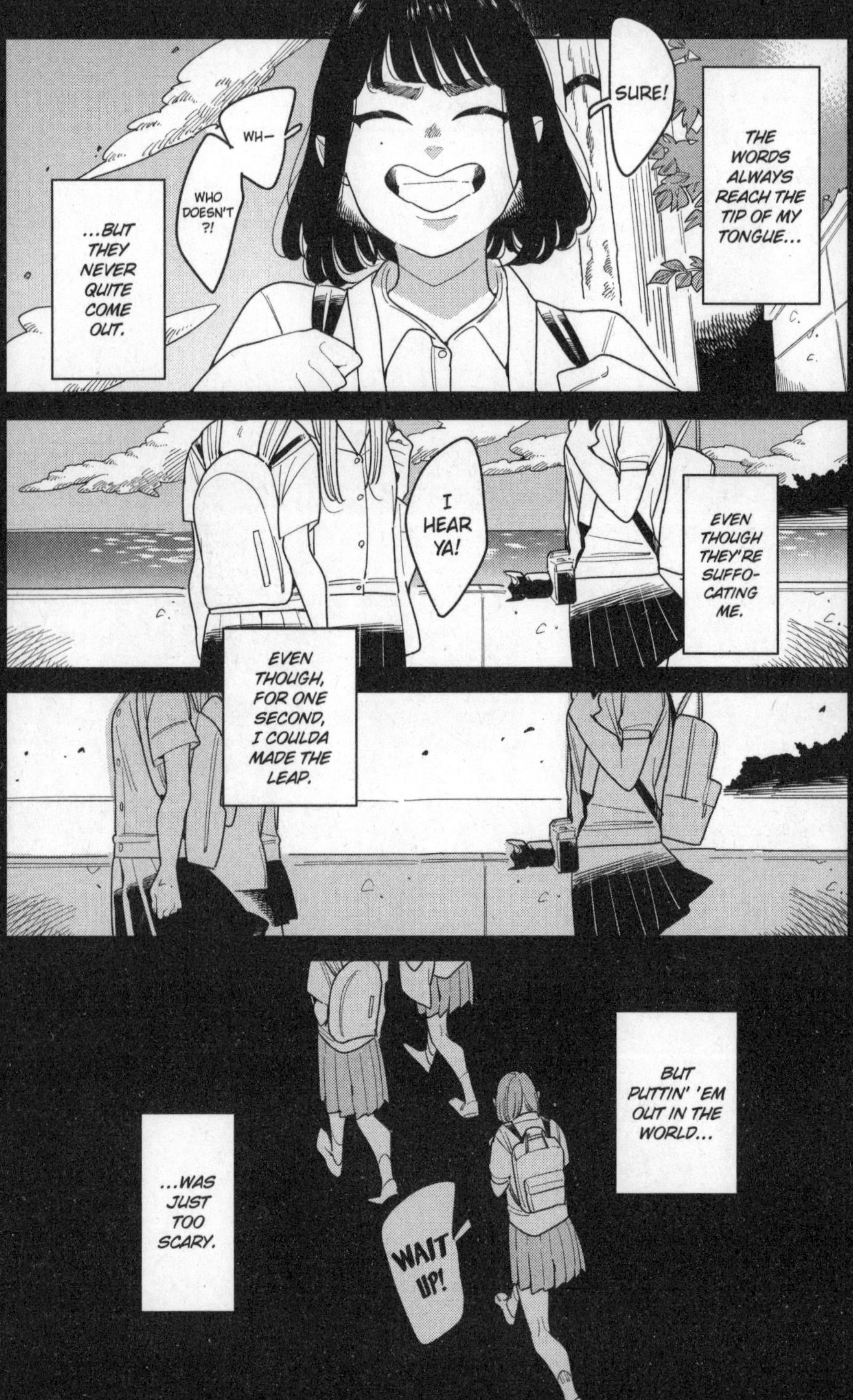
THE WORDS ALWAYS REACH THE TIP OF MY TONGUE...
SURE!
WH–
WHO DOESN'T?!
...BUT THEY NEVER QUITE COME OUT.
EVEN THOUGH THEY'RE SUFFOCATING ME.
I HEAR YA!
EVEN THOUGH, FOR ONE SECOND, I COULDA MADE THE LEAP.
BUT PUTTIN' 'EM OUT IN THE WORLD...
WAIT UP!
...WAS JUST TOO SCARY.

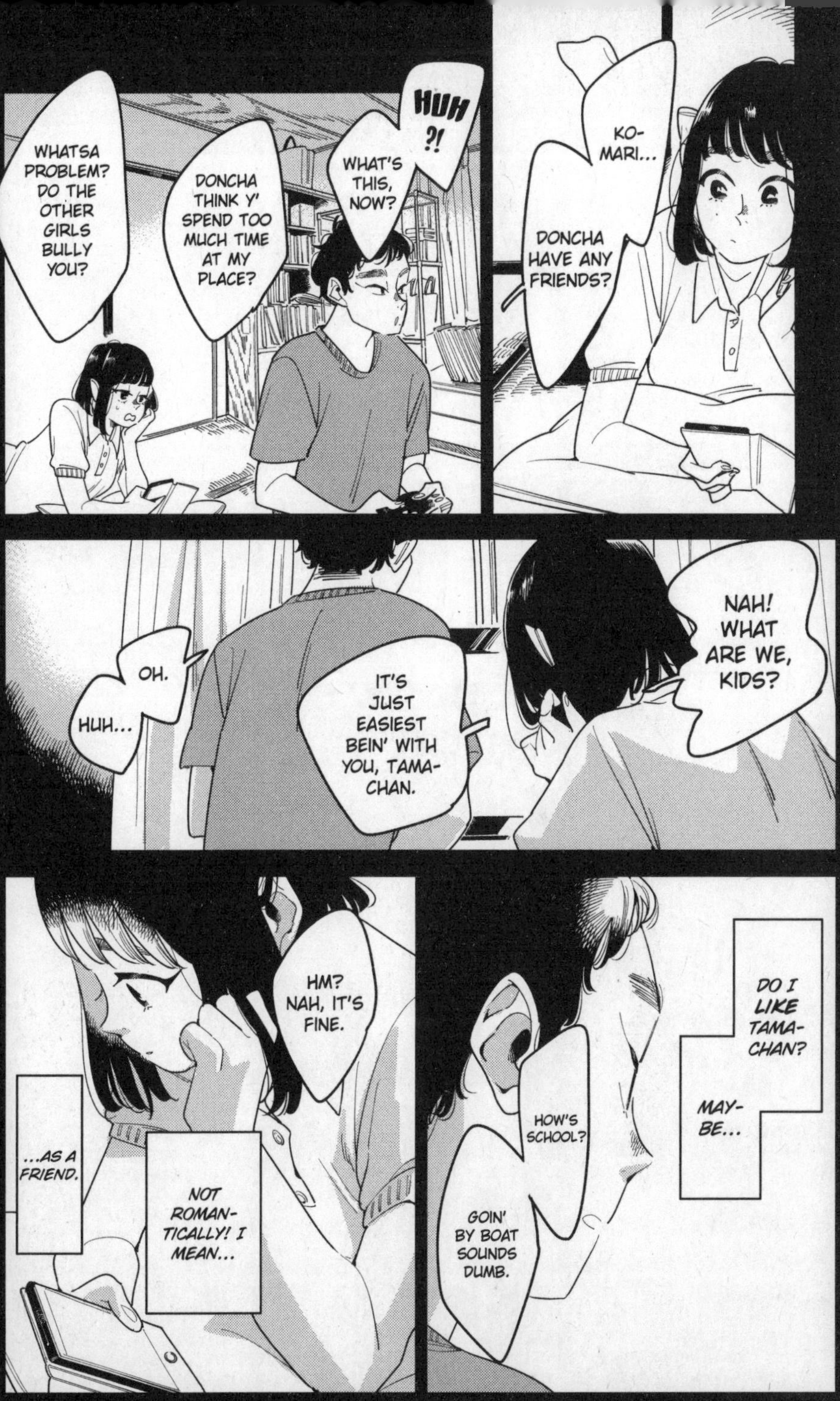
KO-MARI...
DONCHA HAVE ANY FRIENDS?
HUH ?!
WHAT'S THIS, NOW?
DONCHA THINK Y' SPEND TOO MUCH TIME AT MY PLACE?
WHATSA PROBLEM? DO THE OTHER GIRLS BULLY YOU?
NAH! WHAT ARE WE, KIDS?
IT'S JUST EASIEST BEIN' WITH YOU, TAMA-CHAN.
OH.
HUH...
DO I LIKE TAMA-CHAN?
MAY-BE...
HOW'S SCHOOL?
GOIN' BY BOAT SOUNDS DUMB.
HM? NAH, IT'S FINE.
NOT ROMAN-TICALLY! I MEAN...
...AS A FRIEND.

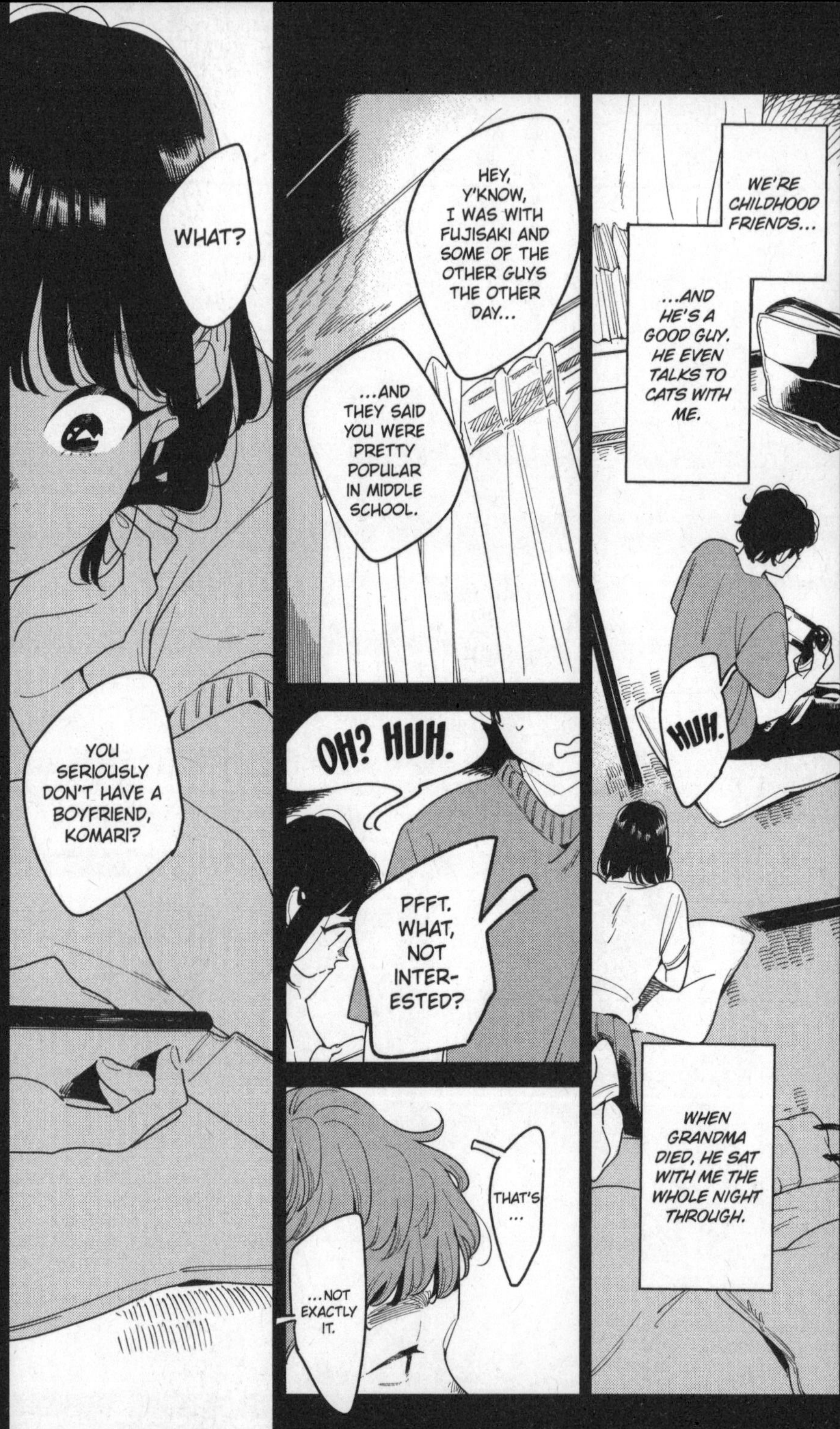
WE'RE CHILDHOOD FRIENDS...
...AND HE'S A GOOD GUY. HE EVEN TALKS TO CATS WITH ME.
HUH.
WHEN GRANDMA DIED, HE SAT WITH ME THE WHOLE NIGHT THROUGH.
HEY, Y'KNOW, I WAS WITH FUJISAKI AND SOME OF THE OTHER GUYS THE OTHER DAY...
...AND THEY SAID YOU WERE PRETTY POPULAR IN MIDDLE SCHOOL.
OH? HUH.
PFFT. WHAT, NOT INTER-ESTED?
THAT'S...
...NOT EXACTLY IT.
WHAT?
YOU SERIOUSLY DON'T HAVE A BOYFRIEND, KOMARI?

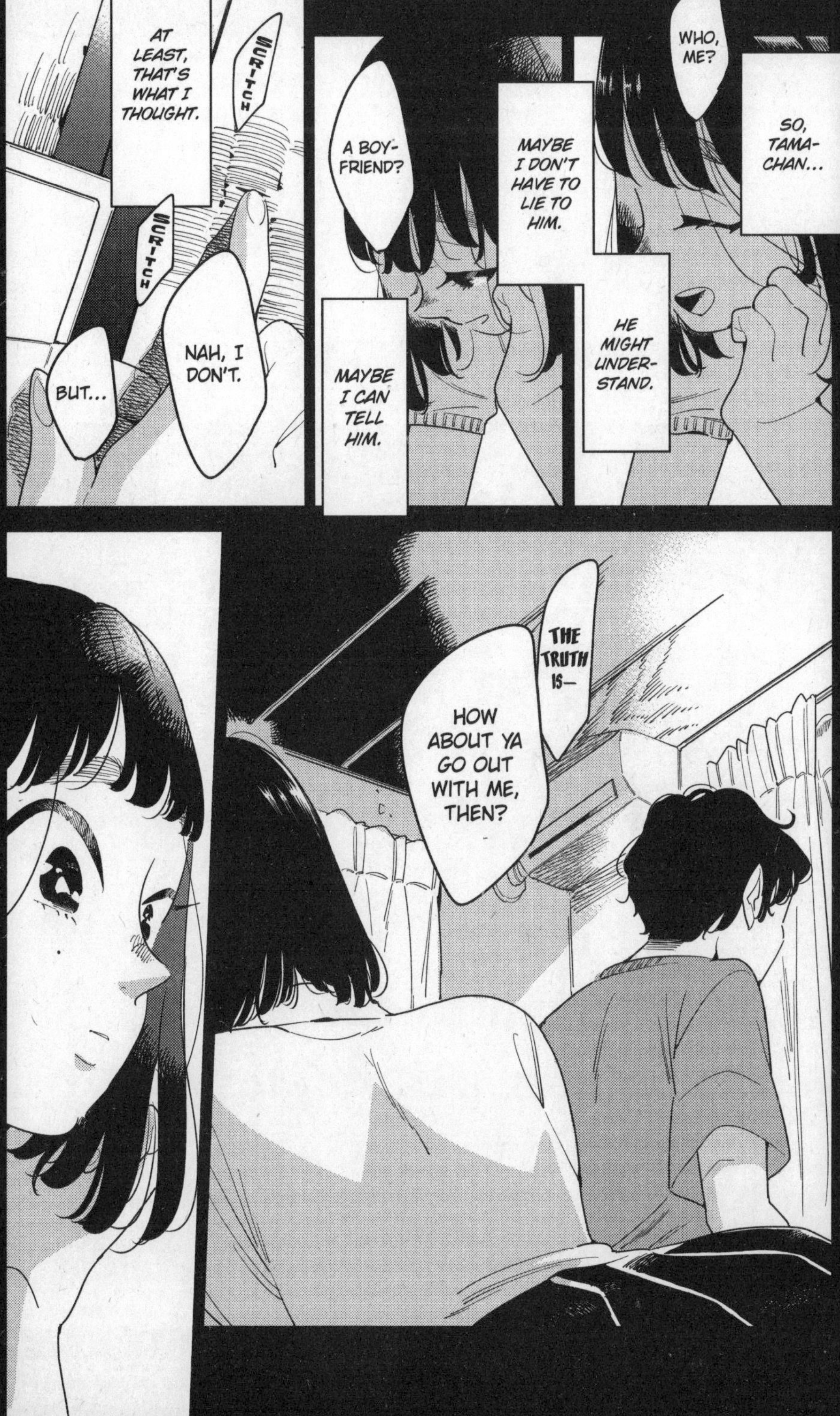
SO, TAMA-CHAN...
WHO, ME?
MAYBE I DON'T HAVE TO LIE TO HIM.
HE MIGHT UNDERSTAND.
A BOY-FRIEND?
MAYBE I CAN TELL HIM.
AT LEAST, THAT'S WHAT I THOUGHT.
SCRITCH
SCRITCH
NAH, I DON'T.
BUT...
THE TRUTH IS—
HOW ABOUT YA GO OUT WITH ME, THEN?

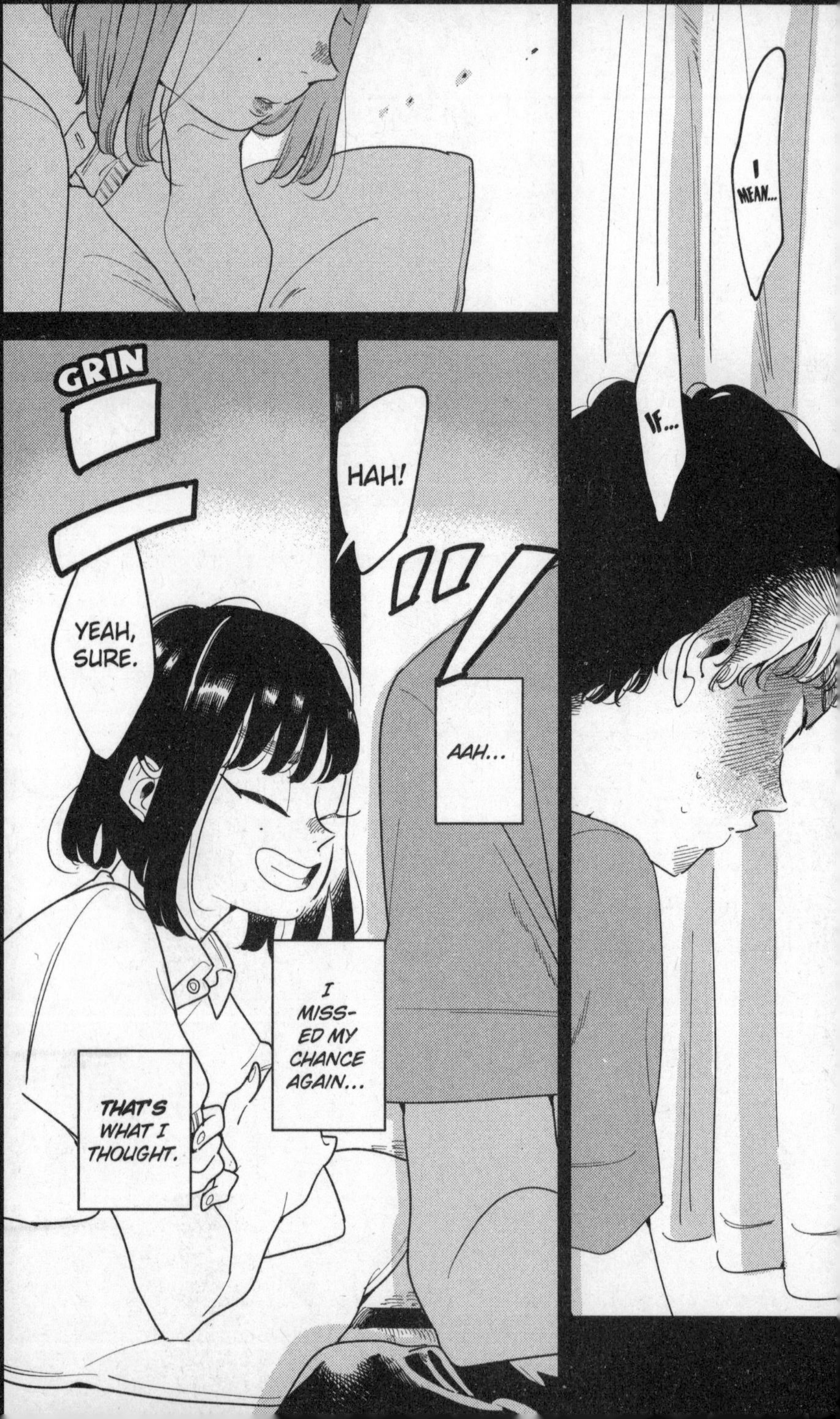
I MEAN...
IF...
HAH!
AAH...
GRIN
YEAH, SURE.
I MISSED MY CHANCE AGAIN...
THAT'S WHAT I THOUGHT.

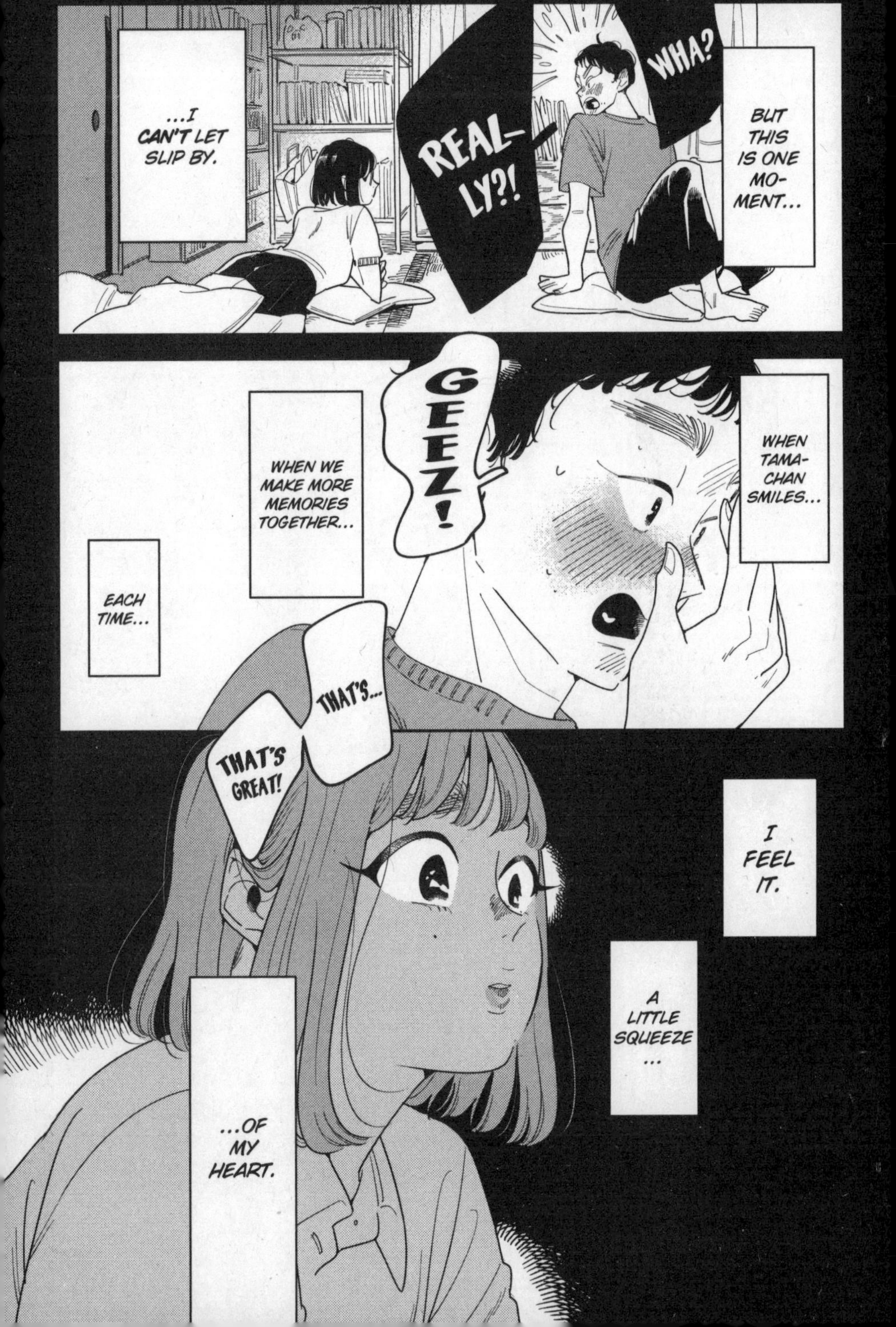
BUT THIS IS ONE MOMENT...
WHA?
REALLY?!
...I CAN'T LET SLIP BY.
WHEN TAMA-CHAN SMILES...
GEEZ!
WHEN WE MAKE MORE MEMORIES TOGETHER...
EACH TIME...
THAT'S...
THAT'S GREAT!
I FEEL IT.
A LITTLE SQUEEZE ...
...OF MY HEART.

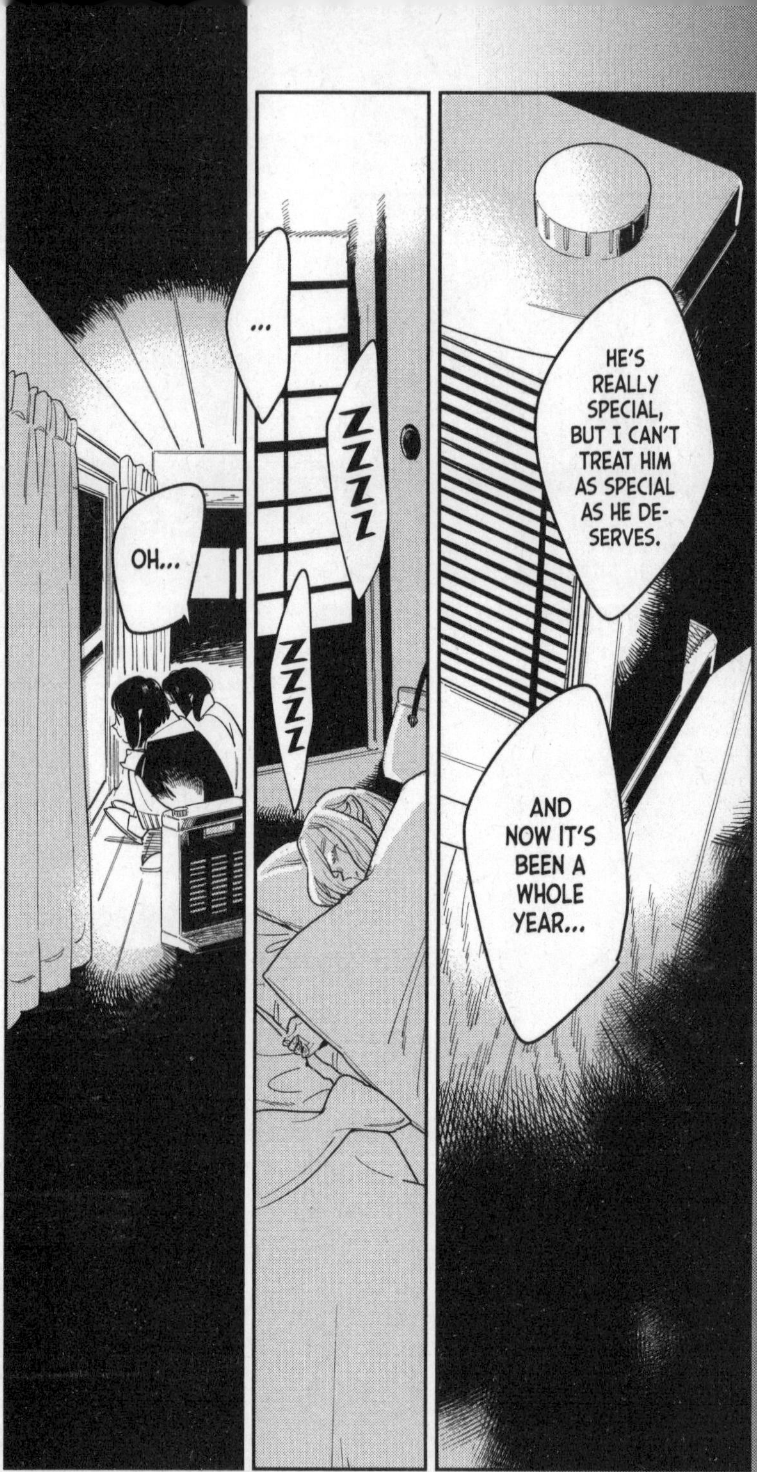
HE'S REALLY SPECIAL, BUT I CAN'T TREAT HIM AS SPECIAL AS HE DE-SERVES.
AND NOW IT'S BEEN A WHOLE YEAR...
...
ZZZZ
ZZZZ
OH...

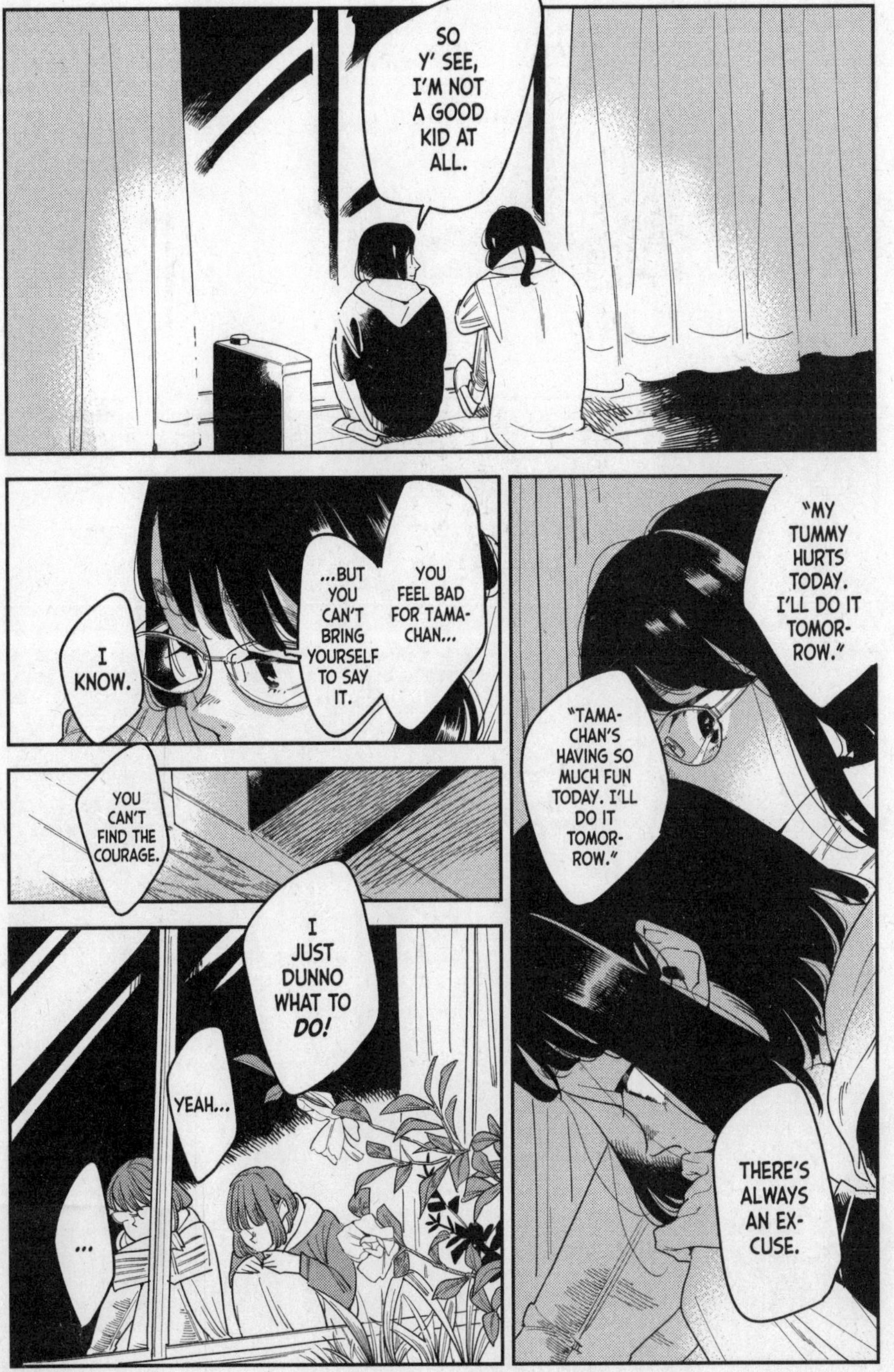
SO Y' SEE, I'M NOT A GOOD KID AT ALL.
"MY TUMMY HURTS TODAY. I'LL DO IT TOMORROW."
"TAMA-CHAN'S HAVING SO MUCH FUN TODAY. I'LL DO IT TOMORROW."
THERE'S ALWAYS AN EXCUSE.
YOU FEEL BAD FOR TAMA-CHAN...
...BUT YOU CAN'T BRING YOURSELF TO SAY IT.
I KNOW.
YOU CAN'T FIND THE COURAGE.
I JUST DUNNO WHAT TO ***DO!***
YEAH...
...

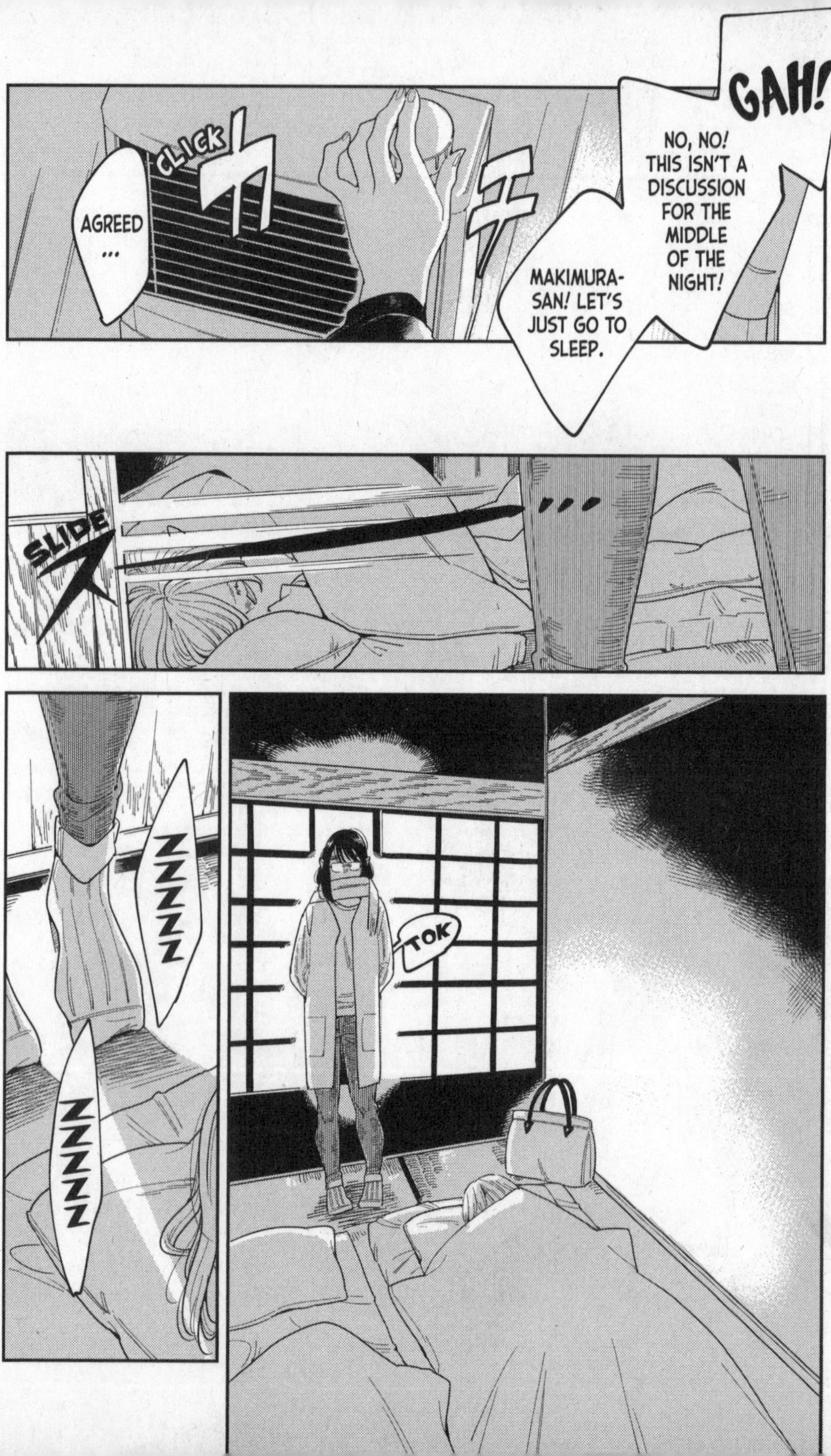
GAH!
NO, NO! THIS ISN'T A DISCUSSION FOR THE MIDDLE OF THE NIGHT!
MAKIMURA-SAN! LET'S JUST GO TO SLEEP.
CLICK
AGREED ...
...
SLIDE
TOK
ZZZZZ
ZZZZZ

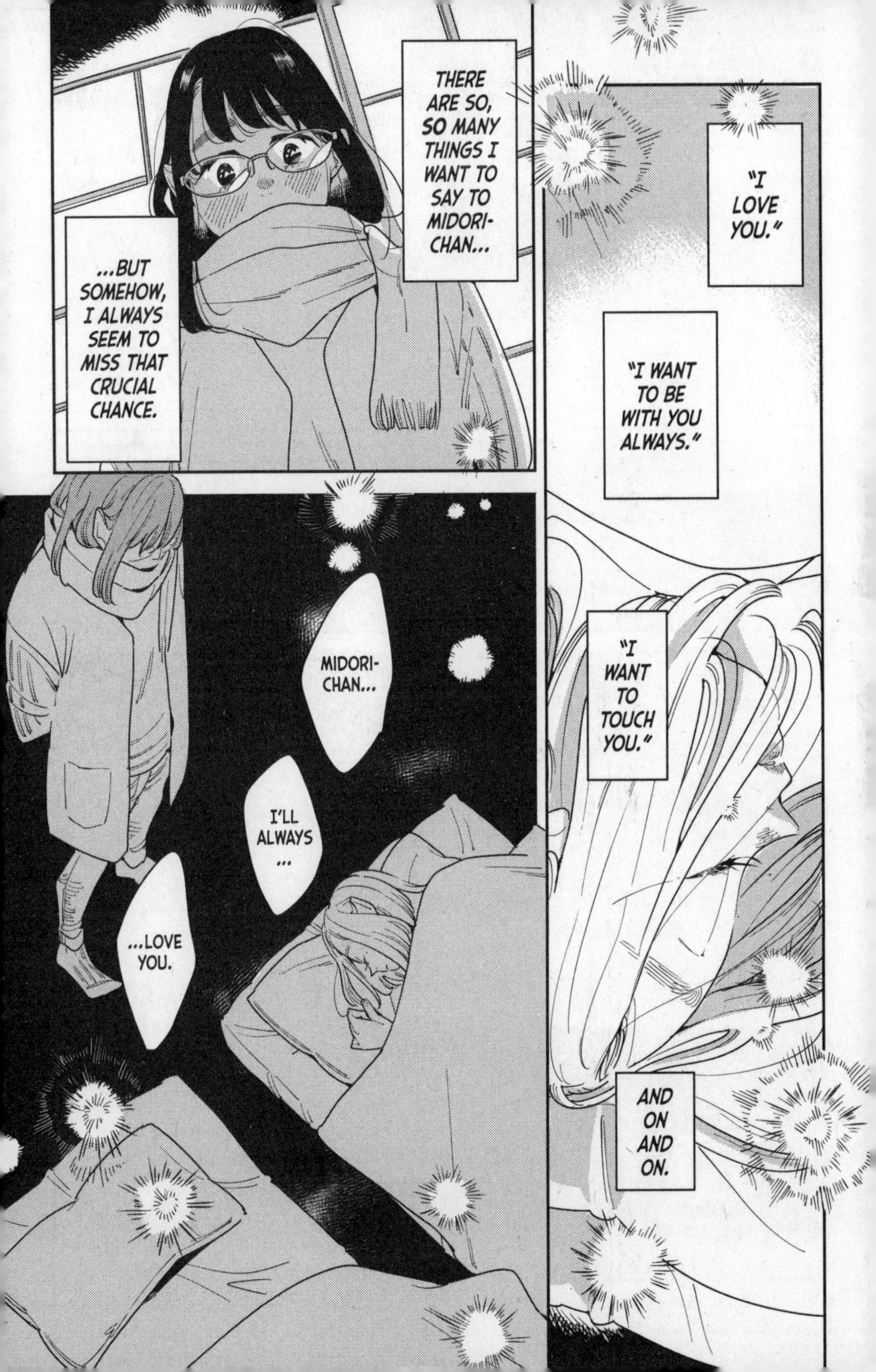
"I LOVE YOU."
"I WANT TO BE WITH YOU ALWAYS."
"I WANT TO TOUCH YOU."
AND ON AND ON.
THERE ARE SO, SO MANY THINGS I WANT TO SAY TO MIDORI-CHAN...
...BUT SOMEHOW, I ALWAYS SEEM TO MISS THAT CRUCIAL CHANCE.
MIDORI-CHAN...
I'LL ALWAYS ...
...LOVE YOU.

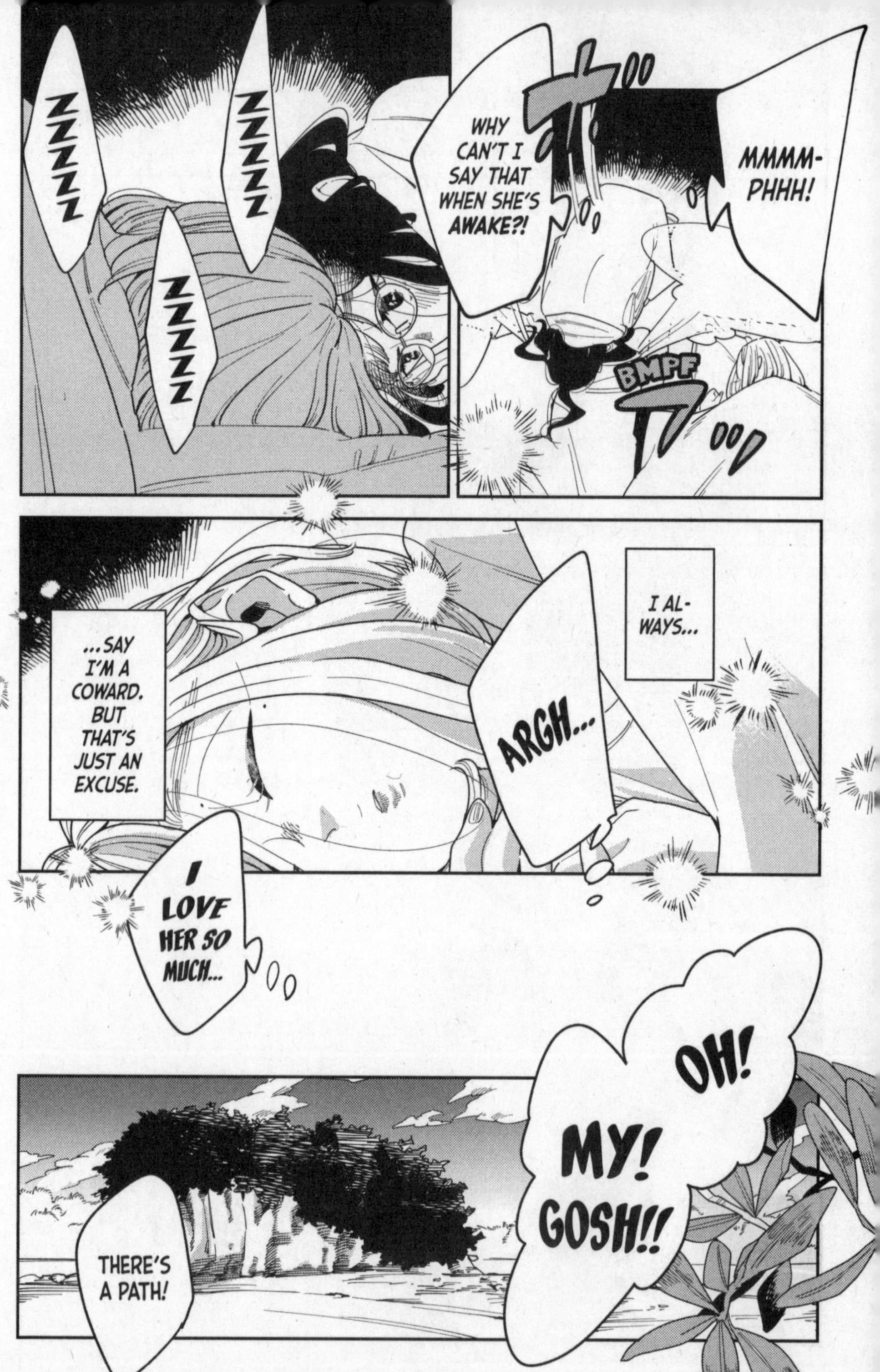
WHY CAN'T I SAY THAT WHEN SHE'S AWAKE?!
MMMM-PHHH!
BMPF
ZZZZZ
ZZZZZ
ZZZZZ
I AL-WAYS...
ARGH...
...SAY I'M A COWARD. BUT THAT'S JUST AN EXCUSE.
I LOVE HER SO MUCH...
OH! MY! GOSH!!
THERE'S A PATH!

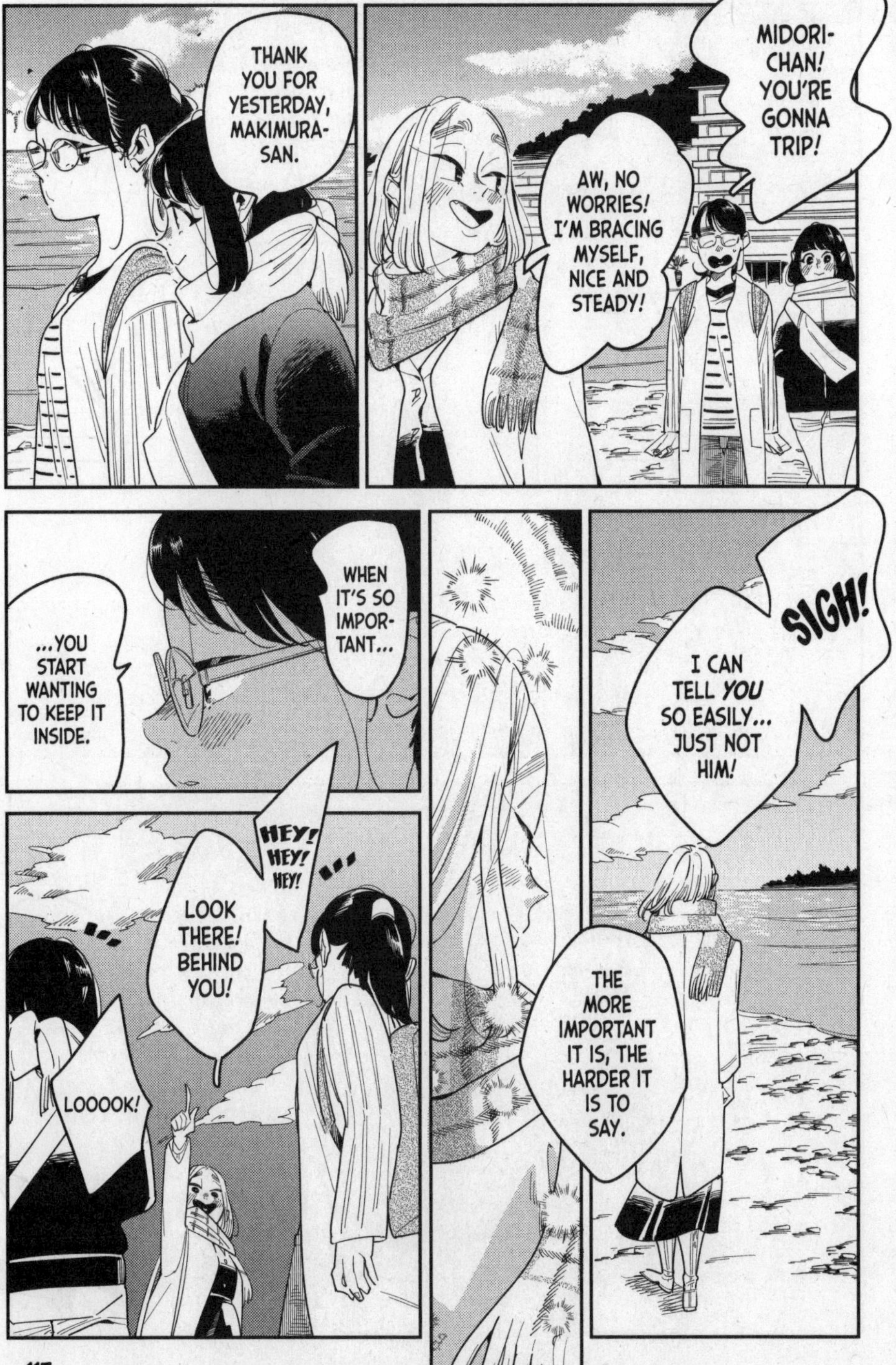
MIDORI-CHAN! YOU'RE GONNA TRIP!
AW, NO WORRIES! I'M BRACING MYSELF, NICE AND STEADY!
THANK YOU FOR YESTERDAY, MAKIMURA-SAN.
SIGH!
I CAN TELL *YOU* SO EASILY... JUST NOT HIM!
THE MORE IMPORTANT IT IS, THE HARDER IT IS TO SAY.
WHEN IT'S SO IMPORTANT...
...YOU START WANTING TO KEEP IT INSIDE.
HEY! HEY! HEY!
LOOK THERE! BEHIND YOU!
LOOOOK!

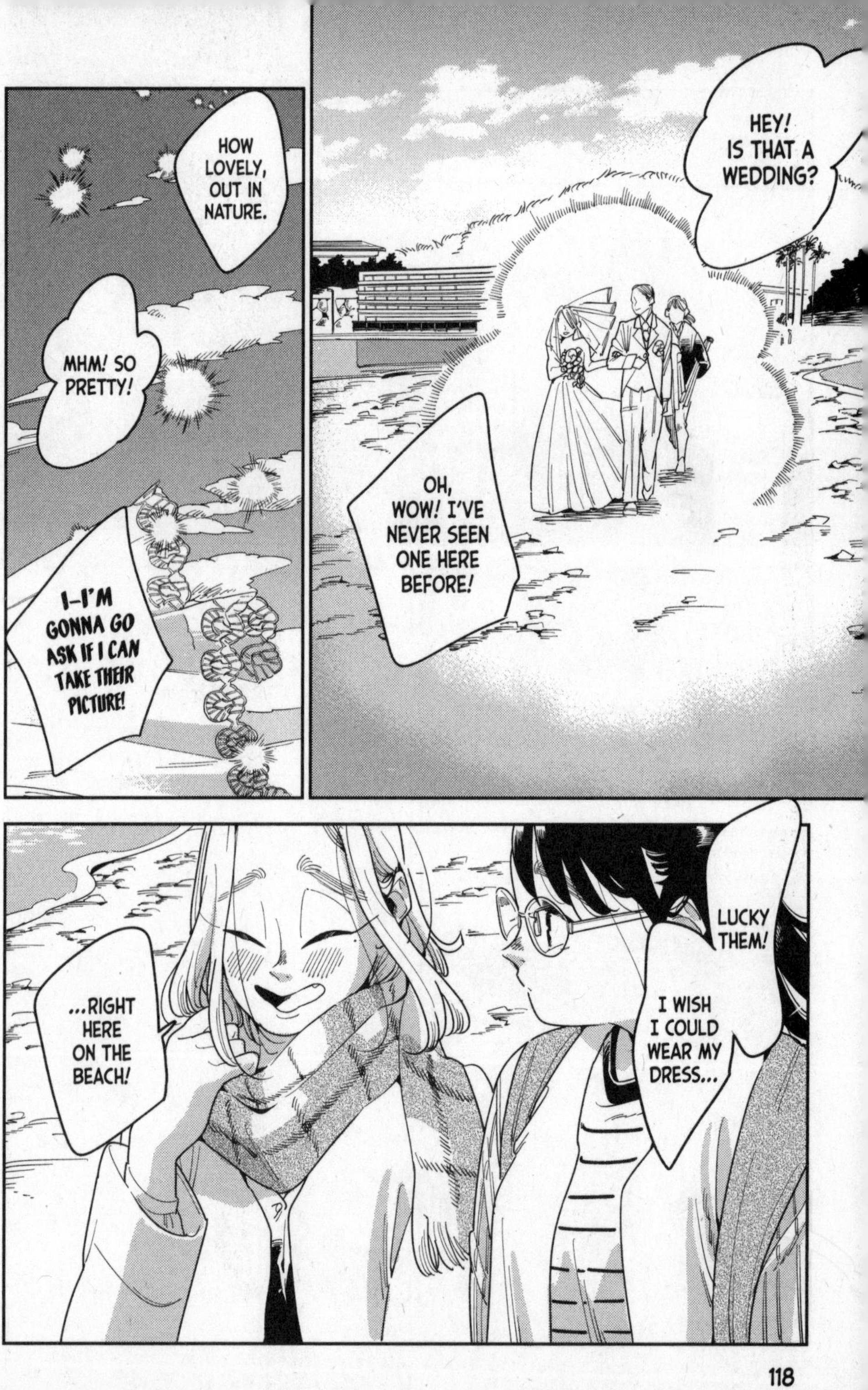
HEY! IS THAT A WEDDING?
OH, WOW! I'VE NEVER SEEN ONE HERE BEFORE!
HOW LOVELY, OUT IN NATURE.
MHM! SO PRETTY!
I-I'M GONNA GO ASK IF I CAN TAKE THEIR PICTURE!
LUCKY THEM!
I WISH I COULD WEAR MY DRESS...
...RIGHT HERE ON THE BEACH!

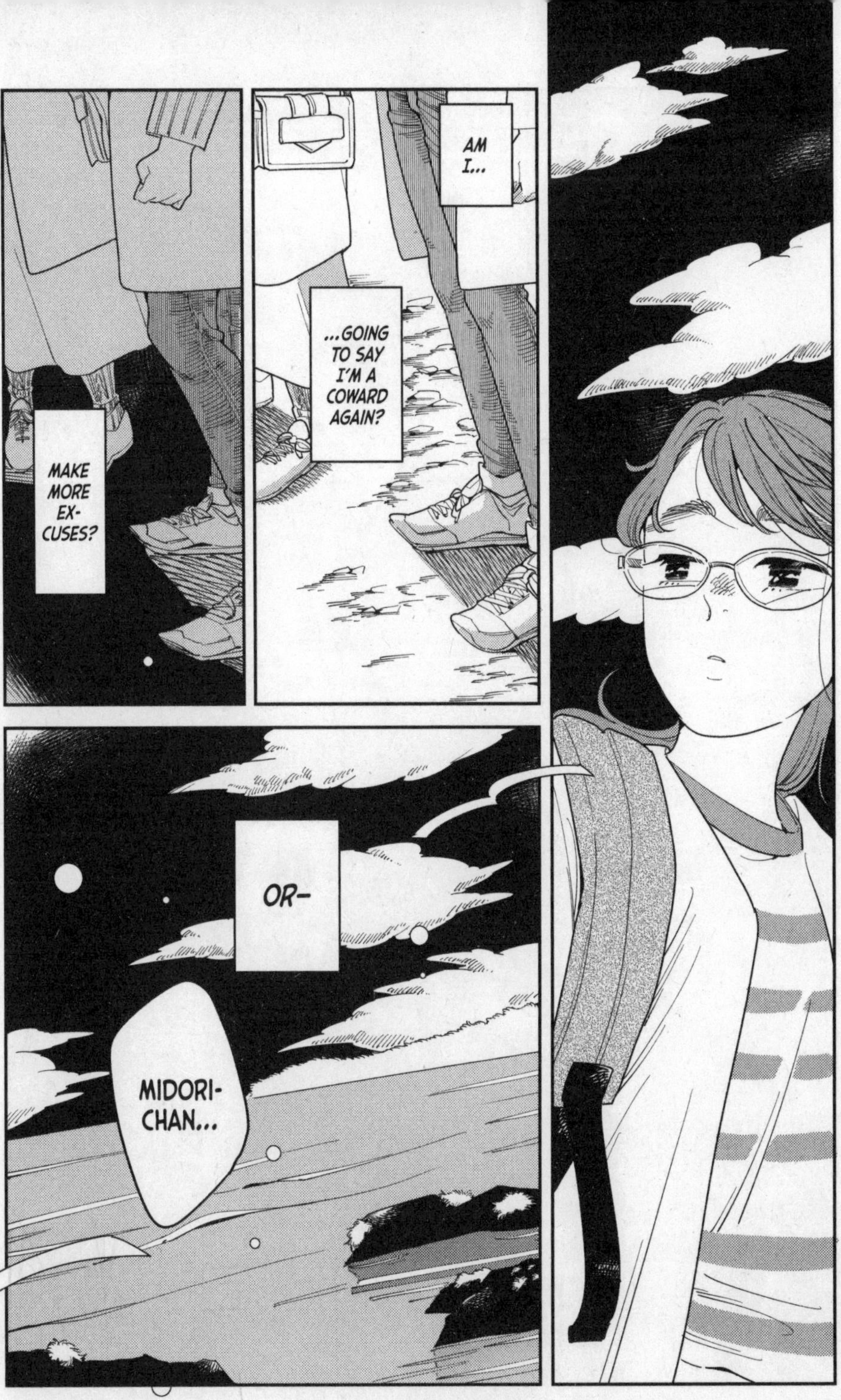
AM I...
...GOING TO SAY I'M A COWARD AGAIN?
MAKE MORE EX-CUSES?
OR-
MIDORI-CHAN...

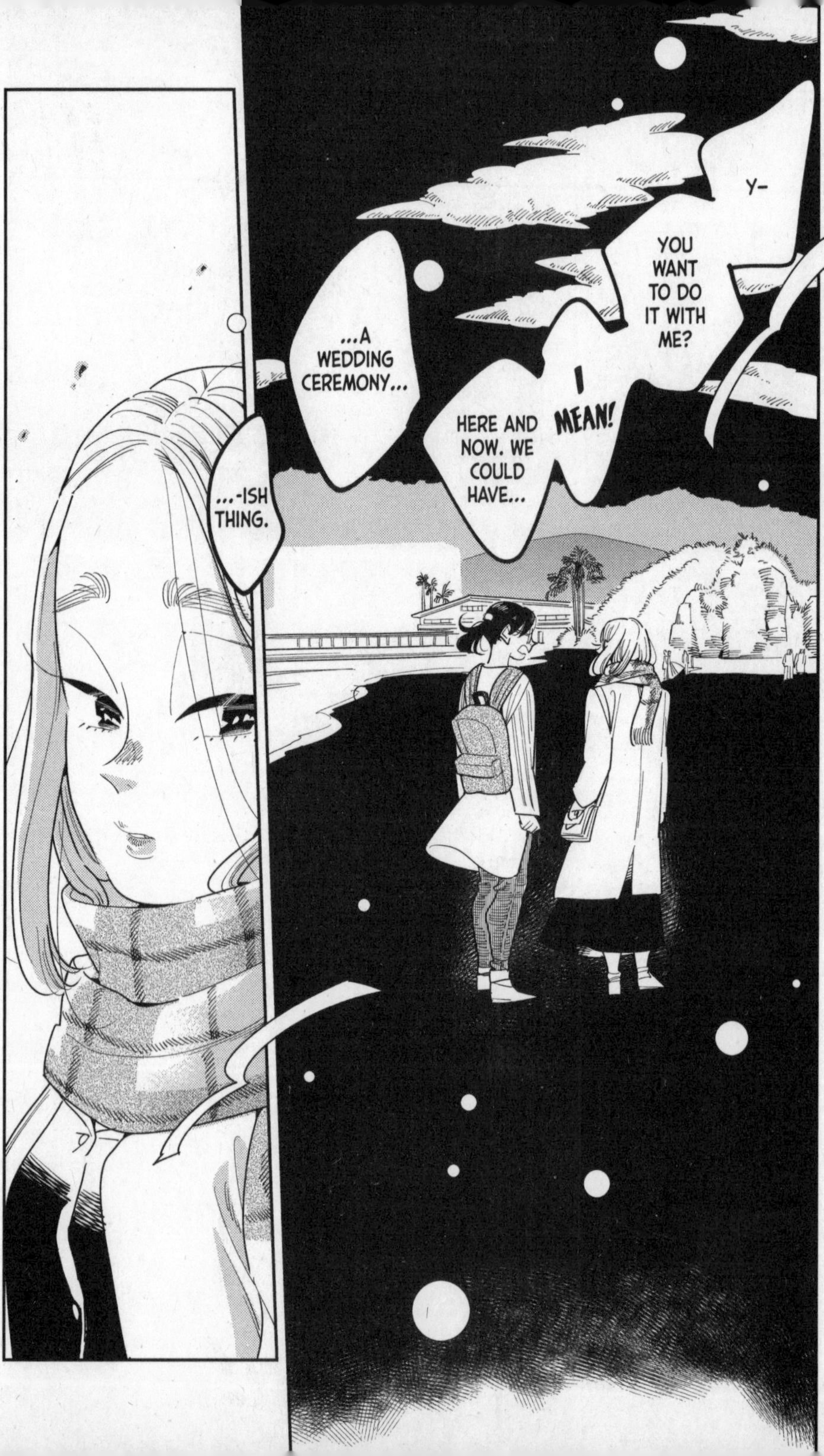
Y-
YOU WANT TO DO IT WITH ME?
I MEAN!
HERE AND NOW. WE COULD HAVE...
...A WEDDING CEREMONY...
...-ISH THING.

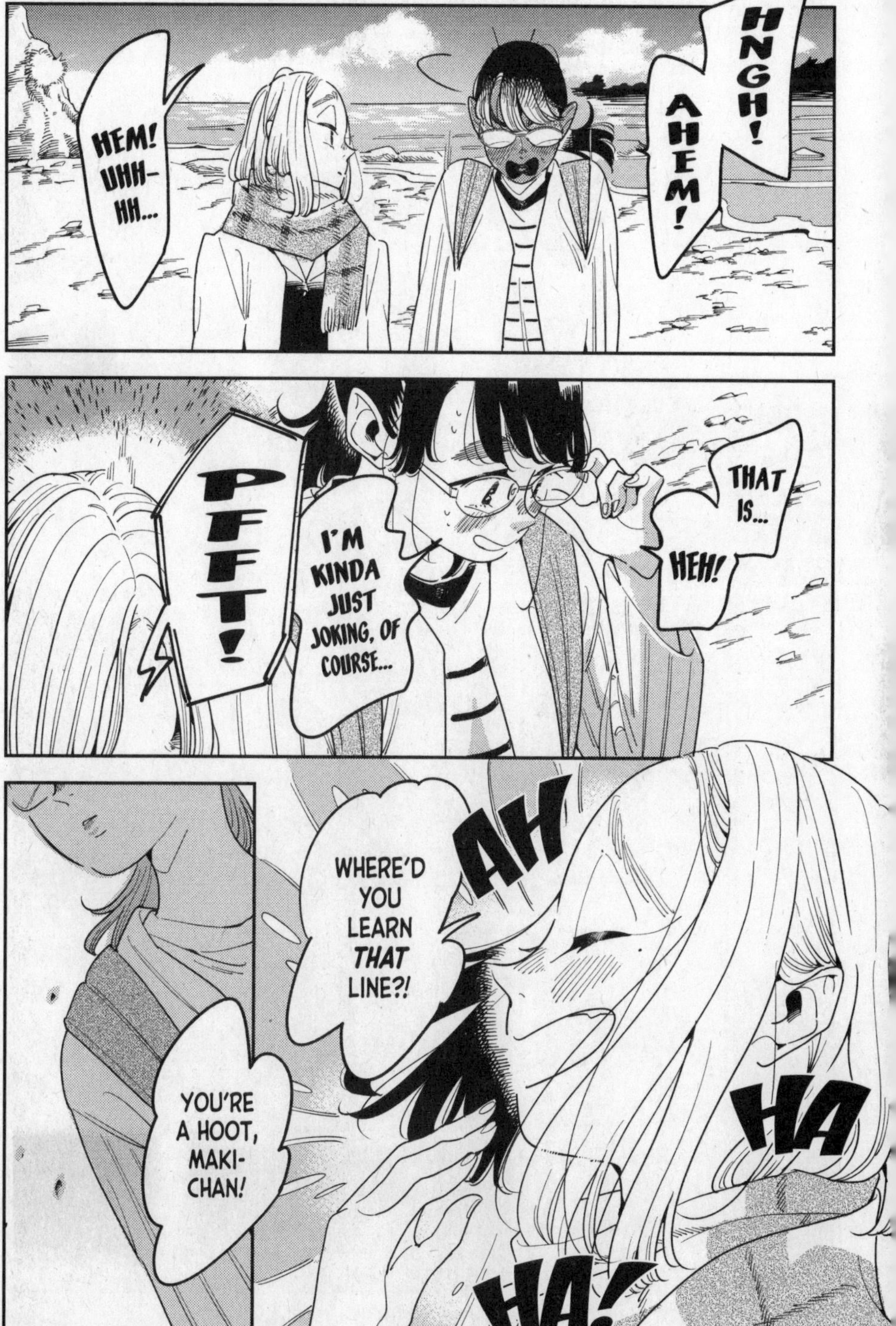
HNGH!
AHEM!
HEM! UHHHH...
THAT IS...
HEH!
I'M KINDA JUST JOKING, OF COURSE...
PFFT!
AH
WHERE'D YOU LEARN *THAT* LINE?!
HA
YOU'RE A HOOT, MAKI-CHAN!
HA!

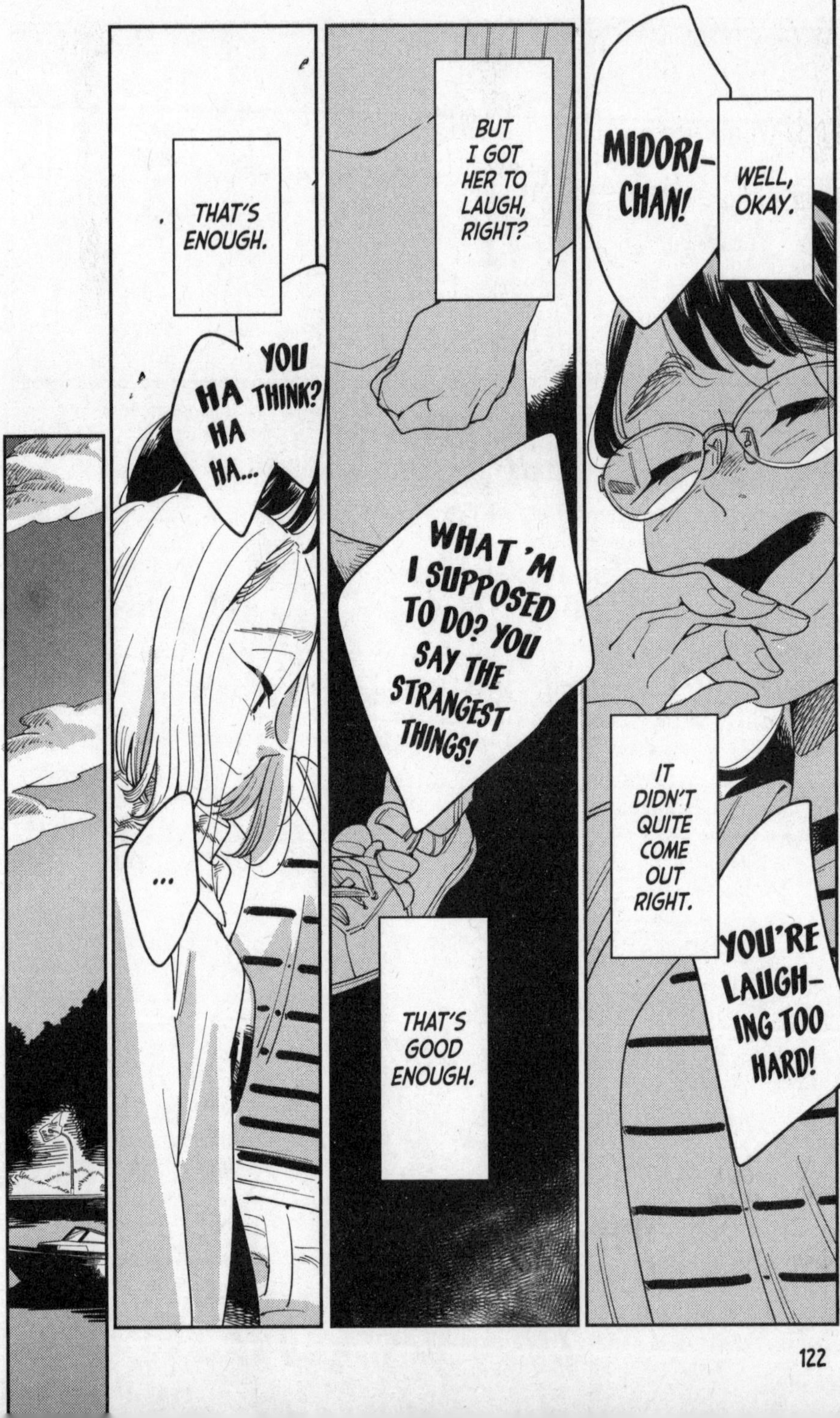
WELL, OKAY.
MIDORI-CHAN!
IT DIDN'T QUITE COME OUT RIGHT.
YOU'RE LAUGHING TOO HARD!
BUT I GOT HER TO LAUGH, RIGHT?
WHAT 'M I SUPPOSED TO DO? YOU SAY THE STRANGEST THINGS!
THAT'S GOOD ENOUGH.
THAT'S ENOUGH.
YOU THINK?
HA HA HA...
...

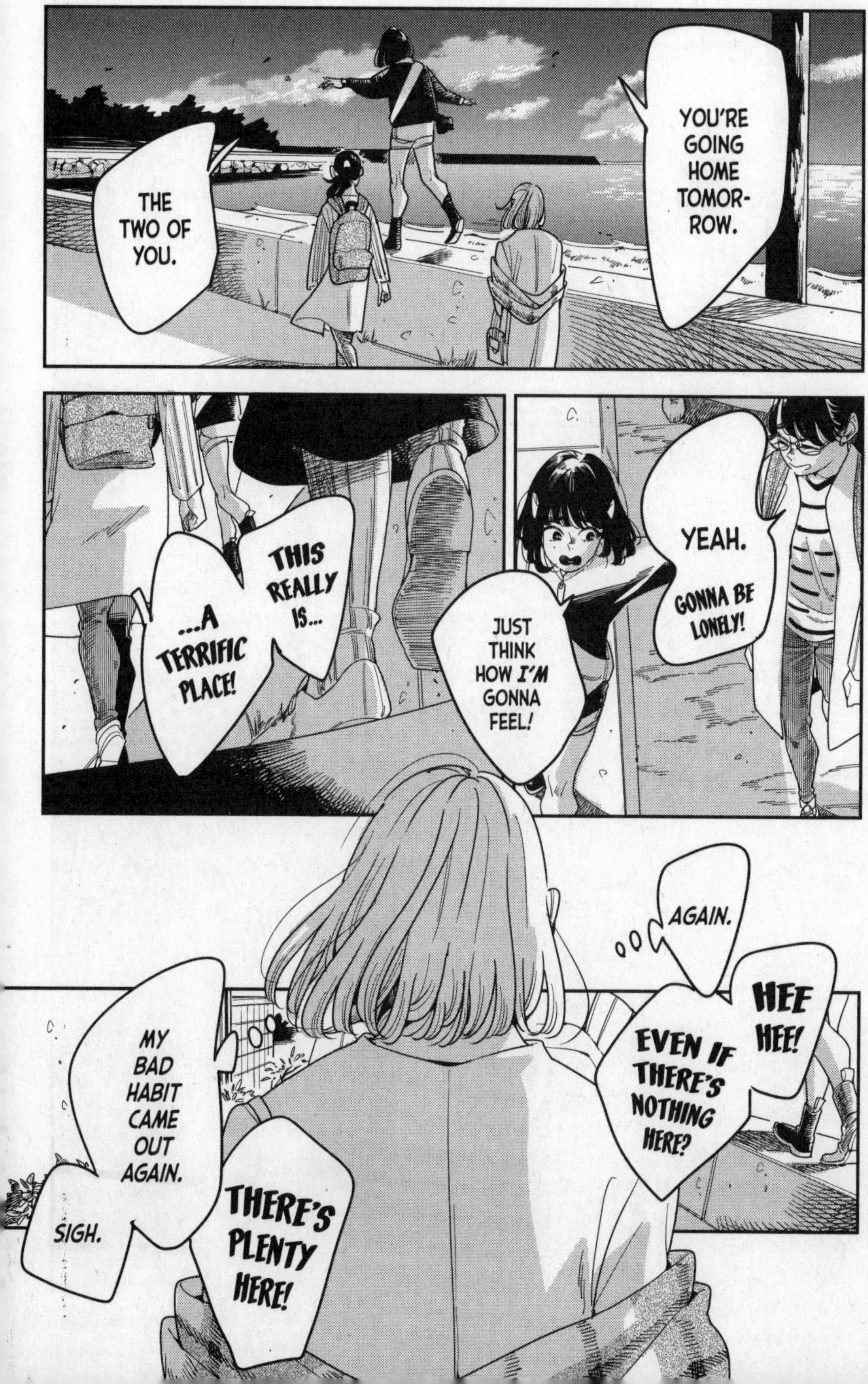
YOU'RE GOING HOME TOMORROW.
THE TWO OF YOU.
YEAH.
GONNA BE LONELY!
JUST THINK HOW *I'M* GONNA FEEL!
THIS REALLY IS...
...A TERRIFIC PLACE!
HEE HEE!
EVEN IF THERE'S NOTHING HERE?
THERE'S PLENTY HERE!
AGAIN.
MY BAD HABIT CAME OUT AGAIN.
SIGH.

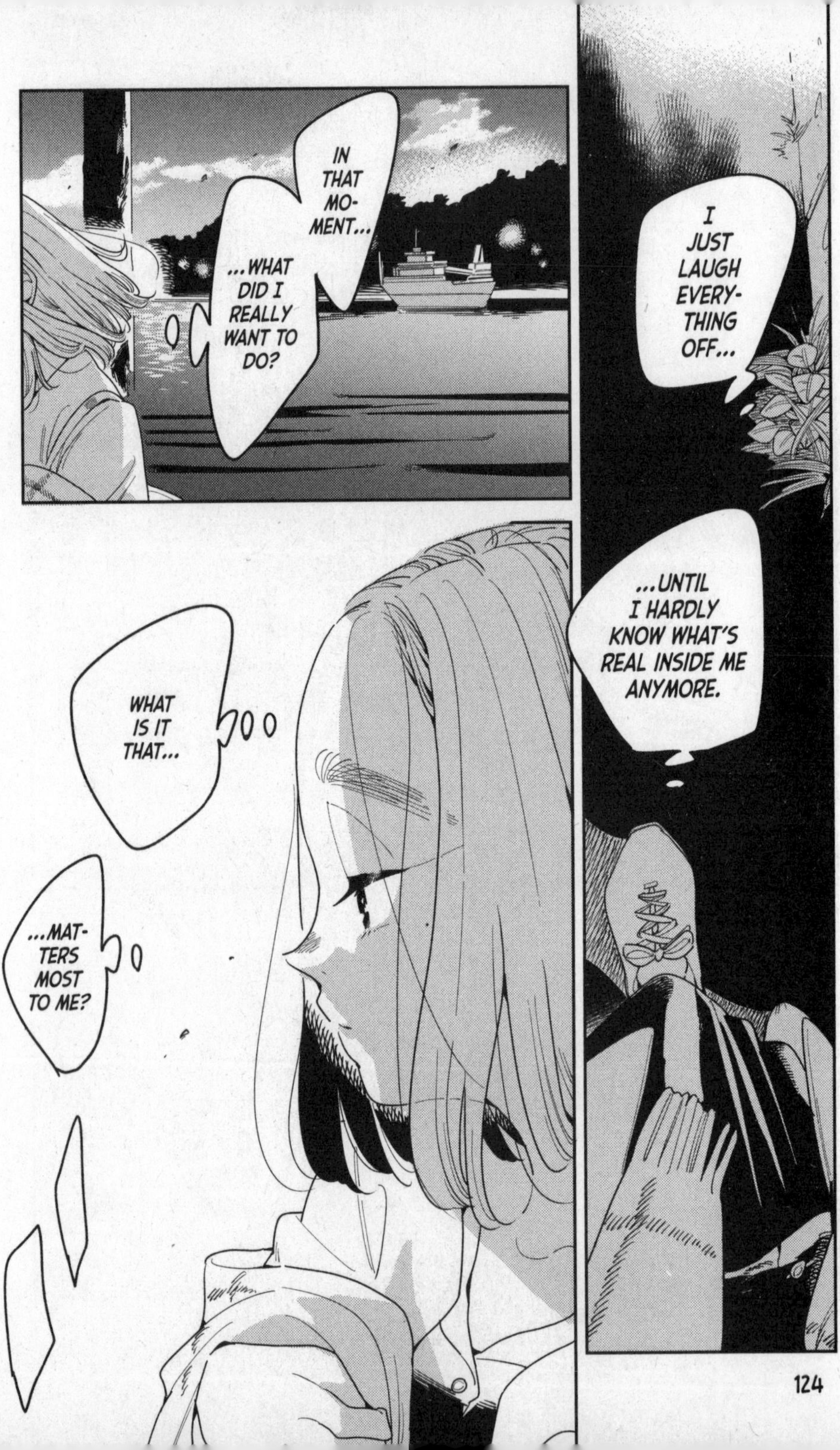
I JUST LAUGH EVERYTHING OFF...
...UNTIL I HARDLY KNOW WHAT'S REAL INSIDE ME ANYMORE.
IN THAT MOMENT...
...WHAT DID I REALLY WANT TO DO?
WHAT IS IT THAT...
...MATTERS MOST TO ME?

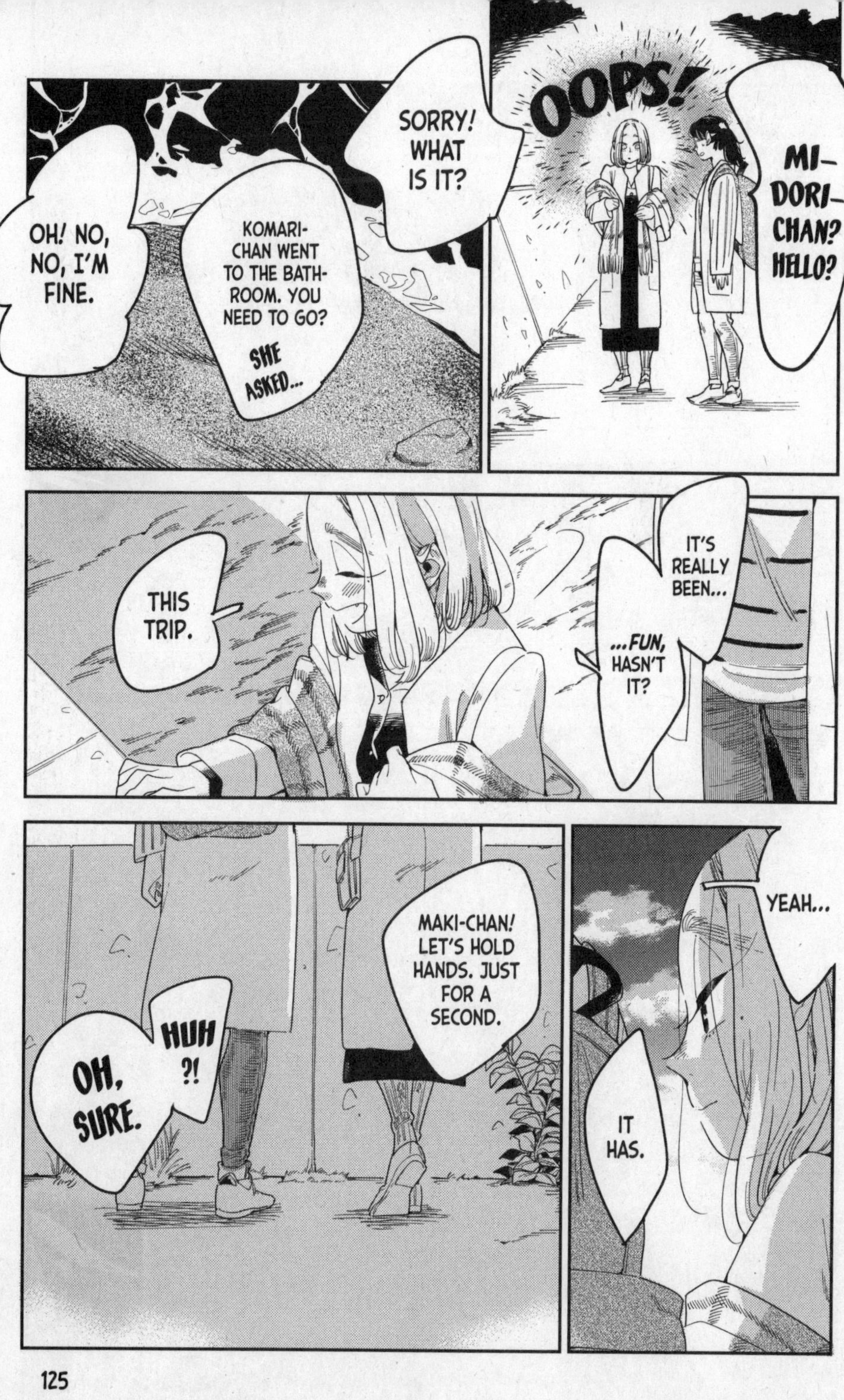
MI-DORI-CHAN? HELLO?
OOPS!
SORRY! WHAT IS IT?
KOMARI-CHAN WENT TO THE BATH-ROOM. YOU NEED TO GO?
SHE ASKED...
OH! NO, NO, I'M FINE.
IT'S REALLY BEEN...
...FUN, HASN'T IT?
THIS TRIP.
YEAH...
IT HAS.
MAKI-CHAN! LET'S HOLD HANDS. JUST FOR A SECOND.
HUH ?!
OH, SURE.

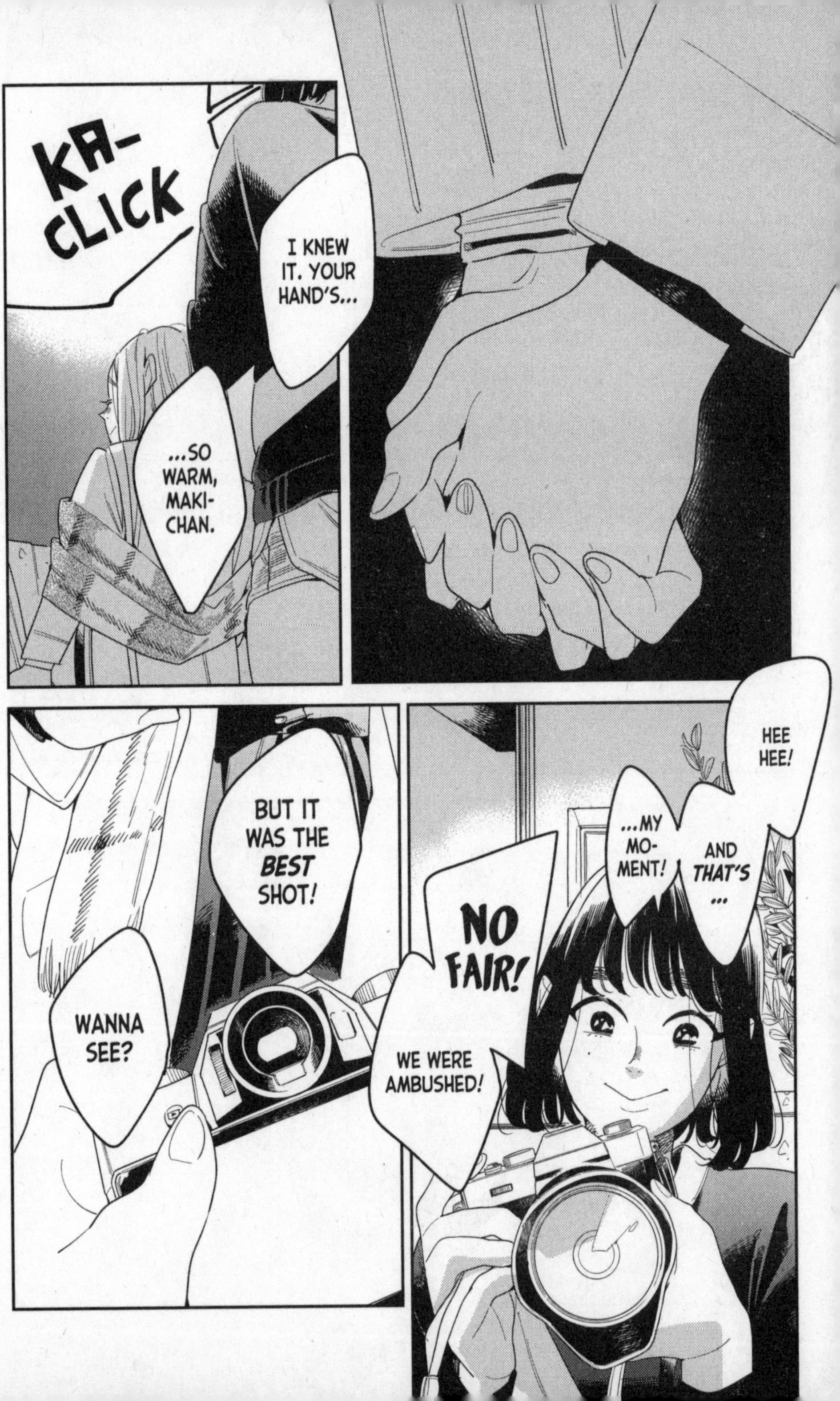
I KNEW IT. YOUR HAND'S...
KA-CLICK
...SO WARM, MAKI-CHAN.
HEE HEE!
AND *THAT'S*...
...MY MOMENT!
NO FAIR!
WE WERE AMBUSHED!
BUT IT WAS THE *BEST* SHOT!
WANNA SEE?

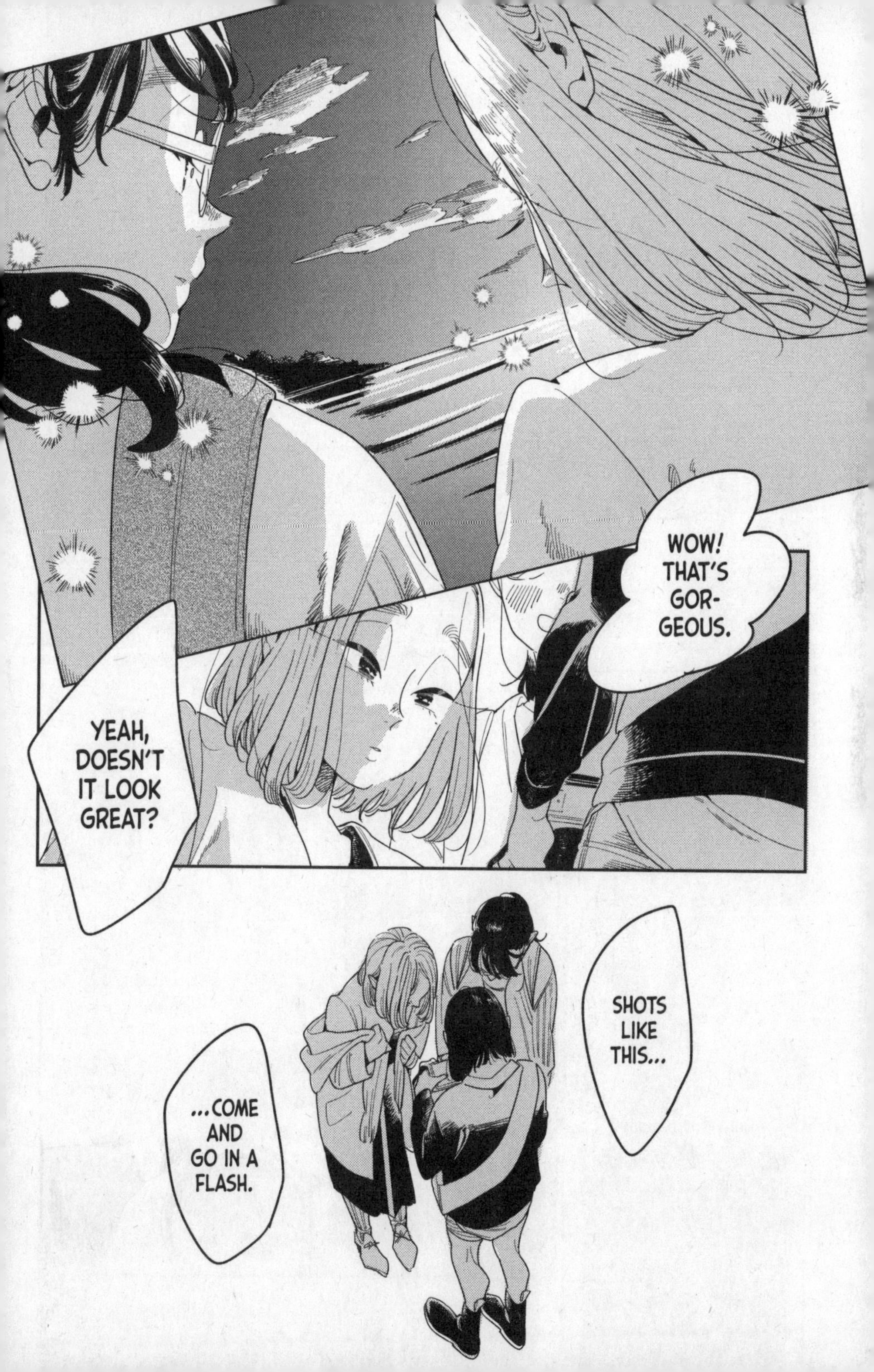
WOW! THAT'S GOR-GEOUS.
YEAH, DOESN'T IT LOOK GREAT?
SHOTS LIKE THIS...
...COME AND GO IN A FLASH.

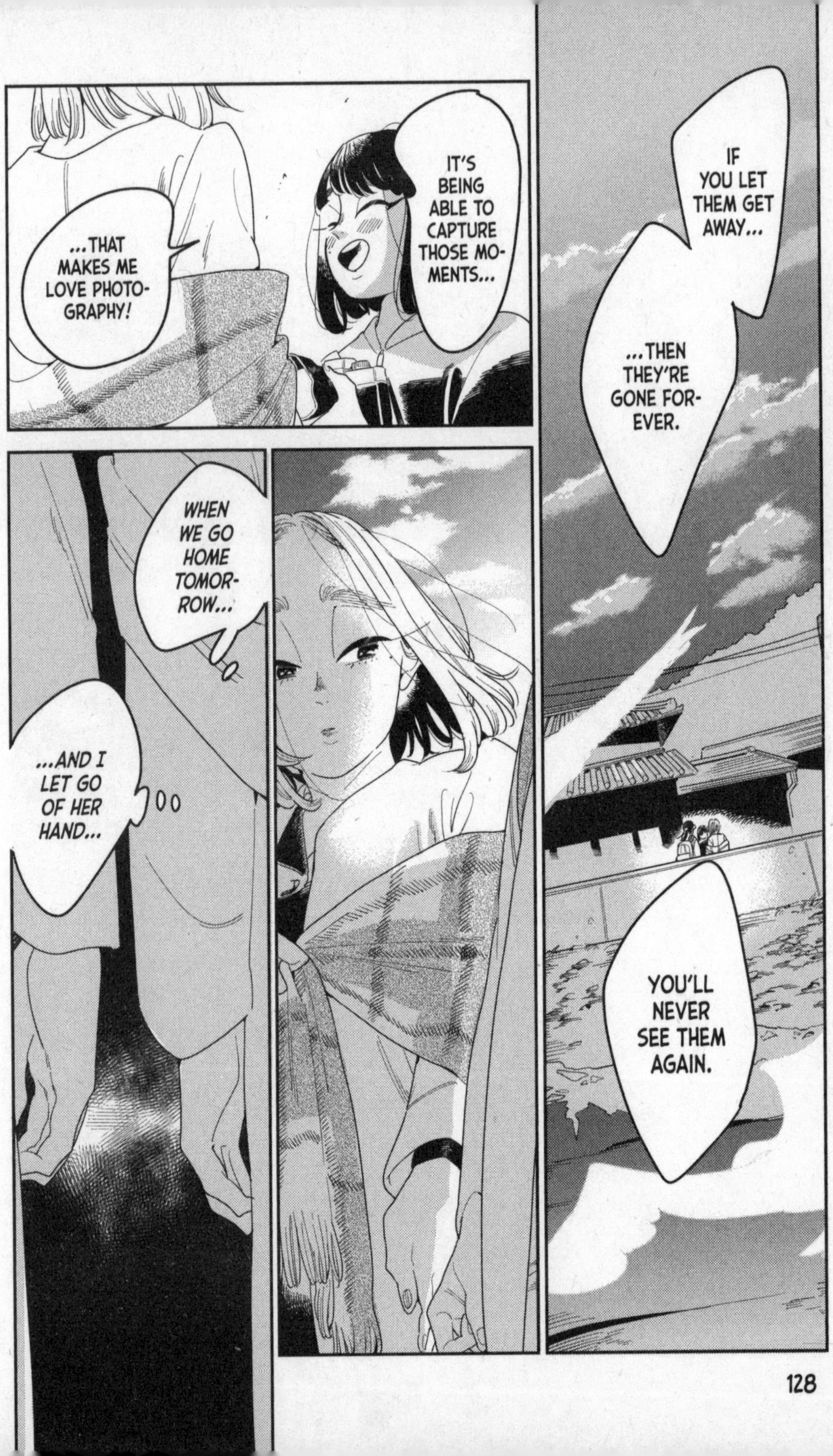
IF YOU LET THEM GET AWAY...
...THEN THEY'RE GONE FOR-EVER.
YOU'LL NEVER SEE THEM AGAIN.
IT'S BEING ABLE TO CAPTURE THOSE MO-MENTS...
...THAT MAKES ME LOVE PHOTO-GRAPHY!
WHEN WE GO HOME TOMOR-ROW...
...AND I LET GO OF HER HAND...

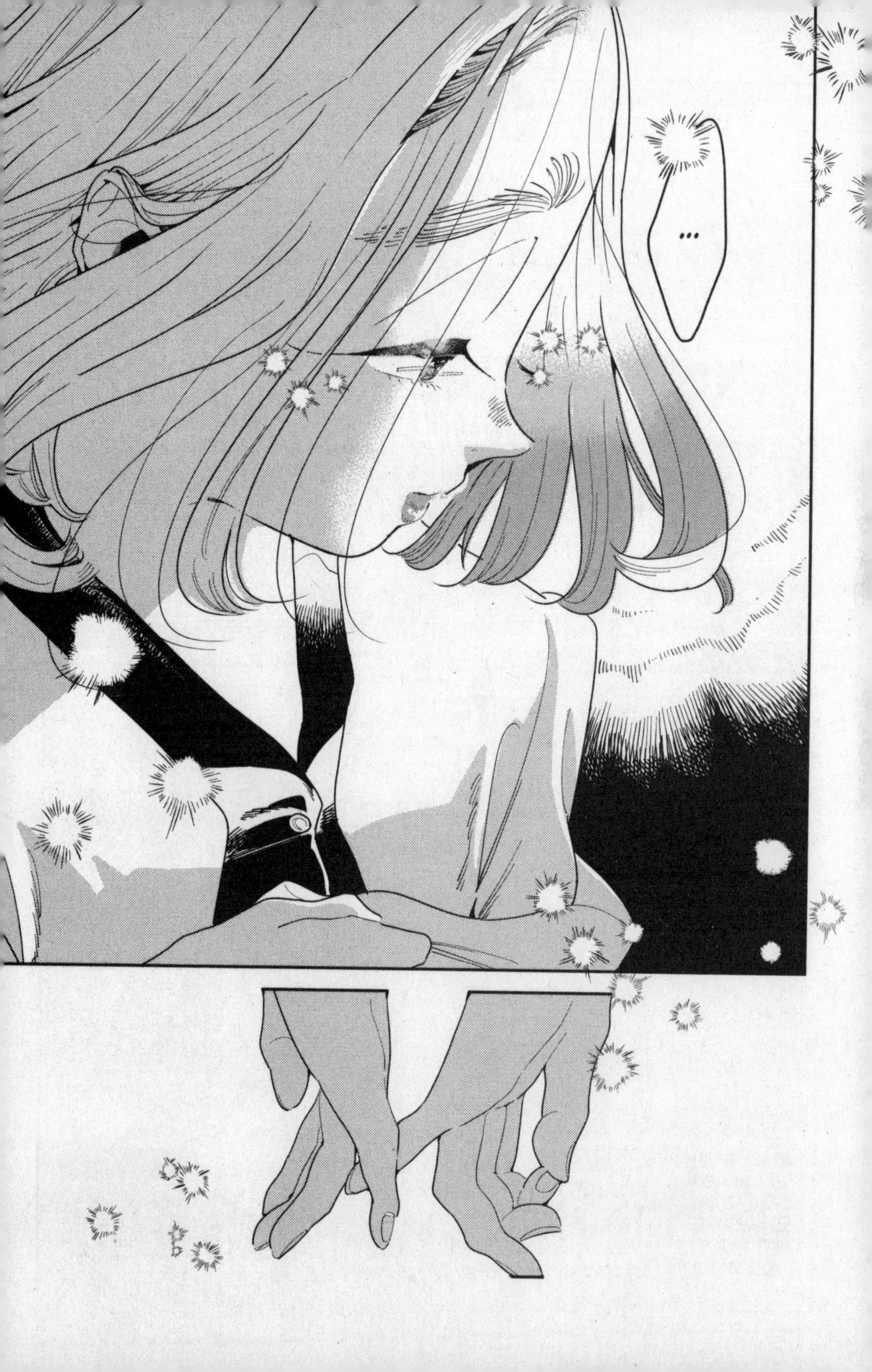
...

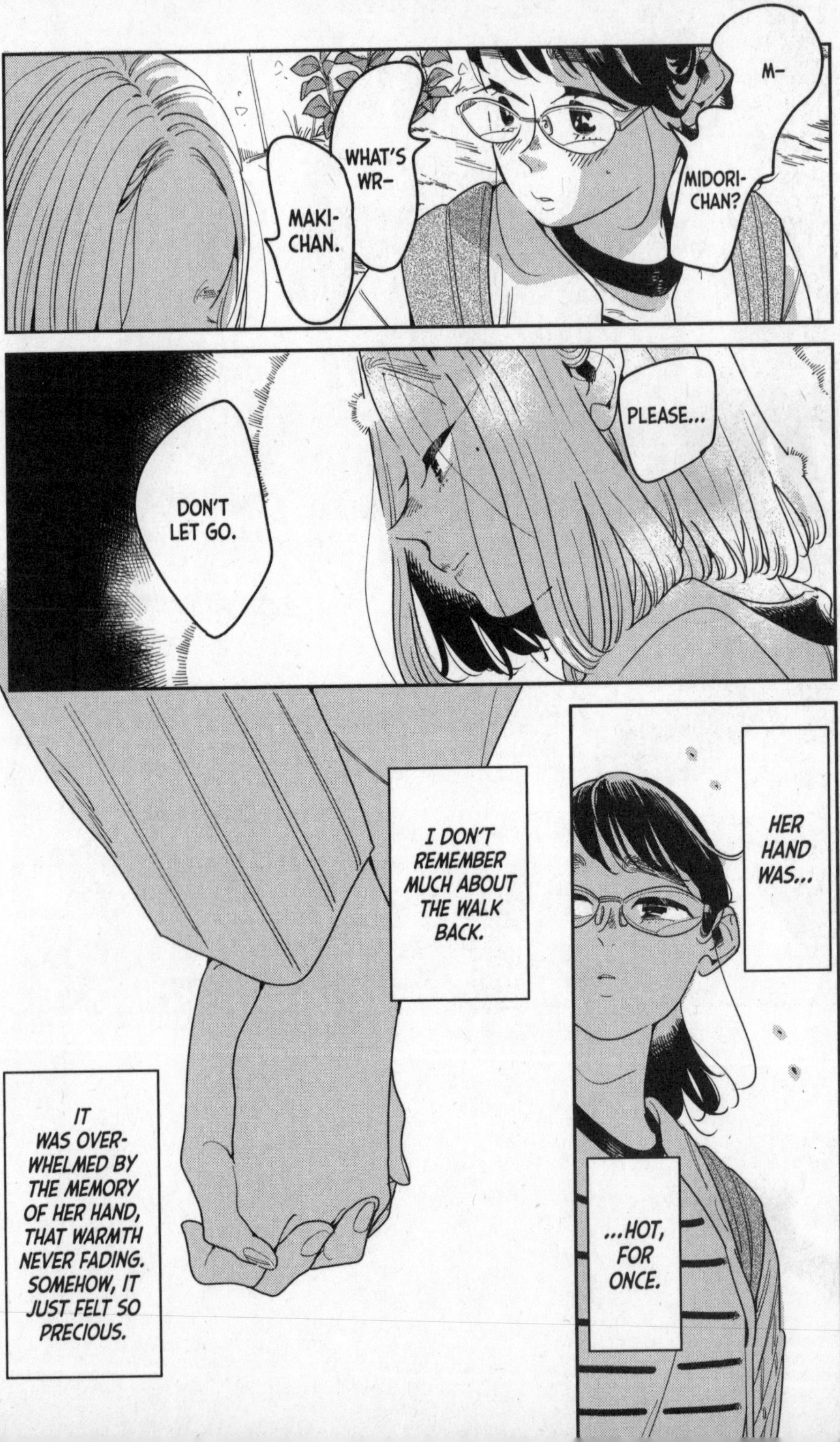
M- MIDORI-CHAN?
WHAT'S WR-
MAKI-CHAN.
PLEASE...
DON'T LET GO.
HER HAND WAS...
...HOT, FOR ONCE.
I DON'T REMEMBER MUCH ABOUT THE WALK BACK.
IT WAS OVER-WHELMED BY THE MEMORY OF HER HAND, THAT WARMTH NEVER FADING. SOMEHOW, IT JUST FELT SO PRECIOUS.

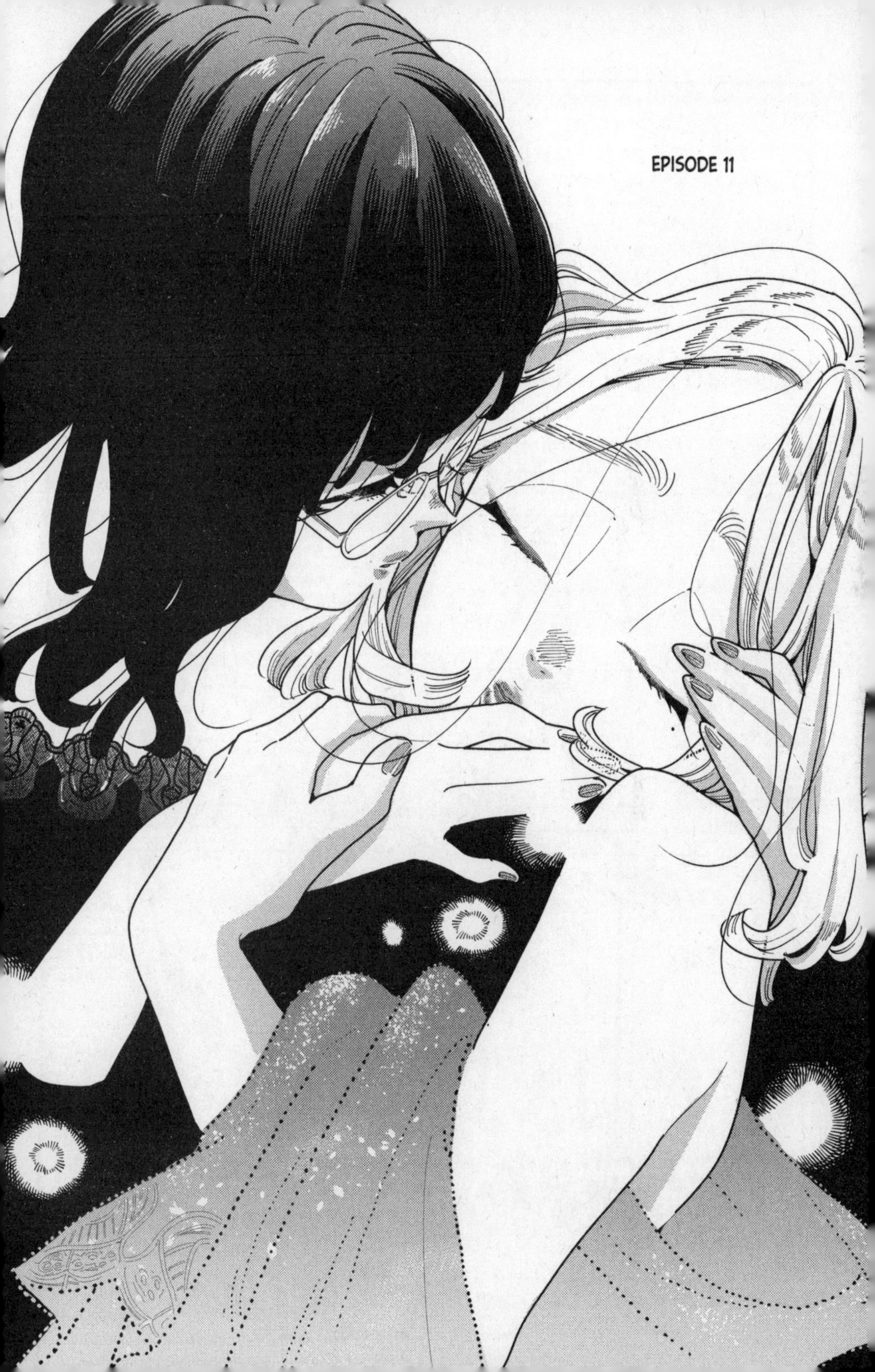
EPISODE 11

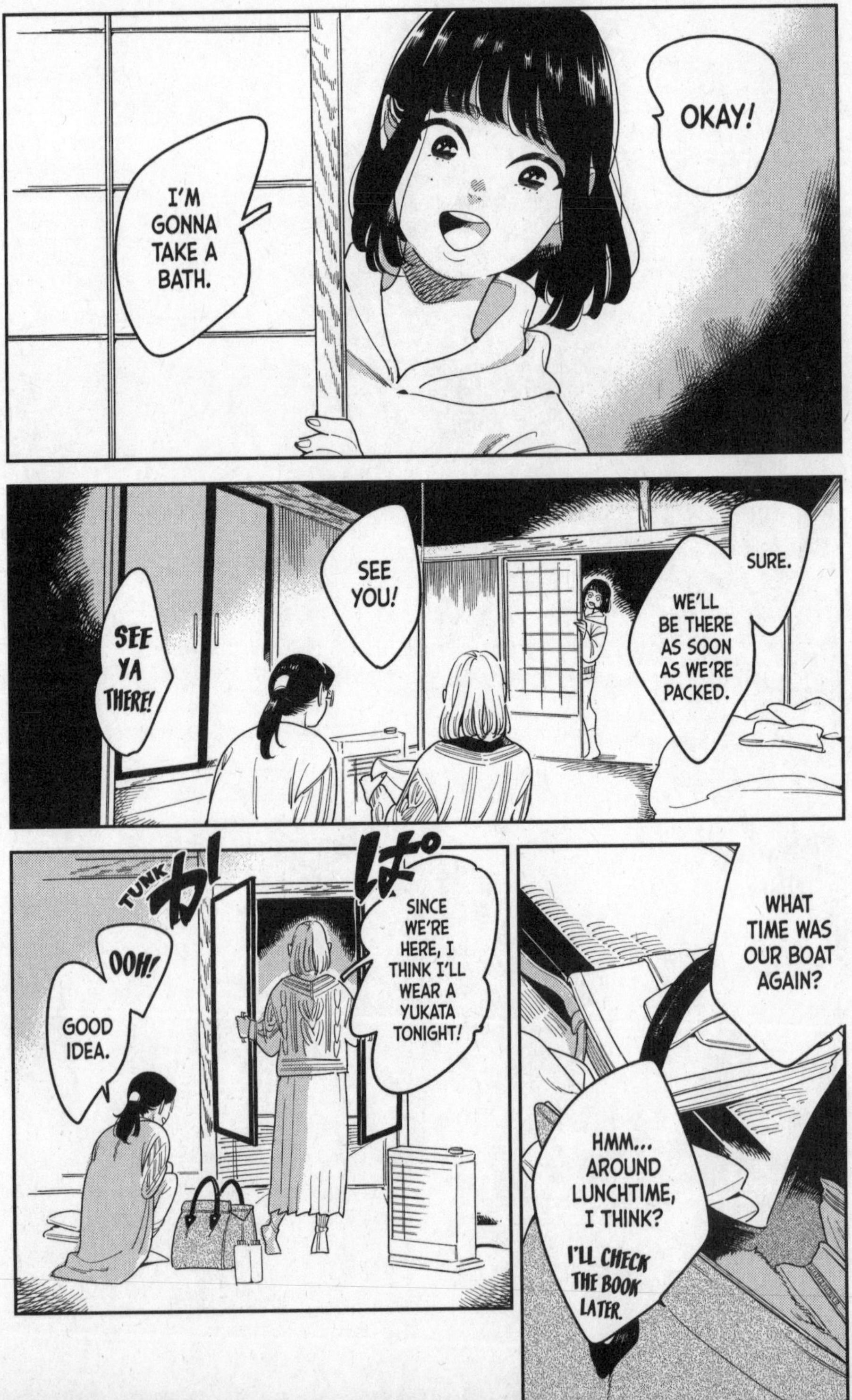
OKAY!
I'M GONNA TAKE A BATH.
SURE.
WE'LL BE THERE AS SOON AS WE'RE PACKED.
SEE YOU!
SEE YA THERE!
WHAT TIME WAS OUR BOAT AGAIN?
HMM... AROUND LUNCHTIME, I THINK?
I'LL CHECK THE BOOK LATER.
ぱ
わ
TUNK
SINCE WE'RE HERE, I THINK I'LL WEAR A YUKATA TONIGHT!
OOH!
GOOD IDEA.

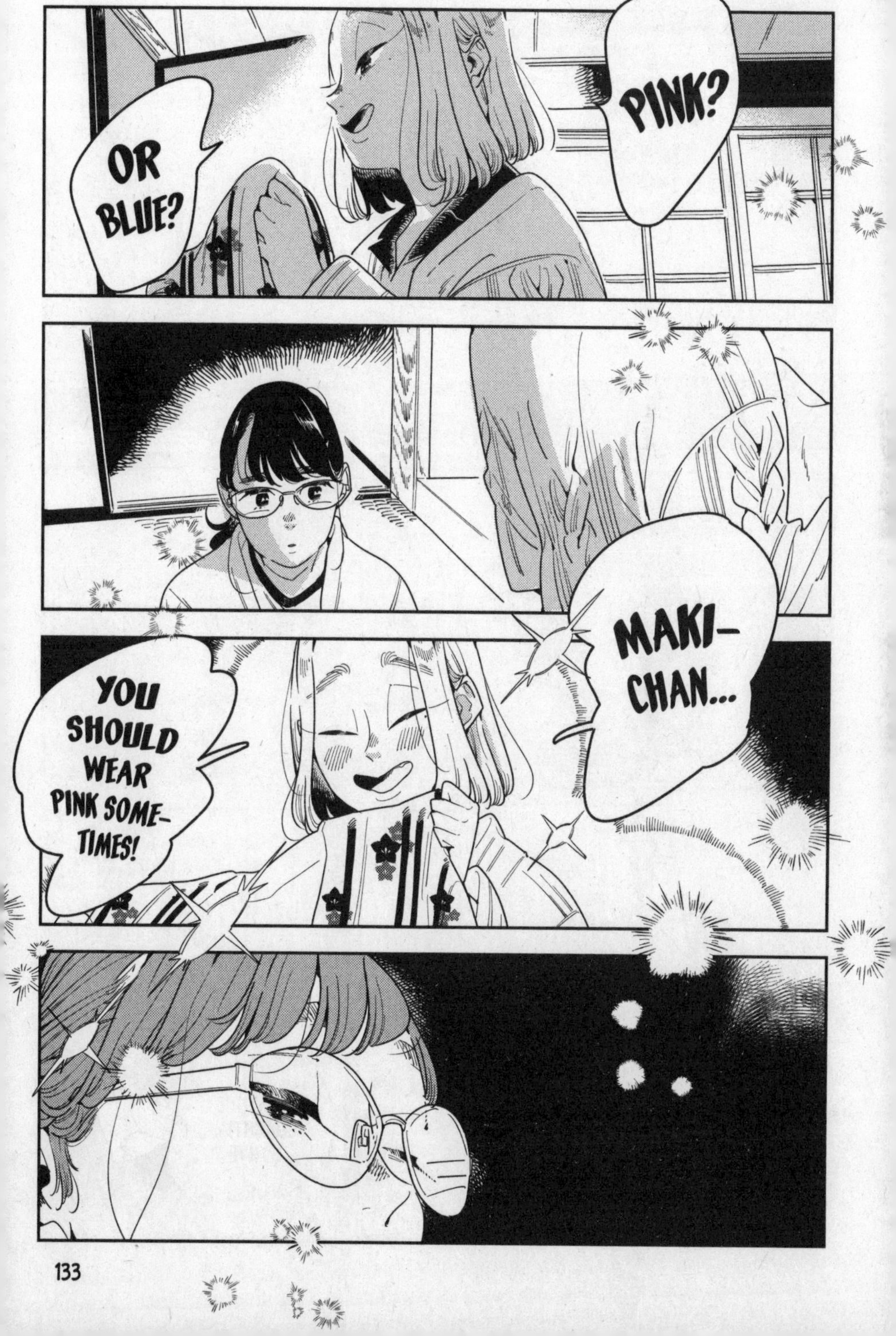
PINK?
OR BLUE?
MAKI-CHAN...
YOU SHOULD WEAR PINK SOME-TIMES!

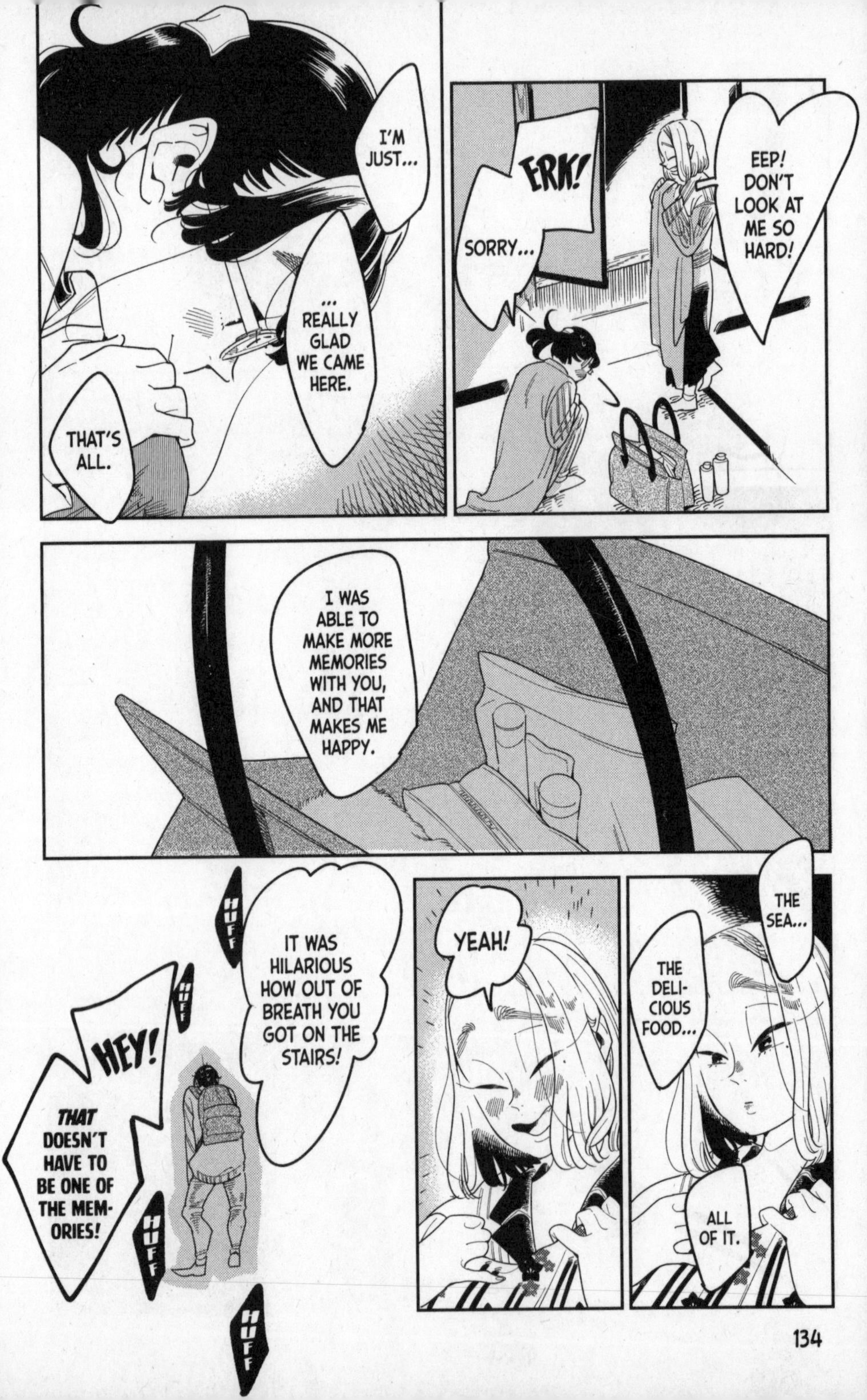
EEP! DON'T LOOK AT ME SO HARD!
ERK!
SORRY...
I'M JUST...
... REALLY GLAD WE CAME HERE.
THAT'S ALL.
I WAS ABLE TO MAKE MORE MEMORIES WITH YOU, AND THAT MAKES ME HAPPY.
THE SEA...
THE DELICIOUS FOOD...
ALL OF IT.
YEAH!
HUFF
IT WAS HILARIOUS HOW OUT OF BREATH YOU GOT ON THE STAIRS!
HUFF
HEY!
THAT DOESN'T HAVE TO BE ONE OF THE MEMORIES!
HUFF
HUFF

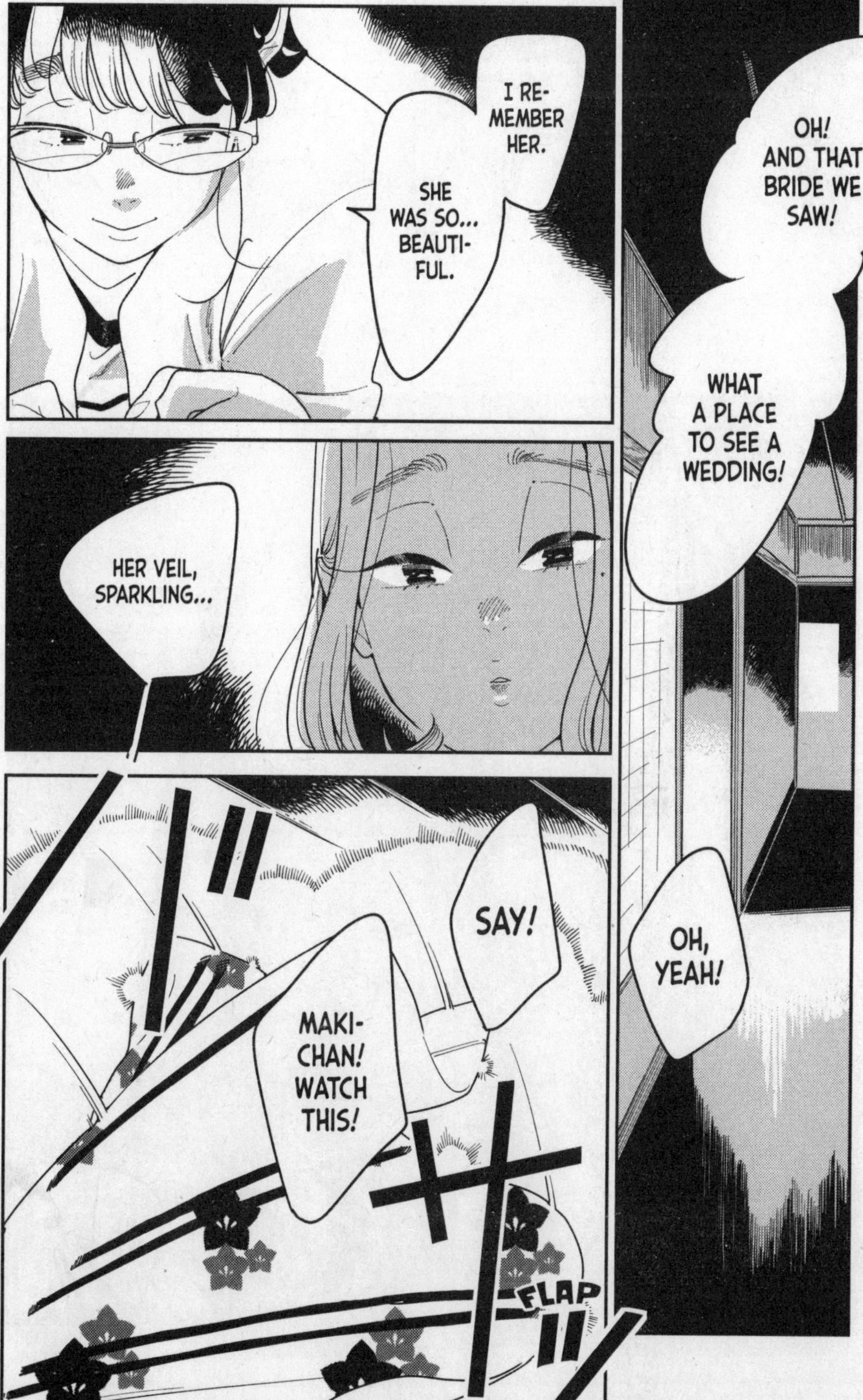
OH! AND THAT BRIDE WE SAW!
WHAT A PLACE TO SEE A WEDDING!
OH, YEAH!
I RE-MEMBER HER.
SHE WAS SO... BEAUTI-FUL.
HER VEIL, SPARKLING...
SAY!
MAKI-CHAN! WATCH THIS!
FLAP

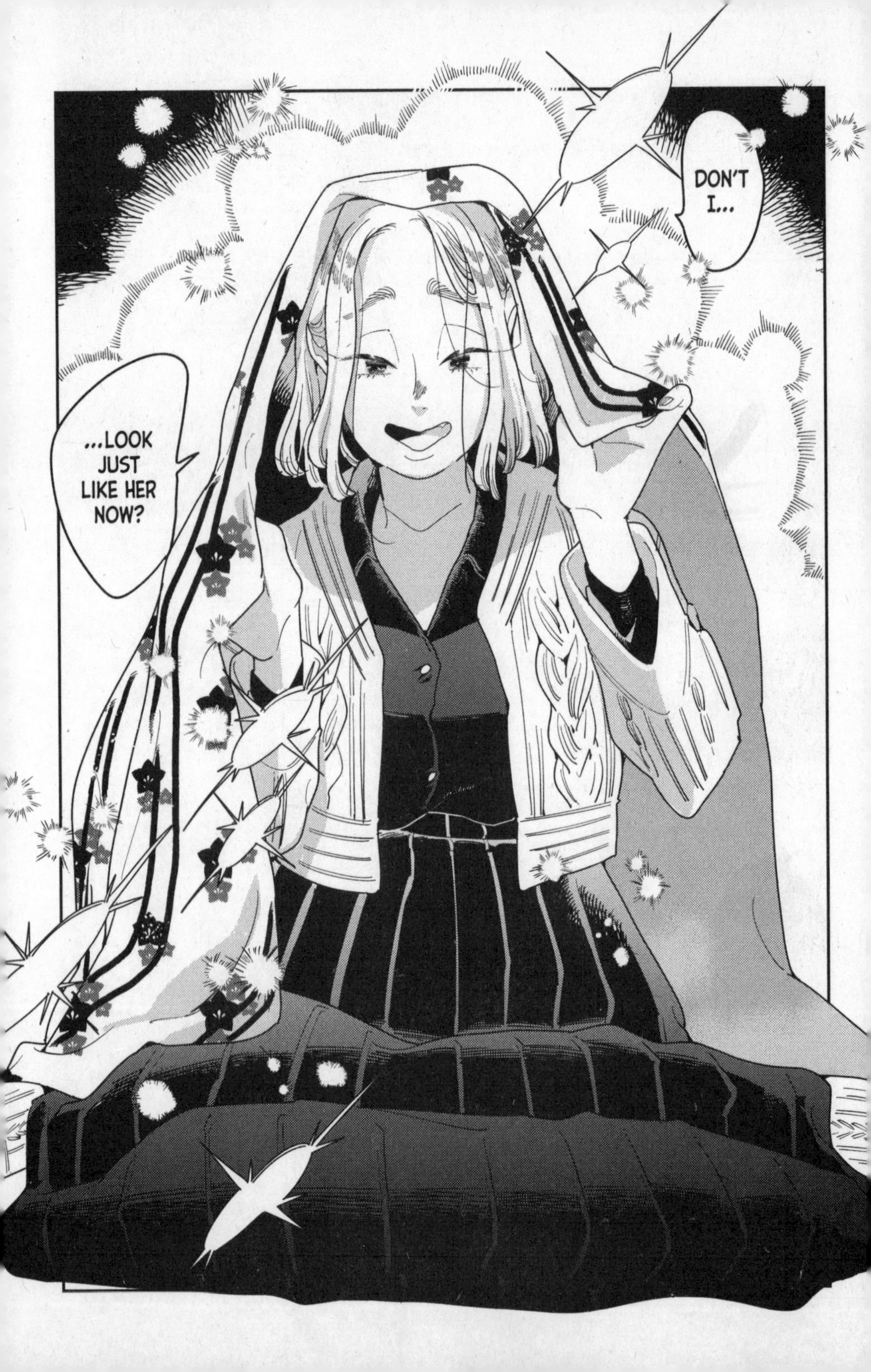
DON'T I...
...LOOK JUST LIKE HER NOW?

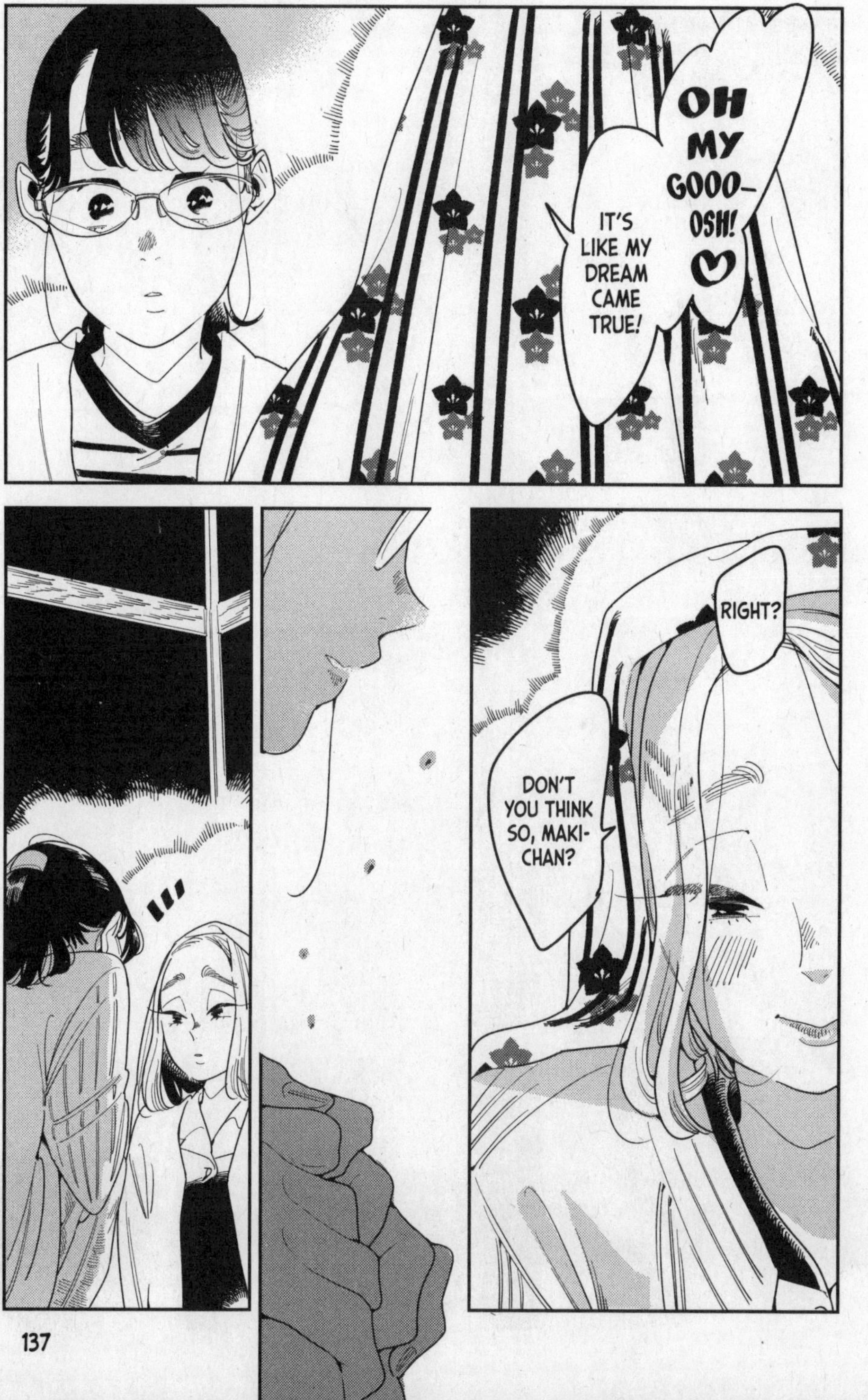
OH MY GOOOO-OSH! ♡
IT'S LIKE MY DREAM CAME TRUE!
RIGHT?
DON'T YOU THINK SO, MAKI-CHAN?

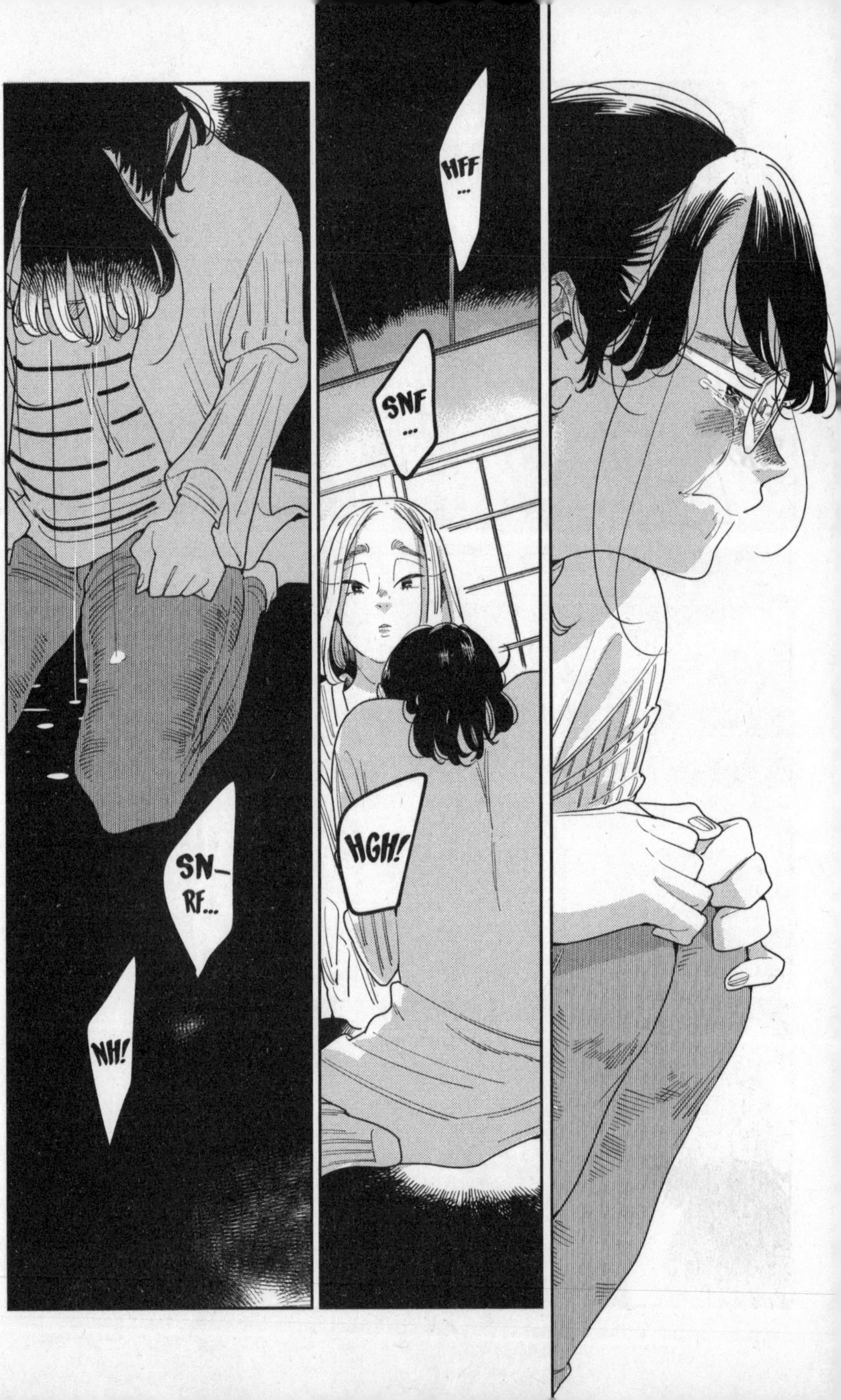
HFF ...
SNF ...
HGH!
SN-RF...
NH!

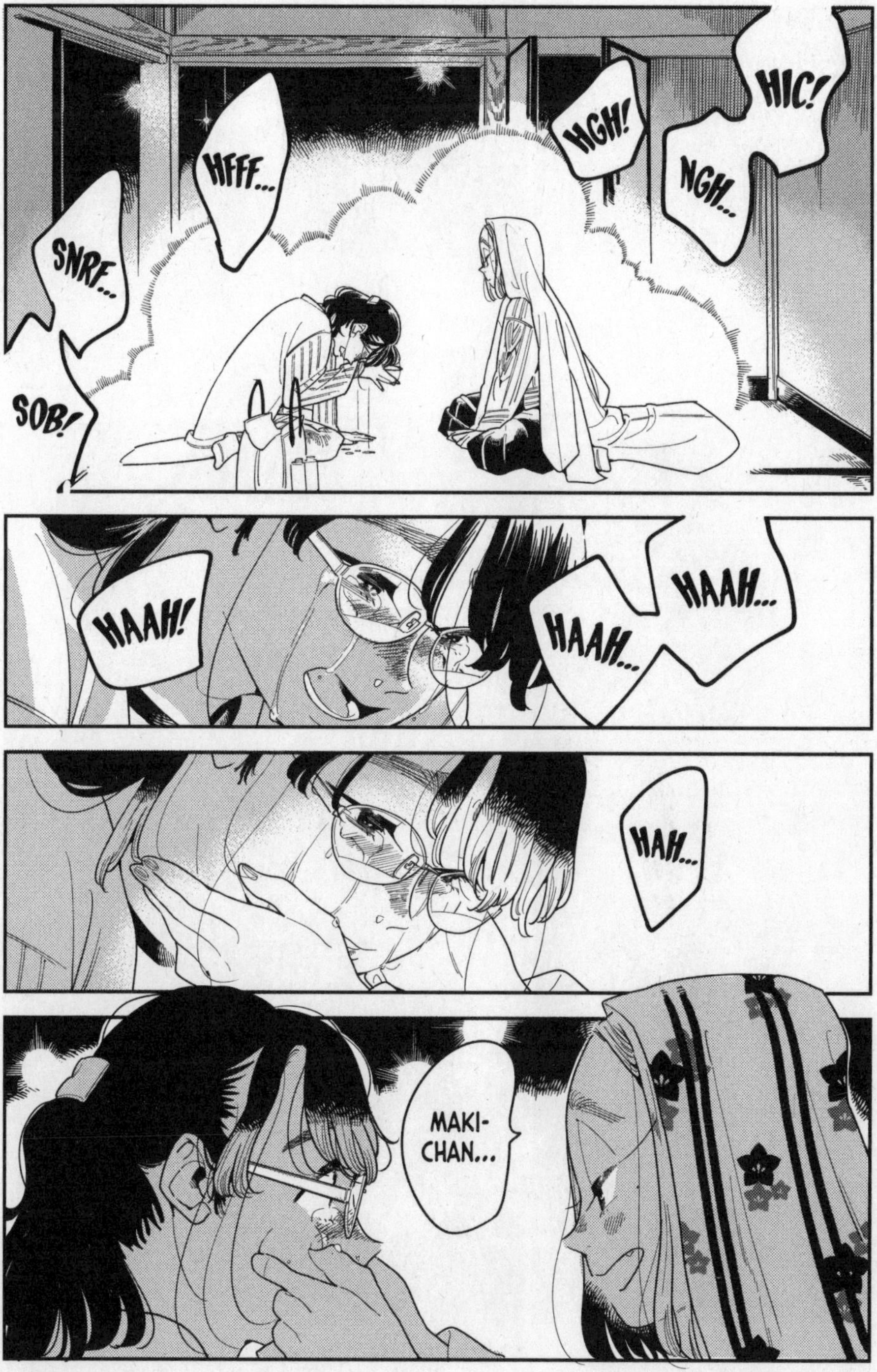
HIC!
NGH...
HGH!
HFFF...
SNRF...
SOB!
HAAH...
HAAH...
HAAH!
HAH...
MAKI-CHAN...

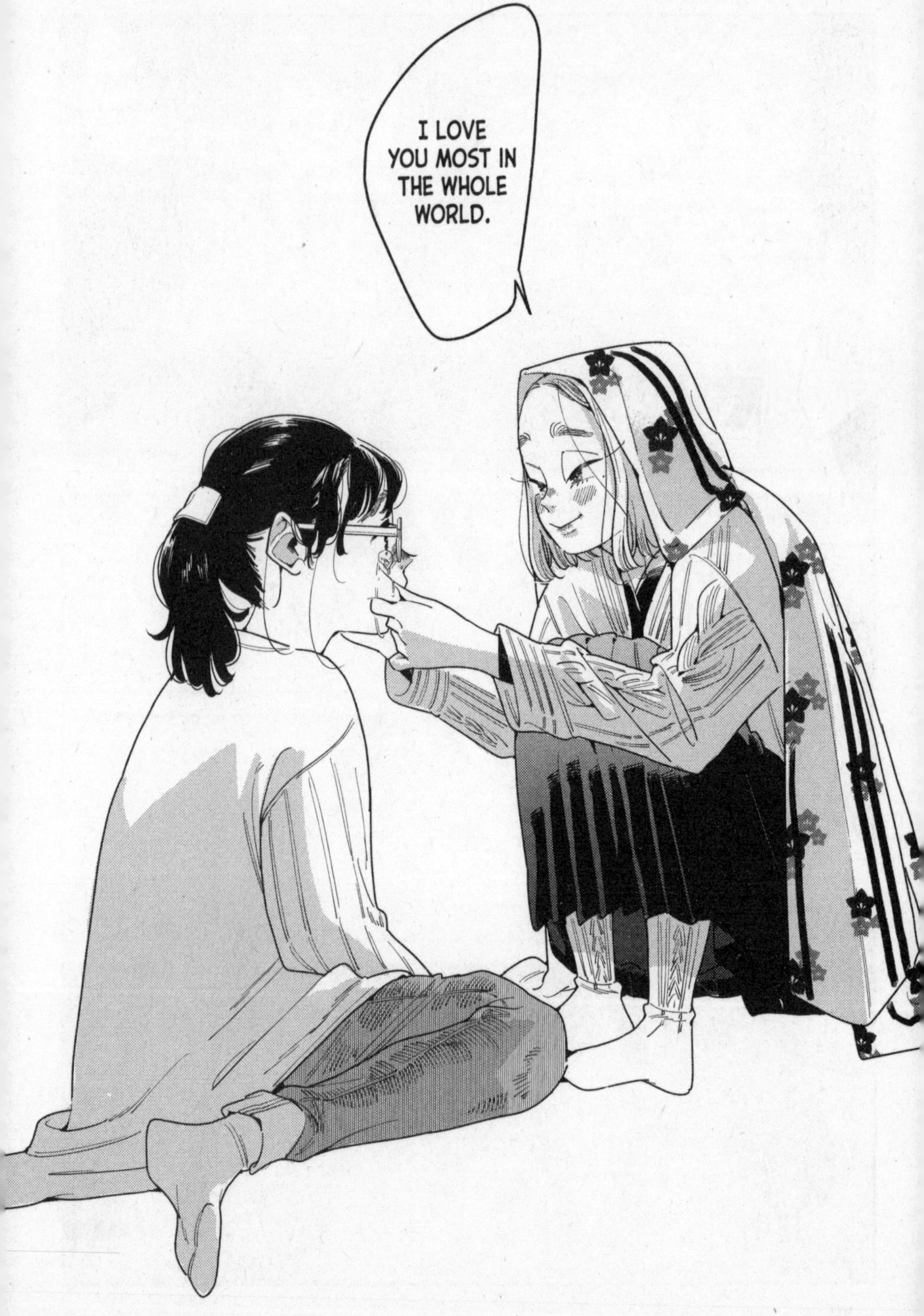
I LOVE YOU MOST IN THE WHOLE WORLD.

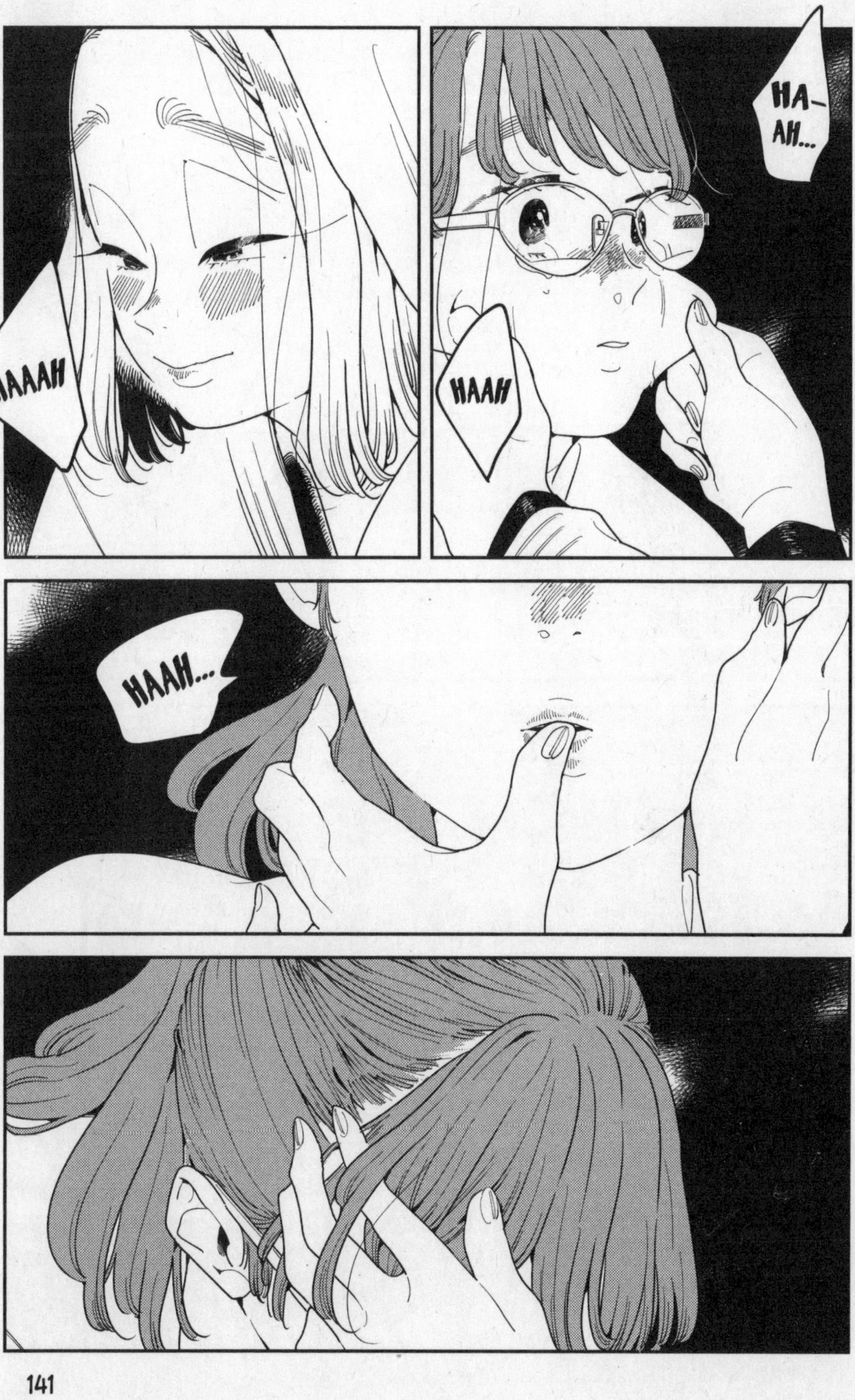
HA-AH...
HAAH
HAAAH
HAAH...

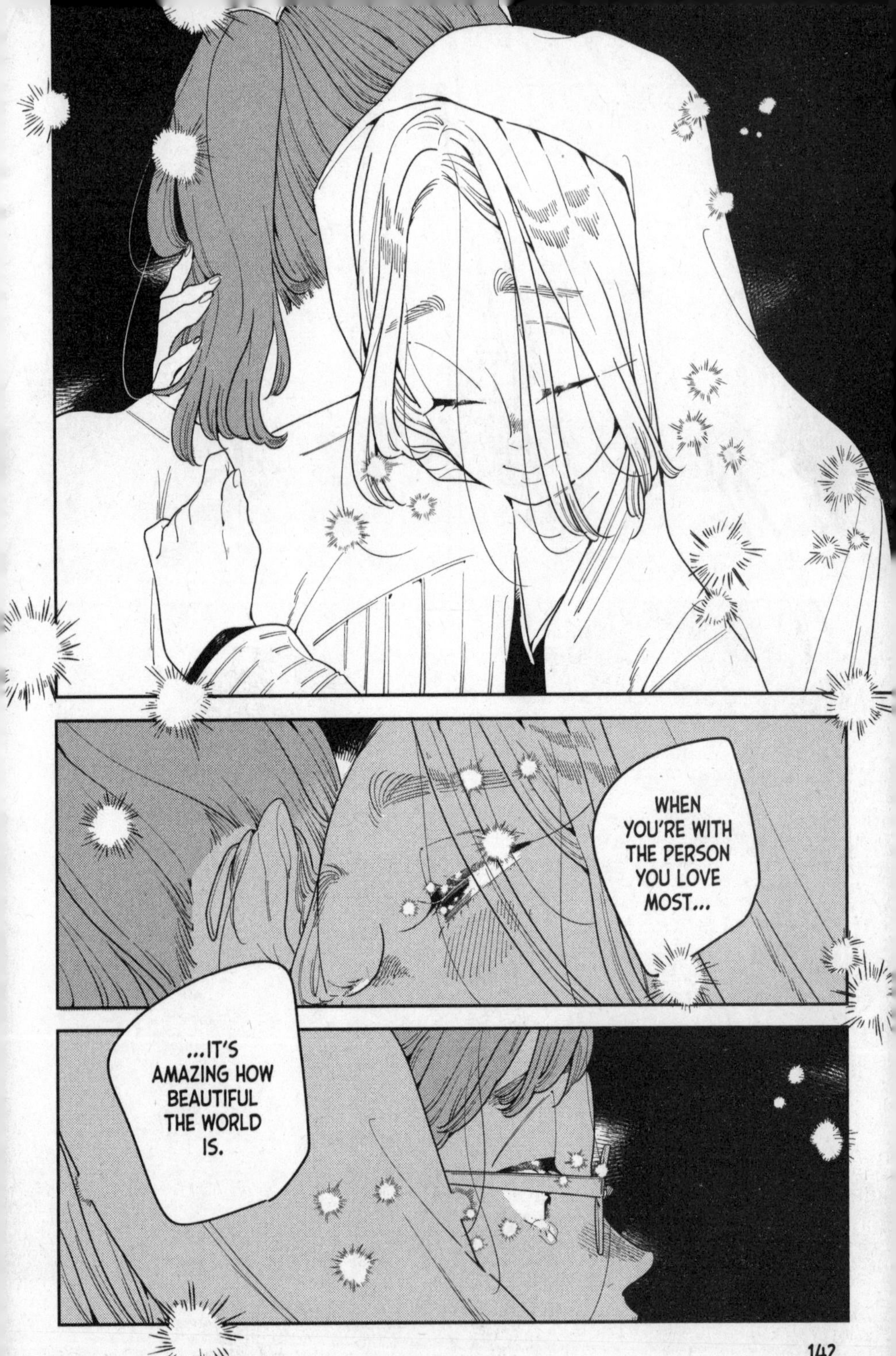
WHEN YOU'RE WITH THE PERSON YOU LOVE MOST...
...IT'S AMAZING HOW BEAUTIFUL THE WORLD IS.

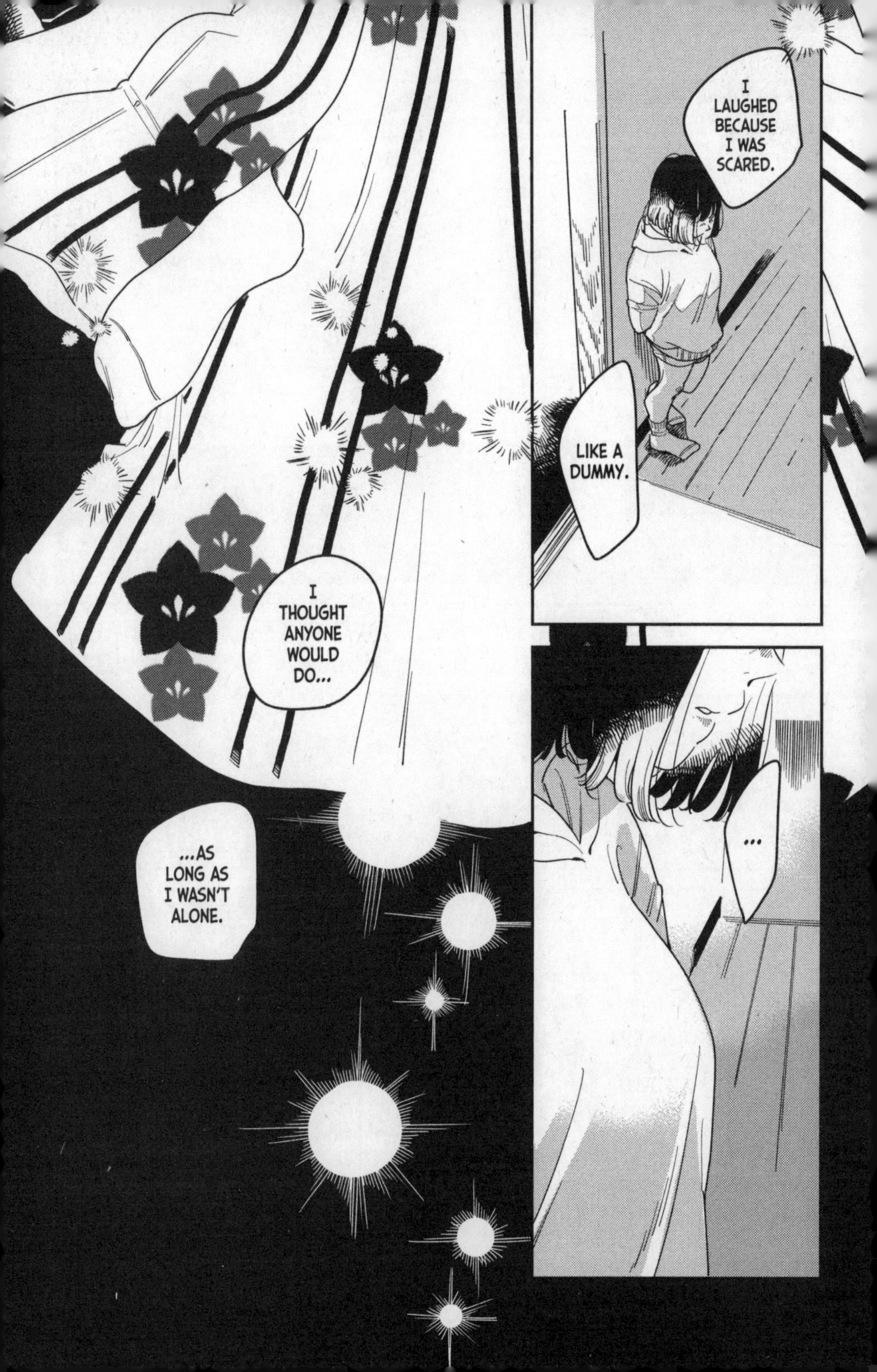
I LAUGHED BECAUSE I WAS SCARED.
LIKE A DUMMY.
...
I THOUGHT ANYONE WOULD DO...
...AS LONG AS I WASN'T ALONE.

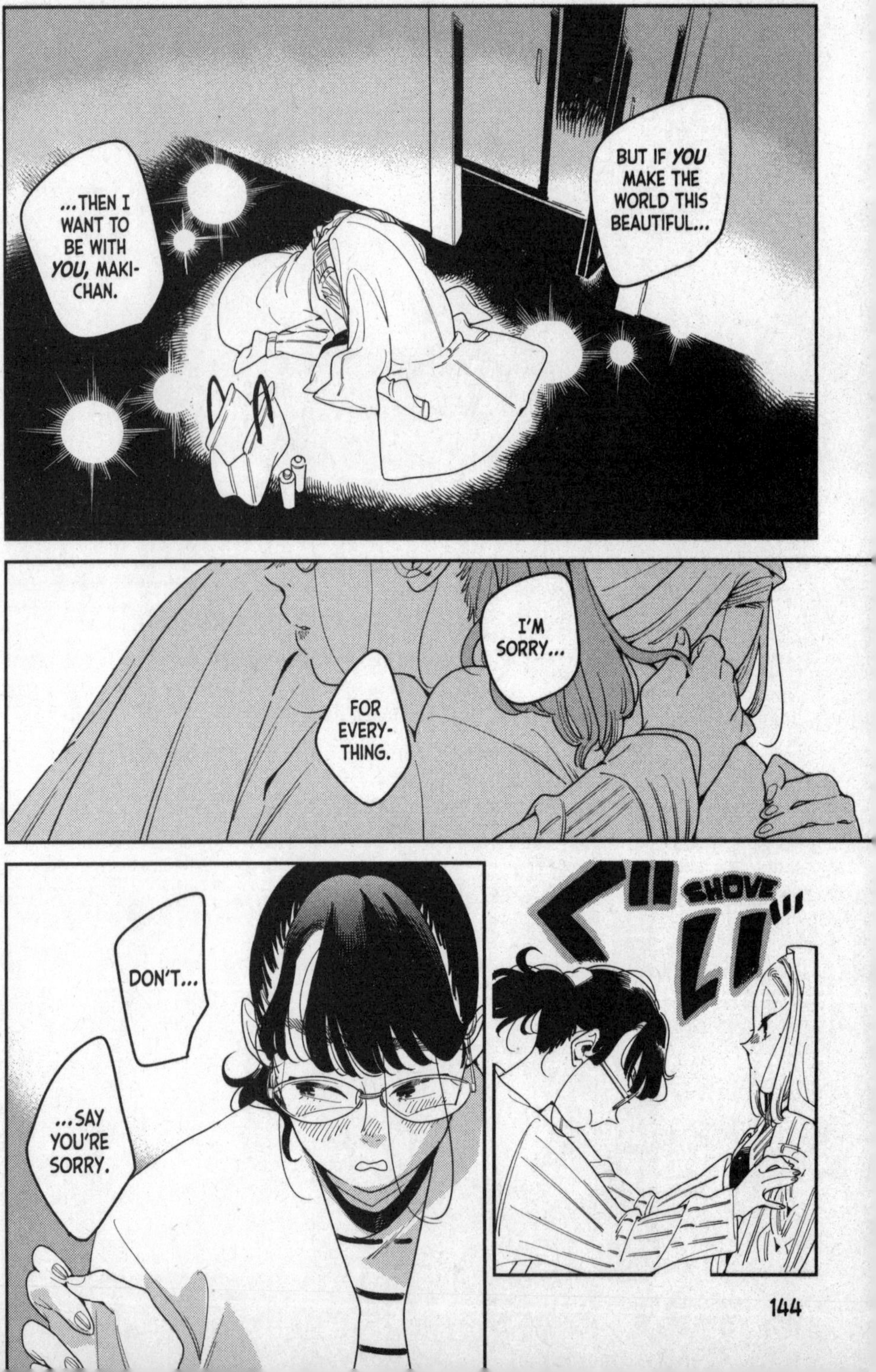
BUT IF *YOU* MAKE THE WORLD THIS BEAUTIFUL...
...THEN I WANT TO BE WITH *YOU,* MAKI-CHAN.
I'M SORRY...
FOR EVERY-THING.
SHOVE
DON'T...
...SAY YOU'RE SORRY.

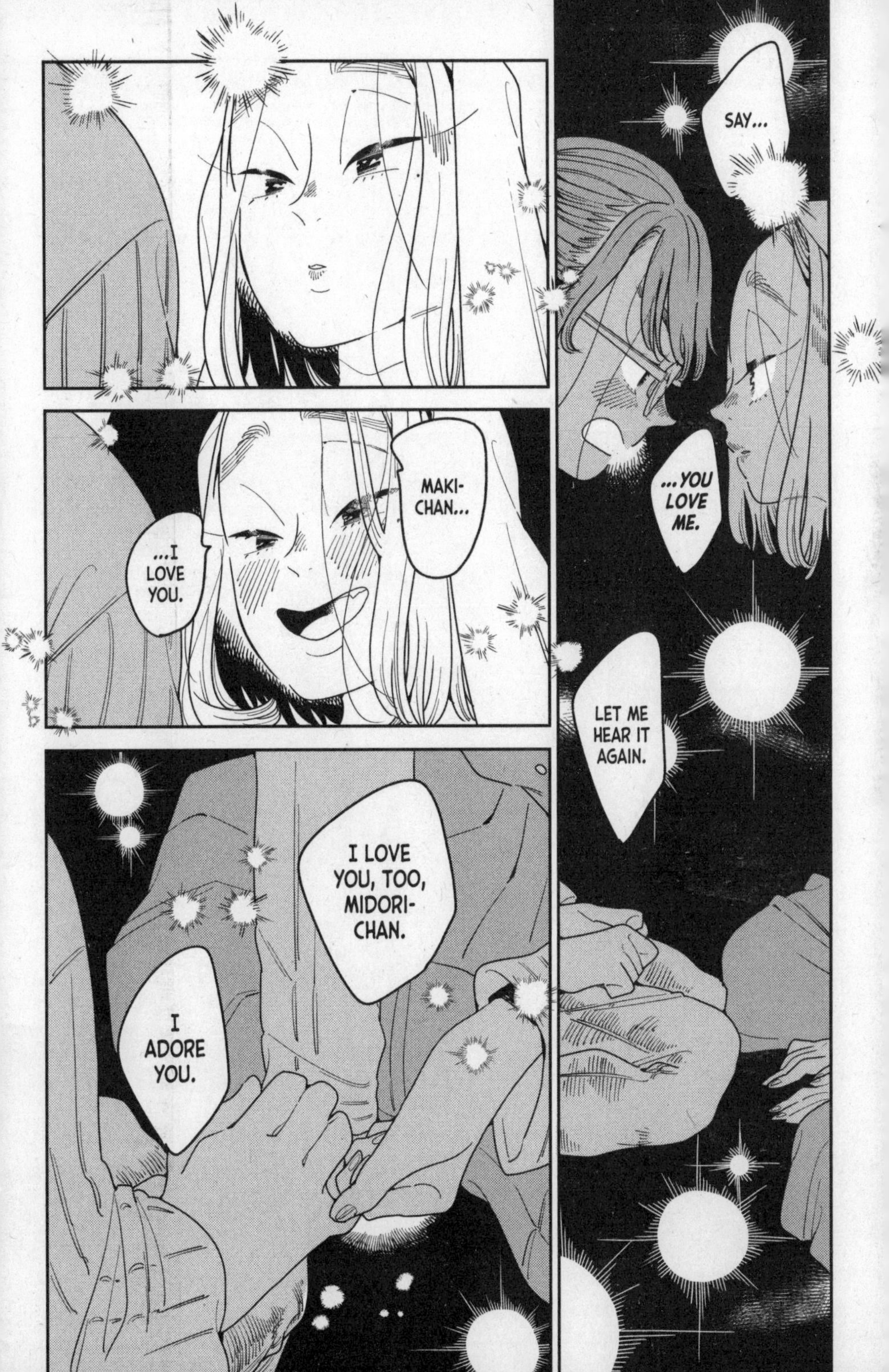
SAY...
...YOU LOVE ME.
LET ME HEAR IT AGAIN.
MAKI-CHAN...
...I LOVE YOU.
I LOVE YOU, TOO, MIDORI-CHAN.
I ADORE YOU.

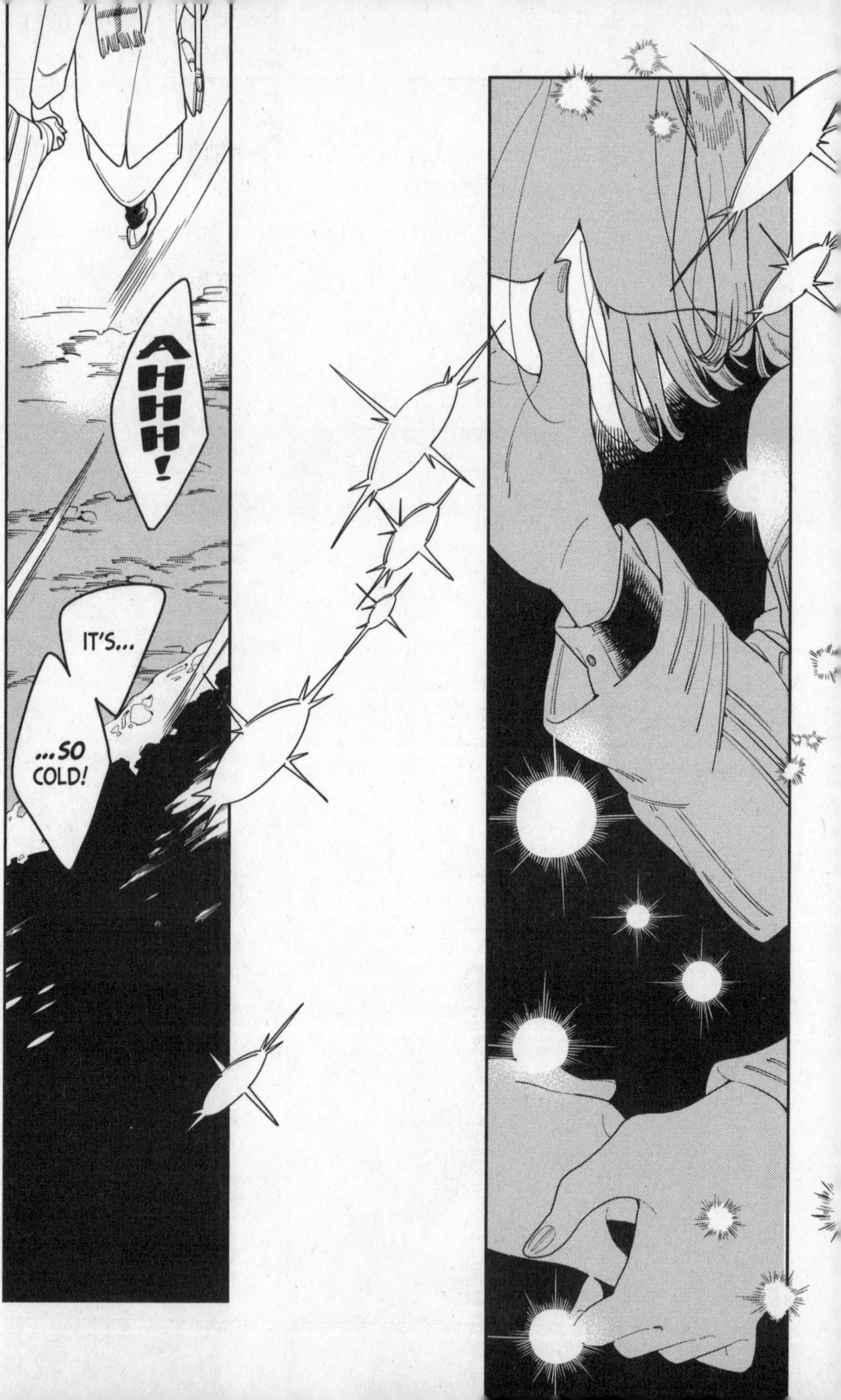
AHHHH!
IT'S...
...SO COLD!

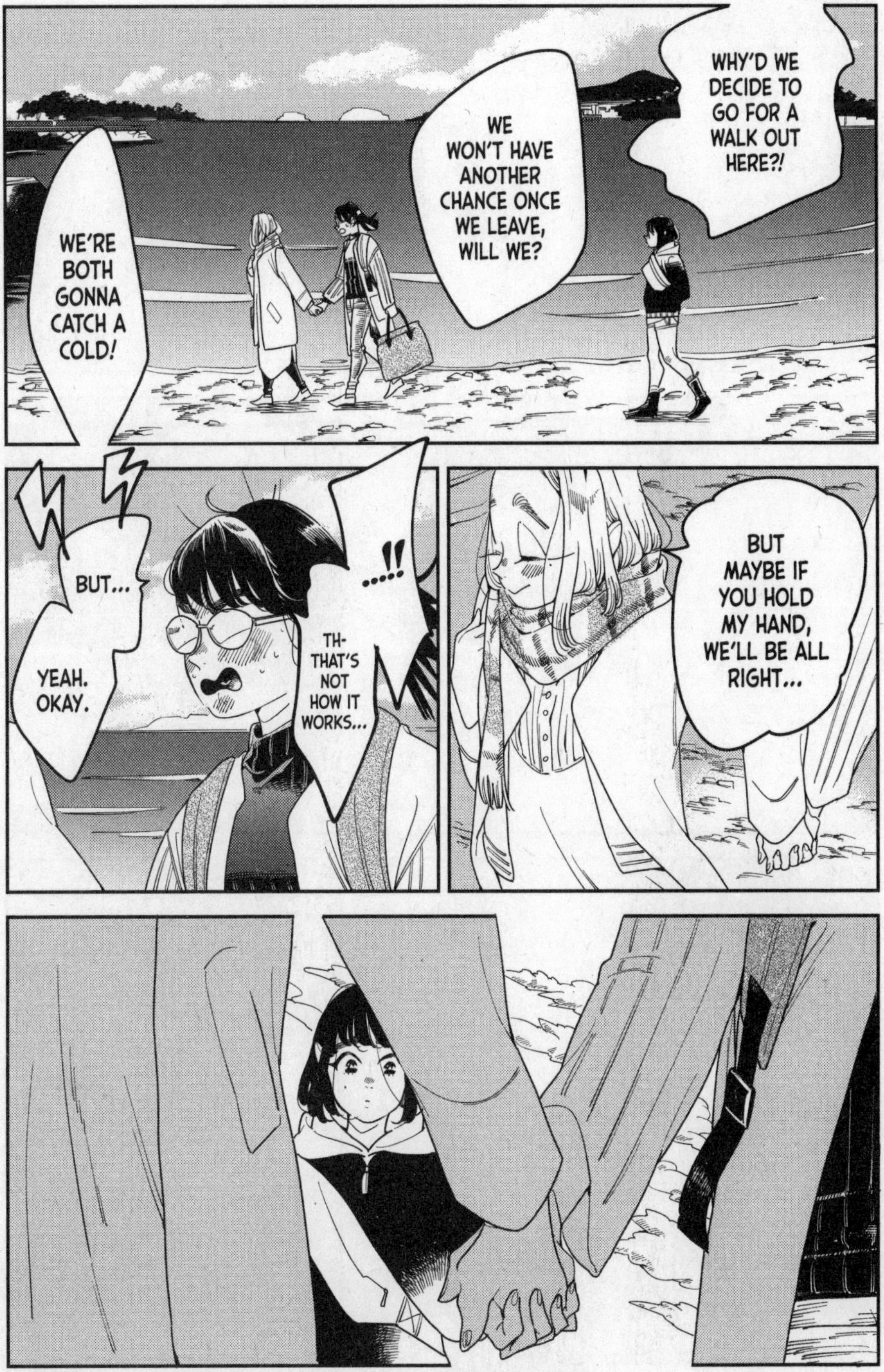
WHY'D WE DECIDE TO GO FOR A WALK OUT HERE?!
WE WON'T HAVE ANOTHER CHANCE ONCE WE LEAVE, WILL WE?
WE'RE BOTH GONNA CATCH A COLD!
BUT MAYBE IF YOU HOLD MY HAND, WE'LL BE ALL RIGHT...
...!!
TH-THAT'S NOT HOW IT WORKS...
BUT...
YEAH. OKAY.

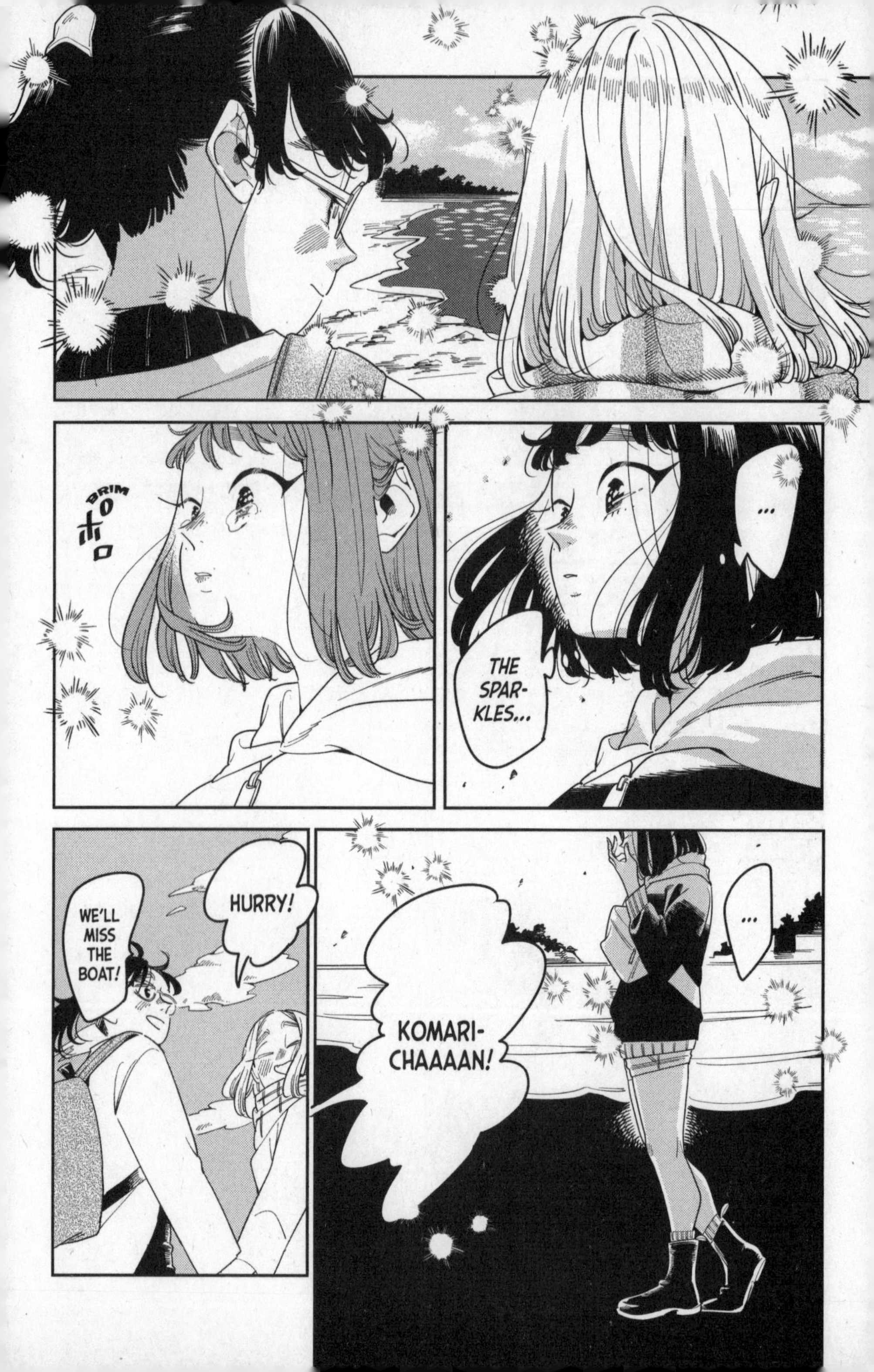
...
THE SPARKLES...
BRIM
ホロ
...
KOMARI-CHAAAAN!
HURRY!
WE'LL MISS THE BOAT!

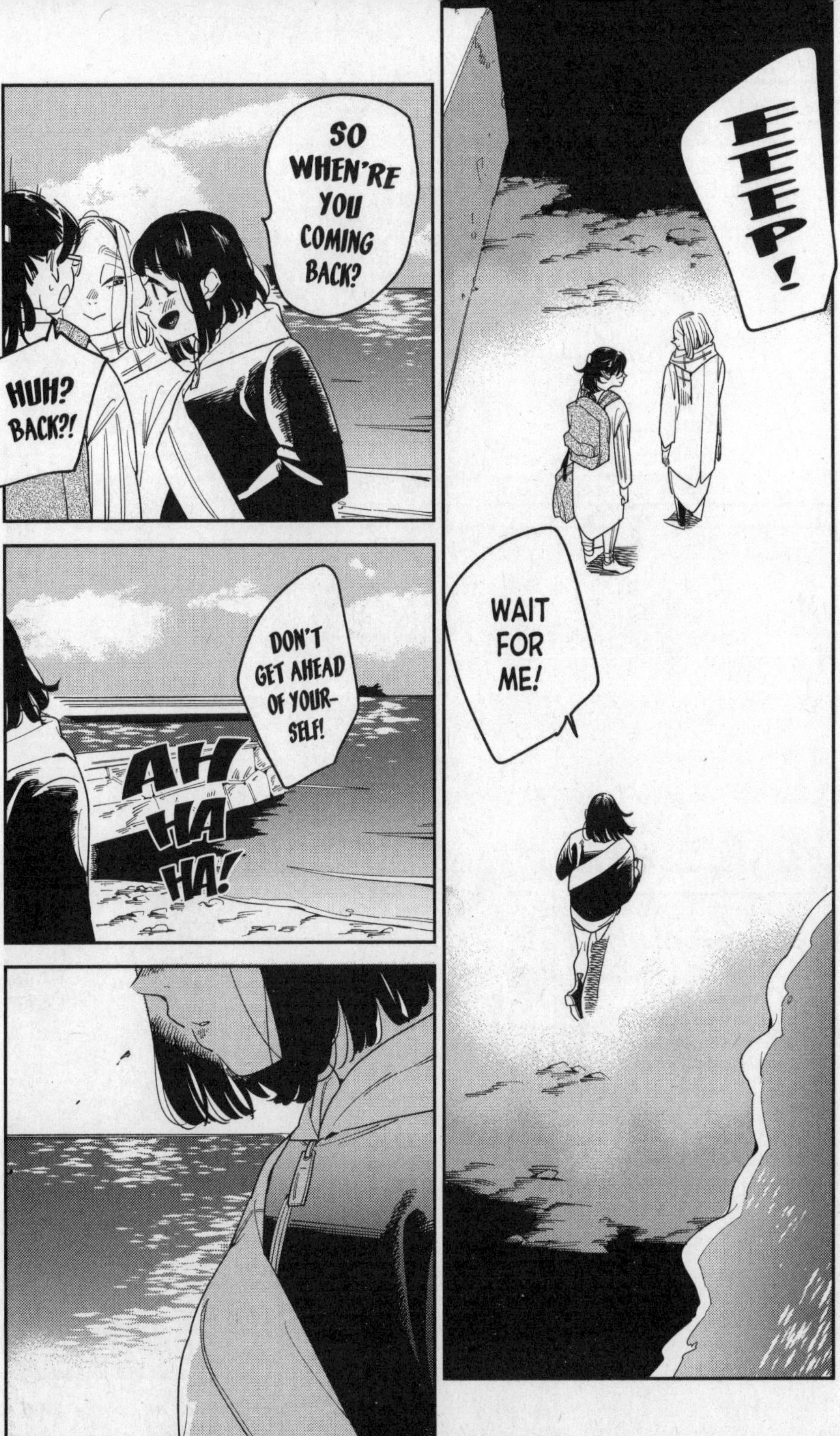
EEEEP!
WAIT FOR ME!
SO WHEN'RE YOU COMING BACK?
HUH? BACK?!
DON'T GET AHEAD OF YOUR-SELF!
AH HA HA HA!

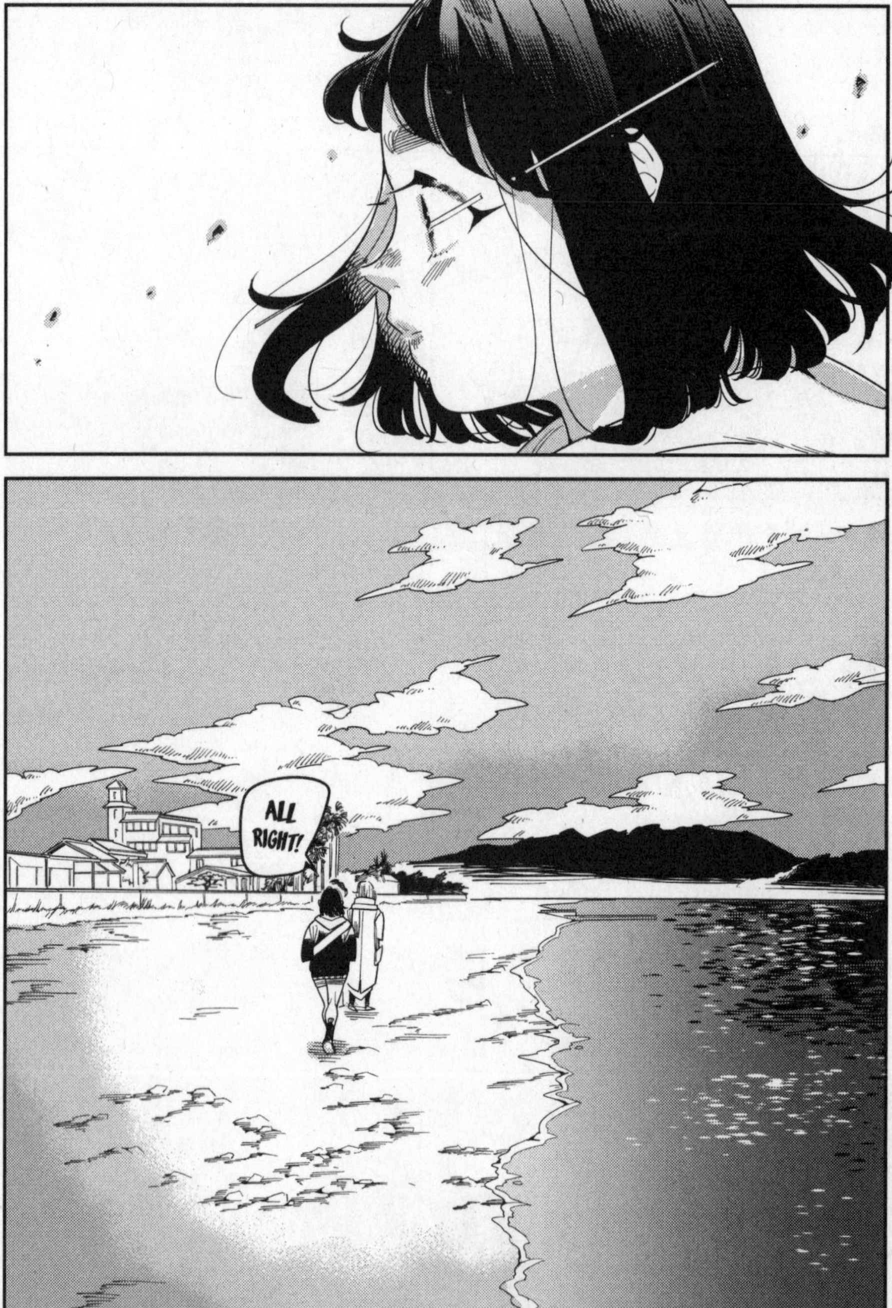
ALL RIGHT!

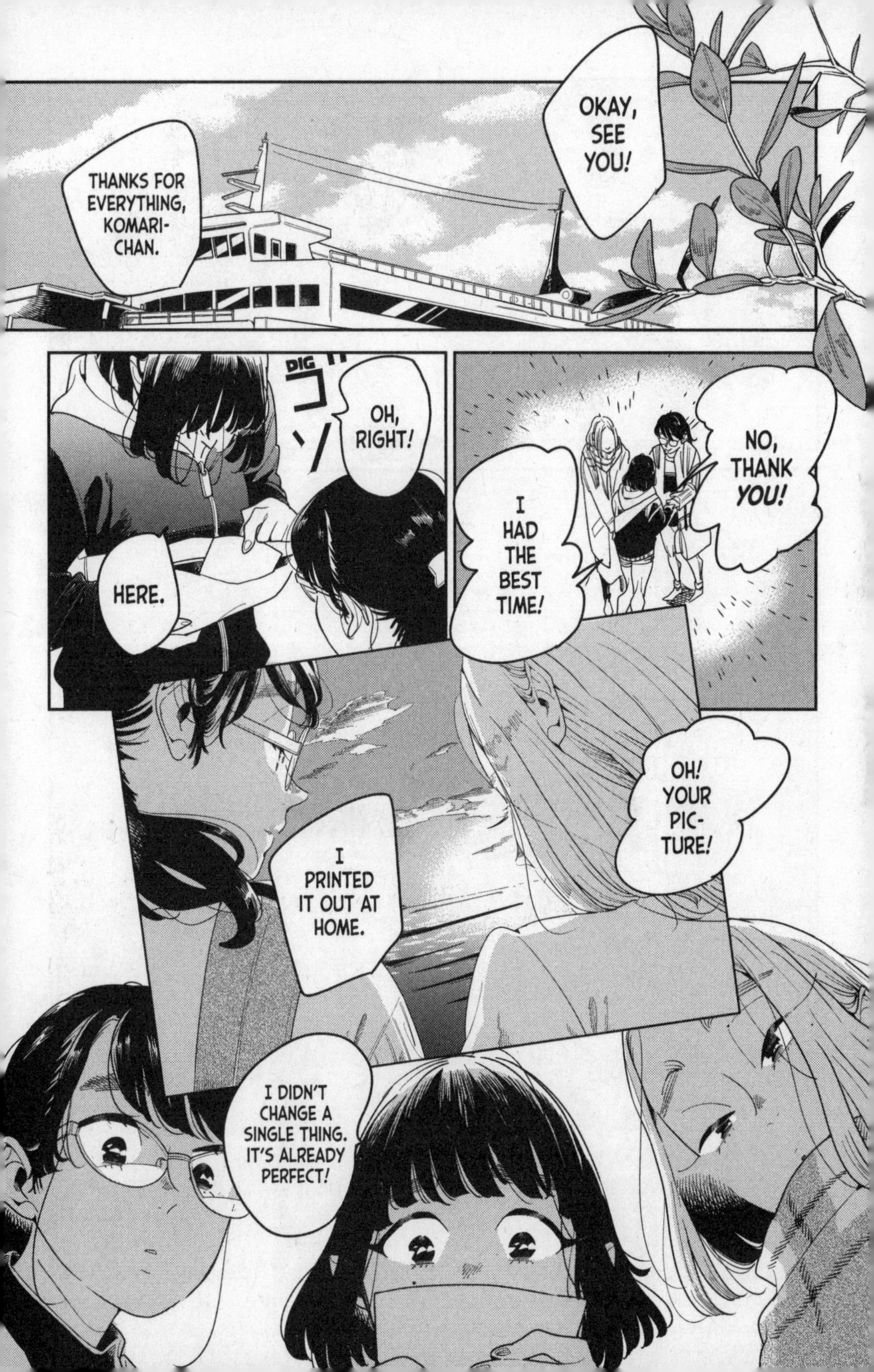
OKAY, SEE YOU!
THANKS FOR EVERYTHING, KOMARI-CHAN.
NO, THANK *YOU!*
I HAD THE BEST TIME!
DIG
OH, RIGHT!
HERE.
OH! YOUR PIC-TURE!
I PRINTED IT OUT AT HOME.
I DIDN'T CHANGE A SINGLE THING. IT'S ALREADY PERFECT!

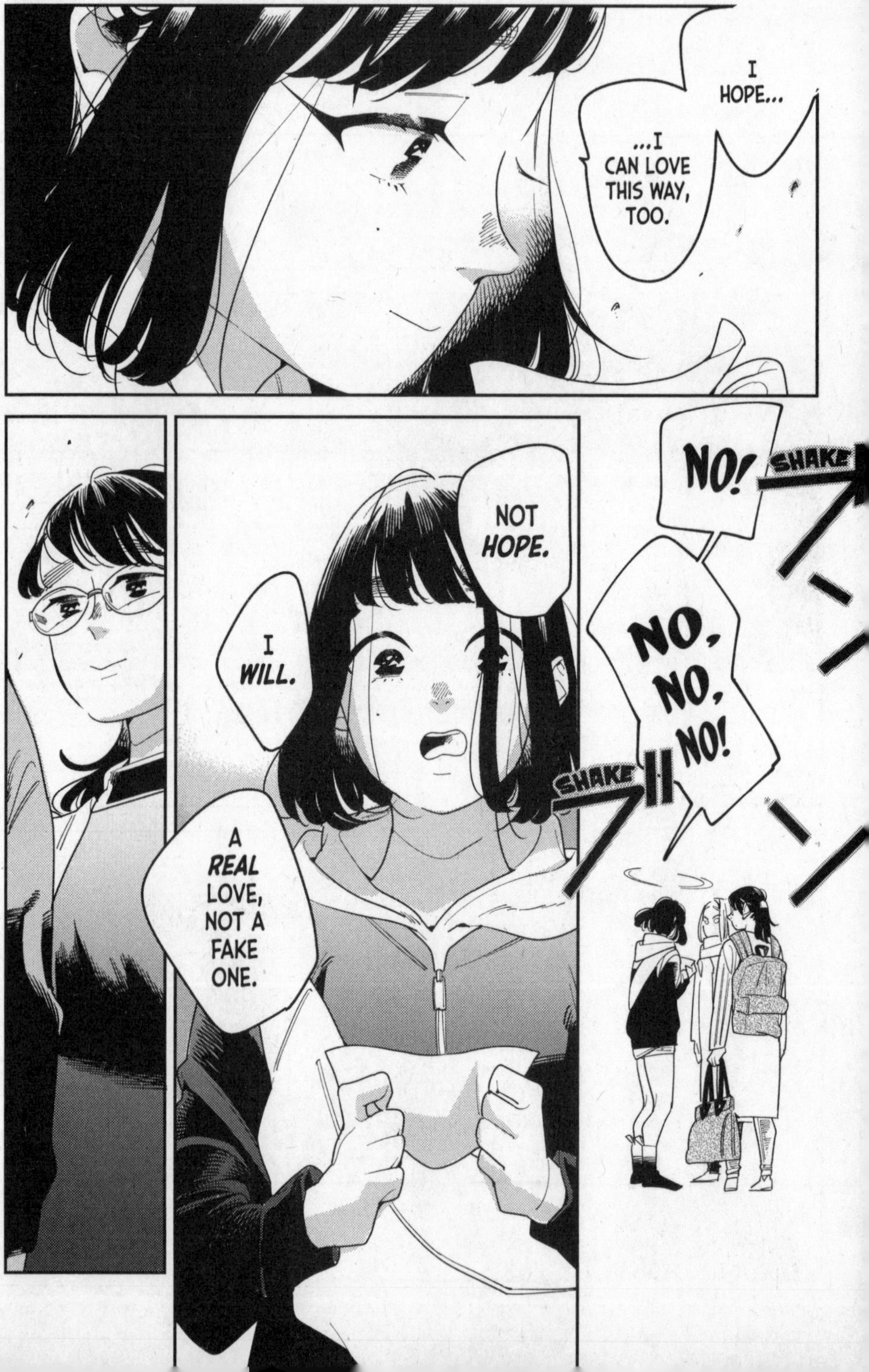
I HOPE...
...I CAN LOVE THIS WAY, TOO.
NO!
SHAKE
NO, NO, NO!
SHAKE
NOT HOPE.
I WILL.
A REAL LOVE, NOT A FAKE ONE.

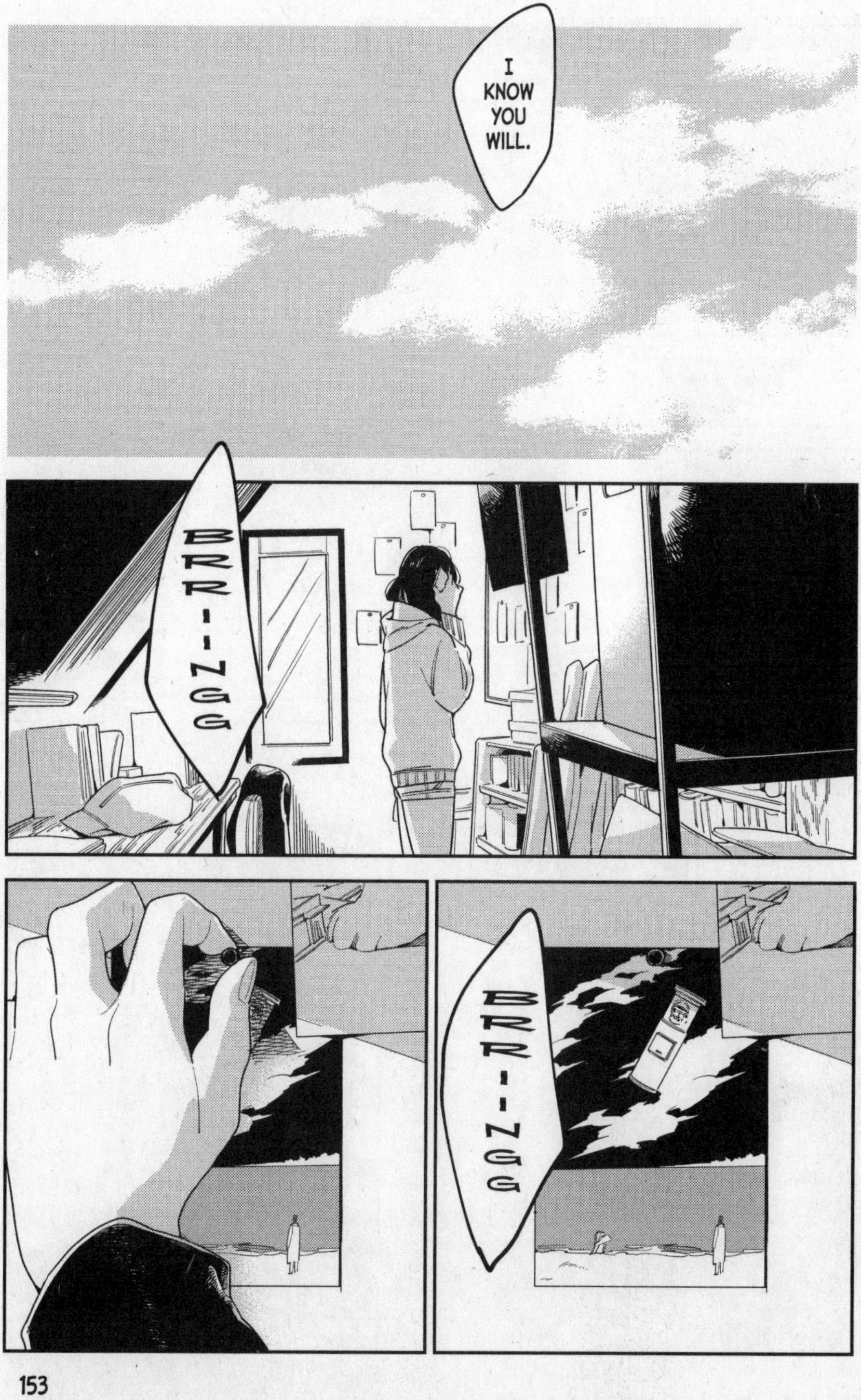
I KNOW YOU WILL.
BRRINGG
BRRINGG

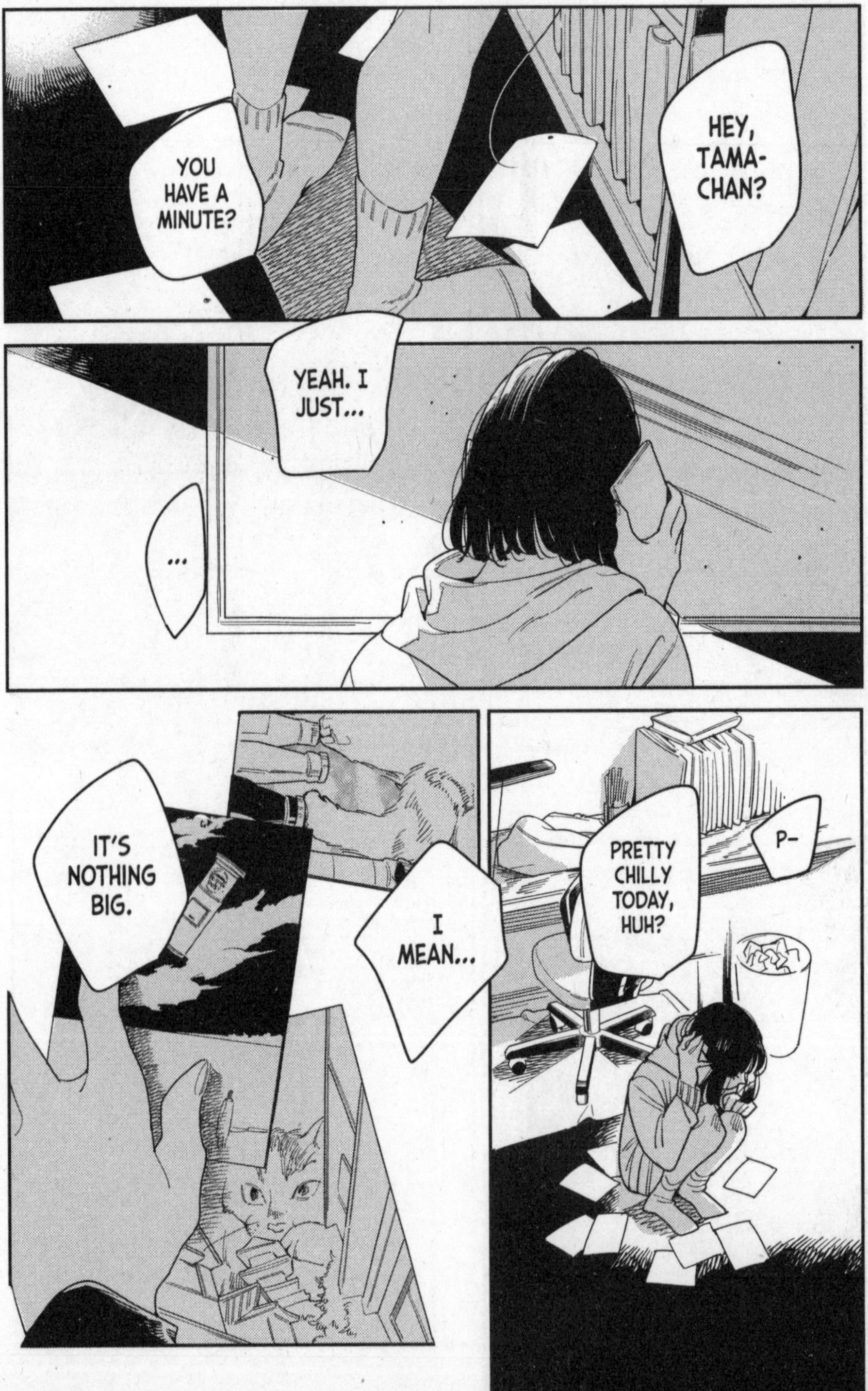
HEY, TAMA-CHAN?
YOU HAVE A MINUTE?
YEAH. I JUST...
...
P-
PRETTY CHILLY TODAY, HUH?
I MEAN...
IT'S NOTHING BIG.

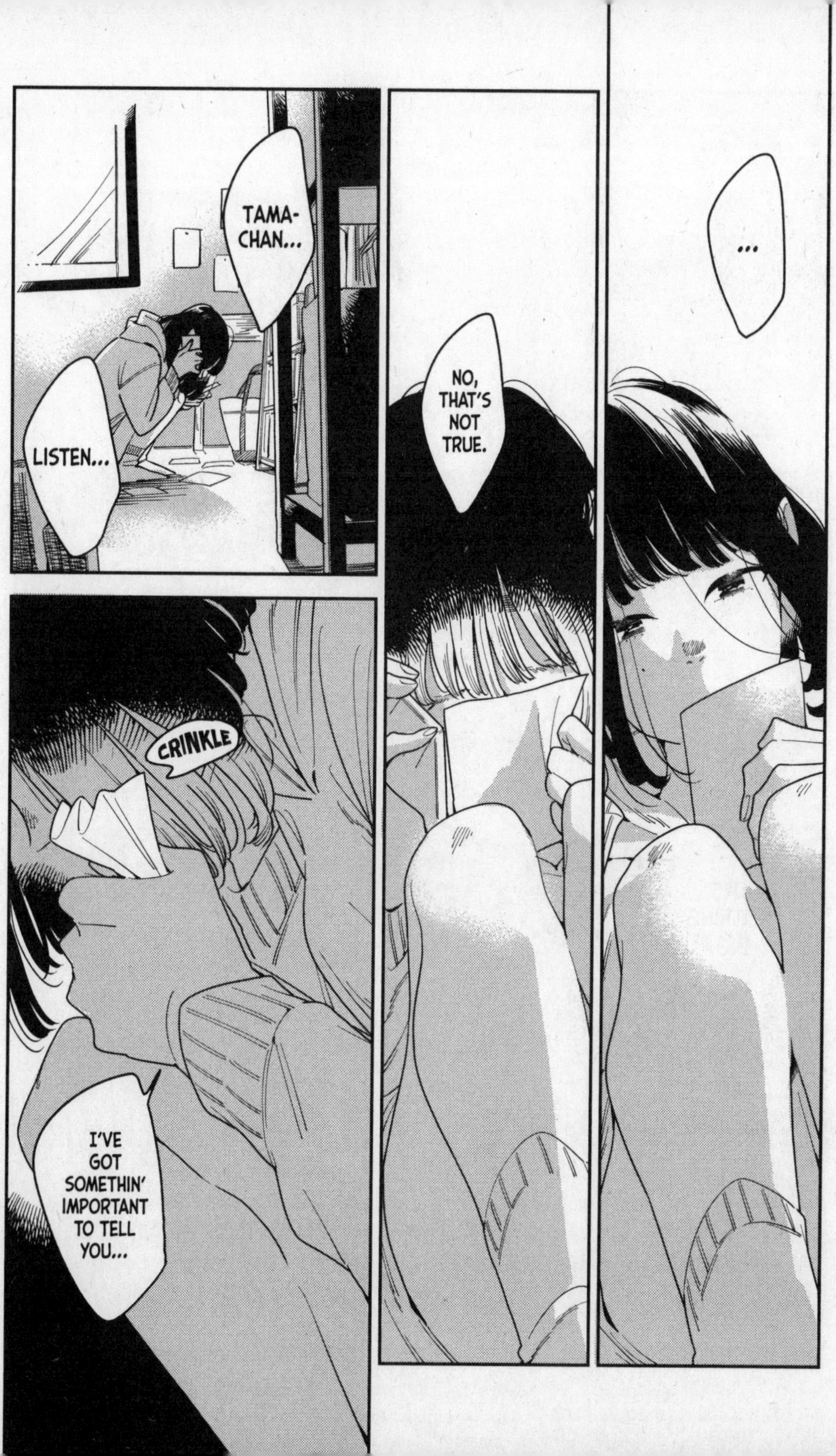
...
NO, THAT'S NOT TRUE.
TAMA-CHAN...
LISTEN...
CRINKLE
I'VE GOT SOMETHIN' IMPORTANT TO TELL YOU...

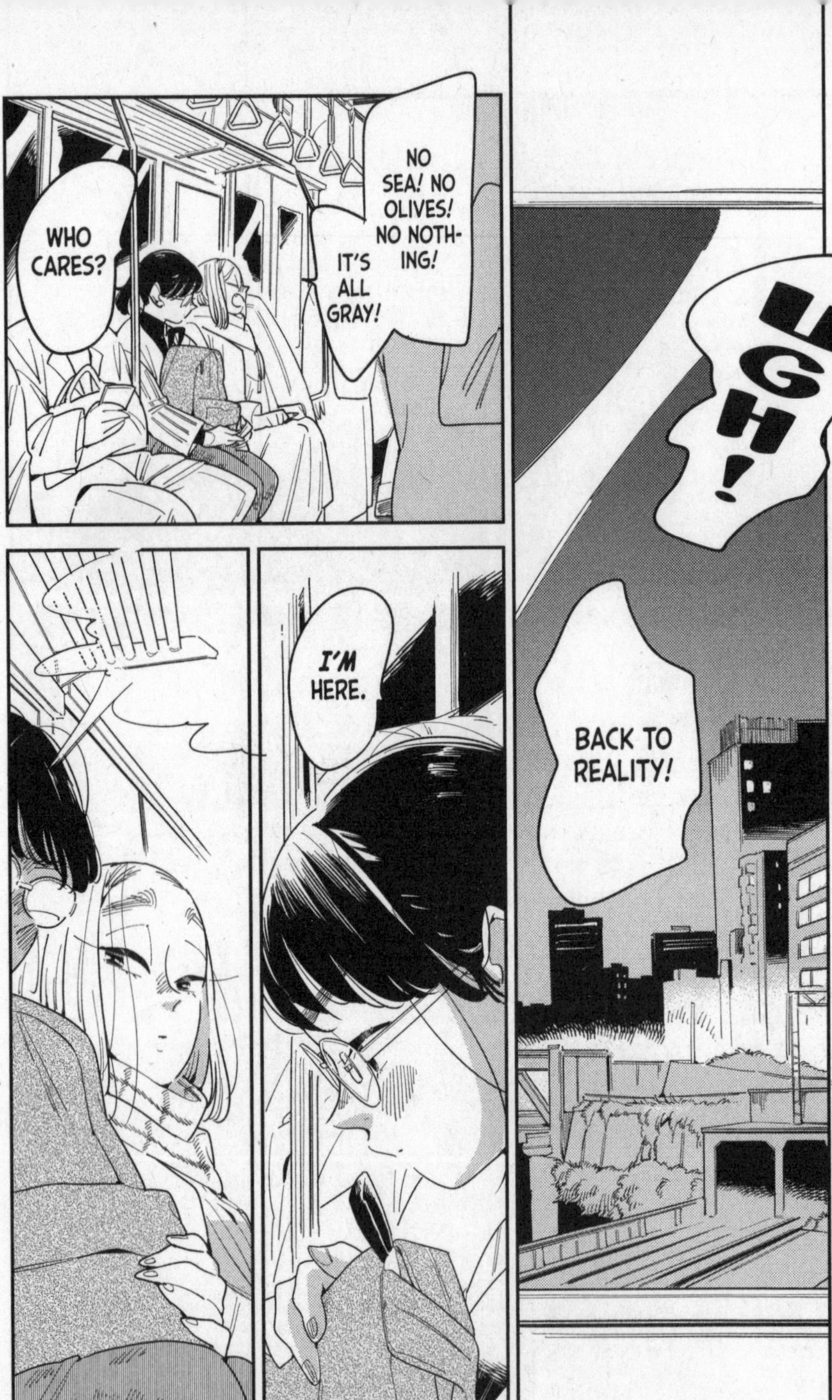
UGH!
BACK TO REALITY!
NO SEA! NO OLIVES! NO NOTHING!
IT'S ALL GRAY!
WHO CARES?
I'M HERE.

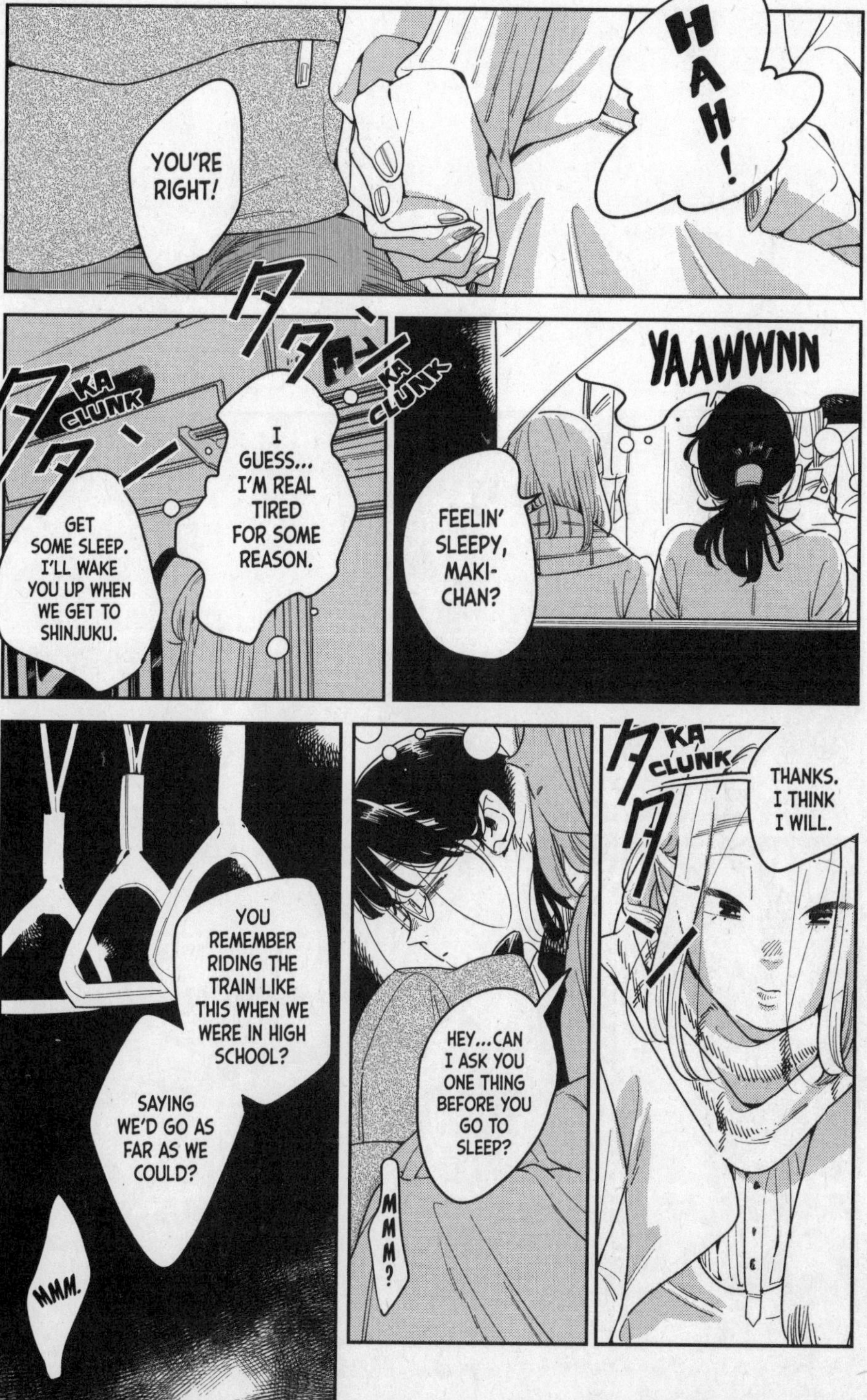
HAH!
YOU'RE RIGHT!
YAAWWNN
FEELIN' SLEEPY, MAKI-CHAN?
タタン
KA CLUNK
I GUESS... I'M REAL TIRED FOR SOME REASON.
タタン
KA CLUNK
GET SOME SLEEP. I'LL WAKE YOU UP WHEN WE GET TO SHINJUKU.
タタン
KA CLUNK
THANKS. I THINK I WILL.
HEY...CAN I ASK YOU ONE THING BEFORE YOU GO TO SLEEP?
MMM?
YOU REMEMBER RIDING THE TRAIN LIKE THIS WHEN WE WERE IN HIGH SCHOOL?
SAYING WE'D GO AS FAR AS WE COULD?
MMM.

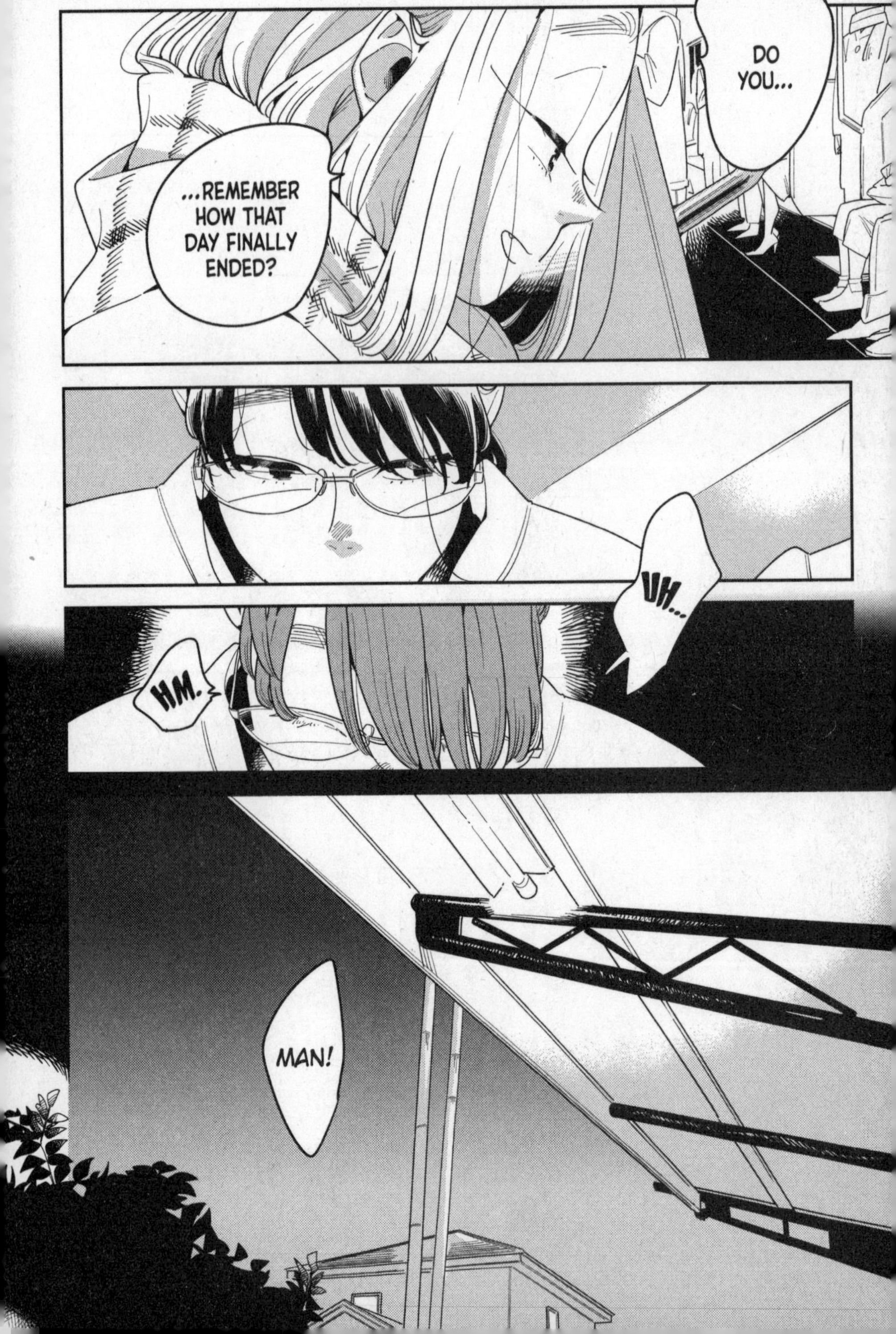
DO YOU...
...REMEMBER HOW THAT DAY FINALLY ENDED?
UH...
HM.
MAN!

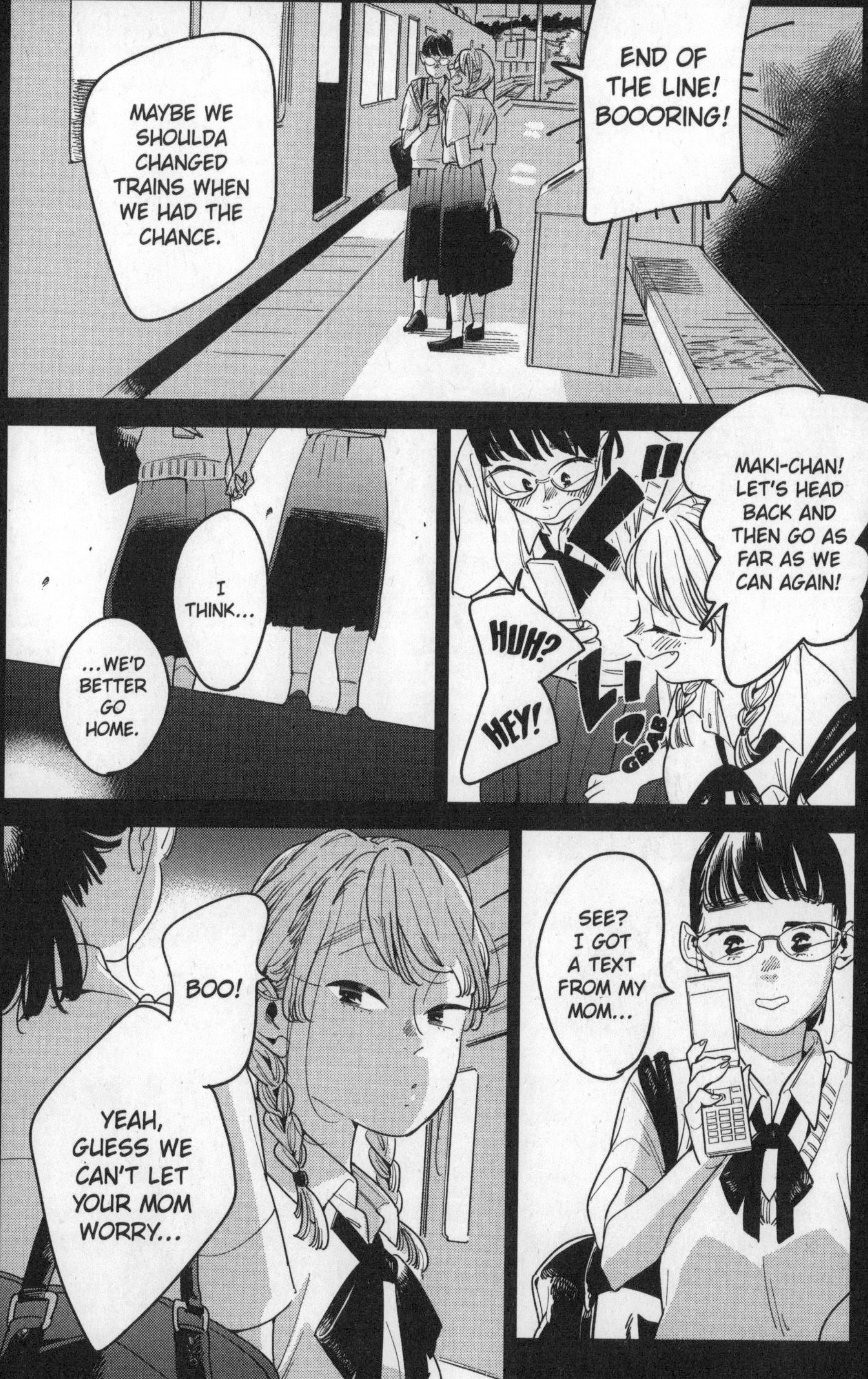
END OF THE LINE! BOOORING!
MAYBE WE SHOULDA CHANGED TRAINS WHEN WE HAD THE CHANCE.
MAKI-CHAN! LET'S HEAD BACK AND THEN GO AS FAR AS WE CAN AGAIN!
HUH?
HEY!
GRAB
I THINK...
...WE'D BETTER GO HOME.
SEE? I GOT A TEXT FROM MY MOM...
BOO!
YEAH, GUESS WE CAN'T LET YOUR MOM WORRY...

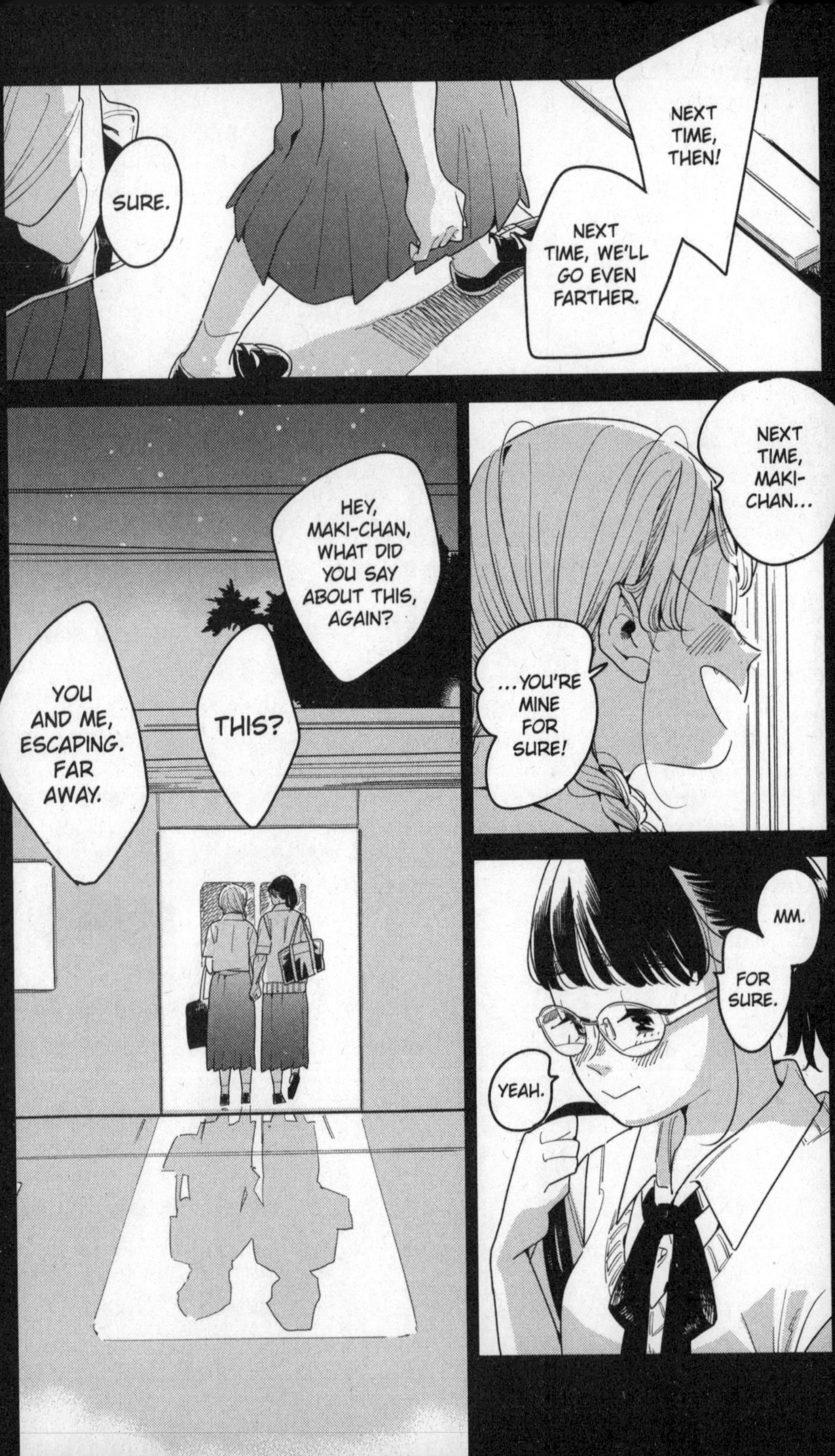
NEXT TIME, THEN!
NEXT TIME, WE'LL GO EVEN FARTHER.
SURE.
NEXT TIME, MAKI-CHAN…
…YOU'RE MINE FOR SURE!
MM.
FOR SURE.
YEAH.
HEY, MAKI-CHAN, WHAT DID YOU SAY ABOUT THIS, AGAIN?
THIS?
YOU AND ME, ESCAPING. FAR AWAY.

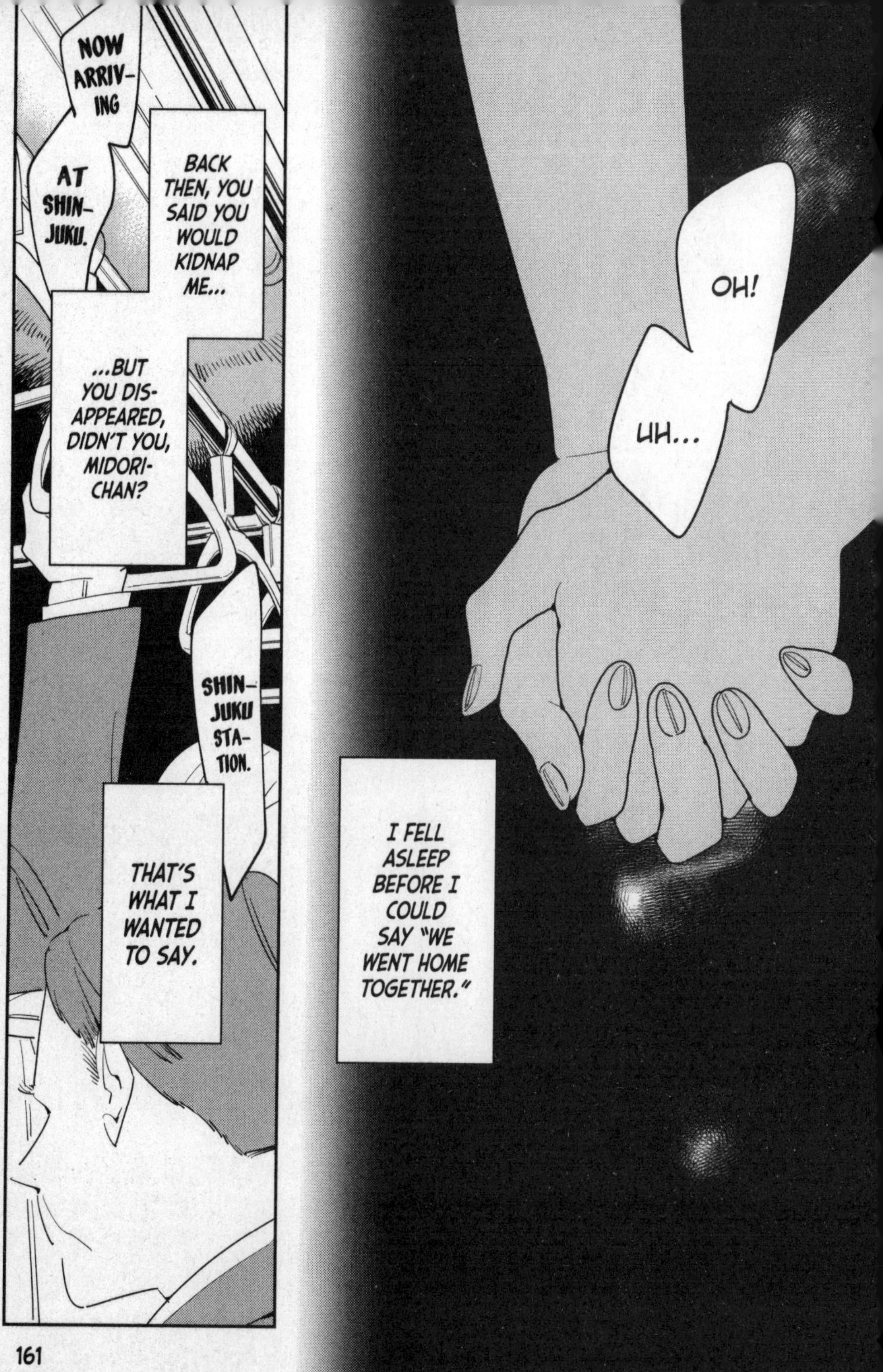
OH!
UH...
I FELL ASLEEP BEFORE I COULD SAY "WE WENT HOME TOGETHER."
NOW ARRIVING
AT SHINJUKU.
BACK THEN, YOU SAID YOU WOULD KIDNAP ME...
...BUT YOU DISAPPEARED, DIDN'T YOU, MIDORI-CHAN?
SHINJUKU STATION.
THAT'S WHAT I WANTED TO SAY.

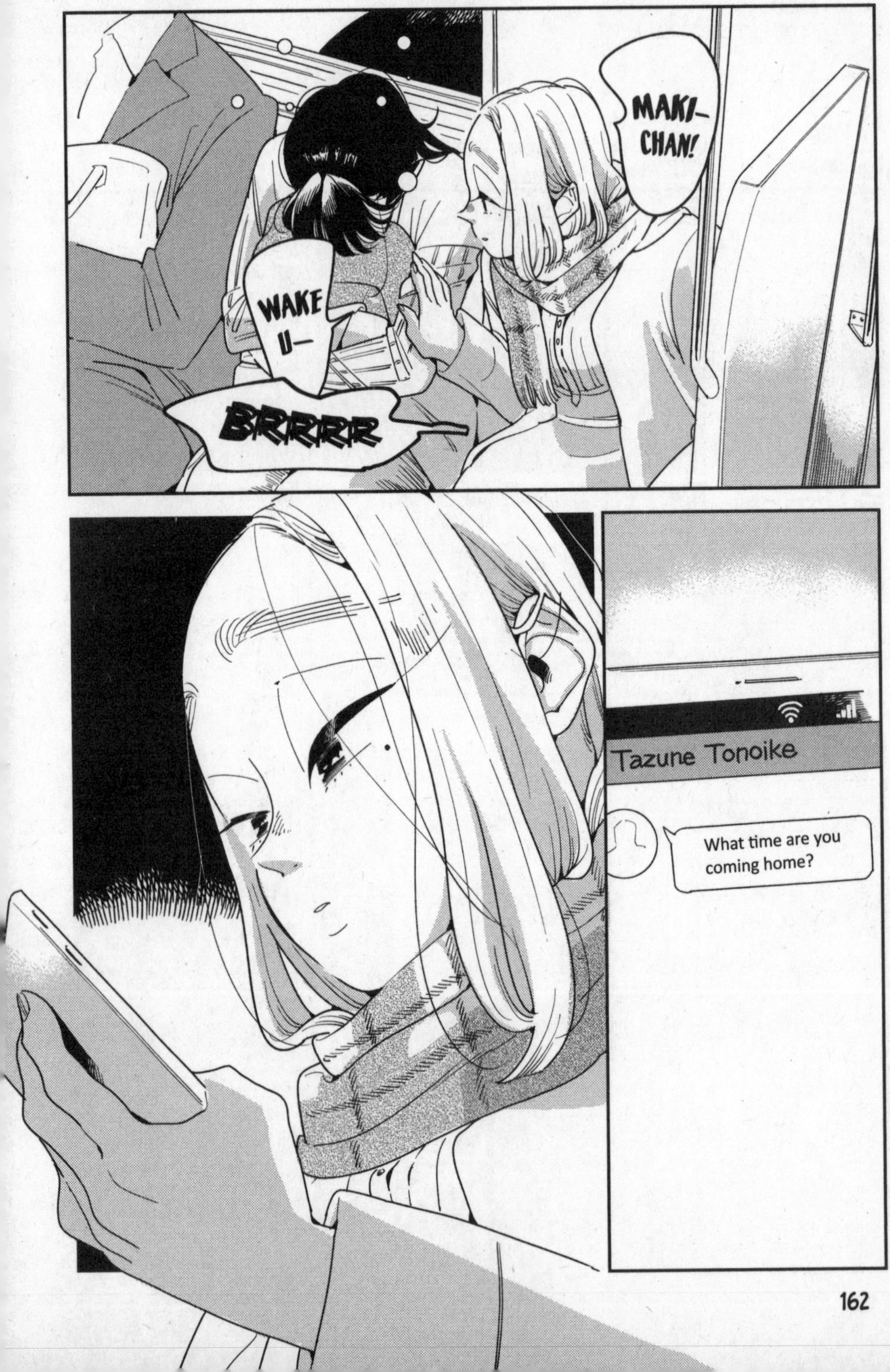
MAKI-CHAN!
WAKE U—
BRRRR
Tazune Tonoike
What time are you coming home?

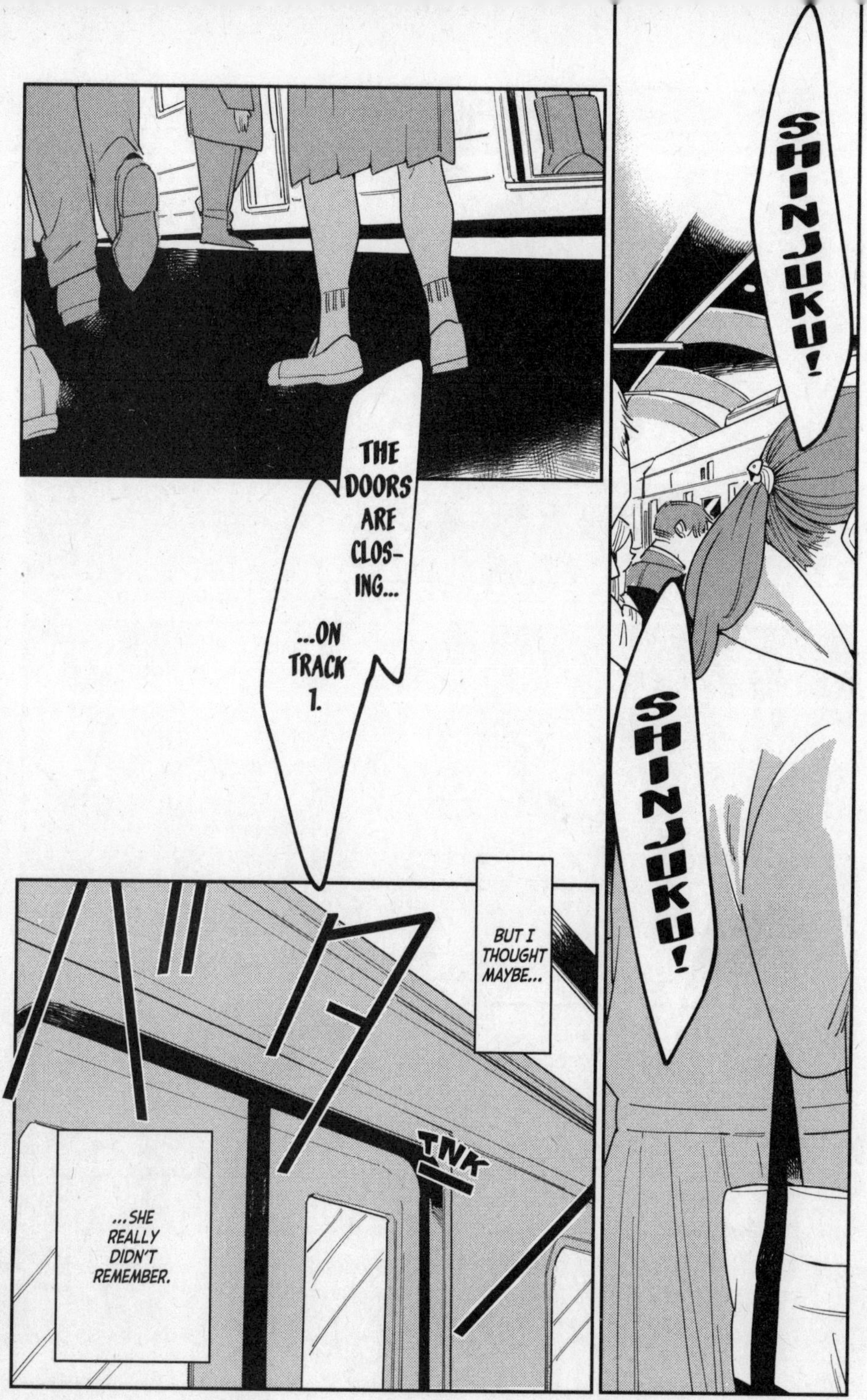
SHINJUKU!
SHINJUKU!
THE DOORS ARE CLOSING... ...ON TRACK 1.
BUT I THOUGHT MAYBE...
TNK
...SHE REALLY DIDN'T REMEMBER.

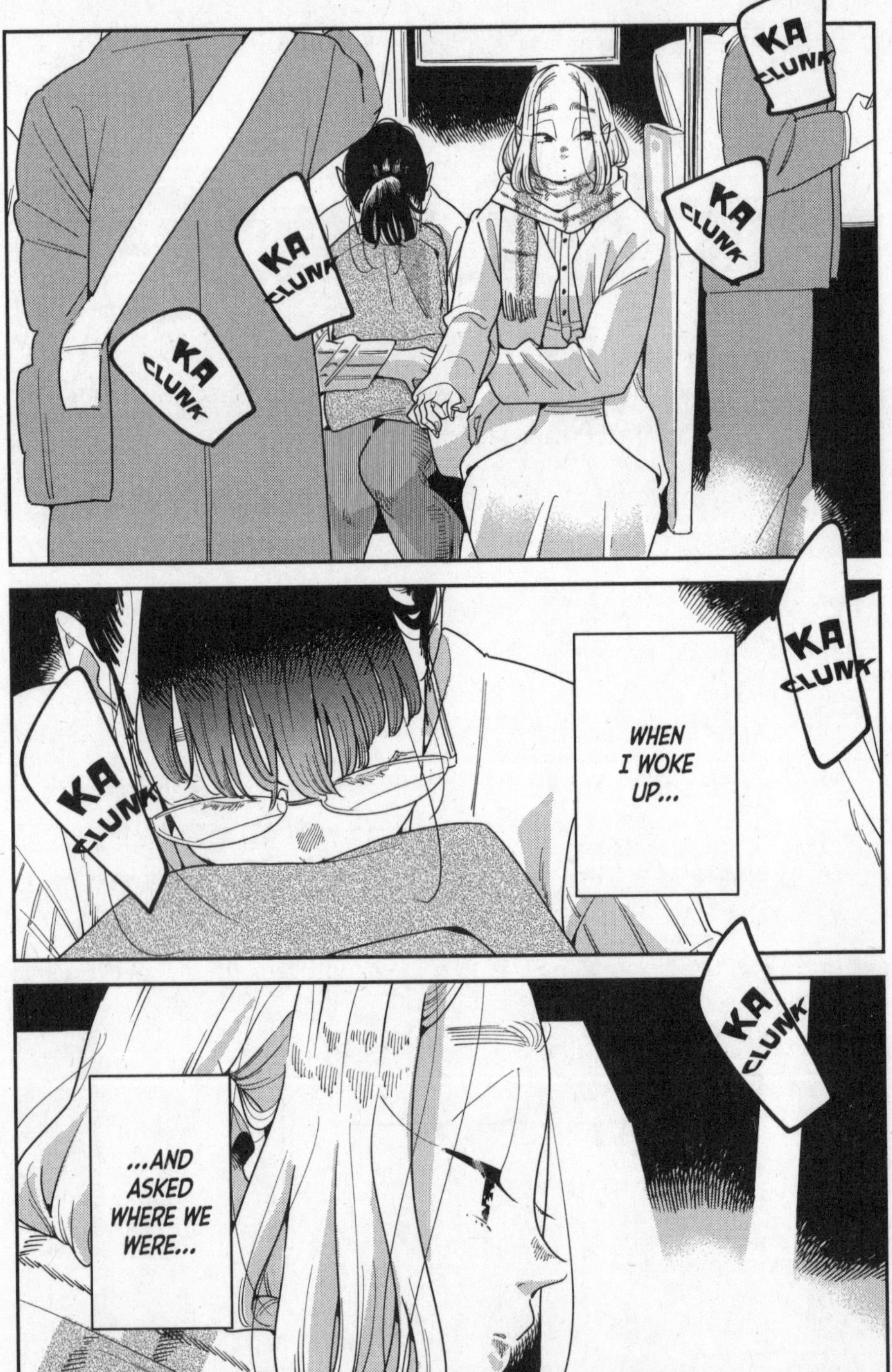
KA CLUNK
KA CLUNK
KA CLUNK
KA CLUNK
KA CLUNK
WHEN I WOKE UP...
KA CLUNK
KA CLUNK
...AND ASKED WHERE WE WERE...

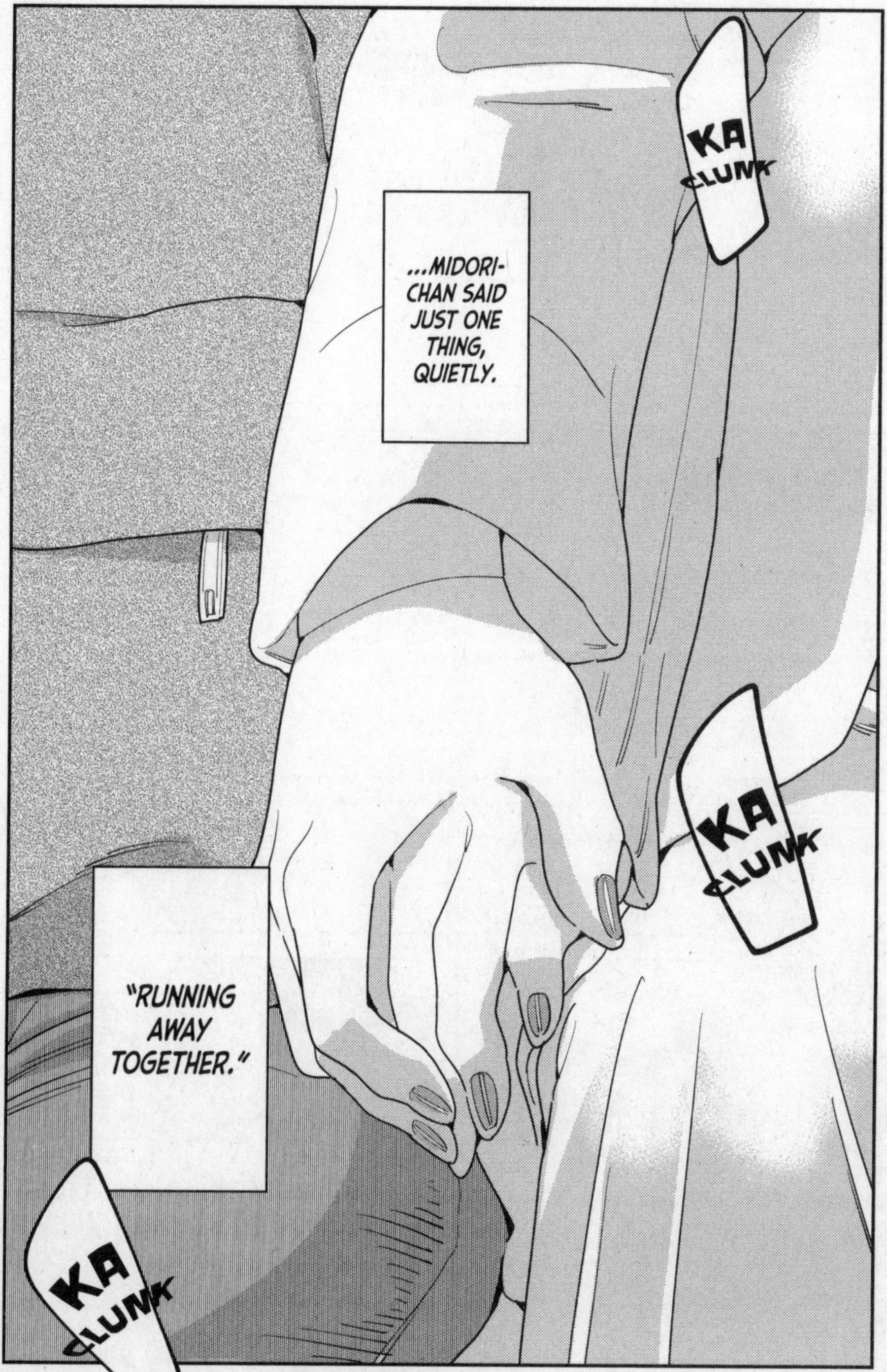
KA CLUNK
...MIDORI-CHAN SAID JUST ONE THING, QUIETLY.
KA CLUNK
"RUNNING AWAY TOGETHER."
KA CLUNK

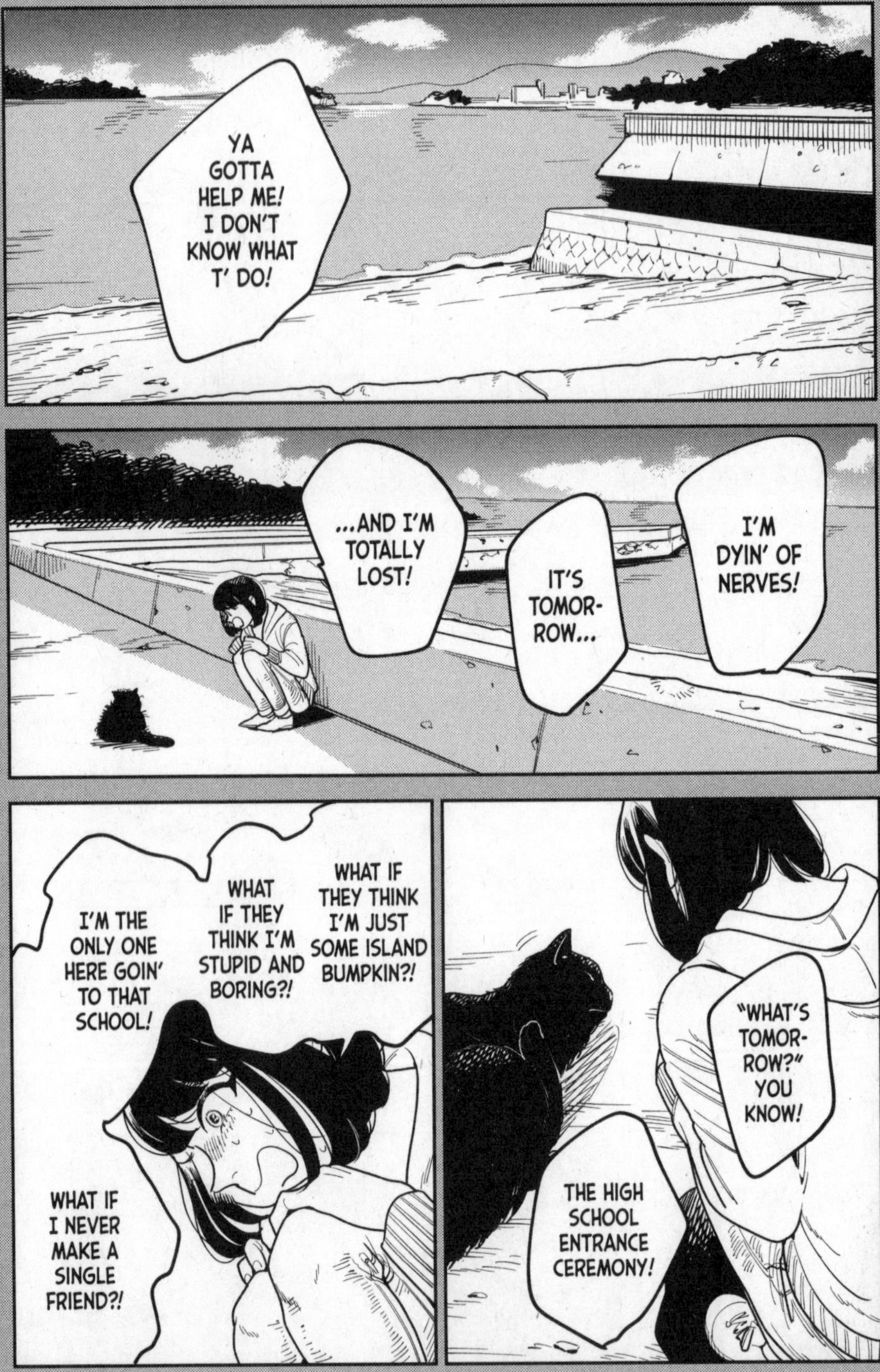
YA GOTTA HELP ME! I DON'T KNOW WHAT T' DO!
I'M DYIN' OF NERVES!
IT'S TOMOR-ROW...
...AND I'M TOTALLY LOST!
"WHAT'S TOMOR-ROW?" YOU KNOW!
THE HIGH SCHOOL ENTRANCE CEREMONY!
WHAT IF THEY THINK I'M JUST SOME ISLAND BUMPKIN?!
WHAT IF THEY THINK I'M STUPID AND BORING?!
I'M THE ONLY ONE HERE GOIN' TO THAT SCHOOL!
WHAT IF I NEVER MAKE A SINGLE FRIEND?!

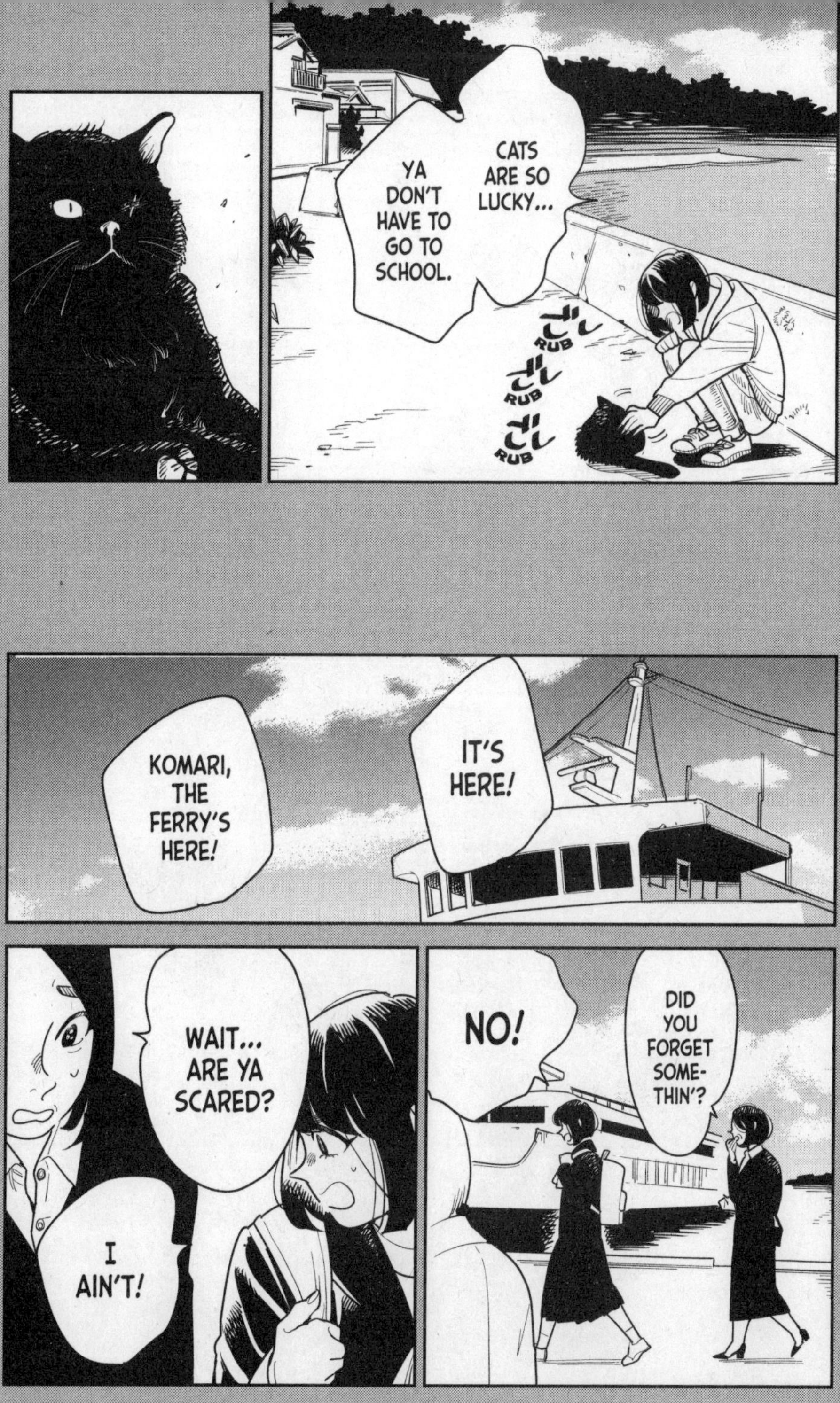
CATS ARE SO LUCKY...
YA DON'T HAVE TO GO TO SCHOOL.
RUB
RUB
RUB
IT'S HERE!
KOMARI, THE FERRY'S HERE!
DID YOU FORGET SOME-THIN'?
NO!
WAIT... ARE YA SCARED?
I AIN'T!

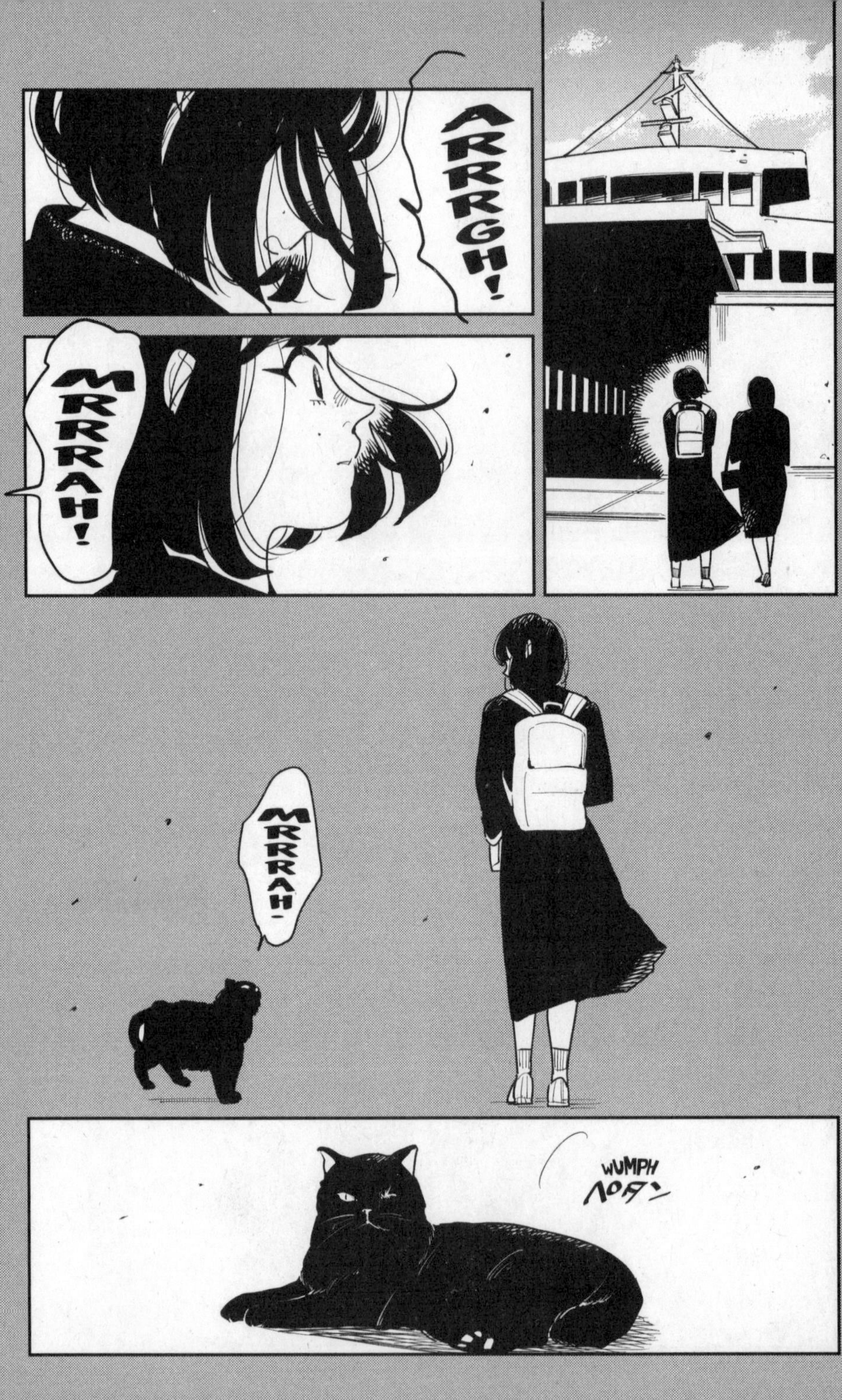
ARRRGH!
MRRRAH!
MRRRAH!
WUMPH

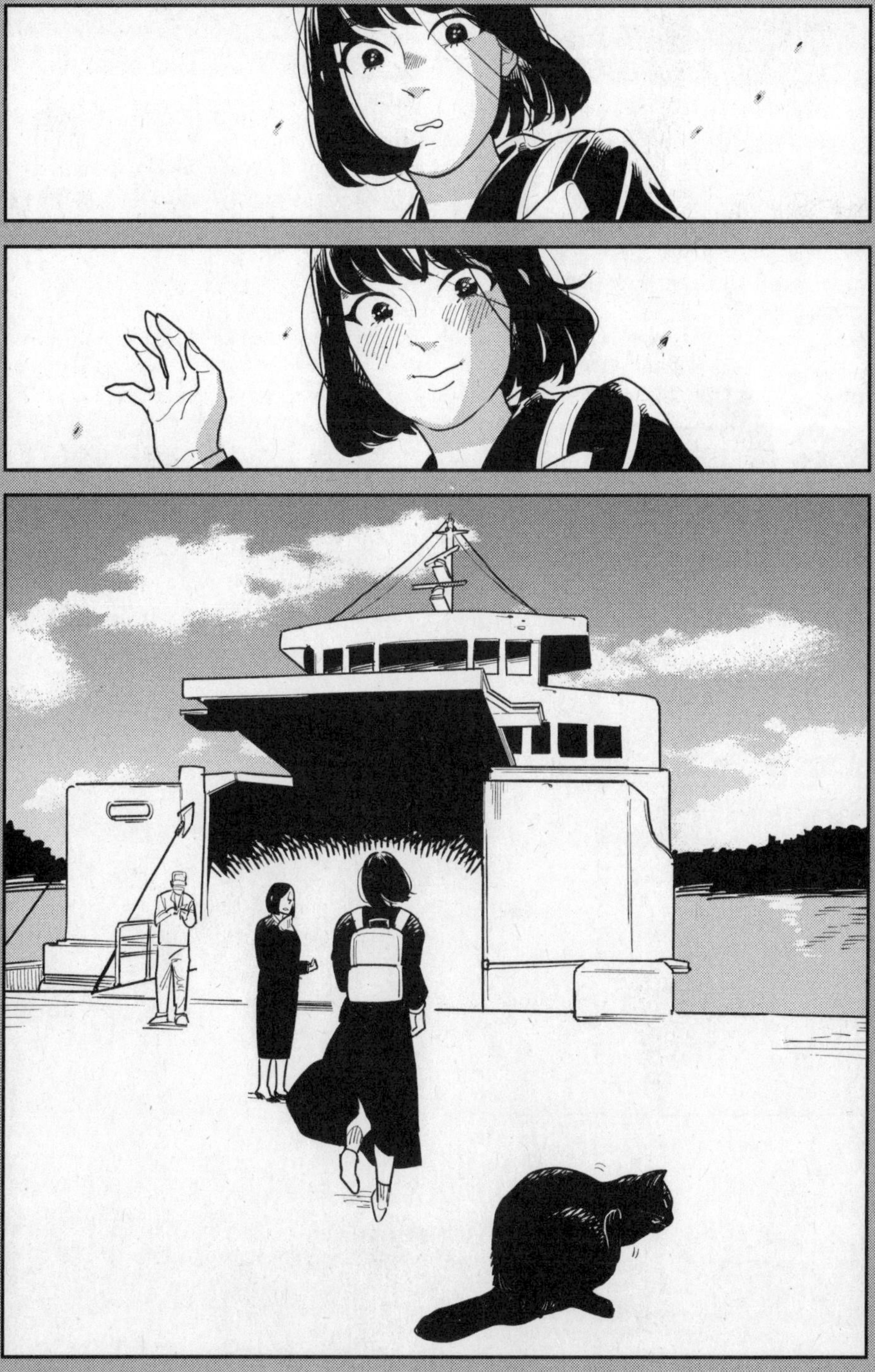

TRANSLATION NOTES

Inland Sea, page 32
The inland sea (formally the Seto inland sea, *seto naikai*) is the body of water that lies between three of Japan's four main islands, Honshu, Shikoku, and Kyushu. Convention considers this area rustic at best, the opposite of a bustling cosmopolitan city like Tokyo. It's not a new notion, but instead goes back centuries: during the Heian era (c. 8th-12th centuries CE), disgraced courtiers were sometimes exiled to locations along the inland sea, such as when Genji is sent off to the coastal area of Suma in *The Tale of Genji*.

Yukata, page 72
Literally meaning "bathrobe," a yukata is a robe, lighter and simpler than a kimono, that can be worn in casual situations. Yukata are associated with hot springs and bathing, but they can also be worn at festivals, around Japanese inns like this one, and in other traditional or festive settings.

Maki-chan-san, page 82
The usage of *-chan-san* is unorthodox and humorous. The implication is that Komari calls Momo "Maki-chan" so readily that it feels like a complete name in its own right to which an honorific, such as *-san*, might be attached.

Masaki Suda, page 103
Masaki Suda is an actor-singer who got his start in *Kamen Rider* movies in the mid-2000s and has played a variety of starring roles since.

Run Away
With Me,
Girl

NEXT VOL.

WHERE DO TWO WOMEN GO WHEN THEY RUN AWAY?

WHEN THEY ARRIVE, A NEW MEETING...

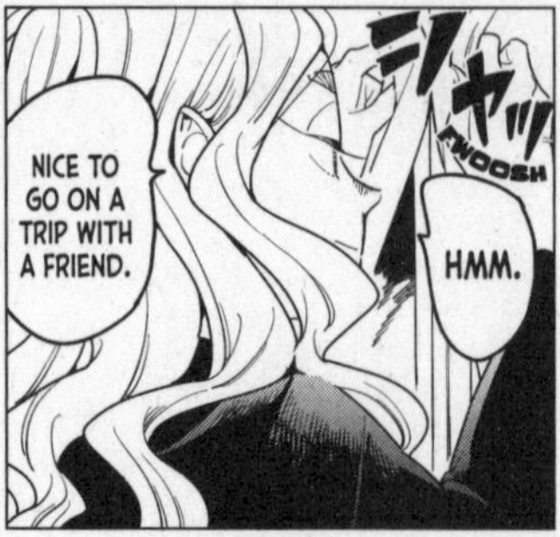
FWOOSH
HMM.
NICE TO GO ON A TRIP WITH A FRIEND.

THEIR PLEASANT TRIP TOGETHER BECOMES A CHANCE TO ESCAPE. MAKI AND MIDORI-CHAN COMMUNE HEART-TO-HEART, BUT EVERY HAPPY MOMENT HAS TO END. THEY CAN'T DENY THEIR LOVE FOR EACH OTHER, BUT WHERE WILL THEIR LOVE TAKE THEM?

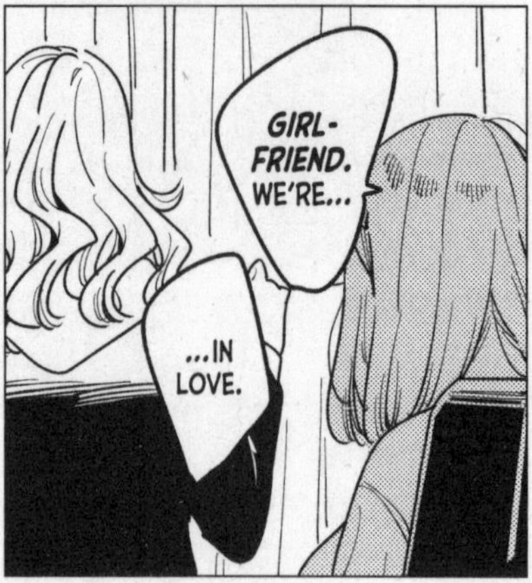
GIRL-FRIEND. WE'RE...
...IN LOVE.

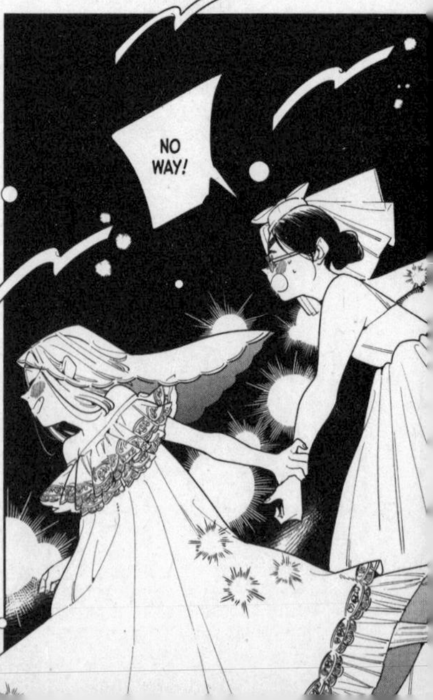
NO WAY!

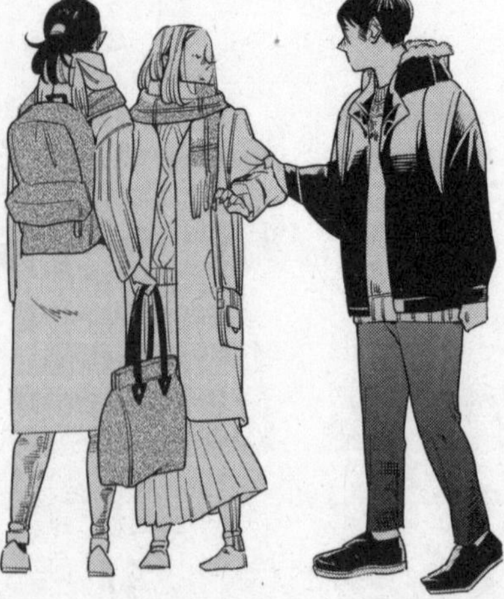

TAZUNE-KUN FINDS THEM...

THEY KNOW EACH OTHER'S FEELINGS...

...DEEPER AND CLOSER THAN EVER BEFORE...

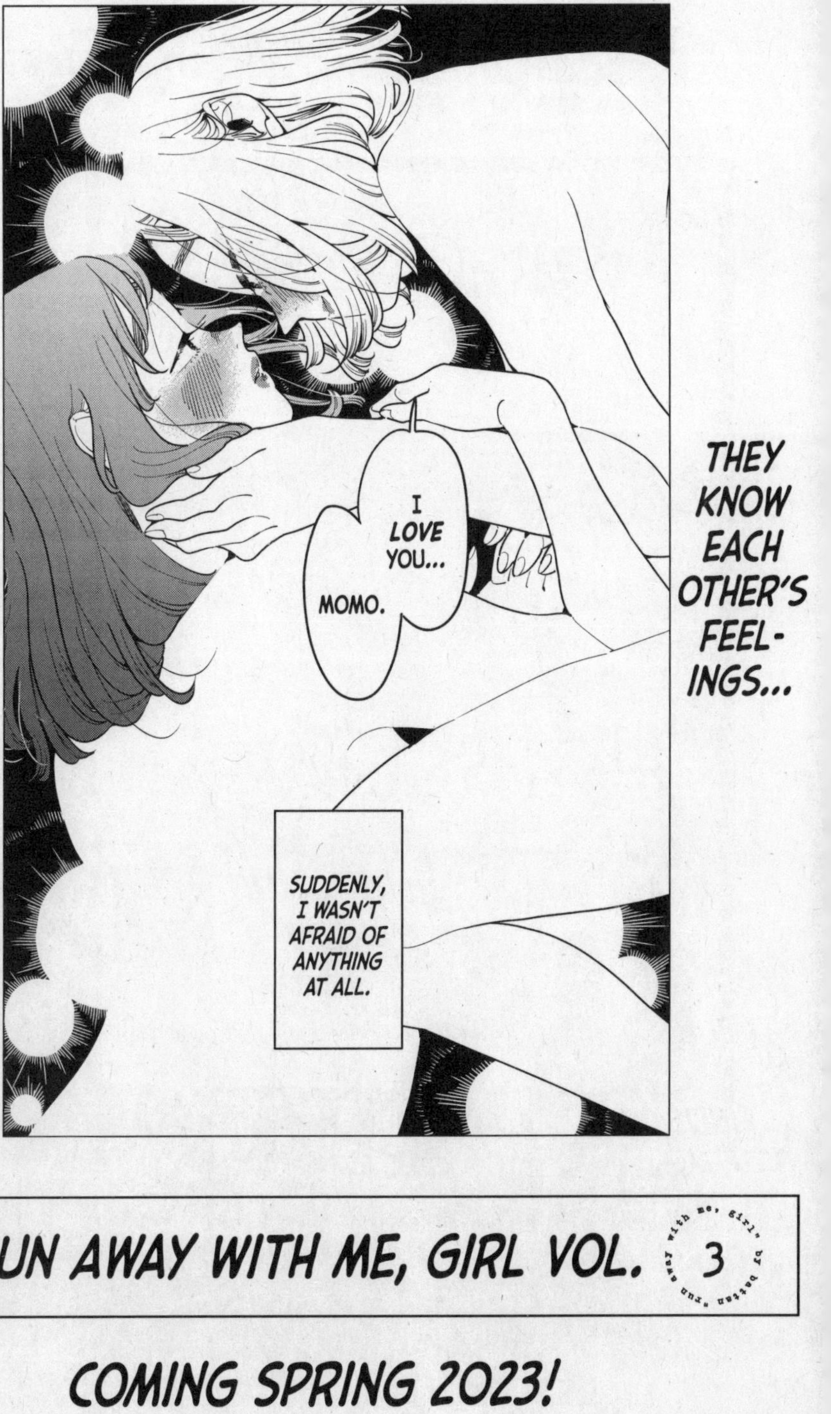
I LOVE YOU... MOMO.
SUDDENLY, I WASN'T AFRAID OF ANYTHING AT ALL.

RUN AWAY WITH ME, GIRL VOL. 3

COMING SPRING 2023!

A SMART, NEW ROMANTIC COMEDY FOR FANS OF *SHORTCAKE CAKE* AND *TERRACE HOUSE*!

Living-Room Matsunaga-san © Keiko Iwashita / Kodansha Ltd.

A romance manga starring high school girl Meeko, who learns to live on her own in a boarding house whose living room is home to the odd (but handsome) Matsunaga-san. She begins to adjust to her new life away from her parents, but Meeko soon learns that no matter how far away from home she is, she's still a young girl at heart — especially when she finds herself falling for Matsunaga-san.

SKATING THRILLS AND ICY CHILLS WITH THIS NEW TINGLY ROMANCE SERIES!

Yayoi Ogawa

Knight of the Ice ©Yayoi Ogawa/Kodansha Ltd.

A rom-com on ice, perfect for fans of *Princess Jellyfish* and *Wotakoi*. Kokoro is the talk of the figure-skating world, winning trophies and hearts. But little do they know... he's actually a huge nerd! From the beloved creator of *You're My Pet* (*Tramps Like Us*).

Chitose is a serious young woman, working for the health magazine *SASSO*. Or at least, she would be, if she wasn't constantly getting distracted by her childhood friend, international figure skating star Kokoro Kijinami! In the public eye and on the ice, Kokoro is a gallant, flawless knight, but behind his glittery costumes and breathtaking spins lies a secret: He's actually a hopelessly romantic otaku, who can only land his quad jumps when Chitose is on hand to recite a spell from his favorite magical girl anime!

KODANSHA COMICS

Run Away With Me, Girl 2 is a work of fiction. Names, characters, places, and incidents are the products of the author's imagination or are used fictitiously. Any resemblance to actual events, locales, or persons, living or dead, is entirely coincidental.

A Kodansha Trade Paperback Original

Run Away With Me, Girl 2 copyright © 2021 Battan
English translation copyright © 2023 Battan

All rights reserved.

Published in the United States by
Kodansha USA Publishing, LLC, New York.

Publication rights for this English edition arranged through
Kodansha Ltd., Tokyo.

First published in Japan in 2021 by Kodansha Ltd., Tokyo
as *Kakeochi Gaaru*, volume 2.

ISBN 978-1-64651-622-3

Original cover design by Kawatani Design

Printed in the United States of America.

9 8 7 6 5 4 3 2 1

Translation: Kevin Steinbach
Lettering: Jennifer Skarupa
Editing: Tiff Joshua TJ Ferentini
Kodansha USA Publishing edition cover design by Pekka Luhtala

Publisher: Kiichiro Sugawara

Director of Publishing Services: Ben Applegate
Director of Publishing Operations: Dave Barrett
Associate Director of Publishing Operations: Stephen Pakula
Publishing Services Managing Editors: Alanna Ruse, Madison Salters,
with Grace Chen
Production Manager: Emi Lotto

KODANSHA.US

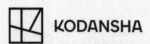 KODANSHA